AN INTRODUCTION TO PROGRAMMING

A Structured Approach Using PL/I and PL/C

Richard Conway

David Gries

<u>Cornell University</u>

WINTHROP PUBLISHERS, INC.
Cambridge, Massachusetts

Library of Congress Cataloging in Publication Data

Conway, Richard Walter
    An introduction to programming.

    1. PL/I (Computer program language) I. Gries,
David   joint author., II. Title.
QA76.73.P25 C65   001.6 424   73-5708
ISBN 0-87626-406-2
ISBN 0-87626-405-4 (pbk.)

Cover design by Harold Pattek

Copyright c 1973 by Winthrop Publishers, Inc.
    17 Dunster Street, Cambridge,Massachusetts 02138

PREFACE

A program is a description of a problem solution that is written in a language and form intelligible to a computer. If someone approaching the programming process for the first time already has a systematic, well-disciplined approach to problem analysis in general, then learning to program a computer just means learning the nature and syntax of a programming language. In this case a book that concentrates upon the syntactic details of a particular programming language is probably adequate. However, some students do not have this prerequisite training in problem solving, and for them a course in programming is a unique opportunity to develop this skill, in a particularly useful and interesting context. The approach and method of analysis are then more significant than the details of a particular programming language. This book is our attempt to provide a text that would be helpful to an instructor who takes this view of his task.

Nothing in our approach is really new. We are simply trying to apply the classical "scientific method" to the production of computer programs. We have been surprised how directly the recommendations of the scientific philosophers -- Descartes, Mills, Polya -- can be applied to this new field, and we have drawn heavily upon their views and procedures.

This approach to programming leads to a strong concern with the organization of programs. The structure of a program should clearly reflect the structure of the problem that it represents, and the pattern of analysis that the programmer has followed. For non-trivial problems this approach offers the only hope of being able to adequately demonstrate the correctness of a program. If necessary, we are willing to accept degradation of program efficiency to achieve clarity of structure and reliability. It makes no sense to use an unclear program of uncertain correctness no matter how efficient it might be. Actually, we find that the major source of program efficiency lies not in clever tricks which obscure the program, but in a clean and logical approach to the problem. In many cases clarity and good programming style lead to the development of more efficient algorithms.

We enthusiastically embrace the philosophy of "structured programming" -- not so much because it is revolutionary, but because it provides a name and an emphasis for what has always been good practice in programming. Emphasis on structure and on the use of program elements that most clearly reflect that structure results in superior programs and more capable

programmers. We are not such structural purists that we
prohibit the use of the GO TO altogether, but we do relegate it
to such subordinate uses as an "exit" from a repetitive section
of program (cases where PL/I does not have a really suitable
control structure).

Programming has too long been regarded as a highly individual
art. Very little attention is given to encouraging consistent
form, style and conventions in programming, and in fact highly
individual and even peculiar styles are tolerated. However, the
practice of programming has long since passed the point where it
is entirely a private activity. To be sure, there are still
many engineers and scientists who write their own programs, use
them once, and then throw them away. But the real difficulties
in programming arise in larger problems. In such cases the
programmer is usually not working on "his own" problem. He is
given an assignment that represents only one aspect of the
complete problem; he must produce a section of program that will
work properly with other sections he has never seen; and the
entire program must be usable by people who know little or
nothing about how it is constructed. Often such programs have a
relatively long lifetime -- measured in months or years rather
than hours or days -- and will almost surely be subject to
significant modification during this time. In this context
programming is not an art form; it is a technical communication
process. It is crucial that programs be cleanly divided into
functional modules and that the interfaces between these modules
be specified in explicit detail in program documentation. We
try to illustrate and encourage this practice by employing it
even for simple introductory examples, where it is obviously not
really necessary and where it may require writing extra
statements. The fraction of lines devoted to control structures
and comments is oppressively large in some of our short
examples, but of course, this proportion diminishes as the same
style is applied to problems of more substance. Programming
practices that are necessary for large problems can be used
(with some short-cutting and informality) for small problems,
but the converse is not true. Although most students who are
introduced to programming will regard it only as one of many
tools, and use it only occasionally, we see no disadvantage in
introducing them to programming as if they were going to be
serious about it.

Most writers of programming texts and teachers of programming
courses are themselves more or less serious programmers,
understand and believe in the virtues of such things as highly
modular, adequately documented programs, and appreciate the
substantial fraction of total programming time and effort that
goes into testing. Yet the usual text or course does relatively
little to convey this concern. Compare the number of pages that
are devoted to syntactic details of the various statements of a
particular language to the pages devoted to discussion of the
strategy and style with which those statements should be used in
constructing programs, and how those programs should be designed
so that they can be systematically and exhaustively tested.

Even worse, whatever material is included on strategy, structure and testing is usually relegated to the final chapters and lectures. In that position it is all too susceptible to omission, if things get behind schedule. It also means that throughout his initial exposure and experience the student is unguided on these important matters (or in some cases encouraged into some very bad habits) and it is not clear that a few parting admonitions can overcome this initial experience. We have tried to emphasize these issues from the very beginning of the introduction. Something must yield, of course, to allow the time and pages for this emphasis and we deliberately sacrifice breadth of coverage and syntactic detail. We hope that our reader and student, who knows less of PL/I than if he had followed a more conventional text, will better understand what he is doing and can perhaps use what he knows more effectively. We would like to give him a clear understanding of the fundamental concepts of computing so that he can later, on his own, expand his knowledge of this particular language, or learn an entirely different programming language.

Some comment on our choice of programming language is in order. This approach to programming could certainly be used with the FORTRAN or COBOL languages, or even with assembly language, and it should result in better programs in any language. However, it is easier to teach this approach using a language whose control structures encourage a natural "top-down analysis". At the risk of enraging the masses of FORTRAN advocates, we think that at least in terms of this approach PL/I and ALGOL are slightly higher-level languages than FORTRAN. That is, in the level-by-level reduction from problem statement to program, one would require an extra level if the target language were FORTRAN rather than PL/I. Stated in another way, given a description in a PL/I-like language as the next-to-last level one could proceed from there to write a FORTRAN program.

Offsetting this advantage, PL/I has some unfortunate characteristics when viewed as an instructional vehicle. In spite of claims to the contrary it is not adequately modular; too much must be known before one really understands certain constructions. Many common student "errors" are not considered errors by the system -- they just invoke hitherto unexplained features of the language. Nevertheless, we have elected to use PL/I -- although we should admit that the choice may have been influenced by our participation in the development of the PL/C compiler for PL/I. We have restricted attention to a small subset and have tried to adopt conventions that will minimize the intrusions from unseen portions of the language. Unfortunately there is no compiler that will enforce this subset and these conventions so that, if his instructor allows it, the student can "get away with" very different practices than those described here.

The body of this book is almost equally applicable to either PL/I or PL/C. Only the material on program testing is particularly oriented to PL/C's unusual diagnostic facilities. The Appendices give a fairly complete definition of PL/I syntax and detail the differences between PL/I and PL/C.

This approach to programming is equally applicable to both "scientific computing" and "business data processing", and this book could be used for an introductory course for students in either area. The subset of PL/I used is common to both fields and the examples and exercises have been carefully chosen so as not to require substantial prior knowledge of either mathematics or accounting. Parts V and VI give very brief introductions to the two major areas of computer application and include suggestions for further reading.

The material in Part VII, on languages and translators, is not essential to the writing of programs. But many students become curious about such matters, and since we are also interested in the subject, we are happy to encourage their curiosity.

It is a pleasure to acknowledge our indebtedness to our colleagues at Cornell, who have enthusiastically debated these matters with us. While they may agree with us in general, they have enjoyed disagreeing in detail. We are especially indebted to John Dennis and Jorge Moré , who contributed Part V, and to Steven Worona, who taught us many things about PL/I, and prepared a set of solutions to the programming exercises.

Ithaca, N. Y.   R. Conway
                                                           D. Gries

TABLE OF CONTENTS

Sections marked with an asterisk are separable topics. These may be skipped without endangering understanding of later sections.

Part I

FUNDAMENTAL CONCEPTS

Section 1 The Computing Process

We are concerned with the process by which a digital computer can be used to solve problems -- or at least aid in the solution of problems. This involves learning to:

1. Choose problems that are appropriate to the computer's abilities, and describe the problem requirements, conditions, and assumptions clearly and precisely.

2. Design a solution to a problem and describe it in a language intelligible to a computer. This description is called a "program", while the process of producing a program is called "programming". Programming is a systematic, level-by-level process in which the original problem description, usually given in a combination of English and mathematics, is translated into a "programming language". This process must also transform a statement of objectives -- what is required -- into a description of an executable procedure -- how the objectives are to be achieved. A third aspect of the transformation is to make explicit and precise those portions of the problem description that are implicit and rely on the intuition, common sense, or technical knowledge of the reader, since the computer is completely lacking in these virtues.

3. Confirm the correctness of the program. This means demonstrating in as convincing a manner as possible that the program precisely satisfies the problem requirements.

The selection of appropriate problems is as difficult and important as the analysis and programming, but it is impossible to discuss this issue until one has some understanding of the nature of computing systems and their special abilities. However, two initial observations might be helpful. Firstly, problems for which computer assistance is sought are generally of substantial magnitude. There is non-trivial effort involved in the mechanics of obtaining computer assistance, and if the problem is simple, not repetitive, and not likely to recur, computer assistance may cost more than it is worth. One must bear this in mind even though the examples that will be used for instruction will necessarily be short and often trivial. They are presumably used to develop a competence which will be useful for subsequent attack on real and substantial problems.

Secondly, the computer can only assist in the solution of problems which can be stated very precisely and for which a detailed and precise method of solution can be given. Roughly speaking, one cannot expect a computer to perform a process that could not be performed by a human--if he lived long enough. The digital computer permits a tremendous increase in the quantity of symbols that may be considered, in the precision and reliability with which they will be manipulated, and above all in the speed with which the process will be carried out. But in principle the computer is only performing operations that could be carried out by a human being. It is true that the orders-of-magnitude differences in volume, speed and reliability combine to produce spectacular capability, but the fundamental process is simple and not unlike what a human could perform.

For example, a computer can "play chess" only because the game of chess has been described to the computer as an elaborate symbol manipulation task. On the other hand, a computer cannot be requested to "solve the vehicle emission problem" because no one has as yet figured out how to describe this problem strictly in terms of symbol manipulation. As another example, a computer is not infrequently asked to "select a date for a person from a set of potential candidates" and sometimes produces rather humorous recommendations. The source of the humor lies not in the computer's execution of the process but in the fact that no one really knows how to precisely describe this complex selection process.

1.1 An Example of a Program

At this point we present an example of a simple but complete computer program. Although you will not understand all the details at this point, you should get a general idea of what the end product of the programming process is going to be.

Suppose one has to determine the maximum of a set of non-negative numbers which are punched on "IBM cards". The program to do this uses a process that is repeated for each of the numbers. It will cause the computer to "read" a number (by analyzing the pattern of holes punched in the card) and compare it to the greatest number encountered "so far". If the new number is greater than the previous maximum it will be retained as a new maximum. The number of numbers is also counted.

This process is straightforward, once it gets started, but some provision is required to make it work properly on the first repetition. Secondly, so that the end of the list can be

recognized we will append a dummy number (in this case a -1,
which cannot occur in the actual data). The program will check
each value as it is read to see if it is this dummy value.

    A program has to be able to store values in the "memory" of
the computer and later retrieve these values. Each location for
storing a value is called a "variable" and is assigned a name so
that the program may refer to it. The names of the variables
used in this program are:

        NUMBER -- the current number being processed
        MAXNBR -- the maximum number encountered "so far"
        COUNT -- the number of times the central process has been
                  repeated "so far"

    The complete program for this problem, written in a
programming language called PL/C, is given below. The numbers
at the beginning of each line below are not part of the program
but have been added so that the notes following the program can
readily reference each line.

```
1)    *PL/C ID='ROBERT CONSTABLE'
2)      /* COMPUTE THE MAXIMUM OF NON-NEGATIVE NUMBERS */
3)      /* DUMMY -1 ADDED FOR STOPPING TEST */
4)      FINDMAX: PROCEDURE OPTIONS(MAIN);
5)
6)        DECLARE (NUMBER,        /* THE CURRENT NUMBER */
7)                 MAXNBR,        /* MAXIMUM VALUE SO FAR */
8)                 COUNT)         /* NBR OF NUMBERS SO FAR */
9)                   FIXED DECIMAL;
10)
11)       MAXNBR = -10;     /* INITIAL VALUE LESS THAN ALL */
12)                         /* POSSIBLE DATA VALUES */
13)       COUNT = 0;
14)       GET LIST(NUMBER);
15)
16)       DO WHILE (NUMBER ¬= -1);
17)           COUNT = COUNT + 1;
18)           IF NUMBER > MAXNBR THEN MAXNBR = NUMBER;
19)           GET LIST(NUMBER);
20)           END;
21)
22)       PUT LIST('NUMBER OF VALUES =', COUNT);
23)       PUT SKIP LIST('MAXIMUM VALUE =', MAXNBR);
24)       END FINDMAX;
25)
26) *DATA
27) 3, 7, 12, 2, 6, -1
```

The printed "output" produced by executing this program with the
data on line 27 is:

        NUMBER OF VALUES = 5
        MAXIMUM VALUE = 12

The following remarks attempt to explain some of the less obvious aspects of the program:

Line 1 announces that the program is written in PL/C, which is a special form of a language called PL/I. Most computing systems accept programs in many different languages and the user must indicate which of these he will use. Line 1 also gives the name of the programmer.

Lines 2 and 3 are program comments. These are intended for human readers and have no effect on the execution of the program. In PL/I comments are denoted by /* preceding and */ following the text of the comment. Comments are also included in lines 6, 7, 8, 11 and 12.

Lines 4 and 24 indicate the beginning and end of this program -- which is named FINDMAX.

Lines 5, 10, 15, 21 and 25 are blank and are inserted to visually indicate the separate sections of the program. They have no effect on execution.

Lines 6-9 define the variables that will be used in the program and specify that they may contain integers ("FIXED" means integer) in the decimal number system.

Lines 11-14 are "initialization" actions -- special steps necessary to make the central, repeated section operate properly on its first execution. GET LIST(NUMBER); means to "read" the first number on the data following the *DATA card (line 26) and store it in variable NUMBER.

Lines 16-20 form the central section, which is repeated for each number. The symbol "¬=" in line 16 means "not equal".

Lines 22-23 are the final steps that cause the results of the process to be displayed.

Line 26 indicates that data follow.

Line 27 consists of the data (including a dummy data value of -1) to be processed by this program.

This example will often be referred to in later sections. In particular, Section 1.4 discusses its "correctness".

1.2 Analysis of a Problem and Design of a Program

The starting point of the analysis process is a problem statement. This is usually given in English or in a hybrid combination of English and the symbols used in that problem area (mathematical symbols, for example). It generally deals with things -- temperatures, automobiles, colors, voters, dollars, etc. -- that cannot themselves be stored and manipulated by a computer. It is also usually stated in terms of commands that are not intelligible to a computer -- words like "solve", "find", "choose", etc. Typically a problem statement is at least initially somewhat vague and imprecise. This is partly because of a tacit reliance on the knowledge and common sense of the human reader, but also partly because the originator has often not completely formulated the exact requirements.

The end point of the process is a program -- a procedure that can be executed on a computer and that represents a solution to the initial problem. This process of transforming a problem description into a program has several different aspects:

1. A translation of language -- from English/mathematics to a programming language (PL/I, FORTRAN, COBOL, etc.)

2. A conversion from a statement of objectives -- what is to be done -- to an executable procedure -- how the task is to be accomplished.

3. The definition of symbols (variables) in a program to represent the real-world objects of the problem. For example, a variable in one problem might represent the status of one of the squares of a chess board; in another problem, the number of dollars in a bank account; in another, the temperature at a particular point on a rocket nozzle.

4. The elimination of all vagueness, imprecision and ambiguity in the description. There is never any vagueness in a computer program -- every program always tells the computer precisely what to do. The trick is to construct a program whose execution exactly solves the particular problem in question.

Only on very simple problems (such as those found in programming textbooks) is there much chance of success if one starts immediately to write the program -- no matter how experienced one might be at programming. On problems of any size and complexity a systematic analysis of requirements, and design of the overall structure of the program, should precede any attempt to write program statements. It is convenient to view this process as a "top down" or "level by level" analysis of the problem. The top level is the initial problem statement; the bottom level is a complete program; the number of intervening levels depends on the complexity of the problem.

Generally the second level is just an elaboration of the problem statement -- an attempt to make complete and precise exactly what is required. This is often achieved by a dialog between the programmer and the "customer" -- the owner of the problem. This dialog can involve questions like the following:

1.   What form will the supplied data be in?

2.   Are there reasonable limits on the values of data that may be expected?

3.   How will the end of the data be recognized?

4.   What errors in the data should be anticipated? What action should be taken?

5.   What form should the output take? What labelling and titling should be provided?

6.   What precision (number of significant figures) of results is required?

7.   What changes in problem statement are likely (or possible) to occur during the lifetime of the program?

There may also be questions and discussion of alternative strategies of solution. There might be two approaches -- one more costly to design and program, and the other more costly to execute. The customer must provide information to guide such a choice.

While the objective of this dialog is ostensibly to convey information to the programmer -- to help him to understand exactly what has to be done -- very often it also causes the customer to discover that the problem is not yet well-formulated, and that he himself is not sure, in detail, what he wants done.

The levels occurring after this refinement of the problem statement are generally designed to accomplish two tasks:

1.   To break up big problems into little problems -- which in turn are attacked by this same approach.

2.   To reduce the commands from English to programming terms. That is, "find", "solve", etc. must be reduced to "read", "print", "assign", "repeat", and then eventually to GET, PUT, DO -- the statements of a programming language.

1.2.1 An Example of Initial Problem Analysis

Suppose a problem statement (level 1) is given in the following way:

Given a list of numbers, print the first, second, third numbers, etc., but stop printing when the largest number in the list has been printed.

After some discussion this statement of the problem might be refined to something like the following (level 2):

A set of not more than 100 integers, each greater than zero, is given on punched cards. A dummy value of zero will be added to denote the end. The ordering with respect to value is unknown. Print a column of numbers corresponding to these numbers in the order given. Begin printing with the first and terminate when the last number printed is the maximum of the entire set. For example, if 1, 7, 3, 9, 5, 0 are given, the output should be:

```
1
7
3
9
```

It should be evident that it is not known how much printing is to be done by this program until the position of the maximum value is determined, and this cannot be done until the last number of the input data has been examined (since the last could be the maximum). Therefore either the numbers will have to be read twice (once to determine the position of the maximum, and a second time to print the values) or the numbers will have to be read once and stored in the computer memory for later use. Card reading is a relatively slow and expensive operation for a computer, so the second strategy is preferable. This could lead to a third level of description:

3.1 Read a sequence of 100 or fewer positive integers from cards until a zero value is encountered; store these integers in memory, preserving order.

3.2 Find the position of the integer with maximum value in this sequence.

3.3 Print the early values of the sequence, from the first to the maximum value, one per line.

One would then attack each of these subproblems to reduce the commands -- "read from cards" and "store in memory" in the first subproblem -- to the corresponding statements in the target programming language. We have carried this analysis far enough here to give the general idea -- the program is completed in Section 5.5.

1.3 Translation to a Programming Language

The level-by-level transformation of the problem description is complete when the entire description is in a language that is intelligible to a computer. However, there is no single, universal programming language into which all problem descriptions are translated; there are literally hundreds of programming languages in use today. The choice of language will have some influence on the manner in which a problem is solved, and may have considerable influence on the difficulty experienced in obtaining a solution. Some programming languages have been designed to facilitate solution of certain classes of problems; they exchange generality for convenience for a particular type of problem. Some exist to serve different makes and models of computers, and many exist just because there are wide differences of opinion as to what a programming language should look like. Opinions on the subject are strongly held, and debated with a fervor normally reserved for politics or religion.

Although there are hundreds of languages in use, a relative handful dominate the field. The most widely used programming language today is COBOL, which was designed for business data processing problems. (The name comes from the first letters of the words: COmmon Business Oriented Language.) The most widely used language for engineering and scientific computation is called FORTRAN (from FORmula TRANslation). Both of these languages were developed in the 1950s -- a long time ago in this field. Other important languages are ALGOL, APL, BASIC, LISP, PL/I, and SNOBOL.

PL/I was developed in the mid-60s in an attempt to serve both the scientific and data processing areas with a single language. The price of this flexibility is complexity. Fortunately one does not have to learn the entire language in order to use part of it. One can learn a small subset of the language initially and then add topics as required to meet new and more challenging tasks. Unfortunately this partitioning of the language is not at all clean, and the unused and unseen portions sometimes intrude upon the initial subset, causing surprising results and forcing one to do things in ways that are not easily explained. One critic compared PL/I to a Swiss Army knife with 100 blades -- there is unquestionably a blade for whatever one might want to do, but there is some risk that in using one blade you will cut yourself with another.

For most students, the first programming language learned will be only the first of several. This is true both because there are many specialized languages available for various different areas of application, and because progress in the field of computer science should eventually lead to languages that will replace all those in use today. PL/I's generality makes it attractive in this regard, for many of the concepts that are emphasized in special-purpose languages are present in some form in PL/I. It is easier for a student who initially

learned PL/I to later learn FORTRAN or COBOL on his own than it
would be to proceed in the opposite order.

PL/C is a special dialect of PL/I. Some features have been
deleted from PL/I and others added in order to facilitate
introductory instruction. (An exact comparison of PL/I and PL/C
is given in Appendix A.)   PL/C is also provided with a
translation program (called a "compiler" -- see Part VII) which
is much more efficient for short programs than its PL/I
counterpart, and which provides considerably more help to a
neophyte programmer. For the most part PL/C and PL/I are
identical, and the student can ignore the differences.

1.4 Confirmation of Program Correctness

Confirming correctness of a program requires a convincing
demonstration that the program actually satisfies the precise
requirements of the problem.   This phase of the computing
process is typically so badly neglected by writers and teachers
that it seems as if they regard the possibility of mistakes as
somewhat remote and distinctly embarrassing. In any but the
most trivial task _many_ _errors_ will be made in each phase.
Anyone who intends to use a computer might as well accept this
unfortunate fact and make plans to systematically track down the
inevitable errors.   Very typically more than half of the total
time, effort, and cost of the computing process is devoted to
testing and "debugging" the program -- and yet in spite of this
effort the process is not often completely successful.   An
embarrassingly large fraction of programs that are declared to
be complete and correct by their authors still contain latent
flaws.   This situation is so prevalent and serious that a large
proportion of society today has diminishing confidence in the
computing process.   Computers are increasingly thought to be
somehow inherently unreliable, but in almost all cases the true
fault lies in a program that was ill-designed and/or
inadequately tested.

The program in Section 1.1 was deliberately constructed to
illustrate this point. It works perfectly for the data given,
and also for many other sets of data, but line 9 restricts this
program so that it can only successfully handle _integer_ values.
However, there is nothing in the problem statement that suggests
that the program will only be used for integer values. As a
consequence any time this program is used for data that are not
all integers (that is, values like 17.3), it is likely to
produce incorrect results without even warning the user that he
is in trouble. The program "works" for some sets of data but it
is _not_ a _correct_ program for the given problem.

Many people seem to regard testing in a negative sense -- as
an extra phase of the computing process that must be performed
only if there appear to be errors. In fact, it is an essential
part of programming.   One must take positive action to try and

force latent errors into revealing themselves -- so that one can reasonably infer correctness if no errors are exposed by determined and persistent testing. This must be done not just for a few simple test cases, but for maliciously contrived test cases that exercise a program more strenuously than is likely to occur in actual use. Contriving sufficiently difficult test cases is something of an art in itself. While testing is listed as a separate phase of the programming process it actually pervades the entire process, and if all consideration of determining correctness is postponed to the final phase it will almost surely be unsuccessful. It is essential that the necessity of demonstrating correctness be considered at the time that the overall structure of the program is chosen and that provision for testing be incorporated in the program as it is written, rather than as an afterthought.

1.5 Loading, Translation and Execution of a Program

When the program is complete and data have been prepared, both must be transmitted to the computer. The usual means of communication is the "punched card" or "IBM card". A machine called a "keypunch" is used to encode information in a card by punching holes in it. Each different character has a different pattern of holes; each character in the program and data is represented by the pattern in one vertical column of the card.

An alternative method of introducing information into a computing system is by means of a "terminal" directly connected to the computer. The keyboard of such a terminal is like that of the keypunch -- but instead of punching holes in a card which will later be detected by the computer, the terminal transmits its information directly to the computer, essentially as the key is struck. This has the virtue of immediate response -- the user is notified of errors after each line of the program, and sees results as the program is being executed. Although the use of such terminals is increasing rapidly it is still more expensive than punched cards, and the majority of introductory instruction still uses cards. For our purposes it makes little difference which type of access is used and we will speak of program lines, input lines, and cards almost interchangeably.

The key point in understanding the loading and execution of a program is the timing of the reading of the cards. The card deck consists of two parts -- the program (lines 1 to 25 of the example in Section 1.1) and the data (lines 26 and 27). The cards for the entire program are read initially -- before any execution of the program begins; the cards for the data are not read until specifically called for during execution of the program. The computer does not read a card and execute the statement on it, read the next card and execute, etc. Instead it reads the entire program, creates a copy of the program in "memory", and then begins execution with the first statement of the program. In the course of execution the "card read"

statements (such as lines 14 and 19 of 1.1) will cause the data
cards to be read.

The initial loading of the cards of the user's program is
controlled by execution of another program called a "compiler"
(or sometimes a "translator" or "interpreter").   As the user-
program cards are read a translation is performed by the
compiler with the result that the "copy" of the program in
memory, while functionally equivalent to the initial program, is
very different in appearance.   During this translation the
compiler   checks   the   program   statements for "syntactical"
(grammatical) errors and reports these to the user.   If any
errors are discovered during this loading-translation process
most compilers will halt after loading and refuse to initiate
execution of the user-program; a few compilers will effect some
repair of minor errors and permit execution to begin.   Most
users will become aware of the existence of a compiler only
through this error checking and will never have occasion to see
the strange form their program has assumed in memory. Readers
who are interested in this aspect of computing should read Part
VII, and then pursue the references cited there.

The printed output for a program can also be divided into two
parts, corresponding to the loading and execution phases
described above. During loading, a copy of the user-program is
printed, including announcement of any errors discovered. This
much of the printing is automatic -- a service performed by the
compiler.   Further printing will be done only as called for by
the "output" statements (such as lines 22 and 23 of 1.1) of the
program. If the user fails to include any such statements there
will be no output during execution and the results of the
computation will never be known.

Section 1 Exercises

The following all refer to the programming example given in
Section 1.1.   You cannot be expected to answer all of these
questions at this point, but attempting to do so should be
interesting and educational.

1. What would have to be done to cause this program to obtain
the maximum of the following eight numbers:
    2, 4, 6, 15, 3, 9, 7, 9

2. What would happen if the program were used to find the
maximum of the following nine numbers:
    6, 45, -3, 14, 0, 2, -1, 52, 143

3. What would happen if line 27 looked like the following:
    5, 5, 5, -1, -1, -1

4. What would happen if the order of lines 17 and 18 were
reversed? Lines 13 and 14? Lines 18 and 19?

5.   Suppose the problem definition were broadened to require the program to work for negative as well as positive numbers. What changes would have to be made?

6. How could the program be changed to obtain the <u>minimum</u> rather than the maximum of the numbers?

7. How could the program be changed to produce both the <u>maximum</u> and the <u>minimum</u> of the numbers?

8. What would happen if line 17 were accidentally left out (say the card was dropped) before the program was submitted to the computer? Line 19? Line 23?

9. What would happen if line 22 were replaced by the following line?

    /* PUT LIST('NUMBER OF VALUES =', COUNT); */

10. How could the program be changed to produce the sum of the numbers in addition to the maximum?

11. What would happen if line 2 were replaced by the following line:

    /* COMPUTE THE PRETTIEST OF THE GREEN NUMBERS */

and no other change were made in the program?

12. Construct a set of test data (a replacement for line 27) that would cause the program to produce incorrect results.

Section 2 <u>Variables</u>

A program consists of a description of how a certain set of values are to be manipulated. However, the description rarely deals directly with these values; instead it deals with entities called "variables". For example, instead of writing

    2 + 3   one could write   X + Y

and make arrangements so that "X had the value 2" and "Y had the value 3". The difference is essentially the same as that between arithmetic and algebra, and yields roughly the same advantage. In this way one gains the ability to specify a procedure which may be applied, without change in the written form, to many different sets of values.

A <u>variable</u> is a named place or location in the memory of a computer, into which a value may be placed. For example:

    A <u>20</u>   TOTAL <u>456.003</u>   ACCOUNT <u>-20.7</u>

The first variable is named A and has the value 20 in its location (on its line). The second variable is named TOTAL and has the value 456.003. Variable ACCOUNT has the value -20.7.

A variable is relatively permanent -- it is created at the beginning of the execution of a program and lasts until the execution is completed. The value is generally more transient, and may change often during the execution of the procedure. At any given instant during execution a variable has exactly one value. That is, its physical location contains a single, specific value, which is referred to as the <u>current value</u> of the variable. The current value of the variable named A above is 20. The phrase "current value of the variable named A" is long, and is often shortened to "value of A". A's value changes whenever a different value is placed in the location named A.

It is important to clearly distinguish between the different actions of <u>creating</u> a variable and <u>assigning a value</u> to a variable. A variable is created only once -- at the time that a physical location in the memory of the computer is set aside to hold its value. The creation process is also referred to as "declaring" or "defining" a variable. Once a variable has been created it may have a value assigned to it, and that value may be frequently changed. This is done by the "assignment process" -- which is the topic of Section 3.

In PL/I, one declares the variables and kinds of values they
can contain in a "declaration". For example,

    DECLARE (A, TOTAL, ACCOUNT) FIXED DECIMAL;

defines three different variables named A, TOTAL and ACCOUNT.
(The terms FIXED and DECIMAL will be explained in Section 2.3.)
The declaration does not automatically assign an initial value
to the newly created variables; hence they exist, they have a
location ready to receive a value, but have not as yet received
one.

Variables play a very important role in programs.   Each
variable contains a value with a specific meaning -- for
example, the minimum value of a list of numbers, or the
cumulative sum of a list of numbers. Knowledge of the variables
and their meaning is essential for any person trying to
understand a program. In order to help the reader, we place all
declarations for all variables at the <u>beginning</u> of the program,
before any statement which uses the variables.

Secondly, it is a good practice to describe the use of each
variable with a "comment". In PL/I, "/*" marks the beginning of
a comment and "*/" marks the end. The comment may contain any
characters on the keypunch -- except the sequence "*/" which
would be interpreted as the end of the comment. For example:

    DECLARE (MINVALUE, CUM_SUM) FIXED DECIMAL;
        /* MINVALUE SAVES MINIMUM VALUE OF THE X'S SO FAR   */
              /* MINVALUE SHOULD NEVER BECOME NEGATIVE. */
        /* CUM_SUM IS THE CUMULATIVE SUM OF THE X'S SO FAR. */

Clarity and precision in defining the role of each variable
in a program is of vital importance in producing a correct and
understandable program. An appreciable fraction of students'
programming difficulties can be traced to fuzziness in the
meaning of key variables. We find it useful, when asked to help
"debug" a program, to start by asking questions along this line:

    "What does this variable represent?"
    "Does it have the same meaning everywhere in the program?"
    "What are the extreme limits on the values it may contain?"

This approach is aided by following a consistent practice of
supplementing the declaration of each variable with comments.

During execution of a program each variable is actually
assigned a particular physical location in the memory of the
computer to hold its value. This assignment of memory locations
is performed automatically by the computing system and, in
general, the programmer does not have to be concerned with it.
In writing about programs, and in tracing their execution, we
will employ the convention of a "named line" to represent a
variable, as in the examples above.

2.1 Identifiers

The sequence of characters that forms the name of a variable
is called an "identifier". Each programming language has a set
of rules that control the choice or construction of identifiers.
These rules sometimes seem arbitrary (although there are more-
or-less reasonable explanations for them) but at this stage it
is best just to accept and learn them. Among the most widely
used programming languages -- FORTRAN, COBOL, PL/I and ALGOL --
the rules are quite similar, but just enough different to be a
nuisance to the unwary programmer. In almost every language, <u>an
identifier can consist of a letter, followed by a sequence of
other letters and digits</u>, and this is the kind of identifier you
will use most often. The PL/I rules for forming identifiers are
given in Appendix A.2.

You should choose <u>variable names that suggest the role</u> the
variables play in the program. While it may seem clever to name
variables after girls or flowers, it doesn't help to make a
program understandable. For example, although SUSAN is a legal
identifier, using SUSAN as the name of a variable which holds
the average of 10 numbers is not helpful. AVERAGE or AVG would
be better since it would help to indicate the role of the
variable.

The PL/I keywords (such as GET, PUT, LIST, SKIP, DO, END,
DECLARE) should not be used as identifiers. Using these words
for the names of variables makes a program hopelessly hard to
understand. A list of keywords that <u>cannot</u> be used as
identifiers is given in Appendix A.2.

2.2 Values

Programming languages allow a variety of different types of
values to be stored in variables. The most important types for
ordinary numeric computation are signed <u>integers</u> (..., -2, -1,
0, 1, 2, ...) and <u>real numbers</u> -- such as 20.3, -463.2,
.000043, and 4.3×10^{-5}. (Note that the last two real numbers
look different but represent the same quantity.) Since each
value is placed in a physical location in the computer's memory,
there must obviously be a limit on the number of digits allowed.
Such restrictions are important and eventually one must be aware
of them, but we will postpone a detailed discussion (see
Appendix A.5 on "Attributes") until more vital subjects have
been covered. We assume here that all numerical values will be
represented in the computer in the conventional decimal
notation, and that a reasonably adequate number of digits are
permitted in each value.

Constant values are often written in a program. In general,
they can be written in their usual form:

    -20   10365   .4   0.15   -.00043   49.65

Alternatively, constants can be written in "scientific" or "exponential" form:

   -20E0   1.0365E+4   4E-1   0.15E0   -4.3E-4

The exponent "E0" following the number specifies that the fractional number is to be multiplied by 10^0, which is 1. In general, one can put any integer after the "E" to represent a power of 10. Thus, the following are all equivalent:

   4.3E-5   .43E-4   .000043E0   .00000043E+2

This is often called "floating point format", since the position of the decimal point "floats" depending on the exponent following "E".

   In general, one can use the exponential form whenever it is convenient, but Section 3.2.3 describes one situation where it is necessary to use this form.

   Some programming languages allow other types of values. A value may also be a string (or sequence) of characters, such as 'ITHACA'. Variables with such "character" values are discussed in Section 9. The values "true" and "false" are important in certain contexts and we will discuss them in Section 4. For the moment we will consider only values that are integers and real numbers.

2.3 Type Attributes

   In PL/I each individual variable is restricted to one particular type of value. The value may change, but the type of value (like the name) is permanent for the life of the variable. For example, if variable COUNT is defined to hold only integer values it might, at different times during the execution of a program, have values such as 2, 1501, -3 and 0, but it could never have values such as 20.3 or 'JONES'.

   The properties that determine the type of value that can be stored in a variable are called "attributes" of the variable. We represent attributes by putting them in brackets [and] after the variable. The following examples illustrate how the names, values and attributes of variables will be indicated in the text:

   MAX   20 [fixed decimal]   MAX may only contain integers
                                    (e.g. -3, 0, 1, +5)

   TB42 -.002 [float decimal]   TB42 may contain real numbers
                                    (e.g. 20.3, 20, -.82)

   Z4   -20.0 [float decimal]   Z4 may contain real numbers

"FIXED" and "FLOAT" are PL/I's way of saying "integer" and "real", respectively. The term DECIMAL means that the value of MAX will be represented in the computer memory in the decimal number system. (The reader may have assumed that this would be the case, but in fact, the "binary number system" is extensively used in computing. See the exercises in Section V.1.)

A variable <u>always</u> has some particular set of type attributes. If, on occasion, we neglect to mention them it is only because the type of value is not relevant to the point under discussion -- not because attributes do not exist for that variable.

In PL/I type attributes are specified by listing them in the declaration that causes the creation of the variable. For example:

    DECLARE MAX FIXED DECIMAL;

    DECLARE TB42 FLOAT DECIMAL, Z4 FLOAT DECIMAL;

When several variables have the same set of attributes, the names may be given in parentheses, and the attributes given only once. For example, the following declarations are equivalent:

    DECLARE (TB42, Z4) FLOAT DECIMAL;

    DECLARE TB42 FLOAT DECIMAL, Z4 FLOAT DECIMAL;

Section 2 <u>Summary</u>

1. A variable is a named location in computer memory into which a value may be placed.

2. All variables to be used in a procedure should be defined (created) by specifying their names and type attributes in declarations placed at the beginning of the program.

3. We will use the type attributes FIXED DECIMAL for integer values and FLOAT DECIMAL for real values.

4. Numeric constants may be written in a program in either conventional form: 32, -61, 4.3, 0.198, or in exponential form: 3.2E1, -61E0, 4.3E0, 198E-3.

5. Each identifier should be chosen to reflect the role that the variable plays in the program, and the declaration of the variable should be supplemented by a comment that describes the role fully and clearly.

Section 2 _Exercises_

Exercises 1 to 4 concern the following variables:

       LAST_ONE   <u>-20 [fixed decimal]</u>

       ANSWER   <u>-30.2 [float decimal]</u>

       BAD20   <u>0 [fixed decimal]</u>

       COSINE   <u>-30.2 [float decimal]</u>

       TEXT   <u>30.0 [float decimal]</u>

       MINIMUM   <u>+30.2 [float decimal]</u>

1. a) What is the current value of variable ANSWER?
    b) What is the current value of variable COSINE?
    c) What is the current value of variable TEXT?
    d) Which variables have the value -30.2?
    e) Which variables have the value 20?

2. Which of the following values:

      -30, -30.1, 0, .0050, 43891, 43891.5, 4.3891E4

    can be stored in variable:

      a) LAST_ONE ?
      b) BAD20 ?
      c) MINIMUM ?

3. Define the term "variable".

4. Write a PL/I declaration for the variables given above.

5. Consider the following declaration:

    DECLARE POSTOT FLOAT DECIMAL, /* TOTAL OF X'S > 0 */
      (SUM, COUNT) FIXED DECIMAL; /* SUM OF Y'S, NO. OF PTS*/

    a) Write a declaration that is exactly equivalent but does
    not use parentheses.

    b) Write three separate declarations (one for each
    variable) that are exactly equivalent to the single
    declaration given.

Section 3 <u>Assignment of Value</u>

The essence of the computing process is the assignment of values to variables. The basic assignment process, in any programming language, has two distinct stages:

1. The production of a new value.
2. The assignment of that new value to a variable.

The construction for specifying a new value is called an "expression". Examples are:

26

X

Y+1

(X3+ABC)/ZZZ

where X, Y, X3, ABC, and ZZZ are variable names. In the evaluation of an expression the current value of each variable referenced is used, but this does not change the values of those variables. Regardless of the length and complexity of an expression the result of its evaluation is a <u>single value</u>.

The second stage of the assignment process is the disposition of the new value. A logical form for describing this would be:

X + Y -> Z

A precise description of the execution of this process is:

Evaluate the expression X + Y, by adding a <u>copy</u> of the current value of the variable named X to a copy of the current value of the variable named Y. Store this sum as the new value of the variable named Z (replacing and destroying whatever previous value the variable named Z may have had).

Note that the values of X and Y are only copied and are not changed in the process. Typical values of X, Y and Z before and after such an assignment are:

before: X <u>1</u>   Y <u>3</u>   Z <u>2</u>
after: X <u>1</u>   Y <u>3</u>   Z <u>4</u>

3.1 The PL/I Assignment Statement

The syntax for an "assignment statement" in PL/I is:

        variable name = expression;

The "expression" on the right gives the formula to obtain a new
value. It can be short -- for example, a constant -- or so long
and complicated that it requires several lines to write.   The
variable named on the left is the "target variable" -- the
variable that is to receive the new value. The "=" denotes the
assignment process (instead of the arrow used on the previous
page) and the ";" denotes the end of the statement.   The
following are examples of PL/I assignment statements:

        A = 4.3;

        Z = X + 1;

        I = I + 1;

        LOW = CTR - 1.43E-1;

        SUM = 0;

        SUM = A1 + A2 + A3;

        SUM = SUM + NUMBER;

        TEMP = (A3 + B4)/BASE;

        RATIO = (A+B) / (C+D);

        SUP = Z3 + P / (A + B/4E0);

    It is unfortunate that most programming languages use this
syntax. Normal left-to-right reading does not suggest the order
in which the different actions are performed. For example,

    X = Y;

should be read "get a copy of the value of Y, and store it in
X". It might seem that this is equivalent to saying "let X take
on the value of Y", but consider the following statement:

    X = X + Y;

It is clearer to read this as "add together the current values
of X and Y, and store the result in X", than it would be to say
"let X take on the value of X plus the value of Y".

    Furthermore, the use of "=" improperly suggests a similarity
to an algebraic equation. The assignment statement is a command
to perform a sequence of actions, whereas an equation is a
statement of fact. If equality between the left and right sides

already existed, there would be no point in writing the statement at all, since no action would be required. One might try to salvage this "equation interpretation" by suggesting that it is a command to "make the equation become true". However, this interpretation just cannot explain examples such as:

    X = X + Y;   and   W = W + 2;

The assignment statement can only be considered a command to perform two distinct actions: first -- produce a value from the expression on the right; second -- assign this value to the variable on the left.

    Note also that the two sides of an assignment statement are not symmetric in role:

    X = Y;   and   Y = X;

have different meanings, although as equations they would be equivalent.

    Assignment statements are executed in the order in which they appear (reading from left to right, and top to bottom). Consider the statements:

    X = Y + Z;   and   Z = X + Y;

Assuming a set of initial values, the effect of executing these statements in one order would be:

		X		Y		Z	
before		X	3	Y	5	Z	2
after	X = Y + Z;	X	7	Y	5	Z	2
after	Z = X + Y;	X	7	Y	5	Z	12

With the same initial values the effect of executing these same statements in the opposite order would be:

	X		Y		Z	
before	X	3	Y	5	Z	2
after Z = X + Y;	X	3	Y	5	Z	8
after X = Y + Z;	X	13	Y	5	Z	8

    As a further example, consider the task of interchanging, or "swapping", the values of two variables. For example, we might want to change

	A	3	B	5
to	A	5	B	3

Since there is no single statement in PL/I to perform this, it must be done with a sequence of assignment statements. Moreover, it requires three statements and the use of an extra variable. Let T be a variable not used in the program so far. The following sequence uses T as a "temporary" variable to accomplish the swap:

```
/* SWAP VALUES OF A AND B */
   T = A;
   A = B;
   B = T;
```

Given the initial values of the variables as shown below, we show the contents of the variables after execution of each statement. Slashes /// are used as the value of a variable that has been created, but has not yet been assigned a value.

before	A 3	B 5	T ///
after T = A;	A 3	B 5	T 3
after A = B;	A 5	B 5	T 3
after B = T;	A 5	B 3	T 3

The comment /* SWAP VALUES OF A AND B */ is used to summarize the actions of the group of statements that follow it (and are indented with respect to it). When reading a program that included this segment, to find out <u>what</u> is being performed we need only read the comment <u>instead</u> of the statements indented underneath it. The detailed statements under the comment need be read only to find out <u>how</u> the swap is being performed. Comments are entirely for the benefit of human of the program -- they have no effect on the execution of the program by the computer. When used properly, comments make it significantly easier for a human to read and understand a program, but when badly used they can obscure rather than clarify. (See Section 4.6.)

3.2 <u>Arithmetic Expressions</u>

Expressions are used in many different contexts in a programming language. Wherever they occur they always have the same basic purpose -- to provide a <u>formula by which a value can be obtained</u>. The simplest expressions are just constants, like 3 or 20.6E0, or variables, like I or TOTAL. In general, an expression can include a number of terms or "operands", and "operations" by which the operand values are to be combined to yield a single value. Examples of expressions are shown in the right side of the assignment statements of Section 3.1. (The semi-colon is the symbol to end the assignment statement and not part of the expression.)

3.2.1 <u>Symbols for Operations</u>

The PL/I symbols for arithmetic operations are:

   +   for addition
   -        for subtraction, or to indicate negation
   /   for division
   *   for multiplication
   **   for exponentiation   (X^2 is written as X**2)

The symbol for an operation is often called an "operator". The * operator is used for multiplication by most programming languages. This convention was invented because all of the familiar means of indicating multiplication in algebra would give rise to confusion in programming. For example, no small letter x is available, while the capital letter X is too popular as a variable to permit it to be reserved for use as a multiplication sign. A period could get confused with a decimal point -- does 2.34.5 mean 2.34 times 5 or 2 times 34.5? Juxtaposition conflicts with the freedom of constructing identifiers -- AB can be a variable, so it cannot represent A times B. Parentheses -- A(B) -- would be confused with subscripts, as explained in Section 5.

Similarly, the usual convention of denoting exponentiation by a superscript is not possible in a programming language because there is no way to indicate on a punched card that one symbol is to be elevated above another. Most programming languages use the double asterisk. (The asterisks must be adjacent -- no blanks between them.)

Other operations exist which can be used with operands whose values are not numeric. For example, the operations performed on string-valued variables are described in Section 9.

3.2.2 <u>Precedence of Operations</u>

Some concern must be given to the order in which arithmetic operations are performed. For example, should the expression

   A + B * C

be evaluated as A+(B*C) or (A+B)*C? In any expression, however complicated, a lavish enough use of parentheses will remove any possible ambiguity. However, to avoid too many parentheses, PL/I has conventions corresponding to normal algebra to indicate, for example, that:

         $a + bc, \quad a - b + c, \quad -a^2$

mean $a + (bc), (a - b) + c, -(a^2)$

and not $(a + b)c, a - (b + c), (-a)^2.$

The PL/I rules for evaluation of an expression are:

1. Expressions in parentheses are evaluated first, from the innermost set of parentheses, to the outer.

2. Subject to rule 1, the order of operations is:
       first: exponentiation (**) and negation (-)
       next: multiplication (*) and division (/)
       last: addition (+) and subtraction (-)

3. Sequences of operations in the same category under rule 2 are evaluated:
       exponentiations and negations - right to left
       multiplications and divisions - left to right
       additions and subtractions - left to right

   For example:

   X**Y**Z is equivalent to X**(Y**Z)

   -X**Y is equivalent to -(X**Y)

   X/Y*Z is equivalent to (X/Y)*Z

   X-Y+Z is equivalent to (X-Y)+Z

It is not really necessary to memorize these rules; use enough parentheses to specify the desired order, and secondly keep a programming language manual handy so you can look the rules up if necessary. The important thing to note is that PL/I does remember these rules and will always follow them in determining the order of execution.

3.2.3 Conversion of Values

   PL/I is usually quite accommodating with regard to the conversion of values between FIXED and FLOAT forms. FIXED and FLOAT variables, and conventional and exponential constants can all be used in the same expression. When the operands of an arithmetic operator are of different type (one FIXED and the other FLOAT) the non-FLOAT operand will be converted to FLOAT form. (Actually, a copy of the value is converted.) For this purpose, a conventional constant (even one with a decimal point) is considered to be in FIXED form and an exponential constant is in FLOAT form.

   However, there are a few surprises. The one that seems to cause a new programmer the most trouble is the fact that a FIXED variable will only accept an integer value no matter what kind of value is produced by the expression on the right side of the assignment statement. For example, if the variable INDEX is FIXED, the statement

INDEX = -17.3;

is legal (no error warning) but upon execution the value of
INDEX becomes -17. The value -17.3 has been "truncated" to -17
by dropping the digits to the right of the decimal point. This
truncation **may** be intended by the programmer, but if not, it is
a particularly insidious kind of error. The program could be
tested on data that happened to be all integers, and work
satisfactorily. Then later, if it is used for data that are not
all integers, this supposedly correct program could give
incorrect results.

Another type of surprise can occur when arithmetic operations
are performed with FIXED operands. Multiplication, addition and
subtraction are straightforward, but division is not. Division
with two FIXED operands is permitted in PL/I, but the rules that
would allow you to understand what the result will be are very
complicated and do not always produce an answer that you would
have expected. For example, the expression 25 + 1/3 yields the
value 5.333333 in PL/I, and .333334 in PL/C (and an "overflow"
error in either). The only reasonable course for a beginner is
to carefully avoid the problem by making sure that in any
division <u>at least one of the operands is in FLOAT form</u>. This
means, for example, that one must not write 1/2, but should use
1/2E0 or .5. If J is a FIXED variable then one must write J/4E0
and not just J/4. If J and K are FIXED variables write
J/(1E0*K) rather than J/K.

3.3 <u>Built-in Functions</u>

Some common "functions" are used so often in programming that
they have been included as part of the language. (This is
essentially a convenience for the programmer since the task of
each of these functions could be accomplished by explicitly
writing all the statements needed to evaluate the function.)
For example, to obtain the square root of the value of a
variable X write

SQRT(X)

and to evaluate the square root of the value of an expression
X+Y/Z write

SQRT(X+Y/Z)

The expression whose square root is sought is called the
"argument" of the function.

This functional form can be used as an operand in an expression, just as one would use a variable:

    X + SQRT(Y)

    SQRT(TEMP - SQRT(T4K/PRESSURE))

    B4 * (SQRT(SQRT(J3) + R2PEAK) + SIDE4)

Another function gives the maximum of a set of values:

    MAX(A,B)

yields a value equal to the greater of the values of A and B. The MAX function may have a long list of arguments, and these may be expressions as well as variables:

    MAX(A,B,C)

    MAX(X+Y, 0, QLOW/4.5E0)

    MAX(A, MAX(B,C))   is equivalent to   MAX(A,B,C)

    MAX(A**B, SQRT(ZTOP), MEAN)

An analogous MIN function obtains the minimum of a set of arguments.

The built-in functions included in a language depend heavily on the problem area for which the language is designed. FORTRAN, designed primarily for scientific and engineering computation, has a different set of built-in functions from COBOL, which was designed for business data processing problems. PL/I, which was intended to be used in both of these areas, has a particularly large collection of built-in functions.   A complete list is given in Appendix A.8.

A problem can arise in distinguishing between a function name and a variable name -- especially since one type of variable name is always followed by parentheses (see Section 5 on "subscripted variables").   One could prohibit the use of the function names as variable names, but this would force the programmer to memorize a list of about 90 names he could not use for variables, including such useful ones as HIGH,   INDEX,   LOW, LENGTH, ALL, SUM, MAX, MIN, COUNT, DATE, and TIME. To avoid this, PL/I requires only that the same name not be used as a variable and a function in the same part of the program. That is, if you are using the SQRT built-in function you cannot use SQRT as a variable name, but if you are not using the COUNT function (and perhaps had forgotten that such a function even existed) you can use COUNT as a variable name. The declaration of such a name as a variable indicates that it will not be used as a built-in function.

3.4 Assignment from External Data

The expression in an assignment statement generates a new value in terms of values that are already in the computer memory. One also needs a mechanism to permit values to be introduced from outside of the computer. Execution of an "input" statement causes some auxiliary device -- such as a punched card reader, a magnetic tape reader, or a typewriter terminal -- to deliver one or more data values to the main memory of the computer. The simplest form of input statement in PL/I is the following:

    GET LIST(variable names, separated by commas);

An example is:

    GET LIST(AMOUNT);

Execution of this statement causes the next value to be read from the data list (which was given on cards after the program) and assigned to the variable named AMOUNT. The values are assigned using the same rules as in an assignment statement: if AMOUNT is a FIXED variable the data value will be truncated to an integer if necessary. Execution of the statement

    GET LIST(X, Y);

would cause the next two values to be read from the data list; the first is assigned to X and the second to Y.

Recall (from Section 1.5) that the cards bearing data at the end of the program are not read automatically into memory as the program is being loaded. Loading ends with the last card of the program body, and the cards bearing data are waiting in the card reader to be read if and when the program calls for them by executing GET statements. The cards supply a list of values; the reading process moves through this list from left-to-right, one card to the next, as demanded by the execution of GET statements. Each value is read only once from this list. Suppose there are three GET statements in a program, where all variables are FLOAT DECIMAL:

    ...
    GET LIST(BASE, HEIGHT);
    ...
    GET LIST(WIDTH, TEMP, TIME);
    ...
    GET LIST(LIMIT);
    ...

and the data list for this program is:

```
*DATA
17.5
83.72
23.05
76
2314
964.122
```

When the first GET statement is executed the first   two   values
are   read   from the data list (two values because there are two
variables listed in the statement) and 17.5 becomes the value of
BASE   and   83.72 becomes the value of HEIGHT.   When the next GET
statement is executed the next three values are read; 23.05   is
assigned   to WIDTH, 76 to TEMP and 2314 to TIME.   When the third
GET statement is executed the value 964.122 is   read   from   the
list and is assigned to LIMIT.

   A total of six values are read in by the three GET statements
and   exactly six values are provided in the data list. If there
had been more than six provided the extra   values   would   simply
have   been   ignored since the program never calls for them to be
read.   This could be intentional -- the amount   of   data   to   be
processed   might depend upon some test the program performs upon
the early data values.   This could also happen   by   accident   if
the   programmer did not properly coordinate his input statements
and data list.

   The opposite condition is more common -- a program   runs   out
of   data   when   a   GET   statement   is executed and an inadequate
number of data values remain on the list to satisfy all   of   the
variables   in   the   GET.   Different   languages   react   to   this
situation in different ways.   It is essentially an error, but is
often   considered   a   legitimate   way to stop the execution of a
program.   (PL/I has a special way of   handling   this   situation.
See   the   discussion   of   the ENDFILE condition in Part IV.)   At
least initially it is preferable to add some marker value at the
end ·of the actual data.   This should be a value that is clearly
recognizable -- it cannot be a possible data value   --   so   that
the   program   can   test   for   it after each GET statement.   This
technique was used in the example of Section 1.1.

   The variables listed in the GET statement and the   values   on
the data list must be <u>synchronized with respect to order</u> as well
as quantity.   The variable to which each particular   value   will
be   assigned   is   entirely   determined by the order in which the
variable names appear in the GET statements.   (For this   purpose
the   order of the GET statements is the order in which they will
be <u>executed</u>, not   necessarily   the   order   in   which   they   are
<u>written</u>.   This   distinction   is   the topic of Section 4.)   Hence
the programmer must know exactly what the order of the variables
in   the   "GET   lists"   will   be   and   arrange   the   data   values
accordingly.   This is not always easy and is a common source   of
errors.   For example, in the data list above there is nothing in
the list that suggests that 17.5 is intended to be   assigned   to
BASE   and   83.72 to HEIGHT.   If the position of these two values

had been reversed the computer would have uncomplainingly
assigned 83.72 to BASE and 17.5 to HEIGHT.

Sometimes there is a question as to whether an assignment
statement or a GET statement should be used. The statement

    LIMIT = 75.4E0;

would assign the same value to LIMIT as the following input
statement and data list (assuming that the order in both program
and data is such that the value shown is read by the statement
shown):

    ...
    GET LIST(LIMIT);
    ...
    *DATA
    ...
    75.4E0,
    ...

In general, only constants that are unlikely to be changed
should be supplied in assignment statements in the body of a
program. Control values that may be changed on different runs
of a program should always be supplied as data.

3.4.1 Data Format

The data format associated with the GET LIST statement is
quite simple; it is just a list of values. There can be no
blanks separating adjacent characters of one value, and adjacent
values must be separated by a comma, by one or more blanks, or
by both. The entire card may be used, with column 1 considered
to come immediately after column 80 of the previous card. (It
is generally a good idea to avoid splitting a single value onto
two cards -- that is, avoid punching 23 with the 2 in column 80
of one card and the 3 in column 1 of the next. PL/I doesn't
mind, but it is hard for humans to follow.) Values can be given
in either conventional or exponential form.

In the example above the six data values were given on six
different cards. Each of the following forms would produce the
same results:

(3.4.1a)   *DATA
             17.5, 83.72,23.05,   76 2314 ,964.122

(3.4.1b)   *DATA
             17.5, 83.72, 23.05, 76, 2314, 964.122

(3.4.1c)   *DATA
             1.75E1, 8.372E1, 2.305E1, 7.6E1, 2.314E3, 9.64122E2

(3.4.1d)   *DATA
               17.5, 83.72
               23.05, 76, 2314
               964.122

Although these are equivalent to PL/I (3.4.1d) is best for a human reader since it suggests by arrangement on cards which values will be read by each GET statement. (3.4.1a) is the least attractive because of the inconsistent (although legal) means of separating values.

   Only values can be given as data. It would not make sense to give a variable as a datum -- each datum will be assigned as the value of a variable, and variables of the kind we are using cannot have another variable as value. Arithmetic operations are not allowed in the data -- .5 cannot be given as 1/2.

Section 3 Summary

1.   The form of an assignment statement is:

     variable = expression ;

To execute an assignment statement, evaluate the expression and assign the result to the variable on the left of the =.

2.   +, -, / denote addition, subtraction and division. * is the only way of denoting multiplication. ** denotes exponentiation. In every division at least one of the operands should be in FLOAT form.

3.   Parenthesized subexpressions are evaluated from inside out.

4.   When not overruled by parentheses the order of operations is:
     a.   Exponentiation and negation
     b.   Multiplication and division
     c.   Addition and subtraction

Within these categories a sequence of exponentiations and negations proceeds from right to left; the others from left to right.

5.   When a value is assigned to an integer variable any fractional part of the value is dropped.

6.   A library of built-in functions such as SQRT(...) is provided.

7.   The form of the simplest input statement is:

     GET LIST(variable names, separated by commas);

8.   The order of data values on cards is crucial, but format   is
immaterial.   The entire card may be used; adjacent values should
be separated by a comma and/or one or more blanks.

Section 3 <u>Exercises</u>

1.   In each of the following assignment   statements   delete   all
"redundant"   parentheses   -- that is, parentheses whose deletion
does not change the result of the statement:

  a) ALT = ALT + (BASE + COL4) + DIV;

  b) PRESSURE = (TEMP + ENTROPY) * SPEC22;

  c) GRADIENT = (GRADIENT - (HGT-SLOPE));

  d) EFF = (EFF + (FULL * (LOSS**H3)));

  e) X = -B + SQRT((B*2 -(4*(A*C))));

2.   Suppose the following were the values of four variables at a
certain point in a program:

        BASE 4   [float decimal]
        HGT   3   [float decimal]
        SIDE 0   [float decimal]
        TOP   14.2 [float decimal]

Starting at that point, the following four assignment statements
are executed in the order shown below:

        SIDE = SIDE + BASE/HGT;
        SIDE = SIDE + BASE/HGT;
        TOP = BASE + HGT + SIDE + TOP;
        TOP = TOP/HGT;

What are the resulting values of the four variables?

3.   The following are all intended to be assignment statements.
Which ones contain at least one syntax error?

    a) A = B + C

    b) A = B, C;

    c) A = (B + C);

    d) A + B = C;

    e) (A = B + C);

    f) A = (B) + C;

    g) A = B (+) C;

    h) A = (B + C;)

4.   Write a GET statement and a data list that will assign the
same values as the following pair of assignment statements:

    XPLUS = 93.17;
    XMINUS = -45.93;

5.   Suppose the data given after a program is the following:

    *DATA
    2, 4, 6, 8, 10, 12, 14

What would be the values of the variables T4, LOW and VAL after
execution of the following statement (assuming that it is the
first GET statement to be executed in the program):

    GET LIST(VAL, LOW, LOW, T4, LOW, VAL);

Give a different data list and GET statement that will produce
exactly the same result (but are shorter and more reasonable
than the example shown).

Section 4 <u>Flow of Control</u>

The essential work of a computer program is performed by the assignment statements. Other statements are used to describe the structure of the program and to specify the order in which different statements are to be executed. These are said to specify the "flow of control" in the execution of a program.

4.1 <u>General Program Structure; Executing Programs</u>

A complete "job" to be processed by a computer consists of a <u>program</u> and <u>data</u>, in that order. In PL/C, the form of a job is:

```
*PL/C ID='name of programmer'
 /* program name comment */
 /* comment summarizing program function */
 identifier : PROCEDURE OPTIONS(MAIN);
    declarations
    body of procedure (imperative statements)
    END identifier ;
*DATA
    data cards
```

The program consists of a "main procedure". The identifier that appears before PROCEDURE and after END is called the "entry-name" of the procedure, and can be used to refer to the program as a whole. Entry-name identifiers are chosen subject to the same rules as variable identifiers (Appendix A.2) and should be chosen to suggest the action that the procedure performs. The entry-name should be different from every other identifier used in the program.

A procedure consists of <u>declarations</u> and <u>imperative statements</u>. The declarations specify the names and attributes of the variables used in the procedure. The declarations are written immediately after the procedure heading and are effectively part of the heading. They describe variables to be created before execution of the procedure body begins.

The body of the procedure consists of imperative statements that direct the computer to perform certain actions -- such as assign a new value to a variable, read new data values from cards, and print results. Normal execution order of the statements is like the normal order of reading English text -- from left to right, top to bottom, from the beginning to the end of a procedure.

4.1.1 Writing Simple Programs

At this point you have seen almost enough of PL/I to be able to write simple programs; we need only explain how to get "output" -- how to cause the computer to write numbers out in a readable form.

The simplest form of output statement is

PUT SKIP LIST(list of variables, separated by commas) ;

Thus, execution of a statement

PUT SKIP LIST(X, Y, Z);

causes the values of variables X, Y and Z to be printed in a readable form, on one line. The output resulting from execution of such PUT LIST statements will accompany the "listing" of the program you receive after your program has been executed on the computer. A more detailed discussion of the control and interpretation of output is given in Sections 6 and 7.

We now show two examples of complete programs -- the kind you should be able to write, keypunch and submit for execution.

```
        *PL/C ID='JAMES BUNCH'
         /* ADDING PROGRAM */
            ADDER: PROCEDURE OPTIONS(MAIN);
                DECLARE (X, Y, Z) FLOAT DECIMAL;
                        /* X, Y ARE NUMBERS TO BE ADDED */
                        /* Z IS RESULT */
(4.1.1a)        GET LIST(X, Y);
                Z = X + Y;
                PUT SKIP LIST(X, Y, Z);
                END ADDER;
        *DATA
        15.5, 10.2
```

The second example is:

```
        *PL/C ID='BOB TARJAN'
         /* PROGRAM TO TAKE SQUARE ROOT */
            SROOT: PROCEDURE OPTIONS(MAIN);
                DECLARE ARG FLOAT DECIMAL;
                        /* NUMBER WHOSE ROOT IS WANTED */
                DECLARE SRARG FLOAT DECIMAL;
                        /* SQUARE ROOT OF ARG */
                GET LIST(ARG);
                SRARG = SQRT( ARG );
                PUT SKIP LIST(ARG, SRARG);
                END SROOT;
        *DATA
            25.01
```

4.1.2 <u>Tracing Execution</u>

1769316

You should understand both the meaning of each PL/I statement and the manner in which they are executed, well enough to be able to follow the execution of a program on a statement by statement basis. In fact, you should be able to <u>simulate the action of the computer</u> and "trace" the execution of a program on paper, by executing the statements of the program yourself. You should be able to completely trace the execution of a short program, or to trace the execution of a critical section of a large, complex program. Your action should differ from the computer's only in speed (by a factor of 10^6 or more).

For example, a detailed trace of the loading and execution of (4.1.1a) is given below:

1. The cards, from *PL/C through *DATA are read; a copy of the program (in translated form) is created in memory.

2. Execution begins by entering the main procedure ADDER.

3. As ADDER is entered three variables are created (recall that /// is used to indicate that no value yet exists):

        X /// [float decimal]
        Y /// [float decimal]
        Z /// [float decimal]

4. The first statement in the body of ADDER is GET LIST(X, Y);. Execution of this statement reads the two numbers on the first (and only) data card and assigns them to variables X and Y. At this point, the variables are:

        X 15.5 [float decimal]
        Y 10.2 [float decimal]
        Z /// [float decimal]

5. Execution of the next statement, Z = X + Y;, changes the value of Z. The variables now are:

        X 15.5 [float decimal]
        Y 10.2 [float decimal]
        Z 25.7 [float decimal]

6. Execution of the next statement, PUT LIST(Z);, causes an output line to be printed:

        2.57000E+01

7. The end of ADDER is reached; execution of the program is finished.

Having completed ADDER, the computer begins execution of some other program. The next program "overwrites" and destroys the ADDER program, and its variables X, Y and Z.

4.2 Repetitive Execution

Almost all computer programs require certain statements, or groups of statements, to be executed repeatedly, so it is essential to have convenient mechanisms to control repetition. In PL/I a sequence of consecutive statements whose execution is to be repeated, or "iterated", may be formed into the "body" of a "DO group" or "loop", which has the general form:

```
DO control-phrase ;
     body of group (imperative statements)    END;
```

The two principal types of control phrase that may be used in a DO statement are considered in Sections 4.2.1 and 4.2.2.

The complete loop is considered to be a single unit -- a single complex statement. It can appear wherever any other statement can appear.

4.2.1 Conditional Repetition

One can specify that the iteration of the body of a DO group is to continue as long as a certain condition remains "true". This is written:

```
DO WHILE (condition);
     body of loop (imperative statements)    END;
```

This is called a "WHILE loop". It is executed as follows:

First the condition is evaluated. If the result of evaluation is "true" then the body of the loop is executed. After that execution, the process is repeated -- the condition is re-evaluated, etc.

If (or when) the result of evaluation is "false" the execution of the entire DO group has been completed.

The action is suggested by the English meaning of the keywords -- the body is iterated while the condition remains true. The action can be shown graphically by a "flow-diagram":

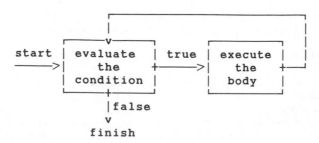

A WHILE loop was used in the example in Section 1.1. As
another example, suppose one wished to sum the integers from 14
through 728. (There is a simple formula to sum consecutive
integers so this program would not actually be used, but it
provides a simple and clear example of the   control   of
repetition.) The following program could be used:

```
          /* SUM INTEGERS FROM 14 THRU 728 */
          I = 14; SUM = 0;
(4.2.1a)      DO WHILE (I<729);
              SUM = SUM + I;
              I = I + 1; END;
```

The first two assignment statements establish initial values for
the variables I and SUM.   Then   the WHILE loop is executed.
Since the condition I<729 is true (the value of I is   14) the
body is executed. These assignment statements add the first of
the required integers to the variable SUM and increase the value
of I.   Then the condition is re-evaluated. It is still true
(since the value of I is now 15) so the body is again   executed.
This   repetition   continues until finally the value of I becomes
729.   At this point the condition is found to be false, and the
execution of the WHILE loop is finished. The required task has
been accomplished -- the variable SUM contains the sum of the
integers from 14 to 728.

  The body of a WHILE loop ought to provide some   action   that
affects   the   condition   in the control phrase -- so that
eventually the condition can become false. In the example above
an assignment statement increases the value of I to serve this
role. If the body never affects the condition, then if it is
initially true it will   remain true and the body of the WHILE
loop will be iterated indefinitely. This a classic program
error called an "infinite iterative loop" and every programmer
produces one once in a while.   In practice, of course, each
program is subject to a time limit so that repetition does not
continue forever.

  Of course, the condition may be false when the WHILE loop is
first encountered.   In this case the body of the loop is not
executed -- not even once -- so the statements of the body have
no effect upon the condition or upon anything else.

  It is very important to the understanding of the action of a
WHILE loop to know when the condition is evaluated. This is
done before the body itself is executed. If the condition is
true then the entire body is executed.   That is, although
certain statements in the body may change the value of variables
so that the condition would be false, the condition is not under
continuous review during the execution of the body.   The
condition is not re-evaluated until after the execution of the
body is completed.

4.2.1.1 <u>Simple Conditions</u>

A "condition" or "relational expression" is a special type of expression that involves a "relation". The symbols for the PL/I relations are the following:

<u>symbol</u>	<u>meaning</u>
=	is equal to
¬=	is not equal to
>	is greater than
¬>	is not greater than
>=	is greater than or equal to
<	is less than
¬<	is not less than
<=	is less than or equal to

(The double-character symbols cannot have a blank between characters.) A condition consists of two arithmetic expressions (as described in Section 3.2) separated by a relation:

           arith-expr   relation   arith-expr

A condition describes a relationship that is either <u>true</u> or <u>false</u>. For example, $2<3$ is a condition that is always true; $2=3$, a condition that is always false; $J=K$, a condition that may be either true or false depending upon the values of the variables J and K at the instant the condition is evaluated.

Other examples are:

    TEST = 0
    J+2 < K
    TEMP*(PRESSURE - 4*PI) <= STATIC

4.2.1.2 <u>Compound Conditions</u>

Conditions can be made more complex by the use of "Boolean operators". These are "and", "or" and "not". "And" and "or" are used to combine two conditions to form a "compound condition". "Not" is used to reverse the truth of a condition. The symbols and meanings are the following:

<u>English</u>	<u>symbol</u>	<u>meaning</u>
"and"	&	A=B & C=D is true if <u>both</u> A=B <u>and</u> C=D are true
"or"	|	A=B | C=D is true if <u>either</u> A=B <u>or</u> C=D is true
"not"	¬	¬(A=B) is true if A=B is <u>not</u> true

The following table gives the values of these compound
conditions for different values of the variables A, B, C and D.

A	B	C	D	A=B	C=D	A=B&C=D	A=B|C=D	¬(A=B)
2	2	2	2	true	true	true	true	false
2	3	2	2	false	true	false	true	true
2	2	2	3	true	false	false	true	false
2	3	2	3	false	false	false	false	true

WHILE loop conditions can be simple or compound:

```
DO WHILE (I>56 & I<729);
DO WHILE (PRESSURE > PRESSMIN & TEMP < TEMPMAX);
DO WHILE ((REG_GAP <= 15.2*GAP) | (FLAG = 2));
```

Precedence rules for these operators are analogous to those
for arithmetic operations given in Section 3.2.2. "And" is
considered before "or", so that

A=B & C=D | E=F   is equivalent to   (A=B & C=D) | E=F

It is a good idea to use parentheses in compound conditions to
be certain that the order of consideration is what you intended.

"Not" should be used sparingly, since it tends to make
programs harder to understand. In simple cases, it can often be
avoided by the choice of the opposite relation:

¬(A=B) is equivalent to A¬=B
¬(A<=B) is equivalent to A>B

When "¬" must be used, <u>parentheses should always be given</u> to
enclose the condition to which it applies.

We have used the terms "true" and "false" quite often in this
section. Actually, any condition evaluates to a value which is
'1'B if it is true, and '0'B if the condition is false. '1'B
and '0'B are <u>constants</u>, which mean true and false respectively
in PL/I. They are called "bit string" constants of length 1;
such bit string values are described briefly in Appendix A.2.

These two bit string constants can be used as values in
conditions, just the way arithmetic constants can be used in
arithmetic expressions. Thus, the condition ¬('0'B) yields the
value true, or '1'B, while '1'B & '0'B yields the value false,
or '0'B.

4.2.2 Repetition with Different Values

An alternative form of DO group can be used to specify that the execution of the body is to be repeated with different values of a key variable, called the "index" variable. Example (4.2.1a) could be rewritten in this form:

```
              /* SUM INTEGERS FROM 14 THRU 728 */
                  SUM = 0;
(4.2.2a)          DO I = 14 TO 728 BY 1;
                      SUM = SUM + I; END;
```

The index variable I is set equal to 14 and the body is executed; then I is set equal to 15 and the body is executed; etc. The final execution of the body has I equal to 728.

The general form of this type of DO group is:

```
              DO index-var = exp¹ TO exp² BY exp³;
(4.2.2b)          body of group
                  END;
```

where "exp^1", "exp^2", and "exp^3" are arithmetic expressions. "exp^1" gives the value of the index variable for the first repetition; "exp^3" gives the "increment" to be added to the index variable after each iteration; and "exp^2" gives the termination test value. Iteration continues until the incremented value of the index variable "passes" this test value. If the increment is positive it continues until the incremented value is greater than the test value; if the increment is negative, until the incremented value is less than the test value.

Execution of such a DO group can be explained in terms of an equivalent WHILE loop. Let INCR and TERM be two new variables that are not used in the body of (4.2.2b). If the initial value of exp^3 is positive, then (4.2.2b) is exactly equivalent to:

```
              index-var = exp¹;
              TERM = exp²;
              INCR = exp³;
              DO WHILE (index-var <= TERM);
(4.2.2c)          body of (4.2.2b)
                  index-var = index-var + INCR; END;
```

If the initial value of exp^3 is negative then the equivalent WHILE loop would be written with the condition

```
              (index-var >= TERM).
```

Studied carefully, the equivalent WHILE loop reveals some interesting, and not altogether obvious, properties of the new form of DO group:

1.   There is a form of assignment embedded in the control

phrase -- the value of the index variable is changed just as if it were the left-side variable of an ordinary assignment statement.

2. Since the index variable will be incremented and tested <u>after</u> the last execution of the body, the final value of the index variable after execution of the DO group is finished is <u>not</u> the same as the value during the last execution of the body.

3. Since the value of the index variable must <u>pass</u> the value of exp^2 to indicate the completion of execution, different control phrases can be effectively equivalent. For example, consider:

     DO K = 2 TO 8 BY 2;   and   DO K = 2 TO 9 BY 2;

In either case the variable K will have value 8 for the last iteration of the body and then be incremented to 10. Since 10 is greater than either 8 or 9 as a test value, in both cases execution is finished after four iterations.

4. It is not necessary for the index variable to be used in the body. Frequently it serves only as a "counter" to determine the number of iterations of the body.

5. If statements in the body <u>alter the value of the index variable</u> this will affect the control of iteration. This is a dangerous practice, and usually leads to considerable confusion.

6. If the statements of the body alter the values of variables that appear in any of the control expressions -- exp^1, exp^2 or exp^3 -- this has no effect whatever on the control of iteration since the only evaluation of these expressions takes place <u>before the first iteration of the body</u>.

This second form of the DO group can be quite useful. However, you should recognize that it is just a special case of the more general WHILE loop. When iteration is of this special form it is certainly easier to write I = 14 TO 728 BY 1; than the assignment statements necessary to initialize and increment the index variable in a WHILE loop. However, not all iteration is of this form and one should not try to force this form of DO group to do work for which it was not intended. The WHILE loop is the general form -- always to be used except when this special form of iteration is required.

To illustrate the use of a negative increment, (4.2.2a) could be rewritten:

```
               /* SUM INTEGERS FROM 728 DOWN THRU 14 */
                   SUM = 0;
(4.2.2d)           DO I = 728 TO 14 BY -1;
                       SUM = SUM + I; END;
```

The DO groups in (4.2.2a) and (4.2.2d) produce the same final
value of SUM, but different final values of I. After executing
(4.2.2a) the value of I is 729; after (4.2.2d) it is 13.

4.2.3 <u>Nesting of DO Groups</u>

   Since the body of a loop can include any <u>complete</u> statement,
and since an entire loop is itself effectively a statement, one
loop can be included in the body of another.   Continuing the
integer summing example (4.2.1a), suppose one wished to obtain
the sum of integers for a series of different values.   The
following program segment, in which one loop is "nested" within
another, could be used:

```
    /* PRINT INTEGER SUMS FOR VARIOUS PEAK VALUES */
        DO PEAK = LOW TO HIGH BY PKINCR;
            /* SUM INTEGERS FROM BASE TO PEAK AND PRINT */
                PKSUM = 0;
                DO PK = BASE TO PEAK BY 1;
                    PKSUM = PKSUM + PK; END;
                PUT SKIP LIST(BASE, PEAK, PKSUM); END;
```

The <u>body</u> of the outer loop consists of an   initializing
assignment statement, the inner loop and a PUT statement to
display the results. Each iteration of this body requires the
execution of each of these three "statements" -- hence execution
of the entire inner loop.

   Perhaps the flow-of-control is more clearly illustrated by
the following segment of program:

```
    OUTSUM = 0;
    INNERSUM = 0;
    DO OUTINDEX = 1 TO 5 BY 1;
        OUTSUM = OUTSUM + 1;
        DO ININDEX = 1 TO 4 BY 1;
            INNERSUM = INNERSUM + 1; END; END;
```

Both index variables OUTINDEX and ININDEX are counters that
control the number of iterations but are not used within the
body. The segment does nothing interesting, but study it until
you understand very clearly why after its execution the values
of the variables are:

```
OUTSUM     5
INNERSUM  20
OUTINDEX   6
ININDEX    5
```

Notice that each program segment in the examples above could
be presented and discussed out of context -- it was not
necessary to specify whether it was part of some larger, unseen
DO group.   Each of the segments could in fact be buried in the
interior of a nest of DO groups several layers deep, so that its
execution would be repeated many times.

4.3 Conditional Execution

It is often necessary to make the execution of a particular
statement depend upon values produced during execution. For
example, this had to be done in the program in Section 1.1 to
find the maximum of a set of values:

    IF NUMBER > MAXNBR THEN MAXNBR = NUMBER;

Each candidate number was compared to the largest that had been
encountered up to that point. If the new candidate was larger,
then the assignment statement had to be executed to record this
new value as the largest encountered. If the new number was not
larger, then that assignment statement had to be skipped.

There are two forms for the conditional execution of a
statement.   The simpler one, used in the example above, has the
general form:

    IF condition THEN statement[1]

The interpretation is suggested by the English meaning of the
keywords "IF" and "THEN":

    If the condition is true then execute statement[1].   If the
    condition is false, do not execute statement[1].

This flow-of-control is as follows:

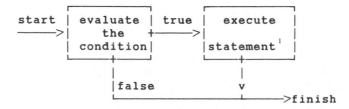

The second form of the IF statement is very similar:

IF condition THEN statement[1]
             ELSE statement[2]

The interpretation is:

If the condition is true then execute statement[1].   If   the
condition is false execute statement[2].

That is, one or the other of statement[1] and statement[2] will be
executed, depending upon the truth or falsity of the condition.
The flow-of-control is:

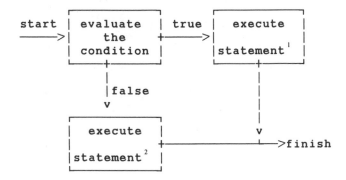

Either   simple   or   compound   conditions   can   be   used,   as
described in Sections 4.2.1.1 and 4.2.1.2.   In this context the
condition does not need to be enclosed in parentheses, unlike
the condition in the WHILE loop where parentheses are required.
(A programming language should not have such inconsistencies of
syntax, but PL/I does, and you will just have to learn to live
with them.)

Examples of conditional statements are:

IF (NEWVALUE > MAXVALUE) THEN MAXVALUE = NEWVALUE;

IF QTY < 0 THEN NEGCOUNT = NEGCOUNT + 1;
          ELSE POSCOUNT = POSCOUNT + 1;

IF (B**2 - 4*A*C) < 0 THEN PUT SKIP LIST('IMAGINARY ROOT');

IF (CONTROL = J+1) | (VALUE = 0) THEN GET LIST(VALUE);

None of the parentheses in the conditions in these examples is
required by PL/I -- in each case the action would be the same if
they were removed. They have been added only to make the
meaning clearer to a human reader.

The "THEN statement" following the condition is mandatory;
the "ELSE statement" is optional, since it is only present in
the second form. Situations will arise where it seems like it
would be useful to have only an "ELSE statement" -- that is, a

statement to be executed only if the condition is false. Since
this is not possible (except by the clumsy artifice of using a
"dummy THEN statement") one should reverse the sense of the
condition. For example:

    replace A>B with A <= B

    replace (A=B) | (C<D) with ¬((A=B) | (C<D))

The required statement can then be given as the "THEN statement"
-- to be executed when the reversed condition is true.

4.3.1 Compound Statements

    Any single statement may follow the THEN or ELSE in a
conditional statement. Thus an assignment statement, a GET
statement, a loop, or another conditional statement may appear
in this position. (Also see Section 4.3.4.) Sometimes one
wants to execute a sequence of statements conditionally. To do
this, a "compound statement" of the following form is used:

    DO;
            body of compound statement   END;

This form of DO group is not repetitive -- the body is executed
only once. The DO and END serve only as "delimiters" to mark
the beginning and the end of the compound statement. They
indicate that the enclosed statements are to be considered as a
single unit. Examples are:

```
/* TEST FOR NEGATIVE VALUES, CORRECT TO +1 */
    IF VALUE < 0
        THEN DO; ERRORCOUNT = ERRORCOUNT + 1;
            PUT SKIP LIST('IMPROPER VALUE', VALUE);
            VALUE = 1; END;

/* SUM AND COUNT NEG AND NON-NEG VALUES */
    IF NEWVAL < 0
        THEN DO; NEGCOUNT = NEGCOUNT + 1;
            NEGSUM = NEGSUM + NEWVAL; END;
        ELSE DO; POSCOUNT = POSCOUNT + 1;
            POSSUM = POSSUM + NEWVAL; END;
```

4.3.2 Exit from a Program Segment

Greater flexibility in choosing program structures is possible if one can "exit" from a program segment "prematurely" -- that is, if one can terminate the execution of a certain segment of program before its normal completion. In the case of a DO group this means being able to terminate one particular iteration of the body, or terminate the execution of the entire DO group. In PL/I this type of exit must be accomplished by a "conditional branch". In addition to the conditional statement, this involves the "GO TO statement" and the concept of a "statement label".

A statement label is an identifier that assigns a name to an individual statement. Label identifiers are chosen subject to the same rules as variable identifiers (Appendix A.2) and should be chosen to suggest the role of the statement being named. A label identifier should not be exactly the same word as any other identifier in the program. The label is given as a "prefix" and punctuated with a colon. The GO TO statement refers to such a label:

```
GO TO label;
...
label: statement
```

Execution of the GO TO statement causes control to "branch" or "jump" to the statement whose label is specified. That is, the next statement to be executed is the one whose label is referenced in the GO TO, rather than the statement immediately following the GO TO. If a GO TO statement is made conditional:

```
IF condition THEN GO TO label;
```

one has the ability to "conditionally branch" -- to cause execution to follow different courses depending upon computational results.

For example, if a label prefix is specified on the END of a DO group it is possible to terminate or shortcut one iteration of the body of the group:

```
            /* SUM POSITIVE INTEGERS FROM BASE TO TOP */
                KSUM = 0; KCOUNT = 0;
                DO K = BASE TO TOP BY 1;
                    IF K <= 0 THEN GO TO SUMINT;
(4.3.2a)            KSUM = KSUM + K;
                    KCOUNT = KCOUNT + 1;
                SUMINT: END;
```

The GO TO exit is not really necessary in this example, since the same result could be achieved much more clearly with a compound statement:

```
            /* SUM POSITIVE INTEGERS FROM BASE TO TOP */
               KSUM = 0; KCOUNT = 0;
               DO K = BASE TO TOP BY 1;
(4.3.2b)           IF K > 0
                      THEN DO; KSUM = KSUM + K;
                           KCOUNT = KCOUNT + 1; END;
               END;
```

The style of (4.3.2b) is certainly preferable in this case, and should be employed whenever practical. However, as DO groups become larger and more complex, situations will arise in which the structure is made clearer if one can branch directly to the END and thus terminate (or skip) a particular iteration of the body.

It is also useful to be able to escape from a DO group earlier than provided by the DO control phrase. This can be done by branching to a statement outside of the group -- preferably to the statement immediately following the end of the group. For example:

```
            /* SUM INTEGERS FROM BASE TO TOP, SUBJECT TO KLIMIT */
               KSUM = 0;
               DO K = BASE TO TOP BY 1;
                   IF KSUM + K > KLIMIT THEN GO TO INTSUM;
(4.3.2c)           KSUM = KSUM + K; END;
               INTSUM:;
```

In this example a "null statement" (a semi-colon) has been placed immediately after the DO group just to provide a target for the escape branch. The same result would be achieved by assigning the label to the first statement of the next section of the program -- but the logical role of the exit is less clear if this is done. The GO TO is being used to <u>exit</u> from this program segment, and not to <u>enter</u> the next segment. Hence the target label should be positioned, and the label name should be chosen, as the <u>last</u> statement of this segment, rather than as the <u>first</u> statement of the next.

As in the case of (4.3.2a), the GO TO exit is not necessary in (4.3.2c). It would be better to use a WHILE loop and include the exit condition in the main control phrase. (4.3.2d) is equivalent to (4.3.2c) in function and preferable in style:

```
            /* SUM INTEGERS FROM BASE TO TOP, SUBJECT TO KLIMIT */
               KSUM = 0; K = BASE;
               DO WHILE ((K <= TOP) & (KSUM + K <= KLIMIT));
(4.3.2d)           KSUM = KSUM + K;
               K = K + 1; END;
```

As another example, suppose we are given integer variables A, B, C, and Y, and we desire a program segment which will print Y if the following is true:

(4.3.2e) There is <u>no</u> integer n such that
$$1 \leq n \leq Y \quad \text{and} \quad Y = A + B \cdot n + C \cdot n^2$$

This can be detected by examining values of $A+B\cdot n+C\cdot n^2$ for n = 1,2,...,Y. The following segment uses a GO TO to end execution of the segment when it has attained its goal:

```
        DO I = 1 TO Y BY 1;
(4.3.2f)   IF A + B*I + C*I*I = Y THEN GO TO EXIT_YPRINT; END;
        PUT LIST(Y);
        EXIT_YPRINT:;
```

Suppose we wish to write a segment which prints up to 5 values of Y, for Y = 1, 2, ..., 50, which satisfy property (4.3.2e). The following segment illustrates the use of a GO TO to end execution of a loop body, in performing this function.

```
    /* PRINT UP TO 5 VALUES OF Y (FOR Y=1,2, ..., 50) WHICH*/
    /* SATISFY PROPERTY (4.3.2E) */
    Y = 0; COUNT = 0;
    DO WHILE (Y < 50 & COUNT < 5);
      Y = Y + 1;

      /* PRINT Y IF IT SATISFIES PROPERTY (4.3.2E) */
        DO I = 1 TO Y BY 1;
          IF A + B*I + C*I*I = Y THEN GO TO EXIT_YPRINT;
          END;
        PUT LIST(Y);    COUNT = COUNT + 1;
        EXIT_YPRINT:;

    END;
```

The GO TO should be used sparingly. It <u>can</u> be used much more widely, and many programming texts consider it to be the principal control mechanism. It is true that with ingenious use of labels, IFs and GO TOs one can "hand craft" control structures equivalent to all of the others described in Section 4. It does not follow that this is desirable. Such programs are not necessarily more efficient and very often do not exhibit their logical structure as clearly as programs using the more complex control statements. One philosophy of programming -- called (by some) "structured programming" -- considers the GO TO statement to be both inelegant and dangerous (with respect to the demonstration of correctness of a program). We agree wholeheartedly, but will resort to the use of a GO TO when PL/I does not offer a more natural alternative. The principal example of such use is as an exit, as has been described in the preceding paragraphs. (Further discussion of this "exit problem" is given in Section 4.5.)

As a general rule, never resort to the use of a GO TO until you have tried to design the program in another way that would avoid it. <u>Use a GO TO only when the alternative is even more awkward</u>. This should occur very rarely in the relatively simple exercises of an introductory course.

4.3.3 Indefinite Repetition

In some cases, a program is clearer and more logical if the control of iteration is performed entirely within the body of the DO group. The exit technique described in 4.3.2 can be used, but some mechanism must be provided to continue the iteration until the exit takes effect. PL/I offers no way of doing this directly, so one must choose the least unattractive way of contriving a mechanism.

We prefer the use of a WHILE loop, with a condition that is always true. Any simple condition, such as 0=0, would suffice, but the best solution is to write

```
DO WHILE('1'B);
```

Again, '1'B is PL/I's way of saying "true", while '0'B is used for "false". By giving '1'B as an always-true condition, the programmer's intention is unmistakable.

For example, consider the following problem:

The input consists of values which are to be read and printed until one is read which satisifies one of the following three conditions:
a) the number is negative
b) the number ends in "3"
c) the number is a power of two (4,8,16,...)

The requirement is not complicated or difficult, but the termination test cannot be conveniently written as the condition of a WHILE loop. The following is a reasonable solution (using the built-in function MOD(x,y) which yields the remainder when an integer x is divided by an integer y):

```
            /* PRINT NON-NEGATIVE NUMBERS WHICH DO NOT END IN 3 AND */
                /* WHICH ARE NOT POWERS OF TWO.  */
            DO WHILE ('1'B);
                GET LIST(A);
                IF A<0 THEN GO TO PRINT_EXIT;
(4.3.3a)    IF MOD(A,10)=3 THEN GO TO PRINT_EXIT;
                POWER_OF_TWO = 1;
                DO WHILE (POWER_OF_TWO < A);
                    POWER_OF_TWO = POWER_OF_TWO * 2; END;
                IF POWER_OF_TWO = A THEN GO TO PRINT_EXIT;
                PUT SKIP LIST(A); END;
            PRINT_EXIT:;
```

4.3.4 <u>Nesting of Conditional Statements</u>

The statement following THEN or ELSE in a conditional statement <u>can be another conditional statement</u>. When this occurs they are said to be "nested". For example, the form of a complete, symmetric nest of three conditional statements, each with both THEN and ELSE statements, is:

```
          IF condition¹
              THEN IF condition²
                      THEN statement¹
(4.3.4a)              ELSE statement²
              ELSE IF condition³
                      THEN statement³
                      ELSE statement⁴
```

The flow-of-control in this nest is:

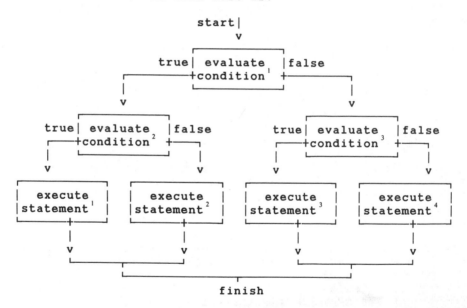

Great care is required in using nested conditional statements since it is very easy to write nests that are syntactically correct (hence do not receive any warning messages) but do not do exactly what was intended. For example, suppose in (4.3.4a) the second conditional statement did not have an ELSE statement. If the fourth line were simply removed from (4.3.4a) the program would look like:

```
          IF condition¹
              THEN IF condition²
                      THEN statement¹
(4.3.4b)      ELSE IF condition³
                      THEN statement³
                      ELSE statement⁴
```

The indenting in (4.3.4b) is deceptive and does not accurately
show the program structure. The lines should be indented as:

```
IF condition¹
    THEN IF condition²
              THEN statement¹
              ELSE IF condition³
                        THEN statement³
                        ELSE statement⁴
```

This is because of the rule that an ELSE belongs with the <u>last
preceding conditional statement that lacks an ELSE</u>. To achieve
the intended flow-of-control a null ELSE statement could be
provided for the second conditional statement:

```
IF condition¹
    THEN IF condition²
              THEN statement¹
              ELSE ;
    ELSE IF condition³
              THEN statement³
              ELSE statement⁴
```

A preferable way of writing this to avoid the clumsiness of
the null statement is:

```
IF condition¹
    THEN DO; IF condition²
              THEN statement¹ END;
    ELSE IF condition³
              THEN statement³
              ELSE statement⁴
```

If the reader finds the schematic nests above hard to follow
he may well believe that when written with actual conditions and
statements (including compound statements), and even deeper
nesting this construction becomes very difficult to understand.

Fortunately the most obvious and common type of nested
conditional statements can usually be replaced by a single
conditional statement with a compound condition. The following
examples are effectively equivalent:

```
IF condition¹
    THEN IF condition²
              THEN statement¹

IF condition¹ & condition²
    THEN statement¹
```

4.4 Tracing Execution

The tracing of execution was introduced in Section 4.1.2. To
trace the execution of a loop, construct a table with a row for
each variable, and a column for the execution of each statement
that changes the value of at least one variable. For example,
consider the following program:

```
*PL/C ID='JOHN WILLIAMS'
 /* SUMMING PROGRAM */
 WILL_SUM: PROCEDURE OPTIONS(MAIN);
     DECLARE N FIXED DECIMAL; /* NUMBER OF DATA */
     DECLARE I FIXED DECIMAL; /* LOOP COUNTER */
     DECLARE X FLOAT DECIMAL; /* NEW DATUM */
     DECLARE SUM FLOAT DECIMAL; /* SUM OF DATA */

     GET LIST(N);
     SUM = 0;
     DO I = 1 TO N BY 1;
         GET LIST(X);
         SUM = SUM + X; END;
     PUT LIST('SUM IS:', SUM);
     END WILL_SUM;
 *DATA
     3, 5.6, 42.1, 31.7
```

The first part of the tracing table for this program is:

```
Vari-
able      Values as execution proceeds ->
___    _____

N      ///    3     3     3     3     3     3     3     3     3     3
I      ///   ///   ///    1     1     1     2     2     2     3     3
X      ///   ///   ///   ///   5.6   5.6   5.6   42.1  42.1  42.1  31.7
SUM    ///   ///    0     0     0    5.6   5.6   5.6   47.7  47.7  47.7
       _____
```

Tracing execution is for the programmer's benefit -- to help
him understand a program or to help him detect an error in it.
Thus, tracing occurs mainly when the programmer is in difficulty
of one sort or another. It must be done with care, one step at
a time. While tracing, the programmer must execute the program
the way the machine does, without thinking about the task being
performed. Too often, a programmer executes what he thinks is
there, and not what really is there, which of course doesn't
help at all.

It is not always necessary to write down each value in each
column, but only that value that is being changed. For example,
the trace table shown above might have been written

Vari-able	Values as execution proceeds ->							
N	///	3						
I	///	///	///	1		2		3
X	///	///	///	///	5.6		42.1		31.7
SUM	///	///	0			5.6		47.7

Often, the trace table becomes complicated and messy, and it is difficult to go back and analyze it. To aid in studying it, one often uses an extra row to indicate which statement is being executed, or the result of evaluating a condition. For example, consider the program segment

```
START: SUM = 0;
       GET LIST(X);
       DO WHILE (X ¬= 0);
         L: IF X < 0
               THEN SUM = SUM - X;
               ELSE SUM = SUM + X;
           GET LIST(X); END;
       SUM = SUM+1;
       ...
 *DATA
   8, -5, 0
```

In the trace table below, the top row is used to indicate the statement executed (by giving its label), or the result of evaluating a condition of a loop or conditional statement.

Vari-able	STA-RT:	loop true	L: X>0				loop true	L: X<0		
SUM	///	0	0	0	0	8	8	8	8	13	13
X	///	///	8	8	8	8	-5	-5	-5	-5	0

The amount of information needed in the trace table varies from program to program, depending on how difficult it is and how much trouble the programmer is having. But get in the habit, from the beginning, of putting in as much information as possible.

4.5 Initialization and Exit Problems

A majority of the problems with iteration involve starting and stopping the iteration, or equivalently, entering and exiting the program segment that performs the iteration. If one can get the first and last iterations to work properly, the iterations in between generally pose much less of a problem. Developing correct loops is one of the hardest parts of programming. While we give some direction in this matter here, the subject is covered in a more sophisticated manner in Section II.6.

4.5.1 Exit Problems in DO Groups

Exit problems seem to have two principal sources:

1) Design of the stopping condition -- in particular, treatment of the "=" case.

2) Position of the "increment step" relative to the rest of the body.

These problems are more often associated with the DO WHILE form since these tasks are handled more or less automatically in the DO index-var form. However, since the DO WHILE is the more general and important form these questions can neither be ignored nor avoided.

We use the integer summing example, first given as (4.2.1a):

```
            /* SUM INTEGERS FROM 14 THRU 728 */
            I = 14; SUM = 0;
(4.5.1a)    DO WHILE (I<729);
                 SUM = SUM + I;
                 I = I + 1; END;
```

The condition in this segment could just as well have been written (I<=728). That is, it could be written to include the case of equality, and with a test value that is to be used in the body. Either form is equally correct -- they result in exactly the same execution -- and there are no general grounds for preferring one form to the other. However, there are two other possibilities that are likely to occur:

condition	result in (4.5.1a)
(I< 728)	one iteration too few
(I<=728)	correct number
(I< 729)	correct number
(I<=729)	one iteration too many

As indicated, the improper matching of the stopping value and the condition will cause improper timing of the exit. This is an exceedingly common type of error, even among experienced programmers.

Similarly, the position of the increment step can be critical. Changing its position, (4.5.1a) would be written as:

```
            /* SUM INTEGERS FROM 14 THRU 728 */
            I = 14; SUM = 0;
(4.5.1b)    DO WHILE (I<729);
                I = I + 1;
                SUM = SUM + I; END;
```

The comment notwithstanding, (4.5.1b) sums the integers from 15 through 729.

If it is important to have the increment step in the position used in (4.5.1b) other parts of the segment could be changed to permit it. For example, (4.5.1c) is a corrected version of (4.5.1b):

```
            /* SUM INTEGERS FROM 14 THRU 728 */
            I = 13; SUM = 0;
(4.5.1c)    DO WHILE (I<728);
                I = I + 1;
                SUM = SUM + I; END;
```

Whether one increments at the beginning of the body of the loop or at the end is a matter of taste at this point. The matter is discussed further in Section II.6.

4.5.2 Initialization and Entry Problems

Typically, one or more variables must be "initialized" prior to entry of a loop, as for example, SUM in (4.5.1a). This is obvious, and logically straightforward, but nevertheless it is overlooked surprisingly often.

The benign form of error, in this regard, is to accidentally place the initialization action within the body of the loop, as in (4.5.2a). This form of error is annoying but is usually revealed during testing, since it makes the loop ineffective.

```
            /* SUM INTEGERS FROM 14 THRU 728 */
            I = 14;
(4.5.2a)    DO WHILE (I<729);
                SUM = 0;
                SUM = SUM + I;
                I = I + 1; END;
```

The malignant form of error is to omit explicit initialization altogether. For example, if the SUM = 0; statement were omitted from (4.5.1a), the result of execution would depend upon what value SUM happened to have when this

segment was encountered. If this happened to be zero throughout
testing the error might well not be detected and this faulty
program could be proclaimed "correct".   Later, in production
use, different initial values for SUM might arise, and this
latent error would affect the results of the program.   If the
user is fortunate, the effect will be so dramatic that it is
obvious that something is wrong. If he is less fortunate the
error will remain hidden, and it will intermittently injure the
results by varying amounts.

Initialization problems can be much more subtle than the
previous example might suggest.   For example, consider the
following task:

>   Read data from cards and sum the values, until a value of
>   -1 is encountered. Do not include the -1 in the sum.

Execution of a program for this task will involve the following
sequence of actions:

```
Read a value
Add the value just read to a running sum
Read a value
Add the value just read to a running sum
...
Read a value and discover it is -1
```

Obviously this will involve a loop whose body includes a GET
and an assignment statement, but the entry and exit from the
loop are not quite obvious. Note that the sequence must both
begin and end with a read. That is, at least one value must be
read, and when the last value (the -1) is read, it must not be
followed by an addition.

If one thinks of this program in terms of iteration of a pair
of actions

```
Read a value
Add the value just read to a running sum
```

then the simple DO WHILE loop cannot be used, since it is unable
to prevent the addition from following the last read. One could
use the techniques described in Section 4.3.2 and 4.3.3:

```
          /* READ AND SUM DATA UNTIL FIRST -1 */
          SUM = 0;
(4.5.2b)  DO WHILE ('1'B);
              GET LIST(VAL);
              IF VAL = -1 THEN GO TO SUMEXIT;
              SUM = SUM + VAL; END;
          SUMEXIT:;
```

Alternatively, one can think of the program in terms of
iteration of the pair

> Add the value just read to a running sum
> Read another value

This simplifies the exit problem considerably, and a normal
WHILE loop can be used:

```
DO WHILE (VAL ¬= -1);
    SUM = SUM + VAL;
    GET LIST(VAL); END;
```

However, now the problem is to get the loop started properly.
One method would be to read the first value as an initialization
action, outside of the DO group:

```
         /* READ AND SUM DATA UNTIL FIRST -1 */
            SUM = 0;
            GET LIST(VAL);
(4.5.2c)    DO WHILE (VAL ¬= -1);
                SUM = SUM + VAL;
                GET LIST(VAL); END;
```

It is not very clean to have to rewrite a portion of the body of
the loop as initialization, but all things considered, for most
simple tasks the style represented by (4.5.2c) is probably
preferable to that of (4.5.2b). Since <u>at least</u> one number must
be read, having the first number read outside of the loop makes
sense.

The style of (4.5.2c) begins to become burdensome as the size
and complexity of the initialization action grows. If an
appreciable number of statements in the body must be rewritten
outside, the risk increases that they will not be exactly the
same. They might start out identical, but subsequent changes in
one location might not be faithfully repeated in the other. In
such cases, one sometimes contrives a way to get the iteration
started, with minimal initialization. For example:

```
         /* READ AND SUM DATA UNTIL FIRST -1 */
            SUM = 0;
            VAL = 0;
(4.5.2d)    DO WHILE (VAL ¬= -1);
                SUM = SUM + VAL;
                GET LIST(VAL); END;
```

(4.5.2d) differs from (4.5.2c) only in the replacement of
GET LIST(VAL); with VAL = 0; but the difference in philosophy is
quite significant. A dummy value has been contrived that will
force the loop body to be entered, and that will permit the
first statement in the body to execute pointlessly, but
harmlessly. This was done just to avoid having to write a
duplicate of a portion of the body outside the loop. It should
be obvious that this is a tricky and dangerous practice.

The previous examples illustrate three unattractive ways of
performing a very common kind of task: (4.5.2b) requires a GO TO

exit; (4.5.2c) requires rewriting a portion of the body outside the loop; and (4.5.2d) requires a devious contrivance to get the loop started. The least unattractive of these will vary, depending upon context and other circumstances. Basically, the problem is that PL/I (as well as most other programming languages) does not offer a natural and convenient way to perform this task.

4.6 Programming Conventions

Conventions in writing programs are the subject of much controversy. Some people maintain that there should be none, that programming is an artistic and creative process, and that individual variations in style and form must be expected, if not encouraged. We do not subscribe to this view. Programming is a communication process, and considerations of clarity, precision and understanding should dominate. If an analogy must be drawn with literature, a program should be compared to an encyclopedia or a mail-order catalog, and not with a novel or epic poem. Consistency and predictability in both style and format are a great help to the reader. It should be remembered that programs are rarely read for pleasure or aesthetic satisfaction. They are read for understanding and to obtain specific information.

Among those who agree that standardization in programming is desirable, there is substantial disagreement as to what the standard practice should be. Each of us is quite willing to have everyone else adopt our practices. Writers of texts and teachers of classes have a substantial advantage in this regard.

A program must be read and understood by two different types of audience -- computers and human beings. The computer's need is obvious; the human's less so. Student programs are written and almost immediately discarded -- because at least at the moment, the objective is to learn to write programs, and not to solve a specific real problem. Once one passes beyond the initial learning phase, programs are written to be used. That is, they are expected to be able to process "real data", and to produce results that are of some interest and value. These programs will often have lives measured in months or years, rather than hours or days. They will often be written by groups of programmers, and used by people other than those who wrote them, whereas this type of cooperative effort is not always encouraged in programming courses. Finally, "real" programs will generally be subjected to many changes. The problem requirements will evolve over time, and if a program cannot be readily and reliably changed it will soon be discarded and replaced.

All of these considerations mean that programs must often be read and understood by humans. As humans read, they try to understand exactly what a computer will do when it executes the program. To be sure, the human should always be able to achieve such understanding, no matter how the program is written, by simulating the detailed action of the computer in the manner described in Sections 4.1.2 and 4.4. However, such tracing is painfully slow. Programs <u>can</u> be written using conventions so that understanding can be communicated much more rapidly.

Conventions are concerned with both <u>style</u> and <u>format</u>. We use the term "style" to refer to the manner in which the statements, declarations and control structures of the language are used. There are always many distinctly different ways in which a given task could be programmed, but there are valid and important reasons to prefer one program to another, even if both will cause the computer to produce the same correct answer.

These issues of style pervade this text. We try throughout to describe <u>how</u> and <u>for what purpose</u> each element of the language should be used, and not just describe its syntactic form.

<u>Variation in program style is not inherently desirable</u>. We expect a given programmer, when confronted with similar tasks at different points in a program, to solve those tasks in the same way. If we were to observe a difference, we should be able to conclude that the programmer had found a way that was better (and not just different) and would, from now on, consistently use this new way. Except for this learning process, if we find what appears to be the same subtask, solved in two different ways in the same program, we should be able to conclude that there must be some subtle but significant difference between the subtasks that we have not yet understood.

On matters of style, our choices are constrained because both humans and the computer must read the program. On matters of <u>format</u> we have more freedom since this is invisible to the computer. The computer does not "see" what is written in comments, nor does it see how the program is arranged on cards. We take advantage of this convenient blindness to adopt format conventions that are the most useful to the human reader. This is the topic of Sections 4.6.1 and 4.6.2.

4.6.1 <u>Use of Comments</u>

Too often a program is commented as follows:

```
/* CLEAR THE VALUE OF SUM */
SUM = 0;
/* REPEAT LOOP FOR DIFFERENT VALUES OF I */
DO I = 14 TO 728 BY 1;
    /* ADD NEW VALUE TO RUNNING SUM */
    SUM = SUM + I;
    /* END OF LOOP */
    END;
```

The same program segment would be much more usefully documented, with less effort, in the following way:

```
/* SUM INTEGERS FROM 14 TO 728 */
   SUM = 0;
   DO I = 14 TO 728 BY 1;
        SUM = SUM + I; END;
```

In the first case, the comments duplicate the statements. They say nothing that the statements do not already say better. There should be no need to explain the role of PL/I statements -- if the reader does not already know this, the comments are not likely to be of much help. In the second case, the single comment summarizes the function of a program segment. This comment can be read instead of reading all of the statements indented underneath it.

   Comments should usually be written before the program, and not after the program is completed and "checked out". Comments are used not primarily to explain what has been written, but rather to specify what is to be written. Done properly, the comments should actually aid the programmer in developing the program. Many comments are "statements" in an informal programming language. For example, one might write:

```
   ...
   /* READ AND SUM DATA UNTIL FIRST -1, YIELDING K */
   /* SUM INTEGERS FROM JMIN TO K */
   /* USE INTEGER SUM TO FIND ENTRY IN CRACK_LOAD TABLE */
   /* APPLY CRACK_LOAD TO BEAM STRESS CALC */
   ...
```

After the complete program had been outlined in this language, one would return and fill in the PL/I statements to accomplish each requirement, immediately under the comment that specifies it:

```
   ...
   /* READ AND SUM DATA UNTIL FIRST -1, YIELDING K */
      K = 0; GET LIST(A);
      DO WHILE (A ¬= -1);
         K = K+A; GET LIST(A); END;

   /* SUM INTEGERS FROM JMIN TO K */
      SUM = 0;
      DO I = JMIN TO K BY 1;
         SUM = SUM + I;     END;

   /* USE INTEGER SUM TO FIND ENTRY IN CRACK_LOAD TABLE */
      ...

   /* APPLY CRACK_LOAD TO BEAM STRESS CALC */
      ...
```

Note that the program can be read on two levels. One can still
read only the comments, and understand the program at a high
level. To get more detail as to <u>how</u> something is performed, one
must read the <u>indented</u> statements under that comment.

    This use of comments follows naturally from a top-down,
level-by-level analysis of a problem. The comments represent
the second-last level in this process -- the level just before
the actual program is written in PL/I. This development, from
English, through comments, to PL/I, is described in Part II.

    Comments are especially important in two places. One is
following declarations, to explain the role of each variable, as
explained in Section 2. The second is as a preface to each
section of a program (as above). The preface should be a clear
and complete description of the function that the section
performs, the assumptions that it makes, the input that it
requires, and the output that it produces.

    Comments in PL/C cannot cross a card boundary -- that is, the
/ that ends a comment must appear on the same card as the /
that started it. PL/I allows a comment to continue over many
cards. (If the NOBOUNDARY option is given in PL/C, it behaves
like PL/I in this regard.) The reason is simply that the
omission of the closing */ is a very common error. When this
occurs PL/C can supply the missing */ at the end of the card,
whereas PL/I considers the contents of the following cards to be
a continuation of the comment.

4.6.2 <u>Program Format</u>

    Program format is primarily a question of how the program is
arranged on cards. Since PL/I is indifferent to the
arrangement, and just considers the program as a continuous
stream of symbols, the format can be designed entirely for the
benefit of the human reader. This opportunity can be used to
good advantage. For example, consider the following program
segment:

```
(4.6.2a) /* PRINT NON-NEGATIVE NUMBERS WHICH DO NOT END IN 3*/
         /* AND WHICH ARE NOT POWERS OF TWO.*/DO WHILE('1'B);GET
         LIST(A);IF A<0 THEN GO TO PRINT_EXIT;POWER_OF_TWO=1;DO
         WHILE(POWER_OF_TWO<A);POWER_OF_TWO=POWER_OF_TWO*2;END;
         IF POWER_OF_TWO=A THEN GO TO PRINT_EXIT;PUT SKIP LIST(A
         );END;PRINT_EXIT:;
```

(4.6.2a) differs from (4.3.3a) only in card format. While PL/I
considers the two segments equivalent, we find programs
formatted in the manner of (4.3.3a) much easier to understand.

    The purpose of an indenting convention is to make the program
<u>structure</u> quickly and clearly apparent to the human reader. By

indenting the body of a loop, one suggests that these statements
are logically subordinate to the DO WHILE heading. By indenting
the THEN and ELSE statements of a conditional statement (as for
example, in (4.3.4a)) it is clear that these statements are
controlled by the IF condition phrase, and that they are in a
parallel relationship to each other. It is true that since the
computer does not need this visual assistance, the human reader
could get along without it also, but it seems to help -- and the
human needs all the help in programming he can get.

The guiding principle in our indentation convention is that
statements (and comments that represent statements at a higher
program level) that begin in the same card column should have
the same logical importance. One should be able to understand
the general outline of a program by reading only the lines
(either comments or statements) that project farthest to the
left. As one needs increasing detail about how some particular
subtask is performed, one reads farther to the right.

The significance of the END keyword to the human reader is
somewhat reduced by this convention. In effect, the indentation
is conveying to the human reader the same structural information
that END is conveying to the computer. We would format a
sequence of DO groups in the following way:

```
    DO
        ...
        END;
    DO
        ...
        END;
```

In many cases, where the last statement in the body is not long,
we simply append END to that line:

```
    DO
        ...  END;
    DO
        ...  END;
```

Some programmers prefer to emphasize the END and bring it to the
left to match the heading of the structure:

```
    DO
        ...
    END;
    DO
        ...
    END;
```

This tends to somewhat lessen the ability to read in a vertical
column and find statements of equal significance, but the point
is certainly debatable. The crucial point is that each
programmer adopt and observe a consistent formatting convention.

Any formatting convention is strained when the level of
nesting increases, and the lengths of the bodies of groups grow.
It becomes increasingly difficult to match the beginning and end
of each group. PL/I provides help in this matter by permitting
the labelling of a DO group. The label can be given as a prefix
to the DO, and again after the corresponding END. For example:

```
MAJOR: DO
    ...
    MINOR: DO
        ...
        END MINOR;
    END MAJOR;
SOLVE: DO
    ...
    ...
    END SOLVE;
```

Make a practice of using such labelling whenever the nesting
depth exceeds two, or whenever a DO is separated from the
corresponding END by more than about ten lines. The labels
should be chosen to suggest the role of the group to which they
are attached.

Section 4 Summary

1. A PL/I job consists of a "main procedure", optionally
followed by data. The execution of a program consists of a
single execution of the main procedure.

2. The normal order of statement execution is the order in
which the statements are written.

3. A DO group, or loop, is a control mechanism to provide
iteration of a group of consecutive statements. The two basic
forms of a loop are:

```
DO WHILE (condition);
    sequence of statements
    END;

DO index-var = expr¹ TO expr² BY expr³;
    sequence of statements
    END;
```

4. A condition is an expression involving a relational
operator, and possibly Boolean operators. Its evaluation yields
a value of either "true" or "false". In PL/I, "true" and
"false" are represented by the constants '1'B and '0'B,
respectively.

5. There are two forms of conditional execution of a statement:

IF condition THEN statement[1]

IF condition THEN statement[1] ELSE statement[2]

Statement[1] and statement[2] can be either simple or compound statements.

6. A conditional branch may be used to terminate execution of a program segment. This is the primary use of the GO TO in PL/I:

```
/* PROGRAM SEGMENT TO PERFORM SOMETHING */
    ...
    IF condition THEN GO TO EXIT_SEGMENT;
    ...
    EXIT_SEGMENT:;
```

7. A consistent programming style should be used. Substatements of a statement should be indented, and a comment should precede each logical program segment to explain _what_ it does.

Section 4 Exercises

1. Write a separate, complete program (similar to the examples in Section 4.1.1) to perform each of the following tasks:

 a) Read five data values, compute their sum and print the sum.

 b) Read three data values, compute the product of the first times the sum of the second and third, and print the result.

 c) Without reading any data (no GET statements) compute the sum of the integers from 1 to 8 and print the result.

 d) Read four data values, print the maximum of the four values.

2. Write a single program that will perform all four of the tasks listed in Exercise 1, one after another.

3. Trace the execution of the programs in Exercise 1.

4. Keypunch and run the programs in Exercise 1.

5. Trace the execution of the following program segments:

```
 a) TOTAL = 0;
    DO WHILE (TOTAL < 100);
        TOTAL = TOTAL + 1; END;
```

b) R1 = 0; R2 = 0; R3 = 0;
    DO I = 1 TO 3 BY 1;
        R1 = R1 + 1;
        DO J = 3 TO -1 BY -1;
            R2 = R2 + 1;
            DO K = 3 TO 7 BY 2;
                R3 = R3 + 1; END; END; END;

c) A = 2; B = 5;
        /* COMPUTE Z=A**B, ASSUMING A > 0 AND B > 0 ARE */
        /* INTEGERS */
         Z = 1; X = A; Y = B;
        DO WHILE (Y ¬= 0);
            DO WHILE(FLOOR(Y/2E0) = Y/2E0); /* WHILE Y EVEN*/
            Y = Y/2E0; X = X*X; END;
            Y = Y - 1; Z = Z*X; END;

d) Same as c), but with "A=2; B=5;" replaced by "A=1; B=1;".

e) /* PRINT OUT THE FIRST 7 FIBONNACI NUMBERS */
        N = 7;
        FIRST = 0; PUT LIST(FIRST);
        SECOND = 1; PUT LIST(SECOND);
        DO I = 3 TO N BY 1;
            THIRD = FIRST + SECOND; PUT LIST(THIRD);
            FIRST = SECOND; SECOND = THIRD; END;

f)   GET LIST(N);
        DO I = 1 TO N BY 1;
          GET LIST(X);
          IF X < 0 THEN PUT LIST(X+1); END;
        ...
    *DATA
        0, 8 , 8, 9, 8 3

g) Same as f), but with the data

    *DATA
        5, -30, 40, 50, -60, -70, -80

2. The following exercises are to be written using only
conditional statements, assignment statements, and GET and PUT.

  a) Write a single conditional statement with only an
     assignment statement as a substatement, for the following
     nested conditionals:

        IF X < 0 THEN
            IF Y < 0 THEN
                IF Z = 5 THEN A = X + Y + Z;

b) Write a single conditional statement for the following nested conditionals:

```
IF X < 0
    THEN DO; IF Y < 0 THEN A = X + Y + Z; END;
    ELSE IF X = 5 THEN A = X + Y + Z;
```

c) Given are three variables A, B, and C. Write a program segment to interchange the values of A, B and C so that the largest is in A and the smallest is in C.

d) Write a program segment to print '1' if the values of X, Y, and Z are the lengths of the sides of a triangle. (X, Y, and Z are the lengths of the sides of a triangle if all are greater than 0 and if X+Y>Z, X+Z>Y, and Y+Z>X.)

e) Write a program segment to print '1' if X, Y, and Z are the lengths of the sides of an equilateral triangle, and '2' if they are the sides of a non-equilateral triangle. A triangle is equilateral if all its sides are the same.

f) A, B and C are three variables with different values. One of these variables has the "middle value" -- one other is greater, one smaller. Write a program segment that will set variable D to this middle value. Compare this to the program for c).

3. Exercises with loops.

a) Write a WHILE loop that is equivalent to the following DO group:

```
FACT = 1;
DO I = 2 TO N BY 1;
     FACT = FACT*I; END;
```

b) Write a program segment to read in a sequence of 50 numbers and print out those numbers that are > 0.

c) Given a variable N with a value greater than 0, write a program segment to print N, N**2, ..., N**N.

d) Given variables N and M, both with values greater than 0, write a program segment to print all powers of N that are less than M. That is, print the value N**i for all i such that N**i < M.

e) The Fibonacci numbers are the numbers 0, 1, 1, 2, 3, 5, 8, 13, 21, ... The first one is 0, the second is 1, and each succesive one is the sum of the two preceding ones. The program segment of Exercise 1 d) calculates the first 7 Fibonacci numbers and prints them out. Given a variable N≥2, write a program segment to print out all Fibonacci numbers which are less than N (not the first N Fibonacci numbers).

4.   Write complete programs (and keypunch and run them) for   the
following   problems.   Most   of   these   use the program segments
written in earlier exercises.

   a) The input consists of groups of three   numbers.   The   last
      group   is   an   end-of-list   signal consisting of three zero
      values.   Write a program to read each group in,   print   it
      out,   and   print   an   indication   whether the three numbers
      represent the sides of a triangle.

   b) The input consists of an integer   N $\geq$ 0,   followed   by   N
      groups   of   three   numbers.   Write   a   program to read the
      groups of numbers in, print them out, and   then   print   the
      middle value of the three.   Each group and its middle value
      should appear on a separate line.

   c) The input consists of a single integer N.   Write a   program
      to   read in N and print the first N Fibonacci numbers.   (If
      N < 1, don't print any out.)

   d) The input consists of two positive integers M and N, with M
      $\geq$ N.   Write a program to print all Fibonacci numbers which
      lie between M and N.

   e) The input consists   of   a   positive   integer   N.   Write   a
      program to read N and to print out the first, second, third
      and fourth powers   of   the   integers   2, 3,   ...,   N.   The
      beginning of your output should look like

              2   4   8   16
              3   9   27   81
                                ...

Section 5 <u>Multiple-Valued Variables</u>

5.1 <u>Arrays of Subscripted Variables</u>

Often a set of variables will all be subjected to similar types of processing. While this can be done using the variables and statements that have been described up to this point, it would require rewriting the processing statements for each different variable. A much more convenient and powerful method is available.

Suppose that in the sample problem of Section 1.1 it was necessary to store all of the numbers, rather than just to read, process and discard them one at a time. Storage might be required for processing in a later stage of the program -- say, a later section that would sort the numbers into order of increasing value and print them out in this order. If there were 50 different numbers, using 50 different variables -- each with a different identifier -- would be cumbersome. Such situations, in which essentially the same process is to be applied to many different variables, are very common in computing, and a special type of variable is used. Such a variable is called an <u>array</u>.

An array is a set of variables, each having a separate value just like ordinary simple variables, but with <u>all the variables of the set sharing a common identifier</u>. A "subscript" is added to this common identifier to produce a unique name for each individual element of the set. For this reason these are often called <u>subscripted variables</u>. For example, an identifier X could refer to a set of five variables:

$$
\begin{array}{lll}
 & X(1) & \underline{20} \\
 & X(2) & \underline{-2} \\
(5.1a) & X(3) & \underline{6} \\
 & X(4) & \underline{217} \\
 & X(5) & \underline{8}
\end{array}
$$

Programming languages are unable to use conventional subscripts because the keypunch (and most other input devices) lack the capability of depressing a character below the normal printing line. As a consequence subscripts are generally identified by being enclosed in parentheses.

In the example above, X is called an array of subscripted variables. Each of the variables named X(1), X(2), X(3), X(4), X(5), is itself called a subscripted variable. (Unsubscripted variables -- that is, those discussed before this Section -- where the name of the variable is just an identifier alone, will now be called simple variables.) The "name" of a subscripted variable has the form:

         identifier(signed or unsigned integer)

Thus X(1), X(0), X(+1), and X(-1) are all valid subscripted variable names. X(1) and X(+1) refer to the same variable. Note that the parentheses are necessary: X(2) is a subscripted variable, while X2 is just a simple variable with no relation whatever to the array X of subscripted variables.

Subscripted variables usually have positive subscripts, but zero and negative subscripts can also be used when convenient.

For example, suppose we need a table whose values represent the number of minutes in a day that the temperature is between i and i+1 degrees Fahrenheit. For each integer i, we can store the number of minutes that the temperature is between i and i+1 in the appropriate element of an array named MINUTES. Thus, the value of MINUTES(2) would represent the number of minutes that the temperature is between 2 and 3 degrees; the value of MINUTES(47) would represent the number of minutes between 47 and 48 degrees, MINUTES(-3) the number of minutes between -3 and -2, etc.

The name of a subscripted variable can be used exactly as the name of a simple variable is used. For example,

         A = X(3) * X(1);

specifies that the current value of X(3) (which is given as 6 in (5.1a)) is to be multiplied by the current value of X(1) (which is 20), and the result 120 is to be stored as the value of simple variable A. Similarly, a subscripted variable can be given as the target of an assignment process:

         X(2) = X(4) * 5;

The value of X(4) (which is 217) is multiplied by 5 and the result (1085) is stored in X(2). At this point, then, there seems to be little difference between a simple and subscripted variable, except that the name of the latter has a somewhat more complicated form. The real power of subscripted variables is shown in the next section.

5.1.1 Referencing Subscripted Variables

Suppose we wished to write a program to obtain the sum of the values of 50 different variables. We could use 50 simple variables named V1, V2, V3, ..., V50, and obtain their sum using a single, long assignment statement:

```
/* COMPUTE SUM OF V1 TO V50 */
    SUM = V1 + V2 + V3 + ...  + V50;
```

(The three dots ... commonly used in algebra to indicate repetition are not valid in PL/I, so the statement shown above is not really complete. It would have to be written out with all fifty variables in the expression.) Alternatively the sum could be obtained using a sequence of 51 assignment statements:

```
/* COMPUTE SUM OF V1 TO V50 */
    SUM = 0;
    SUM = SUM + V1;
    SUM = SUM + V2;
    SUM = SUM + V3;
       ...
    SUM = SUM + V50;
```

It is probably not obvious why this second method is interesting, but this will soon become clear; at least the reader will concede that it produces the same result as the single long assignment statement. A slight modification of this second method would be to use an array of subscripted variables:

```
            /* COMPUTE SUM OF ALL VARIABLES IN U */
                SUM = 0;
                SUM = SUM + U(1);
(5.1.1a)        SUM = SUM + U(2);
                SUM = SUM + U(3);
                   ...
            SUM = SUM + U(50);
```

Now suppose there is a simple variable I with value 2:

         I   2̲

and suppose we execute the following assignment statement:

```
    SUM = SUM + U(I);
```

This is interpreted as follows:

Add a copy of the current value of variable SUM to a copy of the current value of one of the subscripted variables of the array U. The subscripted variable to be used is determined by the value of the variable I. Since I's value is currently 2, the term U(I) refers to U(2). Hence a copy of the value of U(2) is added to the value of SUM. The result is stored as a new value for SUM.

Note that the assignment process remained the same <u>except that a</u>
<u>preliminary evaluation of the variable I was required in order</u>
<u>to determine which of the subscripted variables of U was to be</u>
<u>used</u>. This may not seem like a significant change on first
encounter -- but it is, in fact, exceedingly powerful and very
extensively used. Using this method of referencing subscripted
variables and the means of controlling repetition introduced in
Section 4.2 the summation example can be written as

```
                /* COMPUTE SUM OF ALL VARIABLES OF U */
                    SUM = 0;
                    I = 1;
                    DO WHILE (I <= 50);
(5.1.1b)                SUM = SUM + U(I);
                        I = I + 1; END;
```

Assuming a set of values for the array U, after execution of
the first two assignment statements of this program the values
might be the following:

```
            SUM     0
            I       1
            U(1)    5
            U(2)    7
            U(3)    1
```

Execution of the WHILE loop starts with the evaluation of the
condition. The condition is true, since the current value of I,
1, is less than 50, and the body of the loop is executed.   The
first statement in the body is an assignment statement involving
a subscripted variable. The current value of I, which appears
as the subscript, is 1 so the current value of U(1), which is 5,
is added to the value of SUM. Thus 5 is stored as the new value
of SUM.   The next assignment statement is straightforward,
increasing the value of I to 2. At this point in execution the
values of the variables would be:

```
            SUM     5
            I       2
            U(1)    5
            U(2)    7
            U(3)    1
```

The condition is then re-evaluated. The value of I is still
less than 50 so the body is again executed. Since I is now 2,
the value of the subscripted variable U(2) is added to SUM to
give 12.   This is stored as the new value of SUM. I is then
increased to 3.

The reader should continue this exercise until he   is
convinced that the result is the same as that obtained by
(5.1.1a). Of particular interest is the last execution of the
loop body, when I is 50. At this time the value of U(50) is
added to SUM (which by then contains the sum of the first 49
elements of the array U).   I is then increased to 51. On re-

evaluation the condition is finally false and the   execution   of
the loop is finished.

   (5.1.1b) could also be written using the   second   form   of   a
loop:

```
/* COMPUTE SUM OF ALL VARIABLES OF U */
    SUM = 0;
    DO I = 1 TO 50 BY 1;
        SUM = SUM + U(I); END;
```

As a further example, suppose the problem required the sum of
the   variables   U(1),   U(2),   ..., up to the first variable with
zero value. The two alternative DO group forms would be:

```
/* COMPUTE SUM OF U VARIABLES THRU FIRST 0 */
    SUM = 0; I = 1;
    DO WHILE ((U(I) ¬= 0) & (I <= 50));
        SUM = SUM + U(I);
        I = I + 1; END;
```

```
/* COMPUTE SUM OF U VARIABLES THRU FIRST 0 */
    SUM = 0;
    DO I = 1 TO 50 BY 1;
        IF U(I) = 0 THEN GO TO SUMEXIT;
        SUM = SUM + U(I); END;
    SUMEXIT:;
```

   An expression may be given for a subscript -- the   constants
and   variables   in the examples so far are just special cases of
expressions. The only restriction is that   when   evaluated   the
expression   must yield an appropriate integer value. Expression
subscripts can be very useful. For example, suppose there   were
two   arrays,   LEFT   and   RIGHT, each consisting of 15 variables.
The following segment of program would copy the values of LEFT
into RIGHT in inverted order:

```
/* REVERSE COPY 'LEFT' INTO 'RIGHT' */
    DO I = 1 TO 15 BY 1;
        RIGHT(I) = LEFT(16-I); END;
```

5.2 Variables with Multiple Subscripts

   It is sometimes convenient to use more than one subscript to
designate   a   particular   variable   from an array. This is done
when there is more than   one   natural   pattern   for   referencing
variables   from   the array. For example, suppose one had grades
in nine different courses for   fifty   different   students.   One
might store these grades in an array GRADE of doubly-subscripted
variables in such a way that GRADE(I,J) represented the grade of
the   jth   student in the ith course. That is, GRADE(3,17) would
be the grade of the 17th student in the   3rd   course.   Then   to
obtain the average grade in a certain course one could write:

```
/* COMPUTE AVERAGE GRADE IN ITH COURSE */
    TOTGRADE = 0;
    DO J = 1 TO 50 BY 1;
        TOTGRADE = TOTGRADE + GRADE(I,J); END;
    AVGGRADE = TOTGRADE/50E0;
```

To obtain the average for a particular student for his nine
courses one could write:

```
/* COMPUTE AVERAGE GRADE FOR JTH STUDENT */
    SUMGRADE = 0;
    DO I = 1 TO 9 BY 1;
        SUMGRADE = SUMGRADE + GRADE(I,J); END;
    STUDAVG = SUMGRADE/9E0;
```

The overall average (all students in all courses) could be
obtained by executing

```
/* COMPUTE OVERALL AVERAGE GRADE */
    GSUM = 0;
    DO I = 1 TO 9 BY 1;
        DO J = 1 TO 50 BY 1;
            GSUM = GSUM + GRADE(I,J); END; END;
    OVAVG = GSUM/(9*50E0);
```

An array of singly-subscripted variables is a <u>list</u> of
variables -- with the subscript specifying the position on the
list. The analogous interpretation of an array of doubly-
subscripted variables is a <u>table</u> or <u>matrix</u>. The first subscript
specifies the <u>row</u> position and the second specifies the <u>column</u>:

```
GRADE(1,1)  GRADE(1,2)  GRADE(1,3)  GRADE(1,4)  ...

GRADE(2,1)  GRADE(2,2)  GRADE(2,3)  GRADE(2,4)

GRADE(3,1)  GRADE(3,2)  GRADE(3,3)  GRADE(3,4)

...
```

It is also common to visualize the variables of an array as
being distributed in a geometric space. An array of singly-
subscripted variables is said to be a <u>one-dimensional array</u> or
<u>vector</u>. The values are considered to be positioned along a
line, with the subscript giving the position on the line. An
array of doubly-subscripted variables is called a <u>two-
dimensional array</u> or <u>matrix</u> and the pair of subscripts specifies
a position in the plane of values. Although singly and doubly-
subscripted variables are the most commonly used, three or more
subscripts can be used if required.

5.3 <u>Declaration of Arrays</u>

An array declaration specifies the number of subscripted variables to be created and the number of subscripts to be used for referencing each variable, as well as the type of value each of the variables is to receive. The most common form for a one-dimensional array is

DECLARE identifier(bound) attribute-list;

An example would be:

DECLARE TEMPERATURE(50) FLOAT DECIMAL;

This defines an array of 50 variables named TEMPERATURE(1), TEMPERATURE(2), ... , TEMPERATURE(50), each capable of holding one FLOAT DECIMAL number.

If subscript values are to start anywhere except 1, then a lower bound must also be given. For example, to define an array of 22 variables named PRESSURE(-1), PRESSURE(0), ... , PRESSURE(20), use

DECLARE PRESSURE(-1:20) FLOAT DECIMAL;

Multiple subscripts may be indicated by giving two or more bounds, separated by commas. For example, to define an array of 450 doubly-subscripted variables with the values of the first subscript ranging from 1 to 9, and the second from 1 to 50, use

DECLARE GRADE(9,50) FLOAT DECIMAL;

As a final example, the following declaration defines a three-dimensional array of 60 integer variables, each with three subscripts. The values of the first subscript range from -5 to -2; the second from 1 to 3; and the third from 0 to 4.

DECLARE POINT(-5:-2,3,0:4) FIXED DECIMAL;

In referring to arrays in the text we will generally use the same form as the declaration. That is, MAT(1:5,1:9) will refer to the array defined by the declaration

DECLARE MAT(1:5,1:9) FLOAT DECIMAL;

We will use the complete form of the declaration in these references -- MAT(1:5,1:9) rather than MAT(5,9) -- since this will help to distinguish between a reference to the complete array and a reference to the particular subscripted variable with maximum subscript values. We also use the notation to refer to an array segment -- a part of the array. For example, if A(1:100) is an array, we might discuss the segment A(1:50), or A(1:N) where N contains the subscript value. A(1:1) refers to the single element A(1), while A(1:0) refers to the array segment containing <u>no</u> elements, the <u>empty</u> segment.

5.4* Array Expressions and Assignment

In some contexts PL/I permits an array to be treated as a single object. This does not add any power to the language, but it is convenient for the programmer. For example, an array may be specified on the left side of an assignment statement, rather than a single variable -- provided the expression on the right side provides values for all of the variables that constitute the array. The most common usage is to set all of the variables of an array equal to the same constant value. For example, for the array SCORE(1:10),

```
    SCORE = 0;
```

is equivalent to:

```
    DO I = 1 TO 10 BY 1;
        SCORE(I) = 0; END;
```

5.4.1* Array Expressions and Operations

All arithmetic operations can be performed with array operands. The operands of an array operation must have identical bounds or yield scalar values. The best way to understand array expressions is to see how an assignment statement is executed. Suppose A(1:10) and B(1:10) are two arrays, and suppose we execute

```
    A = B*A + 1;
```

This is executed as if it were

```
    DO I = 1 TO 10 BY 1;
       A(I) = B(I)*A(I)+1; END;
```

That is, the assignment statement is expanded into a loop, where during execution the subscript value increases so that array elements are assigned in "row-major order" -- the first row of variables is assigned first, in left to right order; the second row next, etc. In other words, the rightmost subscript varies most rapidly, the leftmost the least rapidly.

As another example, if C(1:20,1:30) and D(1:20,1:30) are two arrays, then the statement

```
    C = D + 2*C;
```

is executed as if it were

```
    DO I = 1 TO 20 BY 1;
       DO J = 1 TO 30 BY 1;
          C(I,J) = D(I,J) + 2*C(I,J); END; END;
```

Note that an array expression like C*D does <u>not correspond to</u>
<u>the usual definition of matrix multiplication</u>.

   Array assignment statements can be very useful, but one must
be careful since an array assignment statement is not executed
as a conventional assignment statement. The expression is not
evaluated and then assigned to the array; an element by element
evaluation and assignment is performed. Consider the assignment
A = A/A(1);.   It does not divide each element of the array by
the value of A(1). Instead, it divides A(1) by itself and sets
A(1) to 1, and then proceeds to divide each other element by 1:

```
    DO I = 1 TO 10 BY 1;
       A(I) = A(I) / A(1); END;
```

5.4.2* External Assignment to Arrays

   If an array name appears in the variable list of a GET
statement (without subscripts), sufficient data values are read
to provide a value for <u>each</u> of the subscripted variables that
constitute   the   array.   For a one-dimensional array the
assignments are made in the order of increasing subscripts. For
example, for the array VALUE(1:6), the statement:

```
    GET LIST(VALUE);
```

is equivalent to:

```
    DO I = 1 TO 6 BY 1;
       GET LIST(VALUE(I)); END;
```

When there is more than one subscript the assignments are made
in row-major order. For the array TAB(1:3,1:4), the statement
GET LIST(TAB); is equivalent to

```
    DO I = 1 TO 3 BY 1;
       DO J = 1 TO 4 BY 1;
          GET LIST(TAB(I,J)); END; END;
```

5.4.3* Array Built-in Functions

   Several built-in functions will accept an array expression as
an argument. These are called "array generic functions" and are
listed in Appendix A.8. Some are used to perform an operation
over all the variables of an array to produce a single value.

   For example, the function SUM(A) returns as its value the sum
of all the elements of the array A. A may have any number of
elements or dimensions. For example, if LIMIT(1:6) is an array,
and TOTAL_LIMIT is a simple variable, then the statement

```
    TOTAL_LIMIT = SUM(LIMIT);
```

is equivalent to:

```
    TOTAL_LIMIT = 0;
    DO I = 1 TO 6 BY 1;
         TOTAL_LIMIT = TOTAL_LIMIT + LIMIT(I); END;
```

Two other useful functions are ALL and ANY; their definitions are given in Appendix A.8.

Actually, many of the conventional built-in functions will accept arrays as arguments and return a result which is an array. Each value of the resulting array is the result of applying the function to the corresponding element of the argument. Suppose B(1:10) and A(1:10) are arrays. Executing

```
    B = SQRT(A);
```

stores in B the square roots of the values of A. Some of the other built-in functions that can be used this way are ABS, FLOOR, CEIL, COS, and SIN.

Allowing these functions to accept arrays as arguments is just a simple extension of the array expression concept discussed in Section 5.4.1. The statement

```
    B = ABS(A) + FLOOR(B)*2;
```

is really executed as if it were

```
    DO I = 1 TO 10 BY 1;
        B(I) = ABS(A(I)) + FLOOR(B(I))*2;
```

5.5 Program for the Example of 1.2.1

In Section 1.2.1 the analysis of a problem description was carried through several levels, but the programming was postponed until subscripted variables could be employed. The analysis in Section 1.2.1 had reached the following stage:

3.1 Read a sequence of 100 or fewer positive integers from cards until a zero value is encountered; store these integers in memory, preserving order.

3.2 Find the position of the integer with maximum value in this sequence.

3.3 Print the early values of the sequence, from the first to the maximum value, one per line.

Each of these subtasks is well defined and detailed program design can begin. The next step is to specify the data structures that will be used.

The principal data structure will be an array -- call it
INTEGER. It must consist of at least 100 variables, since there
may be that many data values, and should be FIXED DECIMAL. (It
will turn out to be convenient to have 101 variables.) There
should be a variable TOP (say) to mark the actual top position
being used in the array, and another variable MAX (say) to mark
the position of the maximum value. Later, as we design the
different subtasks, we may find that other variables will be
needed.

Now the problem statement can be rewritten in terms of the
variables that will be used:

> 4.1 Read data into elements of INTEGER until a zero value
> is encountered. Set TOP to mark the position of the last
> value before the zero.
>
> 4.2 Set MAX to mark the position of the maximum of elements
> 1 to TOP of INTEGER.
>
> 4.3 Print the elements of INTEGER, from 1 to MAX, one per
> line.

This description is now very close to programming language
terms. Although it may not seem so to one who is just learning
the language, the hardest part of the programming process is
bringing the problem description to this level. The analysis
and design have been completed -- from here on it is just a
matter of translating into the proper form.

We will program the sub-tasks one at a time, taking them in
reverse order just to demonstrate their relative independence.

The program for 4.3 is obviously a loop:

```
DO I = 1 TO MAX BY 1;
    PUT SKIP LIST(INTEGER(I)); END;
```

The only problems that might arise in this sub-task concern
extreme values of MAX. If MAX<1 no values will be printed.
This makes sense since MAX<1 means that <u>no</u> values appeared in
the input -- only the end signal 0. If MAX>100 an invalid
subscript will be used. The loop must be protected against this
possibility. If previous actions cannot guarantee such
protection then testing steps will have to be added to this
section.

The program for 4.2 must take into account that no values may
be supplied in the data -- only the end-of-list signal may
appear. We set MAX to zero initially, to indicate that no
maximum has been found yet, and store -1 in MAXVAL. If there is
actually no list then the body of the loop labeled FINDMAX will
never be executed and MAX will remain at zero.

```
      MAXVAL = -1; MAX = 0;
      FINDMAX: DO I = 1 TO TOP BY 1;
          IF INTEGER(I) > MAXVAL THEN DO;
              MAXVAL = INTEGER(I);
              MAX = I; END;
          END FINDMAX;
```

This routine has potential problems if TOP is greater than 100. However, note that if 0≤TOP≤100, this segment automatically guarantees a value for MAX that will be acceptable to the routine for 4.3.

The program for 4.1 is less obvious and could be done in several different ways. It must make provision for a number of extreme conditions with respect to the input data:

1. It must work properly for every valid quantity of data -- as little as none, to as much as 100 values.

2. It must provide adequate warning when it encounters improper data -- no data at all, too much data, data without the proper end signal, or improper values as described in 3 below.

3. The problem statement specifies that the data will be positive integers. A fundamental decision must be made as to whether the program will <u>trust</u> that it will only be presented with such proper data, or whether it will <u>test</u> to make sure that this is the case. As a general philosophy, programs should be <u>suspicious and trust no one</u>.

If each new datum is read directly into a variable of a FIXED DECIMAL array a non-integer datum will simply be truncated and no warning will be given. If it is first read into a FLOAT DECIMAL variable a test for non-integers can be performed. It will also be convenient to have the array INTEGER consist of 101 variables so that if the maximum number of data values is given the dummy stopping value can still be placed in the array without causing an invalid subscript to be generated. The program for 4.1 would then be as follows:

```
      I = 0; TFLOAT = -1; /* DUMMY STARTING VALUE */
      READLOOP: DO WHILE (TFLOAT ¬= 0);
          /* TEST FOR DATA OVERFLOW */
              IF I = 101 THEN DO;
                  PUT SKIP LIST('MISSING STOPPING VALUE');
                  GO TO SETTOP; END;
          GET LIST(TFLOAT);
          I = I + 1;
          INTEGER(I) = TFLOAT;
          /* TEST FOR PROPER DATA VALUE */
              IF INTEGER(I) ¬= TFLOAT | INTEGER(I) < 0
                  THEN PUT SKIP LIST('IMPROPER DATA',I,TFLOAT);
          END READLOOP;
      SETTOP: TOP = I - 1;
```

This routine relies upon PL/I to provide appropriate warning if
it runs out of data unexpectedly, which would occur if no data
were present, or if the dummy zero was omitted when there were
fewer than 101 values.

The complete program would look like the following:

```
/* PROGRAM TO LIST VALUES FROM FIRST TO MAXIMUM */
LISTTOMAX: PROCEDURE OPTIONS(MAIN);
DECLARE INTEGER(1:101) FIXED DECIMAL;
    /* MAIN ARRAY.  LAST VALUE IS DUMMY */
DECLARE TFLOAT FLOAT DECIMAL; /* TEMP LOCN FOR DATUM*/
DECLARE (MAX,TOP) FIXED DECIMAL;
    /* TOP - MARKS TOP REAL VALUE IN ARRAY */
    /* MAX - MARKS POSN OF MAXIMUM VALUE IN ARRAY */
DECLARE MAXVAL FIXED DECIMAL; /* MAXIMUM VALUE SO FAR*/
DECLARE I FIXED DECIMAL;

/* READ DATA INTO 'INTEGER' UNTIL ZERO IS FOUND */
/* SET 'TOP' TO MARK POSN OF LAST REAL VALUE */
    I = 0; TFLOAT = -1; /* DUMMY STARTING VALUE */
    READLOOP: DO WHILE (TFLOAT ¬= 0);
        /* TEST FOR DATA OVERFLOW */
            IF I = 101 THEN DO;
                PUT SKIP LIST('MISSING FINAL ZERO');
                GO TO SETTOP; END;
        GET LIST(TFLOAT);
        I = I + 1;
        INTEGER(I) = TFLOAT;
        /* TEST FOR PROPER DATA VALUE */
            IF INTEGER(I) ¬= TFLOAT | INTEGER(I) < 0
                THEN PUT SKIP LIST
                        ('IMPROPER DATA',I,TFLOAT);
        END READLOOP;
    SETTOP: TOP = I - 1;

/* SET 'MAX' TO MARK POSITION OF MAXIMUM VALUE */
    MAXVAL = -1; MAX = 0;
    FINDMAX: DO I = 1 TO TOP BY 1;
        IF INTEGER(I) > MAXVAL THEN DO;
            MAXVAL = INTEGER(I);
            MAX = I; END;
        END FINDMAX;

/* PRINT 'INTEGER' FROM 1 TO 'MAX', 1/LINE */
    DO I = 1 TO MAX BY 1;
        PUT SKIP LIST(INTEGER(I)); END;

    END LISTTOMAX;
```

Section 5 <u>Summary</u>

1. An array is a set of subscripted variables. These are distinct variables but all have the same identifier and store the same type of value.

2. A subscripted variable is referenced by following the identifier with a subscript -- an expression enclosed in parentheses. On evaluation the subscript expression must yield an appropriate integer value. Multiple subscripts are expressions separated by commas.

3. An identifier is declared to be an array by giving the upper bound on the subscript:

        DECLARE identifier(bound) attribute-list;

If the lower bound on the subscripts is not 1, it must also be specified:

        DECLARE ident(lower-bound : upper-bound) attribute-list ;

For multiple subscripts the bounds are separated by commas.

4. References to an array in the text will generally be in the same form as a declaration, including explicit lower bounds on subscript values. For example, MATRIX(1:5,1:10), SET(0:4).

5.* Arrays (rather than just a subscripted element of an array) can be used in certain contexts. These include the GET statement, the left-side of an assignment statement (the target variable), and expressions. This can be a great convenience -- but it also can be tricky, and you must know how each array operation is performed.

Section 5 <u>Exercises</u>

It is important for the student to gain facility in using arrays, loops, and conditional statements, before proceeding further. Exercises 1-6 should be done by each student.

1. The following are values of certain arrays and simple variables: (/// means no value has been assigned yet.)

B(-3)	20	AGE(1)	1	I	1
B(-2)	25	AGE(2)	13	J	2
B(-1)	42	AGE(3)	21	K	3
B(0)	9	AGE(4)	6	M	4
B(1)	8	AGE(5)	7	SUM	///
B(2)	13	AGE(6)	12	C	///
B(3)	-20	AGE(7)	8	MAX	///
B(4)	-40	AGE(8)	0	MIN	///
B(5)	50				

a) Give the values of B(-2), AGE(5), B(I), AGE(I+J).

b) Give the name of the variable containing the largest value
     in array B(-3:5), in array AGE(1:8).

c) Evaluate the following expressions:

        B(1) + AGE(4)
        B(3) * AGE(1)
        5 + B(5) + AGE(5)
        AGE(6)/6

d) Give the value of B(1), B(I+1), B(I+J).

e) Which of the following refer to existing variables?

        AGE(I-M)   B(I-M)   AGE(I+M)   B(I+M)

f) Give the values of:

        B(AGE(1))   B(AGE(M)-1)   AGE(AGE(4))   AGE(AGE(M+I)-2)

g) Evaluate the following expressions:

        M + AGE(M)
        M + AGE(K)
        B(3)*3 - AGE(3)
        AGE(J+J)/AGE(J)
        B(M-I)

h) Give declarations for all of the arrays and variables shown.
     (Assume FIXED DECIMAL values for I, J, K and M; FLOAT
     DECIMAL for the others.)

i) Write assignment statements that would assign the values to
     the variables as shown.

j) Write GET statements and a data list that would assign the
     values to the variables as shown.

k)* Write GET statements, using arrays rather than subscripted
     variables, and a data list that would assign the values to
     the variables as shown.

2. Assuming variables with initial values as in Exercise 1,
trace the execution of the following program segments and show
the values that result from their execution.

a) /* PUT IN SUM THE SUM OF AGE(J),...,AGE(M) */
        C = J; SUM = 0;
        DO WHILE (C <= M);
            SUM = SUM + AGE(C);
            C = C + 1; END;

b) /* PUT IN MAX THE MAXIMUM OF AGE(I),...,AGE(M) */
    /* I IS NEVER GREATER THAN M */
        MAX = AGE(I); C = I + 1;
        DO WHILE (C <= M);
            IF MAX < AGE(C) THEN MAX = AGE(C);
            C = C + 1; END;

c) /* ADD THE SUBSCRIPT VALUE I TO EACH VARIABLE B(I) */
        C = -3;
        DO WHILE (C <= 5);
            B(C) = B(C) + C;
            C = C + 1; END;

d) /* STORE INTO AGE(1) THE VALUE 0, INTO AGE(2) 1, */
    /* AND INTO AGE(I) VALUE A(I-2) + AGE(I-1) FOR I>2 */
    /* THESE NUMBERS FORM THE "FIBONACCI SEQUENCE" */
        AGE(1) = 0; AGE(2) = 1;
        C = 3;
        DO WHILE (C <= 8);
            AGE(C) = AGE(C-1) + AGE(C-2);
            C = C + 1; END;

e) /* PUT THE ABSOLUTE VALUE OF EACH B(I) INTO B(I) */
        C = 5;
        DO WHILE (C >= -3);
            IF B(C) < 0 THEN B(C) = -B(C);
            C = C - 1; END;

f) /* MOVE EACH VALUE IN B "UP" ONE POSITION */
    /* STORE 0 IN B(-3), DISCARD B(5) */
        C = 5;
        DO WHILE (C > -3);
            B(C) = B(C-1);
            C = C - 1; END;
        B(-3) = 0;

3. Draw lines (locations) as shown in Exercise 1 for variables
declared as follows:

a) DECLARE (A, B) FIXED DECIMAL;

b) DECLARE AGE(3,4) FIXED DECIMAL;

c) DECLARE COST(-3:0) FLOAT DECIMAL;

d) DECLARE (PAY(0:10),AMOUNT(0:10),I) FLOAT DECIMAL;

4. Write program segments to accomplish each of the following
tasks, using the variables declared in Exercise 3:

 a) Set all of the variables in the array AGE(1:3,1:4) to zero.

 b) Set each variable in the array AGE(1:3,1:4) equal to the sum
    of its own subscripts -- that is, AGE(I,J) equal to I + J.

 c) Set each variable in the array COST(-3:0) equal to whatever
    is the minimum of the initial values of the variables in
    COST.

 d) Subtract the value of each   variable   in   the   array
    AMOUNT(0:10)   from   the variable in the corresponding
    position in the array PAY(0:10).

 e) Compute the sum of the values of all of the variables in the
    array PAY(0:10).

 f) Swap the values of PAY(1:10) to put the largest in PAY(10).
    Thus if initially PAY is

         PAY <u>10</u> <u>9</u> <u>8</u> <u>7</u> <u>6</u> <u>5</u> <u>4</u> <u>3</u> <u>2</u> <u>1</u>

    then after execution, the array might be

         PAY <u>9</u> <u>8</u> <u>7</u> <u>6</u> <u>5</u> <u>4</u> <u>3</u> <u>2</u> <u>1</u> <u>10</u>
     or PAY <u>1</u> <u>9</u> <u>8</u> <u>7</u> <u>6</u> <u>5</u> <u>4</u> <u>3</u> <u>2</u> <u>10</u>

5. Suppose an array B(1:N) contains a sequence of values, some
of which appear more than once. Write a program segment which
will "delete" duplicates, moving the unique values towards the
beginning of the array.   Assign to variable M the number of
unique values. The order of the values should be preserved.
For example, if we have

    N <u>7</u>   B <u>1</u> <u>6</u> <u>1</u> <u>8</u> <u>3</u> <u>7</u> <u>6</u>

after execution the variables should be

    N <u>7</u>   M <u>5</u>   B <u>1</u> <u>6</u> <u>8</u> <u>3</u> <u>7</u> <u>?</u> <u>?</u>

(where "?" indicates that the value is immaterial).

6. The following program segment searches array segment B(1:N)
for a value equal to X. When it finds it, it sets J to the
index of X in B so that B(J) = X.   This is a <u>linear</u> <u>search</u>
algorithm.

    J = 1;
    DO WHILE (B(J) ¬= X); J = J + 1; END;

 a) What value is in J after execution if X is not in the array?

 b) Change the program to set 0 in J if X is not in the array.

c) What happens if N = 0? Change the program segment to store
   0 in J if this is the case. (Such a case actually arises
   in programming, and it does not have to be considered a
   mistake.)

7.   The following questions refer to the program in Section 5.5.

a) Suppose that there is a tie for maximum -- several different
   data values have the same value, greater than all others.
   What <u>should</u> the program do in this case; what <u>does</u> the
   program do?

b) What does the program do if several improper data values are
   included?

c) Precisely what happens if 110 data values followed by the
   end-of-input signal appear in the input?

d) What would the output look like if the following data is
   presented?

        *DATA
         14, 13, -3, 15, 2, 7, 15, 12, 0, 23

Section 6 <u>Display of Results</u>

Printed output from a PL/I program is produced by execution
of "output" statements. The detailed discussion of these
statements is prefaced by two general comments on output.

First, <u>output during execution</u> of a program is entirely the
<u>programmer's responsibility</u>. A copy of the program, called a
"source listing", is produced automatically, but once execution
begins no further printing occurs unless the program
specifically calls for it by the execution of output statements.
Whatever information may be produced by the execution of a
program will be lost if it has not been displayed by the time
execution ends, since the next program to be executed will
overwrite the memory.

Second, the statements that control output are typically the
most complex statements in a programming language. If not the
most difficult in concept they are at least the richest in
detail and the most tedious to learn to use. This seems to be
required in order to give the programmer flexible control over
what information is to be displayed and the format in which it
is to appear. PL/I is certainly not an exception in this
regard, and the following paragraphs offer a brief introduction
to only the simplest type of PL/I output statement.

6.1 <u>Display of Values of Variables</u>

The simplest method of obtaining printed output in PL/I is
with a "PUT LIST statement", the type that has been used in
previous examples. The simple form is:

PUT LIST(variable names, separated by commas);

The variables may be simple or subscripted and are separated by
commas. For example:

(6.1a)   PUT LIST(TOTAL, I, PLACE(I), MAXPLACE);

The standard output format that is used by this statement
divides the printed page horizontally into five "fields" of 24
columns each. (This is somewhat analogous to the "tab stops" on
a typewriter.) Each column is one "print position" -- it will
print one character. Each field is used to display the value of

one variable from the list given in the PUT statement. In the
example given above the value of TOTAL will be printed in the
first (leftmost) field; the value of I in the second; the value
of PLACE(I) in the third; and the value of MAXPLACE in the
fourth. (The particular variable from the array PLACE to appear
in the third field will of course depend upon the value of the
subscript I at the time the statement is executed.) Each value
begins at the left of the field and uses as many columns as
required. Any columns of the field unused by the value are left
blank and the next value begins in the leftmost column of the
next field.

    FIXED variables are printed in the obvious integer form,
while FLOAT variables are displayed in exponential form. The
decimal point is always given after the first digit and the
power of ten required to properly position the point is given
after the digits of the number. For example, if the values of
the variables are:

        TOTAL   −.0036 [float decimal]
        I   2   [fixed decimal]
        PLACE(1)   −124.3 [float decimal]
        PLACE(2)   63.7   [float decimal]
        MAXPLACE   806   [float decimal]

the values displayed by the PUT statement (6.1a) would be:

    −3.60000E−03   2   6.37000E+01   8.06000E+02

(The full number of blanks between values are not shown here
since the print line in this book is not a full 120 positions.)

    A PUT LIST statement does not automatically begin a new line.
It begins with the next unused field, wherever that may be on
the line. For example, if one PUT statement completes its list
by placing a value in the third field on some line, then the
next PUT statement to be executed will place its first value in
the fourth field on that same line. This means that consecutive
PUT statements

        PUT LIST(TOTAL,I);
        PUT LIST(PLACE(I), MAXPLACE);

are equivalent to the single statement

        PUT LIST(TOTAL, I, PLACE(I), MAXPLACE);

In effect, the lists of variables in consecutive PUT statements
form one continuous list -- to be assigned to the continuous
sequence of fields on the printed page. After the fifth field
of one line has been filled the first field of the next line is
used.

    The programmer can control the placement of values on a line
by using the "SKIP option". Inserting the keyword SKIP will

cause the statement to begin placement with the first field of a
new line, regardless of where the last PUT statement left off.
For example:

```
    PUT SKIP LIST(TOTAL, I);
    PUT SKIP LIST(PLACE(I), MAXPLACE);
```

will cause two new lines to be printed, with values in the first
two fields of each line. Note, however, that unless the next
PUT statement also specifies SKIP it will begin placing values
in the third field of this second line.

   A number of lines may be skipped by giving an integer after
the keyword SKIP. For example:

```
    PUT SKIP(3) LIST(TOTAL);
```

will leave two lines blank and place the value of TOTAL in the
first field of the third line. SKIP is equivalent to SKIP(1).

   As a further example

```
    /* TABULATE 'HEIGHT' AND 'WIDTH' */
        DO I = 1 TO 10 BY 1;
            PUT SKIP(2) LIST(I, HEIGHT(I), WIDTH(I)); END;
```

will produced ten double-spaced lines with values in the first
three fields of each print line. The following program segment
would also produce double-spaced lines:

```
    DO I = 1 TO 10 BY 1;
        PUT SKIP LIST(A(I),B(I),C(I),D(I),E(I)); END;
```

Since there are exactly five variables to each print line, PL/I
will automatically be prepared to start a new line -- so the
SKIP leaves that line blank and skips to the next.

   The PUT statement can be used with the SKIP option alone to
terminate a logical section of printed output. For example, the
PUT SKIP(4); below ensures that this section of output will be
separated by at least three blank lines from what follows,
regardless of the form of the next PUT:

```
    ...
    PUT SKIP LIST(X, Y, Z);
    PUT SKIP LIST(R, S, T);
    PUT SKIP(4);
    ...
```

6.2 Titling and Labeling Results

The appearance and readability of printed results can be
greatly improved by adding appropriate titles and labels. To a
limited extent this can be done even with LIST format output by
placing a "literal" instead of a variable in the list of the PUT
statement. A literal is a string of characters enclosed in
single quotes. For example:

```
'TOTAL'
'TEMPERATURE ='
'RESULTS FOR 9/23/72 ARE:'
'*-*-*-*-*-*-*'
' '          (blank is a valid character)
```

The character string is printed exactly as given -- without the
quotes. The printing begins in the leftmost column of the
"next" field. For example, if TOTAL and SUM have values

```
TOTAL 642.17  [float decimal]
SUM   -1043.7 [float decimal]
```

then the statements

```
PUT SKIP LIST('TOTAL =', TOTAL);
PUT SKIP LIST('SUM =', SUM);
```

would produce the following output:

```
TOTAL =              6.42170E+02
SUM =               -1.04370E+03
```

The appearance of these lines can be improved by including
blanks in the literals to displace the words toward the right in
the 24 position print field:

```
PUT SKIP LIST('              TOTAL =', TOTAL);
PUT SKIP LIST('                SUM =',SUM);
```

These statements will produce:

```
              TOTAL = 6.42170E+02
                SUM = -1.04370E+03
```

Literals are often used to identify different values, using
their variable names. For example,

```
PUT SKIP LIST('X', X);
```

will print the name X, in the first field of a line, and the
value of X in the second field. It is important to realize that
whatever is included in the literal will be printed -- and that
the content of the literal has no significance whatever to PL/I
or the computer. One could write

```
    PUT SKIP LIST('THE VALUE OF Y IS:', X);
```

and the deceptive label would be printed without complaint.

Blank literals can be used to control the placement of other list elements on the printed line. For example, the following PUT statement causes the value of the variable X to be printed in the <u>second</u> field of a new line, and the value of Y in the <u>fourth</u> field.

```
    PUT SKIP LIST(' ', X, ' ', Y);
```

PUT statements whose list consists of a single literal are frequently used. For example:

```
    PUT SKIP LIST('IMPROPER DATA ENCOUNTERED');
    PUT SKIP LIST('UNEXPECTED NEGATIVE VALUE');
```

Other examples are shown in the sample program in Section 5.5. Such statements announce to the programmer that the flow-of-control has reached a certain point in the program. This can be used to warn the programmer that some exceptional condition has occurred. Such statements are particularly useful during the testing of a new program and one often includes many such statements, removing them after the correctness of the program has been established. This technique is discussed at more length in Part III.

If a literal of more than 24 characters is given it will simply continue into the next field on the line. (If a literal of exactly 24 characters is given it will completely fill one field and cause the next to be skipped. The next element on the list will be placed in the second following field.) If a literal reaches the end of a line it will continue in the first field of the next line. This applies to the printed output line -- a different rule applies to the cards on which the PUT statement itself is punched.

PL/C does not normally permit any "symbol" to be split between two cards -- to be started on one card and continued on the next. Keywords, variables and constants are all symbols. A literal or a comment, however long, is also considered a single symbol. A <u>statement may be continued</u> onto as <u>many cards as necessary</u>, but an individual <u>symbol cannot be split</u> over a <u>card boundary</u>. (This can be permitted under the NOBOUNDARY option for comments and literals; see Appendix B.2.) The reason for this restriction is that the omission of the closing quote (or the closing */ in a comment) is a very common error. When this happens PL/I continues to search for the closing quote on the following cards, interpreting their contents as continuation of the literal, rather than new statements. PL/C automatically supplies the missing quote at the end of the card where the literal started, which localizes the effect of the error. The following would not be a valid PUT statement in PL/C:

```
PUT SKIP LIST(TOTAL,SUM,AVERAGE,MEDIAN,'THESE STATISTICS
ARE OBTAINED FROM 9/23/72 DATA');
```

This same statement would be valid if it was divided between
symbols instead of in the middle of the literal:

```
PUT SKIP LIST(TOTAL, SUM, AVERAGE, MEDIAN,
     'THESE STATISTICS ARE OBTAINED FROM 9/23/72 DATA');
```

Although the statement is now in acceptable form, the format of
the printed output is likely to be disappointing. Since the
variables fill the first four fields, the long literal will
begin in the fifth field of the line and spill over into the
first field of the following line. The following sequence of
statements would produce more attractive and readable output:

```
PUT SKIP LIST('STATISTICS FROM 9/23/72 DATA:');
     PUT SKIP LIST('          TOTAL =', TOTAL);
     PUT SKIP LIST('          SUM =', SUM);
     PUT SKIP LIST('          AVERAGE =', AVERAGE);
     PUT SKIP LIST('          MEDIAN =', MEDIAN);
```

6.3* Display of Arrays

If an array name without a subscript appears on the variable
list of a PUT statement all of the values of the array will be
printed. They will appear in row-major order. For example, if
TAB(1:8) is an array, the statement PUT LIST(TAB); is equivalent
to

```
DO I = 1 TO 8 BY 1;
     PUT LIST(TAB(I)); END;
```

Either form will place values in the next eight fields (starting
a new line whenever the last line has been filled). To begin
placement with a new line, PUT SKIP LIST(TAB); is equivalent to

```
PUT SKIP;
DO I = 1 TO 8 BY 1;
     PUT LIST(TAB(I)); END;
```

As another example, for array MATRIX(1:3,1:15), the statement

```
PUT LIST(MATRIX);
```

is equivalent to the following nested loops: (Either form will
place values in the next forty-five fields.)

```
DO I = 1 TO 3 BY 1;
     DO J = 1 TO 15 BY 1;
          PUT LIST(MATRIX(I,J)); END; END;
```

6.4* <u>Control of Display Format</u>

   More flexible control over the format of output is provided
by the "PUT EDIT statement".   This statement can be very
complex; we give here only a brief introduction.   Nevertheless,
this will permit substantial control of printing format in the
most common situations. The general form of the statement is:

       PUT SKIP(i) EDIT(element list)(format list);

The "element list" is similar to that of the PUT LIST statement
-- a list of variables, arrays and literals, separated by
commas. The SKIP(i) is optional, with the same effect as it has
on PUT LIST. The difference lies in the "format list". This is
a list of "items", separated by commas. Items are "data-items"
(the items A, A(w), F(w,d) and E(w,d) below) or "control-items"
(X(i) below). The element list and format list are processed
concurrently, from beginning to end.   The first data-item
controls the printing of the first value, the second data-item
controls printing of the second value, and so on. Control-items
are "executed" as they are passed over when looking for the next
data-item to use to control printing. (Thus, control-items at
the end of the format list have no effect.)

   Of the twelve items, the following are the most useful for
our purposes.   (Appendix A.9 has a discussion of all of them.)

   A -- print a character string. This can be a literal (or a
   string-valued variable -- see Section 9). The width of the
   printing field is the length of the string.

   A(w) -- print a character string left-justified in a field
   w positions wide (truncating the string if necessary).

   X(i) -- skip i spaces.

   F(w) -- print an integer right-justified in a field w
   positions wide.

   F(w,d) -- print a decimal number with d digits to the right
   of the decimal point, right-justified in a field w
   positions wide. The width w must include a position for
   the decimal point and a position for a minus sign, if that
   can occur. The internal value will be rounded to fit, if
   necessary.

   E(w,d) -- print a number in exponential form, with d digits
   to the right of the decimal point, right-justified in a
   field w positions wide. The width w must include positions
   for the decimal point, the sign, and the exponent. The
   internal value will be rounded, if necessary, to fit this
   format.

The F and E format-items can be used for either FIXED or FLOAT
values; necessary conversions will be performed automatically.

   In EDIT format, fields are not pre-defined (as in LIST
format). Each format-item defines its own field-length, which
begins immediately after the termination of the preceding field.

   We give examples, assuming the following values:

      TOTAL 14.3 [float decimal]   COUNT 25   [fixed decimal]

The output produced by various PUT EDIT statements is shown
below. (Print position numbers are shown to indicate exact
placement. They would not appear on actual output.)

```
    PUT SKIP EDIT(COUNT)(F(5));
    output:        25
    positions: 12345

    PUT SKIP EDIT(COUNT)(F(5,1));
    output:      25.0
    positions: 12345

    PUT SKIP EDIT(COUNT)(E(10,2));
    output:       2.50E+01
    positions: 1234567890

    PUT SKIP EDIT(COUNT)(X(4),F(5));
    output:            25
    positions: 123456789

    PUT SKIP EDIT(COUNT, COUNT)(F(5),F(5,2));
    output:        2525.00
    positions: 1234567890

    PUT SKIP EDIT (COUNT, COUNT) (F(5), X(3), F(5,2));
    output:        25    25.00
    positions: 1234567890123

    PUT SKIP EDIT(TOTAL)(E(10,2));
    output:       1.43E+01
    positions: 1234567890

    PUT SKIP EDIT(TOTAL)(F(6,2));
    output:      14.30
    positions: 123456

    PUT SKIP EDIT(TOTAL)(F(5));
    output:        14
    positions: 12345

    PUT SKIP EDIT('IMPROPER DATA')(A);
    output:    IMPROPER DATA
    positions: 1234567890123

    PUT SKIP EDIT('IMPROPER DATA')(A(8));
    output:    IMPROPER
    positions: 12345678
```

```
PUT SKIP EDIT('COUNT IS:',COUNT,'TOTAL IS:',TOTAL)
       (A,F(4),X(3),A,E(10,2));
output:     COUNT IS:  25    TOTAL IS:  1.43E+01
positions: 123456789012345678901234567890012345
```

Rather than repeat an item in consecutive positions on the
format list, a constant or expression enclosed in parentheses
may be given as a "repetition factor". For example:

```
N=3;
PUT SKIP EDIT('VALUES ARE:',X,Y,Z)(A,(N)E(10,1));
```

is equivalent to

```
PUT SKIP EDIT('VALUES ARE:',X,Y,Z)
            (A,E(10,1),E(10,1),E(10,1));
```

Expressions can be given for the parameters w, d, and i in
the   format-items   described above.   These expressions are
evaluated during execution of the PUT statement to determine the
field width or number of digits. This allows the output format
to depend on computational results, but this capability is not
often used.   Generally, the format is predetermined, and w, d,
and i are given as constants, as shown in the examples.

Section 6 Summary

1. The form of the simplest PL/I output statement is:

    PUT LIST(variables and literals, separated by commas);

2. The "LIST format" print line consists of five fields of 24
characters each.   Fields are filled from left to right, top to
bottom, starting wherever the last PUT statement left off. Each
element on the PUT list starts a new field, and continues
through as many fields as are required to display its value.

3. The SKIP(i) option will cause a PUT statement to skip down i
lines. SKIP(1), or SKIP, will skip to the beginning of the next
line; SKIP(2) will skip to the second line, etc.

4. A literal is a quoted string of characters that will be
printed exactly as given. These can be used to title and label
results, and to print messages.

5*. If an array name (without subscripts) appears in place of a
variable in the list of a PUT statement, all of the elements of
the array will be displayed in "row major order".

6*. The PUT EDIT statement gives control over output format:

    PUT EDIT(elements) (format list) ;

Section 6 Exercises

1. Write a single PUT statement to produce the same printed output as the following sequence:

```
PUT SKIP LIST(TOTAL);
PUT LIST(MAX);
PUT LIST(MINIMUM, AVG);
```

2. What would the output from the following program segment look like?

```
DO I = 1 TO 5 BY 1;
    PUT SKIP LIST(I,I,I,I,I); END;
```

3. What is the result of executing the following statement?

```
PUT LIST(' ',' ');
```

4. What is printed by execution of the following statement?

```
PUT SKIP LIST('PUT SKIP LIST(X);');
```

5. Write a sequence of PUT statements that will print the pattern shown below (where Ƅ indicates a blank):

```
ƄOƄ
OƄO
ƄOƄ
```

6.* Write a PUT EDIT statement that will repeatedly display the value of a FIXED DECIMAL variable named K, whose value is 2, yielding exactly the same output as the following statement:

```
PUT SKIP LIST('22222222');
```

7.* Assuming that X and Y are FLOAT DECIMAL variables, write a PUT EDIT statement that will produce the same output as:

```
PUT SKIP LIST(X, Y);
```

8.* TABLE(1:5,1:5) is a square array of FIXED DECIMAL variables, all of whose values are integers greater than 0 and less than 10. Print the values of this array in rectangular form, on five consecutive lines, with a single blank between the values on each line. For example, if all of the values are 9, the array would be displayed as:

```
9 9 9 9 9
9 9 9 9 9
9 9 9 9 9
9 9 9 9 9
9 9 9 9 9
```

Section 7 <u>The Execution of Programs</u>

    After a program has been written, and painstakingly checked
for   errors   in   logic   and   syntax, it must be transmitted to a
computer for execution. This is usually done by "punching" both
the   program statements and suitable test data onto cards. Each
card generally contains one   line   of   the   program   as   it   was
written   on   paper, and columns should be skipped at the left of
the card to reflect the indentation of the program lines.

    "Keypunching" is a <u>major source of errors</u>. Many programs,
correct on paper, reach the computer in garbled form simply
because the lines are not exactly represented by the information
actually punched in the cards. Much time and effort is saved if
the cards are checked against the written form, with great care,
before the deck is submitted for processing.

    When cards containing keypunch errors have been replaced, the
deck is arranged as follows for presentation to the computer:

```
    *PL/C ID='name of programmer'     options
     /* title comment */
     /* comment summarizing program function */
     entry-name : PROCEDURE OPTIONS(MAIN);
         cards containing declarations
         cards containing imperative statements
         END entry-name ;
    *DATA
         cards containing data
```

The *PL/C and *DATA cards <u>must</u> begin in column 1.   Program   and
comment cards <u>must not</u> begin in column 1. Data cards <u>may</u> begin
in column 1.   (See Appendix B.3 for further information on card
formats.)

7.1 Loading, Translation and Execution

Processing a program takes place in two distinct stages. First, the program is "loaded" into the memory of the computer; second, it is executed. In order to load a program, the deck of cards is placed in a device called a "card reader". The card reader examines the cards one at a time, in the order presented, detects the position of holes in the cards, and transmits this information to the computer. The card-reading operation appears to proceed very rapidly (500 to 1000 cards per minute) but it is in fact very slow compared to the speed with which statements are executed once the program is loaded.

The loading of a program for processing is actually performed by another program, called a "compiler", which is already in the computer. During loading, the compiler scans the program for errors and translates the PL/I statements into an internal form that the computer can understand and execute. This translation is a complicated, but not fundamentally mysterious process; it is described briefly in Part VII.

A crucial point is that the program is not executed as it is loaded. Only after the complete program has been loaded, does the second stage -- execution -- begin. Execution of a PL/I program consists of one execution of the "main procedure".

At the moment that execution begins only the cards containing the program statements have been read. Cards containing data remain in the card reader -- ready to be read when called for by the execution of GET statements in the program.

7.2 Analysis of Printed Output

The amount and type of printed output produced during the processing of a program can vary considerably. Certain portions are always provided, some portions depend upon the choice of "options" for the particular program, and some depend upon the execution of output statements in the program.

Each computing facility has predetermined a set of standard or "default" choices for the various options. These are presumably chosen to be the most appropriate for the greatest number of users of the computer. The default options are automatically assigned to each program -- but you can override the defaults by specifying your own choice of options. In PL/C, options are specified on the *PL/C card -- the first card of the program. Many of the important options are described in the following sections; a complete list is given in Appendix B.2.

The complete printed output produced during loading, translation and execution of a PL/C program can be divided into the following sections:

Header Pages -- several pages produced by a general supervisory program (called the "operating system") to identify the beginning of a new program, report its cost, the language used -- and scores of other statistics that are of little importance to the neophyte programmer.

Source Listing -- a copy of the program, with additional information such as statement numbers and error messages.

Cross-Reference and Attribute Listing -- a listing of all identifiers, where they are declared, their type attributes, and where they are used. This is not typically a standard option -- it will only appear if the programmer requests the ATR and XREF options.

Execution Output -- the result of executing PUT statements (with error messages, if necessary).

PL/C Post-Mortem Dump -- a listing of the final values of variables (values after the end of execution), and various PL/C summary statistics.

Trailer Pages -- additional more-or-less incomprehensible pages supplied by the operating system.

These different portions of output are described in more detail in the following sections.

7.2.1 Source Listing

The source listing is a copy of the program, to which certain other information has been added.

1) At the top of the first page are two lines titled

   OPTIONS IN EFFECT

Any question about what options are standard, or whether the programmer's requests for special options were successful, should be answered by studying these lines.

2) The card following the *PL/C card is used to automatically title the pages of the source listing. The contents of this card are printed as a title at the top of each page. Page numbers are also printed.

3) At the left of the program statements in the main body of the source listing are four columns headed STMT, LEVEL, NEST and BLOCK. The LEVEL and BLOCK columns describe the "block structure" of the program -- a topic discussed in Part IV. For programs that consist of only a main procedure these two columns will contain nothing but 1's.

The column headed NEST shows the nesting level of DO groups.
Statements in the body of an "outer" DO group have "1" in this
column; statements in the body of the next inner DO group will
have a "2", etc.

The column headed STMT gives "statement numbers" that are
assigned by PL/I.   Statements are numbered in the order that
they are loaded. One minor difficulty is that PL/I is very
generous in what it considers a "statement".   Declarations are
numbered as if they were statements, as are PROCEDURE, DO and
END.   This STMT numbering is quite obvious, as long as there is
exactly one statement per line. When there is more than one
statement per line or more than one line per statement, the
numbering is still straightforward, but the printing of the
numbers is not.   In general, with more than one statement per
line, the number of the first statement on the line will be
printed.   When a single statement takes more than one line, the
statement number will be printed only once.

You should give careful attention to these numbers. They are
generated in a very systematic way, so that if they do not run
as you would expect them to, there is a misunderstanding about
the structure of the program. Discouraging as it may seem at
first, it is never the computer that misunderstands the program.
It is always you, misunderstanding what you wrote.

These STMT numbers are used throughout the printed output to
refer to individual statements -- in error messages, in the
cross-reference listing, and in the post-mortem dump.

4) When errors are detected during the initial scanning of a
program, an error message is printed directly following the
offending statement. In almost every such case PL/C attempts to
make some repair of the error, so that the program can be
executed. The statement that results from the PL/C correction
is printed below the error message. For example:

```
        STMT
              . . .
           8           X = Y*(X+Z;
    IN     8  ERROR  SY04 MISSING )
    PL/C USES        X = Y*(X+Z);
              . . .
```

Unfortunately, the repair is not always as successful as in this
example. Sometimes, in its efforts to construct a syntactically
correct program, PL/C constructs statements that are very unlike
what the programmer intended.   The proper attitude is to be
appreciative when the correction is helpful; amused when it is
not; and try to give PL/C as few opportunities to make
corrections as possible. Note that even though a particular
correction does not recreate what you intended, it still permits
execution of the program. This execution may yield information
that will help expose other faults in the program.

5) Certain errors in the meaning of statements are easily detected only after the complete program has been scanned. Since the listing of the program statements is printed as the program is loaded and scanned, these additional error messages cannot be printed immediately after the offending statement. Instead they are collected, and printed in a group after the end of the program statement listing.

These messages are especially confusing when they describe an improper meaning that is a direct consequence of an earlier PL/C "correction". When one of these errors is completely mystifying, see if there has been a previous error message and correction for the same statement.

These messages often include the warning:

WARNING   CG0C NO FILE SPECIFIED. SYSIN/SYSPRINT ASSUMED.

GET and PUT statements have other uses in addition to reading cards and printing lines. Strictly speaking, one should designate the origin or destination of the information by specifying a "FILE phrase" in the statement. For example, when printed output is intended this phrase would be given as:

PUT FILE(SYSPRINT) SKIP LIST(...);

When card reading is intended the statement would be:

GET FILE(SYSIN) LIST(...);

If any GET or PUT is missing a FILE phrase, FILE(SYSIN) or FILE(SYSPRINT) is assumed, respectively, and the warning message is printed.

7.2.2 Cross-Reference and Attribute Listing

Typical default options do not include the production of this section of output, so the ATR and XREF options must be given on the *PL/C card in order to obtain it. These are two distinct options which produce two different types of information, but they are almost always used together.

The attribute listing describes all of the identifiers used in the program, including labels and entry-names as well as variables. Each identifier is listed by name, in alphabetical order, with the STMT number where it was declared and the attributes that were assigned to it. The numbers given after the FIXED and FLOAT attributes specify their "precision" -- the number of digits in their value. DECIMAL FLOAT(6) means a decimal number with six significant figures. DECIMAL FIXED(5,0) means a decimal integer of five digits, with no digits to the right of the decimal point. The attribute list will include several attributes that we have not discussed. "AUTOMATIC" will be considered in Part IV; "ALIGNED" and "UNALIGNED" are irrelevant for our purposes.

The cross-reference (XREF) option adds to the entry for each identifier a list of the statement numbers of all statements that refer to that particular identifier.

If the attribute and cross-reference list is studied carefully it will reveal two important kinds of errors:

    1. Misspellings of identifiers that accidentally create new identifiers.

    2. Missing or faulty declarations of variables, resulting in surprising assignments of attributes.

7.2.3 Execution Output

The output generated by the actual execution of a program is completely dependent upon the execution of PUT statements in the program. If no PUT statements are executed, there will be no execution output. PL/I intrudes in this output only if an error is committed during execution. For example, the program might contain the statement

    BASE_VALUE = SQRT(LEFT_PT);

and this might be executed at a point where LEFT_PT has a negative value. Since the SQRT built-in function requires a non-negative value as argument, an error message would be inserted at that point in the execution output.

This section of output is not automatically titled in any way, nor are the pages numbered. It normally begins at the top of a new page. The end of execution output is denoted by a line that announces the completion of execution of the program:

    IN STMT nn PROGRAM RETURNS FROM MAIN PROCEDURE

7.2.4 PL/C Post-Mortem Dump

The automatic "post-mortem dump" is a feature of PL/C that is not provided by PL/I. This dump supplies information on the final values of variables, and certain other statistics that summarize execution. This information can be very useful in program testing. The different sections of the dump are:

1) The final values of the variables in the main procedure. Although the display is ordinarily limited to the simple (or "scalar") variables, arrays will be included if the DUMPARRAY option has been specified. (The dump refers to "active blocks" and "automatic variables" -- topics that will be discussed in Part IV.)

When a value /// is displayed for a variable, this means that nowhere in the program was a value assigned to this variable. All such instances should be investigated, for they often reveal the presence of a misspelling of a variable name, or a logical error.

2) The number of times that each label and entry-name was encountered during execution.

This can be exploited to provide a complete history of how many times each section of a program is executed. If, during testing of a program, you temporarily insert labelled null statements (for example, CHECKPOINT_1:;, CHECKPOINT_2:;, etc.) at key points in the program, PL/C will automatically count the number of times each such point is reached in execution, and report these statistics in the dump. The optional labelling of DO groups, as described in Section 4.6.2, can be helpful in this regard.

3) The history of the last 18 situations where flow-of-control departed from normal, sequential execution. For example, consider the following program, with STMT numbers shown as they would be assigned by PL/C:

```
STMT 1    INTSUM: PROCEDURE OPTIONS(MAIN);
STMT 2        DECLARE (I, SUM) FIXED DECIMAL;
STMT 3        SUM = 0;
STMT 4        DO I = 1 TO 50 BY 1;
STMT 5            SUM = SUM + I;
STMT 6            END;
STMT 7        PUT LIST(SUM);
STMT 8        END INTSUM;
```

After execution of this program, PL/C would report the flow-of-control history in the following form:

```
*STMT* DYNAMIC FLOW TRACE
*0008*    0000->0001   0050*(0006->0004)   0004->0007   0008->0000
```

The history of the flow-of-control is read from left to right, as follows:

a) The report is issued after execution of STMT 8.

b) Execution began with a transfer to statement 1 (the entry to the main procedure).

c) Progress from 1->2->3->4->5->6 is not reported, since this is the normal, sequential execution.

d) The next 50 departures from sequential order all involved the end of an iteration of the loop.

e) The next transfer was from 4 to 7 (the completion of the loop).

  f) The last transfer was from 8 (the return from the main
  procedure).

Since this program is very short the complete flow-of-control
history is reported.   On larger programs only the final 18
transfers are reported. Complete "flow trace" information can
be obtained in PL/C by other means, described in Part III.

4) Statistics concerning the amount of memory used.

5) The amount of computer time required to load, scan and
translate the program (called the "COMPILE TIME").

6) The amount of computer time required to execute the program.

Section 8 <u>The Declaration of Variables</u>

The declaration of variables has been mentioned in several
earlier sections. Declarations in PL/I are so crucial that
their consideration could not be entirely postponed to this
point, but the previous fragmented presentation is not
sufficient. Section 8 provides a general discussion of
declarations, repeating much of what has been mentioned
previously. Even this is far from complete. The declaration of
string-valued variables is not considered until Section 9.1, and
the relationship between declarations and the "block structure"
of a program is not discussed until Part IV.

The following is a summary of the previous references to the
declaration of variables:

1. Variables are defined by listing their names in a
declaration. Section 2.

2. Declarations are part of the heading of a procedure, and are
placed at the beginning. The creation of the variables takes
place as the procedure is entered -- before the execution of any
statement in the procedure.

3. The type of value that a particular variable can store is
determined by the <u>type attributes</u> that are given in the
declaration of that variable. Section 2.3.

4. A variable can be declared to be an array by specifying the
bounds on its subscript values in its declaration. Section 5.3.

8.1 <u>The Form of a Declaration</u>

The basic form of the declaration of a single, unsubscripted
variable is:

      DECLARE identifier attributes ;

Examples are:

      DECLARE POLYPHASE FLOAT DECIMAL;

      DECLARE K_BOUND DECIMAL FIXED;

Note the following:
    1.   The attributes <u>follow</u> the identifier.

    2.   Order within a list of attributes is immaterial --
        FIXED DECIMAL and DECIMAL FIXED are equivalent.

    3.   <u>No comma is given after the identifier or between the
        attributes</u>.

    Several variables may be included in the same declaration, separated by commas. For example, the following are equivalent:

    DECLARE J FIXED DECIMAL, SUM FLOAT DECIMAL;

    DECLARE J FIXED DECIMAL; DECLARE SUM FLOAT DECIMAL;

    If two or more variables have exactly the same set of attributes, the identifiers can be grouped in parentheses so that the attribute list need not be repeated. The attributes are said to be "factored". For example, the following declarations are equivalent:

    DECLARE I FIXED DECIMAL, J FIXED DECIMAL, K FIXED DECIMAL;

    DECLARE (I, J, K) FIXED DECIMAL;

    These shortcuts in declaration are convenient and widely used. However, they also mean that the declaration is exceedingly sensitive to the placement of each comma and parenthesis. For example, consider the effect of changing the position of commas and parentheses in the following declaration:

    DECLARE (NUMBER, QTY) FLOAT DECIMAL;
        two variables, NUMBER and QTY, each float decimal

    DECLARE NUMBER, QTY FLOAT DECIMAL;
        two variables
            NUMBER default attributes (see Section 8.2)
            QTY float decimal

    DECLARE NUMBER, QTY, FLOAT DECIMAL;
        three variables
            NUMBER default attributes
            QTY default attributes
            FLOAT decimal (and default float)

    DECLARE NUMBER, QTY, FLOAT, DECIMAL;
        four variables
            NUMBER default attributes
            QTY default attributes
            FLOAT default attributes
            DECIMAL default attributes

Each of these declarations is syntactically correct, but each has a distinctly different meaning. Only one of these forms could actually create the proper variables; the others would all create variables in a way that was different from what the programmer intended. Sometimes the effects of such differences are catastrophic. While the programmer may be temporarily mystified as to the cause it is obvious that something is wrong and he eventually will realize that a comma has been misplaced. Unfortunately, the effects are sometimes latent and subtle. If the effects do not happen to appear during testing, a faulty program can be pronounced "correct".

The best protection against such problems is to request the optional listing of the variables that have been created, along with the attributes that have been assigned to them. (See Section 7.2.2.) Careful examination of this list will indicate whether the variables actually created were precisely those intended.

A further shortcut is permitted in the abbreviation of a few keywords:

        DCL is equivalent to DECLARE
        DEC is equivalent to DECIMAL

Using these abbreviations, and factoring the attribute lists, the following are equivalent:

        DCL MAX FIXED DEC, (ZB42,Z4) FLOAT DEC;

        DECLARE MAX FIXED DECIMAL, ZB42 FLOAT DECIMAL,
                Z4 FLOAT DECIMAL;

Any list of popular PL/I errors would have several entries concerning these abbreviations. The use of DEC as an abbreviation for DECLARE is an all-time favorite error. Similarly, neither FIXED nor FLOAT has a valid abbreviation, and any attempt to invent one just creates a new variable named FIX, or FLT, or whatever is used.

8.1.1 <u>Declaration of Arrays</u>

An array is declared by specifying bounds on its subscript values immediately after the identifier. The general form is:

        DECLARE identifier(lb1:ub1, lb2:ub2, ...) attributes ;

where lb1, ub1, lb2, ub2, ... are expressions giving the lower bound and upper bound for the first subscript; the lower bound and upper bound for the second subscript, etc. If only an upper-bound-expression is given, a lower bound of 1 is assumed. For example:

        DCL (X(5), MAT(0:6,J)) FLOAT DECIMAL;

will create two arrays of FLOAT DECIMAL variables.   X consists of five singly-subscripted variables.   MAT is doubly-subscripted -- the first subscript ranging from 0 to 6; the second from 1 to whatever value J had at the time of creation of the array.

8.2 Implicit Declaration and Default Attributes

   The reader will not run many PL/I programs before discovering that PL/I does not demand the explicit declaration of every variable. This discovery will probably occur the first time that he makes a keypunch mistake that misspells the name of a variable. Rather than recognize it as an error, in most contexts PL/I will accept the misspelling as a new identifier, and consider this the "implicit declaration" of a different variable. No announcement is made and unless the ATR or XREF options are in effect, such an error may be difficult to detect.

   Since type attributes are not specified in such an implicit declaration they must be assumed by the system. These "default attributes" depend upon the <u>first letter of the identifier</u>, and not upon the context in which the implicit declaration occurs. The rules are:

     If the identifier begins with one of the letters I,   J,   K, L, M or N the type attributes are FIXED BINARY.

     Otherwise the type attributes are FLOAT DECIMAL.

The BINARY attribute specifies that the value should   be represented in the computer memory in the binary (rather than decimal) number system. The choice of internal representation is of no significance for our purposes, and we mention it here only because you will probably see BINARY on an ATR listing, and wonder what it means.

   These same rules for default attributes apply if a variable is declared explicitly, but no type attributes are given. For example, the following are equivalent:

     DECLARE TOTAL;

     DECLARE TOTAL FLOAT DECIMAL;

The rules that apply when a variable is explicitly declared, but with only partial specification of type attributes, are more complex (and not very reasonable). They are given in Appendix A.4. You are strongly advised to

     a) explicitly declare all variables at the beginning of the procedure, and

     b) completely specify type attributes in each declaration.

8.3* <u>Initial Values</u>

The creation of a variable and the assignment of value are distinctly different actions and initial values are not automatically supplied when a variable is created. (It is such a common mistake to assume that an initial value of zero is automatically supplied that a few languages -- including PL/C -- will in fact supply a zero value for numeric variables. But this action is considered the correction of a user error and a warning message will be printed.)

PL/I does offer an option that permits the programmer to specify both <u>creation</u> and <u>assignment of initial value</u> in a declaration. "Initial value" is considered an optional attribute. The form is:

    INITIAL(constant)   or   INIT(constant)

During creation, the specified constant is assigned to the variable. An example of use would be:

    DECLARE SUM FLOAT DECIMAL INITIAL(0);

The variable SUM would be created and <u>immediately</u> assigned a value of 0. This is <u>almost</u> equivalent to writing:

    DECLARE SUM FLOAT DECIMAL;
    SUM = 0;

The difference lies only in the timing. When an initial value is assigned by the declaration, it takes place with creation -- that is, before the execution of any statement in the procedure.

The INITIAL attribute is especially convenient for arrays. In this case a list of initial values is specified -- usually one value for each element of the array. The form is:

    INITIAL(c1, c2, c3, ...)

where c_1, c_2, c_3, ... are constants. These values are assigned to the elements in "row major order". For example:

    DECLARE X(4) FIXED DECIMAL INITIAL(5,6,7,8);

will cause creation and assignment of initial values as follows:

    X(1) 5
    X(2) 6
    X(3) 7
    X(4) 8

If the same constant would appear in several consecutive positions on the INITIAL list, an expression giving a "repetition factor" may be specified:

    DECLARE XP(5) FIXED DECIMAL INITIAL(6,(3)7,8);

This would create the following:

    XP(1) 6
    XP(2) 7
    XP(3) 7
    XP(4) 7
    XP(5) 8

The repetition factor can be applied to a list of constants,
which for this purpose is enclosed in parentheses. For example,

    DECLARE X(4) FIXED DECIMAL INITIAL ((2) (8,5));

would create

    X(1) 8
    X(2) 5
    X(3) 8
    X(4) 5

    The number of values on the INITIAL list does not need to
coincide exactly with the number of elements in the array.   If
there are fewer values on the list, the final elements of the
array will not receive an initial value; if there are excess
values on the list they will be ignored.

    The INITIAL attribute may be factored:

    DCL (AA, BB) FIXED DECIMAL INIT(5);
    DCL (X(2),Y(2)) FIXED DECIMAL INIT(5,6);

would create the following:

    AA 5
    BB 5
    X(1) 5
    X(2) 6
    Y(1) 5
    Y(2) 6

However, the following is an example of a common error:

    DCL (CC, DD) FLOAT DECIMAL INITIAL(7,8);

This statement is incorrect, and it will not assign 7 as initial
value to CC, and 8 to DD.

Section 8 <u>Summary</u>

1. Variables are created, and have their type attributes assigned by a declaration:

        DECLARE identifier attributes ;

A comma must not be given immediately before any attribute.

2. Declarations are placed at the beginning of a procedure. Variables are created immediately upon entry to the procedure -- before the execution of any statement in that procedure.

3. Several variables can be be given in the same declaration:

        DECLARE ident attributes, ident attributes, ... ;

4. Variables with identical sets of attributes can be grouped in parentheses:

        DECLARE (ident, ident, ...) attributes ;

5. The <u>only</u> allowable abbreviations are:

        DCL   for   DECLARE
        DEC   for   DECIMAL
        BIN   for   BINARY
        INIT   for   INITIAL

6. The form for declaration of an array is:

        DECLARE identifier(lb1:ub1, lb2:ub2, ...) attributes ;

If only an upper-bound-expression is given, a lower bound of 1 is assumed.

7. If no type attributes are specified for a variable:

        If the first letter of the identifier is I, J, K, L, M or N, FIXED BINARY is assumed.

        Otherwise FLOAT DECIMAL is assumed.

8. Initial values are not automatically assigned to a variable when it is created. A value must be assigned before the variable can be used.

9.* An initial value <u>can</u> be assigned at the time of creation by specifying the INITIAL attribute in the declaration. The form for a simple variable is:

        INITIAL(constant)

Section 8 <u>Exercises</u>

1. Write a declaration to create a variable named TOTAL that will hold values such as −123.79 and .00062.

2. Write a declaration equivalent to the following, that does not use parentheses:

        DECLARE X FIXED DECIMAL, (Y,Z) FLOAT DECIMAL,
                (I,J) FIXED DECIMAL;

3. What types of variables are created by each of the following declarations:

        a) DECLARE ITEM;

        b) DECLARE Z_COORDINATE;

        c) DCL A;

        d) DCL TOTAL, FLOAT, DECIMAL;

4. What type of variables are created by the declaration

        DCL (COL(0:1), TABLE(4:10,14)) FLOAT DEC;

5.* Write a declaration that will create variables with the following names, attributes and initial values:

        TOP(1) 5   [float decimal]
        TOP(2) 6.5 [float decimal]
        BOT(1) 5   [float decimal]
        BOT(2) 6.5 [float decimal]
        SIDE   5   [float decimal]
        WIDE   5   [fixed decimal]

Section 9 <u>Character-Valued Variables</u>

Up to this point we have considered numeric-valued variables. We have used non-numeric "strings" of characters as literals in a PUT statement (Section 6.2), but not as values to assign to variables. Some languages are only capable of processing numeric values, and are considered useful primarily for scientific and engineering applications. However, in many types of applications it is useful to be able to store, manipulate, and display values that include characters that are not digits. Values that include letters and special symbols as well as digits are called "character data", or "strings".

For example, there are programs called "text editors" that deal entirely with such values. They take a sequence of words, punctuation marks, and format commands, and format the words and punctuation marks into lines, paragraphs, and pages. This book was produced by such a program.

More important applications involve both numeric and character data. For example, consider a program to maintain a customer charge account system for a retail store. Each account must include numeric information on charges, payments, balance due, arrears, finance charges, etc. It must also contain character information giving the name of the customer, his address, credit references, etc. A brief introduction to such "file processing" programs is given in Part VI. A majority of the world's computers are used primarily for file processing, and computers, in the aggregate, process more character data than numeric data.

Since PL/I was designed to serve both scientific and file processing applications it includes facilities for processing strings.

The characters that may appear in a string are those that occur on the keypunch. They are the following, with "b" representing the <u>blank</u> character:

b.<(+|&$*);¬-/,%_>?:#ə'=ABCDEFGHIJKLMNOPQRSTUVWXYZ0123456789

String processing is in a sense more fun than numeric processing. After learning a few details, you will find it easy to format output nicely, to write programs to print out graphs and pictures, and to perform other interesting tasks.

9.1 Declaration of Character Variables

The declaration of a character-valued variable has the form:

    DECLARE identifier CHARACTER(length);

"Length" specifies the number of characters in the value. Length can be given as an expression, although in most cases a constant is used. As indicated in the examples below, CHAR is a valid abbreviation for CHARACTER, and this attribute can be factored.

    DECLARE TITLE CHARACTER(30);
    DCL (NAME, ADDRESS) CHARACTER(40);
    DCL WORD CHAR(10), LINE CHAR(60);
    DCL STRING CHAR(J+K);

The CHARACTER attribute is incompatible with the numeric value attributes FIXED, FLOAT and DECIMAL; they cannot be given to the same variable. They can, however, appear in the same declaration:

    DCL LINE CHAR(50), LINE_COUNT FIXED DECIMAL;

An array can consist of string-valued subscripted variables. The following declaration describes an array of fifty, singly-subscripted variables, each of whose values is a string of 20 characters. Multiple subscripts and lower bounds other than 1, are declared in the same form as for numeric-valued arrays:

    DCL WORD(50) CHAR(20);

An optional attribute for a character-valued variable is VARYING (abbreviated as VAR):

    DCL PHRASE CHAR(50) VARYING;

When VARYING is specified, the length in the declaration is the maximum length. The actual length of a VARYING string variable will be changed during processing, but will not exceed the given maximum. A VARYING variable may contain the "empty string" -- the string of length zero, consisting of no characters at all. Without the VARYING attribute, the length of the variable is always exactly equal to the declared length.

9.1.1* Initial Character Values

Non-VARYING strings are not initialized upon creation.
VARYING strings are assigned the null string when they are
created. These defaults can be overridden by using an INITIAL
attribute in the declaration. This is similar to the INITIAL
attribute used for numeric variables, except that literals are
given as values instead of numeric constants. For example:

```
DCL KEYWORD CHAR(4) INIT('FOR ');
DCL PAGE CHAR(4) INITIAL('PAGE');
DCL LETTER(1:5) CHAR(1) INIT('A','B','C','D','E');
DCL WORD(50) CHAR(3) INIT((49) (' ') );
```

The last of these examples assigns the initial value 'ƀƀƀ' to
the variables WORD(1), ..., WORD(49), but leaves WORD(50)
uninitialized. In the last example, (49)('ƀ') should not be
written as (49)'ƀ'. This would mean a string of 49 blanks. The
assignments of the literals to the variables is done under the
normal rules of assignment as discussed later in Section 9.2.

9.2 String Assignments and Expressions

Character variables are used as numeric variables are. They
receive values from assignment statements and GET statements,
have values displayed by PUT statements, and are used in
expressions to produce values.

9.2.1 String Assignment

The string assignment statement has the same form as a
numeric assignment:

```
variable = expression ;
```

The string variable denoted by the left side is first
determined, the expression is evaluated to yield a string value,
and this value is assigned to the variable.

The simplest form of expression to be used on the right hand
side of an assignment is a literal -- a quoted string of
characters. Literals, discussed in Section 6.2, are used as
string constants, in the same way that numeric constants are
used.

For example, if WORD has been declared to be CHARACTER(5),
then the assignment statement

```
WORD = 'ABCDE';
```

would assign the value ABCDE to the variable named WORD. The

quotes around ABCDE are crucial -- without them, ABCDE would be
interpreted as the name of a variable, rather than as a value.
To further illustrate the point, consider

    WORD = 'A + B';

Like the previous example, the right side of this assignment
statement is just a five character literal. Without the quotes
the right side would be interpreted as an arithmetic expression
consisting of two variables and an addition. Note that the
quotes enclose the value, but are not part of the value.   The
value consists of the five characters between the quotes:

    WORD A̶ +̶ B [char(5)]

(where "b̶" is used to denote a blank, which is a valid
character).

    If a string variable is not declared to be VARYING, it always
has the same fixed length. A shorter value assigned to a string
variable is automatically extended on the right with blanks
until the required length is achieved. For example, if WORD is
declared CHAR(5), then all of the following are equivalent:

        WORD = 'A';
        WORD = 'A ';
        WORD = 'A ';
        WORD = 'A   ';
        WORD = 'A   ';

If the value to be assigned is longer than the target variable,
the value is truncated on the right to the same length as the
target variable.   This means that

    WORD = 'Ab̶b̶b̶b̶B';

is equivalent to the assignments above, since only the leftmost
five characters of the right-side value are used. This same
adjustment takes place even if the value is the result of the
evaluation of a complex string expression.

    A VARYING string variable always has the length of the last
value assigned to it, up to its declared maximum. For example,
suppose A and B have been declared as follows:

    DCL A CHAR(3) VARYING, B CHAR(3);

Now consider the assignment statements:

    A = '';
    B = '';

The literal on the right side of each statement is the empty
string (since no characters are given between the quotes).
Since A has the attribute VARYING and B does not, after

execution of these statements the values are:

```
A  _____ [char(3) var]        (length is 0)
B  ƀƀƀ  [char(3)]             (length is 3)
```

9.2.2 Expressions

A string expression is an expression which yields a string of characters as a result. The only string operator is concatenation; it is discussed below. Operands may be literals, string variables, and functions which return strings as values.

Concatenation

Strings are built up by combining two smaller strings end to end. The operation is called "concatenation", and the PL/I symbol for it is "||". (These are two adjacent vertical strokes, with no intervening blanks; the vertical stroke is the character above the Y on the keypunch.)

For example, suppose that the following variables and values existed at a certain point in a program:

```
STR(1)  ABCƀ     [char(4)]
STR(2)  DEFƀ     [char(4)]
CHR(1)  ƀƀƀƀƀƀƀƀƀƀ    [char(10)]
CHR(2)  1234567890     [char(10)]
SVAR    1234567890     [char(10) var]
```

After execution of the following assignment statements

```
CHR(1) = STR(1) || STR(2);
CHR(2) = STR(1) || ' ' || STR(2);
SVAR = ' ' || STR(1) || STR(2);
```

the values would be

```
STR(1)  ABCƀ     [char(4)]
STR(2)  DEFƀ     [char(4)]
CHR(1)  ABCƀDEFƀƀ     [char(10)]
CHR(2)  ABCƀƀDEFƀƀ     [char(10)]
SVAR    ƀABCƀDEFƀ     [char(10) var]
```

SUBSTR and LENGTH Built-in Functions

   The substring function is used to refer to a portion of a
string. The form of the function is

     SUBSTR(char-expr, start-pos, length)

where char-expr is an expression whose evaluation yields a
string value, start-pos is the position number (counting from 1,
left to right) of the leftmost position of the desired
substring, and length is the number of positions in the
substring. Start-pos and length are either integers,   or
expressions that evaluate to integers. Their values must be
reasonable -- that is, they must specify a substring that really
exists in the string referred to. For example:

     SUBSTR('ABCDEF',2,3) is 'BCD'
     SUBSTR('ABCDEF',1,1) is 'A'
     SUBSTR('ABCDEF',1,6) is 'ABCDEF'
     SUBSTR('ABC'||'DEF',2,5) is 'BCDEF'

As further examples, if variables and values are

     SA ABC [char(3)]
     SB DEF [char(3)]
     J   2   [fixed decimal]
     K   3   [fixed decimal]

then

     SUBSTR(SA,1,2) is 'AB'
     SUBSTR(SA||'ABC',2,4) is 'BCAB'
     SUBSTR(SA||' '||SB,J,K+2) is 'BC␢DE'
     SA||SUBSTR(SB,3,1) is 'ABCF'
     SUBSTR(SUBSTR(SB,1,2),2,1) is 'E'

   The SUBSTR function can be given without specifying length:

     SUBSTR(char-expr, start-pos)

In this case, the value of the function is the right portion of
the string, starting with the position specified. For example,

     SUBSTR(SA,2) is BC
     SUBSTR(SA||SB,3) is 'CDEF'

   The LENGTH built-in function has the form

     LENGTH(char-expr)

Its value is the actual length of the string expression given as
argument. It is generally used to determine the length of a
VARYING string. For example, if the value of WORD is:

     WORD HOPE [char(10) var]

then

```
LENGTH(WORD) is 4
LENGTH(WORD||'XY') is 6
LENGTH(SUBSTR(WORD,2)) is 3
```

String Values in Conditions

String expressions can be used in conditions. The form is:

        char-expr   relation   char-expr

The relations are the same as those used for arithmetic-expression conditions (listed in Section 4.2.1.1.) These conditions can be made compound in the manner described in Section 4.2.1.2.

The relationship between two string values depends upon an ordering that has been defined over all of the valid characters that might be included in such a value. This ordering is called the "collating sequence". In PL/I it is defined to be:

b.<(+|&$*);¬-/,%_>?:#@'=ABCDEFGHIJKLMNOPQRSTUVWXYZ0123456789

This is an extention of "alphabetical order" with the digits higher than Z, and the special characters lower than A. The blank is lowest of all. Any character in this sequence is said to be "less than" a character to its right in the sequence.

If two strings being compared have different lengths, the shorter one is extended on the right with blanks until it is the same length as the longer. Both this length equalization, and the effect of the collating sequence can be described by the following set of conditions -- <u>all of which are true</u>:

```
'A' = 'A'
'A' = 'Ab'
'A' ¬= 'bA'
'A' ¬= 'AB'
'A' < 'B'
'/' < 'A'
'Z' < '3'
'AA' < 'AB'
'A' < 'AB'
'bB' < 'AB'
'ZZ' < '1.'
'HOROWITZ ELLIS' < 'HOROWITZ, ELLIS'
```

9.2.3 The SUBSTR Pseudo-Variable

While one can refer to a part of a string using the SUBSTR
function, it is often necessary to assign to a part of a string
variable. For example, we might like to change the variable

     S A SECOND ONE   to   S A FIRST ONE

This can be done using the SUBSTR "pseudo-variable", which has
the same form as the SUBSTR function except that the first
argument must reference a variable:

     SUBSTR(string variable, start-pos, length)

The arguments have the same meaning as in the SUBSTR function;
the length can be left out (in which case the longest length
possible is assumed). For example, to effect the change shown
above, execute the statement

     SUBSTR(S, 3, 6) = 'FIRST ';

The SUBSTR pseudo-variable always refers to a fixed length part
of the string variable. One cannot delete that part of the
variable by assigning it the null string; all this does is store
blanks in that part. For example, if we have

     X A SECOND ONE

then executing

```
     SUBSTR(X,1,1) = 'THE';    changes X to    X T SECOND ONE
and  SUBSTR(X,1,3) = 'THE';    changes X to    X THEECOND ONE
```

As another illustration, the segment below changes all
occurences of ';' to 'b' in string variable CARD:

```
     I = 0;
     DO WHILE (I<LENGTH(CARD));
         I = I+1; IF SUBSTR(CARD,I,1)=';';
             THEN SUBSTR(CARD,I,1)=' '; END;
```

The following segment reverses the characters in string S. T is
a CHARACTER(1) variable used to temporarily hold a character:

```
     FIRST = 1; LAST = LENGTH(S);
     DO WHILE(FIRST < LAST);
        T = SUBSTR(S, FIRST, 1);
        SUBSTR(S, FIRST, 1) = SUBSTR(S, LAST, 1);
        SUBSTR(S, LAST, 1) = T;
        FIRST = FIRST+1; LAST = LAST-1; END;
```

9.3 String Assignment from External Data

String variables may appear in the list of a GET statement.
The value assigned from the data will be truncated or extended
with blanks, exactly as discussed under "String Assignment".

The data format is similar to that described in Section
3.4.1, except that any value on a data card to be assigned to a
string variable must be enclosed in quotes. For example, if X
and Y are FIXED DECIMAL, and SA and SB are CHAR(1), then values
could be read from data cards as follows:

```
GET LIST(X, SA, Y, SB);
...
*DATA
...
5, 'P', 7, '9'
```

9.3.1* EDIT Format Character Data

Placing quotes around each string on a data card is a
nuisance.   If only string values are to appear on a card, the
use of quotes can be avoided by reading the entire card as a
single string value.   For example, if CARD is CHAR(80) values
can be assigned to CARD from data with the statement

```
GET EDIT(CARD)(COL(1),A(80));
```

The COL(1) phrase causes reading to start at column 1 of the
card, no matter where reading for the last previous GET left
off. The character positions in CARD correspond to the columns
of the card, so the SUBSTR function can be used to extract
individual strings from CARD.   For example, SUBSTR(CARD,1,8)
gives the first eight columns of the card.

9.4 Display of Character Values

String variables may be included on the list of a PUT LIST
statement.   Values are displayed in the standard printing
format, as described in Section 6.1. The value begins in the
left-most print position of the "next" field. If the length of
the value is greater than 24, it simply continues into the
following field. An array of string variables may also be given
on the list, and all of the values will be printed, in row-
major-order, as described in Section 6.3.

More flexible control of output format can be achieved by use
of the PUT EDIT statement, as described in Section 6.4. The "A"
data-item should be matched with a string variable.   If the
data-item is given as "A" alone, without a field width
specification, the field width is determined by the length of

the variable. If a width is specified in the data-item, the value is either truncated or extended on the right with blanks to fit the specified field. (Width must be specified for a VARYING value.)

9.5 <u>An Example</u>

   Consider the following problem. The input contains the names of 50 people, each consisting of a first name followed by a last name, all enclosed in quotes. A name may be at most 20 characters long. One blank separates the last from the first name. For example, the first two names in the list might be

   'BOB CONSTABLE'   'ROBERT TARJAN'

The program should read in these 50 names, and print out all the <u>last</u> names which begin with 'T'. For the two names shown above, the program should select and print only TARJAN.

   We have chosen a program strategy that first reads all of the names into an array, then selects and prints. In this case, the array is not necessary, since the names could be examined as they are read. Note that the selection criterion is a search for the sequence 'ᵇT'. The blank denotes the beginning of the last name; the T is the required first letter of the last name.

```
    /* PROGRAM TO PRINT LAST NAMES BEGINNING WITH T */
        PRINT_NAMES: PROCEDURE OPTIONS(MAIN);
        DECLARE NAME(50) CHAR(20) VARYING,/* LIST OF NAMES*/
                NM CHAR(20) VARYING,   /* NAME TO BE SCANNED*/
                TNAME CHAR(20) VARYING,   /* LAST NAME*/
                (I,J) FIXED DECIMAL;
        /* READ NAMES INTO NAME ARRAY */
            DO I = 1 TO 50 BY 1; GET LIST(NAME(I)); END;
        /* SCAN ARRAY, SELECT AND PRINT T NAMES */
            LOOK: DO I = 1 TO 50 BY 1;
                NM = NAME(I);
                /* SEARCH FOR ' T' */
                  SCH: DO J = 1 TO LENGTH(NM)-1 BY 1;
                      IF SUBSTR(NM,J,2) = ' T' THEN DO;
                        TNAME = SUBSTR(NM,J);
                        PUT SKIP LIST(TNAME);
                        GO TO ENDLOOK; END; END SCH;
                ENDLOOK: END LOOK;
        END PRINT_NAMES;
```

This program illustrates the topics of Section 9, but it is not a good program. It is highly vulnerable to errors in keypunching the data. For example, both of the following names would be selected for printing:

   ' TOM BROWN'   'ROBERT T JONES'

Section 9 <u>Summary</u>

1. A string variable is declared in the following way:

    DECLARE identifier CHARACTER(length);

CHARACTER may be abbreviated CHAR

2. The length of a string variable is fixed, at the length given in the declaration, unless the optional VARYING (or VAR) attribute is given. With this attribute, the length of the variable is the same as the length of the value most recently assigned to it (but not more than the declared maximum length).

3. Fixed-length string variables <u>do not</u> have an automatic initial value. VARYING string variables are automatically initialized to the null string if no INITIAL attribute is given.

4.* An initial value may be assigned at the time of creation, by the use of the optional INITIAL attribute.

5. A string constant is a literal -- a sequence of characters enclosed in single quotes.

6. In PL/C string variables cannot be subject to arithmetic operations, even if their values happen to be numbers.

7. The only operation that can be performed on string values is "concatenation". The symbol is "||", the action is to join two string values, end to end.

8. The SUBSTR built-in function extracts a portion of the value of a string expression. The form is:

    SUBSTR(char-expr,start-pos,length)

If the length is not specified, the entire right portion of the value is assumed.

9. The LENGTH built-in function gives the length of a string expression. The form is:

    LENGTH(char-expr)

10. The SUBSTR pseudo-variable has the same form as the SUBSTR function, except that the first argument must refer to a variable. The SUBSTR pseudo-variable may be used on the left hand side of an assignment statement to change part of a string variable.

Section 9 <u>Exercises</u>

Write programs for the following problems.

1. Read a string of up to 40 characters, reverse the order of
the characters, and print it out. For example, 'EVIL' becomes
'LIVE'. You may determine the input form.

2. Read a string of up to 40 characters, using GET LIST.
Delete all blanks up to the first non-blank, and print out the
result.

3. Read a string of up to 40 characters, delete all characters
'A', and print the result. You may determine the input form.

4. Read in three strings, call them A, PATTERN, and REPLACEBY.
Replace every occurrence of PATTERN in A by the string
REPLACEBY. Print the result. For example, if we have

     A <u>BIG, BIGGER, BIGGEST</u>   PATTERN <u>BIG</u>   REPLACEBY <u>SMALL</u>

the program should print the string

     'SMALL, SMALLGER, SMALLGEST'.

Be careful. If we have

     A <u>LAST</u>   PATTERN <u>A</u>   REPLACEBY <u>EA</u>

A should not be changed to 'LEAST', then to 'LEEAST', and then
to 'LEEEAST', etc. Stop with 'LEAST'.

5. Write a program to perform the equivalent of the functions
below (see Appendix A.8 for their definition).

     INDEX   VERIFY   TRANSLATE (assume p is always given)

6. Read a three-digit integer and print out the value of the
number in English. For example, print 182 as ONE HUNDRED AND
EIGHTY TWO. You will need string arrays to hold the English
equivalents of the digits.

7. The input consists of three two-digit numbers representing a
date.   The first number is the day of the month, the second the
month, and the third the last two digits of the year.   For
example: 25, 12, 73. Read the number and put it out in English
form. For example, DECEMBER 25, 1963. You will need an array
for the names of the months. Use the PUT EDIT statement to
write it out.

8. Read in a list of words and print out (1) the number of
words made up of 1 to 6 characters, (2) the number with 6 to 12
characters, and (3) the number of times the word 'THE' appears.
The words appear on one card each, left-justified in columns 1
through 12, with no surrounding quotes.

Part II

PROGRAM DEVELOPMENT

Section 1 <u>Introduction</u>

1.1 <u>General Discussion</u>

Now that you have some knowledge of a programming language we can address the more difficult and important question of developing programs. Development starts with a problem statement.   It then involves the choice of an "algorithm" and appropriate data structures, and the analysis of the correctness of the algorithm. The final stage is the production of a program that allows the algorithm to be executed on a computer.

The first phase of program development is simply to <u>understand</u> the problem completely. This may seem obvious, but it is often neglected. To begin programming without a clear understanding of the problem leads to a program that solves a different problem.

Initially, don't even think about the <u>program</u> you have to write. Instead, study the <u>problem statement</u> until it becomes absolutely clear. Make up several sets of input data, and figure out the corresponding output results by hand. The sample data you make up must of course be limited in size so that you can determine the output in a reasonable amount of time, but the data should be designed to test and increase your understanding of the details of the problem, and not just its general nature.

It might seem to be a waste of time to make up input data and perform hand calculations, but in doing so you are actually executing an algorithm to solve the problem. Thus while concentrating on understanding the problem, you are in effect also working toward designing the program.

While studying the problem, you will find yourself asking questions like "What is to be done if the input number is incorrect?", "What happens if this particular input number is 0? Is it correct or incorrect and what should I do with it?", and "What should I do here -- the problem statement seems to be ambiguous?" It is important that these questions be raised and answered <u>before</u> any programming is done, and not after the program is completed and is run with such data.

Proper understanding of the problem <u>before</u> you begin programming is one of the important parts of the process. Without this understanding, the program can never be correct.

For the student, there are two main reasons for programming. One is to write a program to solve a problem; the second is to develop problem solving and programming ability. If you rush from problem to problem without looking back, you are missing an important opportunity to increase your programming competence.

Spend some time going over a program after it is "finished", and see if it is as good as it could have been. Was there a faster method for doing part of it? Could the data have been stored differently? Is it as clear as it could have been? Think about how you developed the program. Why was one part particularly difficult for you -- why didn't you see the solution immediately? Will you have the same difficulty in a similar situation?

One of the hardest things to learn is how to find a mistake in a program. Often, the program must be submitted to the computer several times, with various changes, in order to find the error. When this happens, don't throw the output away; save it for later analysis. When the program is finished, look back and try to discover why the error was hard to find. Look at the very first run where the presence of the error was detected, and see whether there was enough information to find the cause of the error. Quite often there is, but it takes experience to analyze output.

Why did you <u>make</u> the error? How can you avoid making the same error again?

After you have studied your own work in this fashion, compare your program and its development with those of other students. Every solution will be different in some aspect, and much can be learned from other peoples' mistakes too. No one would consider trying to learn to write coherent English prose without studying prose written by others, but many people attempt to learn to program without ever studying examples of good programs.

Almost no problem is ever solved in the best possible way -- there are always changes possible which will increase its readability, make it faster, or decrease the space it requires. At the least, some thought and reflection will increase your understanding of the problem and its solution.

1.2 Algorithms

We will frequently write down sequences of statements to be
executed in order. These statements will not always be written
in PL/I, but will be a mixture of English, PL/I, and any other
suitable notation. The sequence cannot properly be called a
"program segment" since it is not written in a programming
language, and we must use another name for it.

An algorithm is generally regarded to be a sequence of
statements to be executed in order, to produce some desired
result. It may contain comments or descriptions to aid us in
"executing" or understanding it. A cooking recipe, instructions
to put a Heathkit tuner together, or instructions to build a
model airplane are all good examples of algorithms. Note that
each algorithm uses a notation particularly suited to the
problem area. We should attempt to do this with our programs,
also.

A program is an algorithm written in a programming language.
For example, the algorithm

    Swap the values of variables A and B

would be programmed in PL/I as

    T = A; A = B; B = T;

The same algorithm could be written in ALGOL (another
programming language) as

    T := A; A := B; B:= T

Some programming language might have a more suitable, concise
notation for swapping, such as using a "double assignment"
operator. Thus "swap A and B" could be written A:=:B. But
regardless of how it is expressed in a programming language, the
algorithm describes the function or task that must be performed.

Since our algorithms will eventually be programmed in PL/I,
we will write algorithms in a PL/I-like style, and use a
language that is a mixture of PL/I and English. Upper case
phrases are PL/I; lower case phrases are not PL/I. As the
development proceeds and the English statements are refined into
PL/I program segments, we often carry the English statement into
the program as a comment. For example:

    /* SWAP THE VALUES OF A AND B */
      T = A; A = B; B = T;

Section 2 <u>An Example of Program Development</u>

We present here the complete development of a program for a simplified bookkeeping system for a bank in connection with its checking accounts. This is an idealized version of the program development process; we describe the important steps in their logical order. Interspersed with the development are short discussions of techniques and methods used in creating a program; these will be elaborated upon in later sections.

Before reading a section of the development, stop and ask yourself how <u>you</u> would develop the part suggested by the section title. <u>Then</u> proceed to read how we feel it should be done.

2.1 <u>The Problem</u>

A bank would like to produce records of the transactions during an accounting period in connection with their checking accounts. For each account the bank wants a list showing the <u>balance</u> at the beginning of the period, the <u>number</u> of deposits and withdrawals, and the <u>final</u> <u>balance</u>. This is a simplified version of the type of application described in Part VI.

The accounts and transactions for an accounting period will be given on punched cards as follows:

1) First will be a sequence of cards describing the accounts. Each account is described by two numbers: the <u>account number</u> (greater than 0), and the <u>account balance</u> at the beginning of the period, in dollars and cents. The last account is followed by a "dummy" account consisting of two zero values to indicate the end of the list. There will be at most 200 accounts.

2) Following the accounts are the transactions. Each transaction is given by three numbers: the <u>account number</u>, a <u>1 or -1</u> (indicating a deposit or withdrawal, respectively), and the <u>transaction amount</u>, in dollars and cents. The last real transaction is followed by a dummy transaction consisting of three zero values.

The following sample input has been supplied, where the words at the right are <u>not</u> part of the input, but explanatory notes.

```
          Input numbers        meaning
          1025    61.50        (account 1025 contains $61.50)
          1028    103          (account 1028 contains $103)
          1026    100          (account 1026 contains $100)
(2.1a)    0       0            (end of accounts)
          1025    1    500     (deposit $500 in account 1025)
          1028   -1    20      (withdraw $20 from account 1028)
          1025   -1    400     (withdraw $400 from account 1025)
          1025   +1    50      (deposit $50 in account 1025)
          0       0    0       (end of transactions)
```

For this input, the output should be:

```
          ACCOUNT   PREV BAL  WITHDRAWALS   DEPOSITS  FINAL BAL
          1025        61.50       1            2       211.50
(2.1b)    1028        103         1            0        83
          1026        100         0            0        100
```

The first step in solving the problem is to understand it
thoroughly.   The problem definition should be read and studied
until every detail is clear.   The sample input data and
corresponding output should be analyzed in detail. Make up
several sets of input data and try to write the corresponding
output data.   The importance of this preparation cannot be
overemphasized; it is impossible to write a correct program for
a problem you do not understand or one that is not fully and
precisely defined.

2.2 Developing the Program

Step 1.   Discovering the global structure of the algorithm.

Looking at the problem description, note that the account
data precedes the transactions. Thus all accounts must be read
and stored internally, before the transactions can be read and
"processed".   Moreover, while processing the transactions we
must be able to access any account at any time, since no
ordering of the transactions by account number is mentioned in
the description of the problem. The sample data confirm this
lack of ordering. Also, since the last transaction may apply to
any account, no result may be printed for an account until all
transactions have been processed. This analysis indicates that
the structure of the program will be:

(2.2a)   2a1: Read in and set up the accounts in a "table";
          2a2: Read in and process the transactions;
          2a3: Print the results;

(2.2a) is an algorithm using the English commands "read",
"set up", "process" and "print". These are not yet precise
enough to specify the action to be taken, and our task is to
refine them so that they are precise and are expressed in PL/I
terms.

Writing (2.2a) has accomplished a good deal -- the problem has been broken up into three smaller, logically independent parts or "modules", each of which can be attacked separately. This "divide and conquer" strategy is one of the more important techniques at our disposal.

There are now three separate, smaller problems, but they are obviously not entirely independent of each other. All three share the data structures used to contain the accounts and all the information connected with them.

Whenever we split a problem up into several smaller parts, it is important to look at the "interface" or connections between them. Often, several strategies exist for implementing each one, but implementing one in a particular way may reduce the flexibility in designing the others. We must weigh carefully the benefits and disadvantages, including effects on other modules, in choosing a strategy for a given module.

Step 2.   The data structures representing the accounts.

From our previous discussion, we know that we must keep the accounts accessible in a table until all transactions have been processed and the results have been reported. This can be done using an array ACCT (say) to hold the ACCounT numbers and an array IBAL to hold the corresponding Initial BALances. We also need a variable N (say) to hold the number of accounts. Thus, if i is an integer between 1 and N, ACCT(i) contains an account number and IBAL(i) contains the corresponding Initial BALance. Other alternatives for storing the data exist of course, but this is probably the simplest and easiest.

Let us carefully consider the problem definition to make sure the accounts have been described completely and accurately. Certainly this is all we need initially, but look at the sample output (2.1b). After processing the transactions, in addition to the initial balance we must report the number of deposits and withdrawals and also the final balance. This will require three more arrays; we use two arrays to contain the number of withdrawals and deposits, and a third to contain the balances. The arrays holding the number of withdrawals and deposits will be initially set to 0, and will be increased to count the number of withdrawals and deposits that are processed for each account. Similarly, the array holding the final balances will be initialized to the initial balances and will be updated as transactions are processed.

To summarize, we write down the names of the variables which describe the accounts and define as precisely as possible how they will be used:

1. Variable N contains the number of accounts.

2. Five arrays describe the accounts: ACCT, IBAL, WITH, DEP

and CBAL (meaning Current BALance). If i is an integer
between 1 and N, then during execution of the program

    ACCT(i)   is an ACCounT number,
    IBAL(i)   is the corresponding Initial BALance,
    WITH(i)   is the number of WITHdrawals processed so far,
    DEP(i)   is the number of DEPosits processed so far,
    CBAL(i)   is the Current BALance in the account.

CBAL(i) depends of course on the withdrawals and deposits
processed so far. In order to fix these definitions more
clearly in our minds, consider some examples. Just after
reading in all the accounts in the sample input, the arrays are:

	ACCT	IBAL	WITH	DEP	CBAL
(1)	1025	61.50	0	0	61.50
(2)	1028	103	0	0	103
(3)	1026	100	0	0	100

Note that each CBAL(i) is the same as IBAL(i), since no
transactions have been processed. After processing the first
transaction, the arrays are:

	ACCT	IBAL	WITH	DEP	CBAL
(1)	1025	61.50	0	1	561.50
(2)	1028	103	0	0	103
(3)	1026	100	0	0	100

We could at this point write PL/I declarations for these data
structures, but it is better to wait. These structures should
be considered tentative, and may have to be revised as the
detailed design of the program unfolds.

We have looked at the data structures which contain the
accounts from the viewpoint of the information that must be
available as the program executes. Now consider <u>how</u> this
information is accessed and changed -- how the three statements
of algorithm (2.2a) use the information. Statement 2a2, "Read
in and process the transactions", requires us to locate in the
table of accounts the account associated with each transaction.
This means a search in the array ACCT of account numbers for
each transaction account number. That is, given a transaction
like (1028, 1, 100), we have to find an integer i such that
ACCT(i) = 1028. Assuming a linear search (see Exercise 6,
Section I.5), on the average we must look at half of them in
order to find the right one. If there are only a few hundred
accounts this may be feasible. But if there are 5000 to 50,000
accounts, the time to search would be in seconds for each
transaction, and we could not afford to structure the table of
accounts as we have done.

This search time can be drastically reduced if the accounts
are rearranged so that the account numbers are in ascending
order: ACCT(1) $\leq$ ACCT(2) $\leq$ ... $\leq$ ACCT(N). (We will look at
this more efficient searching algorithm in Section 3.2.1.) If

we sort the array of accounts as we read them in, we can process
the transactions more efficiently. But sorting takes time too,
and we must carefully weigh the sorting time against the
efficiency gained in processing, before we decide which approach
to take. This depends on the number of accounts relative to the
number of transactions, and we now realize that we lack such
information. The problem description is not complete, and
without such information we cannot design the best program.

An even better solution would be for the bank to keep their
accounts in ascending order, so that neither sorting nor a slow
search would be required.

This discussion should illustrate the need for thinking about
the various ways of implementing each succesive statement of an
algorithm, and considering the effects of each. For now, assume
that the accounts cannot be kept sorted because of other
considerations, and that a linear search is adequate.

Step 3.   Refining the statement "Read and set up the accounts."

Statement 2a1 is not yet in PL/I, so it must be refined
further. The required action is

    Read and set up the first account;
    Read and set up the second account;
                . . .
    (until the account just read has account number 0)

Such a sequence of similar statements can be replaced by a loop
which iteratively executes a single statement like "Read and set
up the Kth account", where K is of course increased after each
execution.   There are several ways of writing this loop. One
method recognizes that the first statement "Read and set up the
first account" must always be executed and can therefore be put
outside the loop:

            K = 1; Read and set up the Kth account;
            DO WHILE (ACCT(K) ¬= 0);
              K = K + 1; Read and set up the Kth account;   END;
            N = K - 1;

The last statement assigns K-1 instead of K to N because the
last account read was just the end-of-list signal.

The second technique uses a dummy account ACCT(0) whose
account number is set to 1 so that the loop body is always
executed at least once:

            K = 0; ACCT(0) = 1;
            DO WHILE (ACCT(K) ¬= 0);
(2.2b)   K = K + 1; Read and set up the Kth account;   END;
            N = K - 1;

Either refinement could be used. If the refinement of the
statement "Read and set up the Kth account" turned out to be
long and difficult, we would tend to choose the latter because
this difficult statement only appears once. (Recall the
discussion of this issue in Section I.4.5.2.) At this point, we
arbitrarily choose (2.2b).

We have introduced a variable K, and should indicate what it
means. While executing (2.2b) (and only then), K is the number
of accounts read in so far, including the end-of-list signal as
an account.

Note that when we declare the array ACCT we must give an
upper bound on the number of elements in it. If the input
happens to have more than that number of accounts, then (2.2b)
will execute incorrectly. Error checking is an important part
of a program, and it must be considered during the development
process. We postpone it to Section 2.3 only to keep this
discussion to a reasonable size.

Algorithm (2.2b) still contains an English statement which
must be translated into PL/I. To "read and set up account K",
we must obtain values from the input data and store the account
number and balance in ACCT(K) and IBAL(K), and initialize the
other three variables that comprise account K:

(2.2c)   GET LIST (ACCT(K), IBAL(K));
          WITH(K)=0; DEP(K)=0; CBAL(K)=IBAL(K);

As a final step, we insert this refinement into (2.2b) to yield
the following program segment. Note that the original statement
2a1 becomes a comment of the PL/I program which replaces it:

```
          /* READ AND STORE THE ACCOUNTS.*/
             K=0; ACCT(0)=1;      /* EXECUTE LOOP AT LEAST ONCE*/
(2.2d)       DO WHILE( ACCT(K) ¬= 0);
               K = K+1;
               GET LIST( ACCT(K), IBAL(K));
               WITH(K)=0; DEP(K)=0; CBAL(K)=IBAL(K);    END;
             N = K - 1;
```

Step 4.   Refining "Read and process the transactions."

Consider statement (2a2), keeping in mind that the array of
accounts is not sorted. Two actions are required -- reading and
processing the transactions -- and there may be several ways of
performing them. Two possibilities come to mind:

  1) First read and store all the transactions, then process
     all the transactions.

  2) Read and process the first transaction, read and process
     the second transaction, etc.

The first possibility requires arrays in which to store all the transactions. How big should the arrays be? We don't know, since we have no idea how many transactions there may be. To use this method, we would have to determine the maximum number of transactions in any one run.

The question with the second method is feasibility. Is it possible to process a single transaction without having access to the others? The answer in this case is yes.

This is not really such a pointless question to ask as it might seem. For example, consider the task "Read in a list of transactions and print them out in order of the account number." We cannot "Read one and print, read one and print, etc.", so we must read all of them before we can begin printing.

With the second method, an array is not needed to hold the transactions, since we need only keep track of one transaction at a time. This second method seems to have no disadvantages compared to the first, and should be used.

Note that without a change in the problem definition, we are forced to use the second method. Since we don't know how many transactions might appear, we cannot assume any maximum and hence cannot use the first method. Quite often, a careful examination of the problem will answer a question for us. We should be continually asking ourselves questions like: "Have I used everything that was given to me?" "Could the problem definition be changed to make the solution easier, clearer, or more efficient?" "Have I assumed something that is not explicitly stated to be true?"

A second point is the question of efficiency. For example, we use the second possibility rather than the first, because it uses less computer memory but otherwise is essentially the same. We may strive for efficiency with respect to execution time, computer memory, or with respect to the time it takes to program. There is always a trade-off when trying to gain efficiency; usually what executes faster will take more memory, or what is easier to program and understand will be slower. A programmer must know what the value criterion is for each program he is to design.

Our choice, then, for reading and processing transactions is

```
        Read a transaction;
        Process the transaction just read;
            ...
        Read a transaction;
        Process the transaction just read;
        Read a transaction;
             (until transaction acct. number is 0)
```

This is a sequence of (a pair of) statements which is to be executed several times, and we can use a loop. Since the first

statement "Read a transaction" must always be executed and the
last transaction is <u>not</u> to be processed, it is easiest to
perform the first "read" outside the loop and to let the loop
body consist of "Process transaction; Read transaction".   That
is, we are pairing the statements as indicated by the spacing in
the following algorithm:

>   Read a transaction;
>
>   Process the transaction just read;
>   Read a transaction;
>   ...
>
>   Process the transaction just read;
>   Read a transaction
>   (until transaction acct. number is 0)

The algorithm using a WHILE loop is:

>   Read a transaction;
>   DO WHILE (transaction account number $\neq$ 0);
> (2.2e)   Process the transaction just read;
>   Read a transaction;   END;

   Further refinement requires a decision as to how the
transactions are to be stored. We should question the format of
the input transactions.   If we allow a negative amount to
specify a withdrawal, then the withdrawal-deposit code is not
necessary. Let us assume that the bank says the given   form is
indeed necessary, and continue with the development.

   Since only one transaction need be accessed at any time, only
three simple variables are needed:

>   TACCT   contains the Transaction ACCounT number.
> (2.2f)   DEPWITH contains the action code:
>   1 means DEPosit, -1 means WITHdrawal.
>   AMT   contains the AMounT of the transaction.

This leads to the following refinement of algorithm (2.2e):

>   GET LIST(TACCT, DEPWITH, AMT);
>   DO WHILE(TACCT $\neg$= 0);
> (2.2g)   Process the transaction just read;
>   GET LIST(TACCT, DEPWITH, AMT);   END;

The final task is to reduce the phrase "Process the transaction
just read" to PL/I.   Processing a transaction requires us to
find the corresponding account in the array ACCT. Suppose that
while searching ACCT we store in a new variable J an integer so
that TACCT = ACCT(J).   Then account ACCT(J) is to be changed as
follows: If DEPWITH(J) = 1 then add 1 to DEP(J) and add AMT to
CBAL(J); if DEPWITH(J) = -1 then add 1 to WITH(J) and subtract
AMT from CBAL(J).

We have already written a search algorithm (Exercise 6 of Section I.5) which can be used here:

```
        /* PROCESS THE TRANSACTION JUST READ.*/
            J = 1;    /* SEARCH FOR TRANSACTION ACCOUNT.*/
            DO WHILE (ACCT(J) ¬= TACCT);
(2.2h)         J = J + 1;     END;
            IF DEPWITH = 1
             THEN DO; DEP(J)=DEP(J)+1;   CBAL(J)=CBAL(J)+AMT; END;
             ELSE DO; WITH(J)=WITH(J)+1; CBAL(J)=CBAL(J)-AMT; END;
```

Note that we assume that DEPWITH is a 1 or -1, without checking. The program should properly check for other than 1 or -1 and print a message if an error has occurred. See Section 2.3.

Step 5.   Refining "Print the results."

Statement 2a3 is the easiest to translate into PL/I.   Since an order was not specified by the problem description, we will print in the easiest order possible -- the order in which they were read in.

```
        /* PRINT THE RESULTS.*/
            PUT SKIP LIST('ACCOUNT', 'PREV BAL', 'WITHDRAWALS',
                            'DEPOSITS', 'FINAL BAL');
(2.2i)      DO I = 1 TO N;
              PUT SKIP LIST(ACCT(I), IBAL(I), WITH(I), DEP(I),
                            CBAL(I));      END;
```


Step 6.   Assembling the complete program.

The final task is to gather together the refinements for the three statements of (2.2a) into a PL/I program. These refinements are (2.2d), (2.2g) with (2.2h) replacing the single English statement of (2.2g), and (2.2i). We also produce declarations from the descriptions of variables written in steps 2 and 4. We end up with the program below. It should be pointed out that this is not the only possible program. Just considering the same basic algorithm, there are many minor variations when using PL/I. For example, arrays WITH and DEP could be initialized in the declarations, the array IBAL could be assigned to CBAL using an array assignment statement, and the statement "Read and set up the accounts" could have been written so that the array could be declared ACCT(1:200) instead of ACCT(0:201). Many possibilities exist, and one cannot <u>always</u> say which is better.

```
/* PROGRAM TO PERFORM BANK BOOKKEEPING DESCRIBED IN STEP 1*/
BANK: PROCEDURE OPTIONS(MAIN);
DECLARE (                   /* THE ACCOUNTS, IN ORDER READ:*/
     N,                     /* THERE ARE N ACCOUNTS*/
     ACCT(0:201),           /* THE ACCOUNT NUMBERS*/
     WITH(1:201),           /* NUMBER OF WITHDRAWALS*/
     DEP (1:201))           /* NUMBER OF DEPOSITS*/
        FIXED DECIMAL;
DECLARE (
     IBAL(1:201),           /* THE INITIAL BALANCES */
     CBAL(1:201))           /* THE CURRENT BALANCES*/
        FLOAT DECIMAL;
DECLARE (                   /* CURRENT TRANSACTION:*/
     TACCT,                 /* TRANSACTION ACCOUNT NUMBER*/
     DEPWITH,               /* 1=DEPOSIT, -1=WITHDRAWAL*/
     AMT)                   /* TRANSACTION AMOUNT*/
        FIXED DECIMAL;
DECLARE (I, J, K) FIXED DECIMAL;

/* READ AND SET UP THE ACCOUNTS.*/
  K=0; ACCT(0)=1;
  DO WHILE (ACCT(K) ¬= 0);
    K = K+1; GET LIST( ACCT(K), IBAL(K));
    WITH(K) = 0; DEP(K) = 0; CBAL(K) = IBAL(K);      END;
  N = K - 1;

/* READ AND PROCESS THE TRANSACTIONS.*/
  GET LIST(TACCT, DEPWITH, AMT); /* FIRST TRANSACTION*/
  TRAN: DO WHILE ( TACCT ¬= 0);
    /* PROCESS THE TRANSACTION JUST READ.*/
     J = 1;      /* SEARCH FOR TRANSACTION ACCOUNT.*/
     DO WHILE (ACCT(J) ¬= TACCT);  J = J + 1;     END;
     IF DEPWITH = 1
       THEN DO; DEP(J)=DEP(J)+1;  CBAL(J)=CBAL(J)+AMT; END;
       ELSE DO; WITH(J)=WITH(J)+1;CBAL(J)=CBAL(J)-AMT; END;
    /* READ NEXT TRANSACTION.*/
     GET LIST(TACCT, DEPWITH, AMT);       END TRAN;

/* PRINT THE RESULTS.*/
  PUT SKIP LIST('ACCOUNT', 'PREV BAL', 'WITHDRAWALS',
                   'DEPOSITS', 'FINAL BAL');
  DO I = 1 TO N;
    PUT SKIP LIST(ACCT(I), IBAL(I), WITH(I), DEP(I),
                   CBAL(I));     END;
END BANK;
```

2.3 Handling Input Errors

While creating this program, we assumed that the input would
always be correctly punched, in order to keep the discussion to
a reasonable size. Assuming that the input is correct is a
disastrous mistake. Error checking must be a continual concern
during the development process, and should not be left until
after the program is "finished".

A program should always check its input for errors, and
produce output documenting any error it finds. When a data
error is not detected, the best that can happen is that the
program will "blow up" -- an infinite loop will be executed, in
PL/C an array subscript will be out of range, or some similar
indication will be given. The worst that can happen is that the
program processes the erroneous input as if it were correct,
giving no indication that anything is wrong. If and when the
error is eventually detected, it can be embarrassing and costly
to correct.

In the bank problem just discussed, the following kinds of
errors might be detected:

    1) An account is listed two or more times.
    2) The end-of-account signal is missing or incorrect.
    3) A transaction number is not in the list of accounts.
    4) The withdrawal-deposit number is not 1 or -1.
    5) The transaction amount is negative.
    6) The end-of-transaction signal is wrong or missing.

Detecting other situations such as overdrafts (which are not
really input errors) would probably make the program more
valuable. Of course, not all errors can be detected by the
program.   For example, in the bank program, a withdrawal
keypunched as a deposit, or an error in a transaction amount can
not be detected.

With some errors the program should stop and print a message.
For example, if the end-of-account signal is missing, then all
transactions have been read as accounts, and there is no hope of
proceeding usefully. With other errors the program should just
print a message and continue. For example, if a transaction
gives a non-existant account number, that transaction can be
rejected and a message can be printed.

One could conceivably overdo error checking. The programmer
must weigh each type of input error and the damage its
occurrence might cause against the amount of programming
necessary to detect it.   But at least the programmer should
think of all the possible errors and come to a rational decision
on each one.   If necessary the manager should be questioned
about them. Very often the person in charge may not have
thought about all the possibilities and will be delighted to
hear they can be detected. On the other hand, he may be able to
tell the programmer that a particular error will never occur.

Section 2 Exercises

1. Why is ACCT declared as ACCT(0:201) instead of ACCT(0:200)?

2. With each of the 6 errors discussed in Section 2.3, indicate whether the program should stop or whether it may be reasonable to continue.

3. Change the bank account program to detect the 6 errors discussed in Section 2.3. These changes should not be made by trying to revise the final program. Instead, go back to the proper step (3, 4, or 5) and perform the complete analysis and program creation once more, this time with the view of checking and documenting possible input errors.

4. Suppose the signal ending the accounts is a single 0 instead of two 0's. Change the program to reflect this. In making the changes, repeat the program analysis and development from the beginning; don't attempt to just change the final program. Which signal is better and why?

5. Suppose we wish to change the end-of-transaction signal to a single 0 instead of three. Change the program to reflect this.

6. Below are several problem statements. For each, develop an algorithm in English to solve it. This algorithm should contain no details about arrays used, variables used, etc. It should be only the first step toward a final program -- on the same level of detail as algorithm (2.2a). Note that the problem statements do not in fact give you exact details about the input. Compare your algorithms with each other and with (2.2a).

   a) The input consists of two lists X and Y of numbers. Print out the number of times each number in list Y occurs in the first list X.

   b) The input consists of a list of bank accounts and transactions concerning these accounts. Print out the number of transactions for each account.

   c) The input consists of the text of a book, punched on cards, followed by a list of words. Print out the number of times each word on the list is used in the book.

   d) The input consists of a list of student records (name, address, grades in each course, etc.), followed by a list of a few student names. Find and print out the average, highest, and lowest grade point average for the students given in the second list.

7. Below are several problem statements. For each, develop an algorithm, which shows the overall structure of the final program. Your algorithm should probably be along the lines of algorithm (2.2e).

a) The input consists of a list of integers. Print out all those integers which are even.

b) The input consists of a list of integers. Print out those integers which are prime. (An integer is prime if it is greater than 1 and evenly divisible only by 1 and itself. The integers 2, 3, 5, 7, 11, 59 are prime; the integers -2, 0, 1, 4, 9, 100 are not.)

c) The input consists of a list of names of people. Print out all the names that contain the letter A.

8. In developing subalgorithm (2.2e), one problem was preventing the "Process transaction just read" statement from being executed if the transaction just read was the end-of-list signal. Is there another way to write the loop without adding conditional statements? If you produce a different version, with or without conditional statements or GO TOs, is it more efficient? Easier to understand? Easier to modify?

9.* Suppose the account numbers are limited to three digits. Can you think of a way to sort the accounts efficiently? What modifications would you have to make in the program? What are the relative merits of your solution and the one developed here in terms of time and space?

Section 3 <u>Top-Down Program Development</u>

3.1 <u>The General Method</u>

Section 2 contains an example of program development which proceeded as follows. We began (implicitly) with the algorithm "Solve the problem." This was "refined" into algorithm (2.2a):

> Read in and set up the accounts in a "table";
> Read in and process the transactions;
> Print the results;

The third step was to describe the data structures representing the accounts, since this was needed in order to work on each of the three statements of algorithm (2.2a). Each of these three statements was then further refined in a similar manner. This process can be depicted by the "trees" (3.1a) through (3.1d); trees (3.1a), (3.1b) and (3.1c) represent the first three succesive refinements, while (3.1d) represents the final product and how it was developed. For each tree, the lines leading down from a statement represent the sequence of statements (from left to right) which perform the same function as that statement. The sequence is to be executed in left-to-right order. (To save space, we have put the identifying line number of Section 2 in place of the corresponding sequence of statements in a number of places.)

<u>Each successive tree represents a correct program</u>, with successively more detail added. Correctness follows from the fact that the first algorithm "Solve the problem" is correct, and that each refinement specifies a correct way of performing the statement it replaces.

(3.1a)   Solve the problem

(3.1b)   Solve the problem

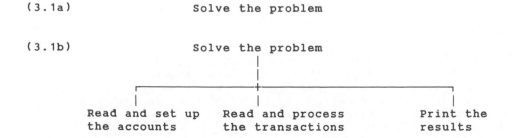

(3.1c)

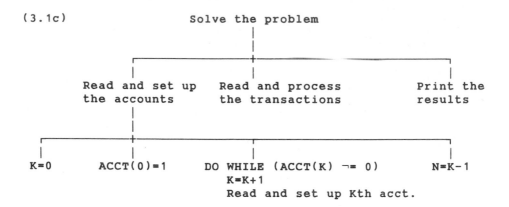

(3.1d)

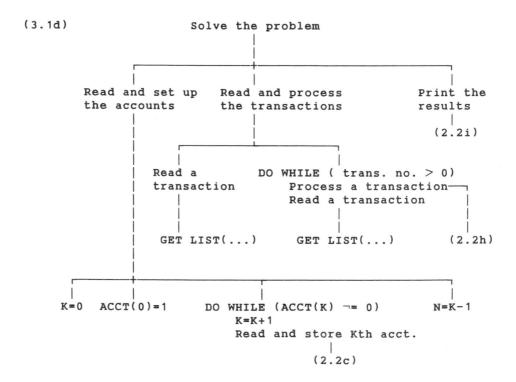

The decisions are made in "outside-in", "top-down" order -- in order of increasing detail. In the bank problem, initially there were a number of questions that could have been raised and answered -- how accounts should be stored, how the transactions should be processed, how the transactions should be stored, etc. Out of all these, we chose the one which helped determine the overall structure and which led to a correct program with just more detail: what were the main subproblems and in which order should they be executed?

This is not to say that your thoughts shouldn't skip to various parts of the program in varying amounts of detail. (They will whether you want them to or not.) There is nothing wrong in beginning by looking at various possibilities for the representation of data and subalgorithms to process them. Sometimes this is necessary in order to obtain a better understanding of the problem and possible solutions. Sometimes this is necessary in order to come up with any idea at all. But this should just be considered a side trip. Any ideas discovered on it should <u>not</u> be accepted as final, and the main program development should then proceed <u>top-down</u>.

This top-down process is not as easy and straightforward as it may seem from the example given in Section 2. Programming, like any problem solving, is a trial and error process. Mistakes will be made, or just the wrong avenue explored, which will cause the programmer to undo several levels of refinements (discarding several parts of the tree) and to repeat the process in a different manner. This "backing up" is discussed in more detail in Section 3.3.

Programming in top-down fashion may seem foreign and difficult, especially to beginners. This is because one has to force himself to think systematically and logically. Yet for most problems it is the best approach, because it will lead to efficient, understandable, and correct programs. Attempt right from the beginning to develop programs in a top-down, outside-in, general statement to fine detail, manner.

In programming in this fashion we attempt to make <u>one</u> clear decision at a time. A decision leads to a refinement of part of the program. The two types of refinement are:

1. A statement is refined.

2. The method of storing data is refined, by describing the variables used to store the data.

We discuss these separately in the next two subsections.

3.1.1 <u>Refining a Statement</u>

<u>Concentrating on "what" rather than "how"</u>

One of the advantages of top-down programming is that it helps us concentrate initially on <u>what</u> is to be done, and then systematically becomes concerned with <u>how</u>. For example, in developing the overall structure of the bank problem in Section 2, we refined "Solve the problem" into algorithm (2.2a):

```
Read in and set up the accounts;
Read in and process the transactions;
Print the results;
```

Here, we were not <u>primarily</u> interested in <u>how</u> the accounts and
transactions were to be stored or processed, but only in <u>what</u>
was to be done, so that we could concentrate on the order in
which the various functions were to be performed.

As another example, consider the problem of sorting the
elements of B(1:N) into ascending order. One way to achieve
this is to first put the largest value in B(N), then put the
next largest in B(N-1), and so on. Once the largest is in B(N),
putting the second largest in B(N-1) is equivalent to putting
the largest of B(1:N-1) in B(N-1). Similarly, putting the third
largest in B(N-2) will be the same as putting the largest of
B(1:N-2) in B(N-2). The following algorithm serves our purpose:

                DO I = N TO 1 BY -1;
    (3.1.1a)   Swap values in B(1:I) to put largest in B(I); END;

Notice that the last execution of the loop body, "Swap values of
B(1:1) so that the largest is in B(1)", is unneccessary. Hence
we change (3.1.1a) to

                DO I = N TO 2 BY -1;
    (3.1.1b)   Swap values in B(1:I) to put largest in B(I); END;

Up to this point, we haven't worried about <u>how</u> to swap the
values of B(1:I). We don't <u>care</u> how it is done, because we are
concentrating on a different decision -- we are concerned with
the main loop and its limits. If we <u>did</u> have the problem of
swapping on our minds, we might not have seen the refinement of
(3.1.1a) into (3.1.1b).

<u>Limiting ourselves to understandable refinements</u>

When refining a statement we replace a statement of <u>what</u> to
do by an algorithm which indicates <u>how</u> to do it. In making such
a refinement it is important to <u>limit ourselves</u> to refinements
we can easily understand, and which we can easily communicate to
others.

Given a statement, what possibilities exist? The most
general possibility we should allow ourselves is a <u>sequence of</u>
<u>statements to execute in order</u>. Thus we should attempt to break
the original statement into <u>successive</u> parts to be executed in
order. Other possibilities for a refinement are:

    1. Use a conditional statement to break the problem up
        into two subcases.

    2. Break it up into several (instead of two) subcases.

    3. Replace it by a loop (with perhaps initialization
        statements).

Faced with these limited possibilities for refining a statement, we can focus our attention on the following questions:

1. How can it be broken up into succesive statements?
2. Does it break up easily into two or more subcases?
3. Is it an iteration problem -- can a loop be used?

As an example, suppose the input consists of words separated
by one or more blanks, in free format on cards. A variable CARD
defined as CHAR(...) VARYING always contains that part of the
input read in but not yet "processed".   We want a program
segment which puts the next unprocessed word in variable WORD
and deletes it from CARD.

Now remember that we can write the segment as a series of
statements to execute in order, a conditional statement, or a
loop. Those are the only possibilities. A little thought, with
these restrictions, leads to the following algorithm:

1: Find the beginning of the word in CARD, and delete the
        blanks preceding it;
2: Find the end of the word;
3: Copy the word into WORD;
4: Delete the word from CARD;

We now have four simpler problems to refine.   The problems of
no word on a card or a word split onto two cards have been
postponed -- in fact, we didn't even have to mention them!

Using Suitable Notation for Statements

Whatever language and notation suits the problem at hand
should be used in order to aid in an orderly development and to
make the final program as lucid as possible.

Usually the initial notation consists of English commands
like "Sort the list", "Process the transactions" and "Generate a
value to ...". Any imperative statement can be used, provided
its meaning is sufficiently clear.

In particular, it is often convenient to invent control
mechanisms that do not exist in PL/I (and perhaps not in any
real programming language). One control mechanism we have been
using all the time is the "exit statement", which we have had to
write as a GO TO statement. As other examples, the meaning of
the following two algorithms should be clear without any formal
definition of how the "FOR EACH" statement is to be executed:

```
FOR EACH account in the list DO;
    IF the account balance < 0 THEN Print a message; END;
```

```
FOR EACH position of the chessboard DO;
    IF the position is occupied by a white piece THEN
        DO; IF the white piece can capture the black king
            THEN Print "check";
            IF the white piece can capture the black queen
            THEN Print "watch out!";   END;   END;
```

Using such statements helps postpone decisions about the order in which the accounts or positions on the chessboard should be processed. These can wait, and will probably depend on how the list and chessboard are stored as variables. Once we decide on an order, translating the FOR EACH loops into PL/I WHILE loops will not be difficult.

As another example, consider a program to simulate a baseball game. We have variables which keep track of the inning, number of outs, men on base, etc., and we have a way of generating an integer I to represent what happens next. A partial list of the values of I and the corresponding actions are given below:

value of I	action after pitch
1	ball
2	strike
3	foul ball
4	single
5	double
etc.	

We want a program segment which tests I and executes a subsegment to simulate the corresponding action by changing the values of the variables which describe the number of strikes, balls, outs, etc. It is convenient to "program" this as

```
DO ONE OF FOLLOWING, DEPENDING ON I;
    1: Process ball;
    2: Process strike;
    3: Process foul ball;
    4: Process single;
    5: Process double;
    etc.      END;
```

Here, I is evaluated to yield an integer, and the statement labeled with that integer is executed. This is a generalization of the conditional statement, with many alternatives instead of two. At some point it will be reduced to a number of nested or sequential PL/I conditional statements.

Such control structures occur naturally in program design, but PL/I and many other languages have no such statements. So we make up our own.

3.1.2 Refining a Data Description

Data refinements are just as important as statement refinements, but decisions about how to store the data should be postponed as long as possible, until no further statement refinements can be made without knowing more about the data structures used.

You will gradually learn that there are many different ways of keeping data in variables. For example, the list of accounts in the bank problem can be kept in unsorted form in an array, or sorted in ascending or descending order. There are also more sophisticated storage structures such as hash tables, singly linked lists, doubly linked lists, circular lists, dequeues, stacks and trees. Each method has advantages and disadvantages, depending on the nature and form of the operations to be performed. In order to intelligently choose a method for data representation, it is necessary to wait until the operations to be performed on the data are well understood.

The method of storing transactions in the bank problem is a good illustration. We could have initially decided to use an array, since there were many transactions. But waiting and later deciding based on what was to be done with the transactions led to the discovery that only one transaction had to be stored at any time.

Whenever you decide upon variables, write down their names with their exact meanings immediately. Don't wait until you write the declaration for them. Every variable is important (or else it shouldn't be in the program) and you must know exactly why it is there. Don't trust these exact meanings to your memory; write them down.

A recent incident will illustrate the importance of this. A student came in with a two-page program, the relevant parts of which are given in (3.1.2a). The program was a simplified "text editor"; it read text -- a sequence of words interspersed with symbols for commands like "begin a new line" and "begin a new paragraph" -- and printed out the text as formatted by the commands. Each output line was "right justified", which means that not only were the left margins lined up, but also the right margins. (Right justification is performed by inserting extra blanks between words, as in the lines you are now reading.)

There was obviously an error, since occasionally a blank at the end of a word was missing -- "the big black fox" might come out as "thebig black fox". The problem was found by examining the exact role of the variables. Looking at the program, it was surmised that OUTLINE would contain the current line to be written out and LENGTHLINE would contain its length. The student was asked what N meant, since its meaning was not written down. After some uncertainty he said "Oh, it's just the length of the word being added to the current line OUTLINE." ("It's just" is used often when one doesn't really know. It

seems to belittle the variable, making it all right not to know
exactly why it is there.)

   The program was then examined to find if N was <u>always</u>
assigned and used in this way. The error was exposed when it
was discovered that in one place, N was the length of the word,
while in the other it was the length plus one, to take into
account the blank character following it.

```
              ...
              IF ...
                   THEN DO; ...  WORD = SUBSTR(LINE,M,N);
                                 WORD = WORD || ' ';
                        ...         END;
(3.1.2a)           ELSE DO; ...  WORD = WORD || ' ';
                                 N = LENGTH(WORD);
                        ...         END;
              ...
              LENGTHLINE = LENGTH(OUTLINE) + N;
              OUTLINE = ...
              ...
```

The importance of clearly understanding and having an exact
written description of each variable cannot be overemphasized.

Using Suitable Notation for Data

   We used notation outside PL/I in Section 2 during development
of the bank program, programming in terms of a "table of
accounts" and a "transaction" as long as possible before
describing how these quantities were to be represented in the
PL/I program. In effect, we talked as if the whole table of
accounts was contained as a value in a variable. Data can often
be represented using variables in many ways, and it is important
to talk in general terms about the "list" or the "records" until
more is known about the operations to be performed on them. For
example, see the "KWIC index" development in Section 3.5.2.

   Some algorithms just <u>cannot</u> be described coherently without
resorting to notation outside of PL/I. A good example of this
is the "heap sort" algorithm developed in Section 4.3.

   Using high-level notation for data structures is just as
important as for statements. However it is difficult to give
good examples of this until you have more programming experience
and are familiar with a variety of different data structures.
We leave this discussion to another book.

3.2 Getting an Idea for a Refinement

"How to invent something" is difficult to describe, and it is not clear that creativity can be effectively taught. Fortunately, the typical programmer is rarely asked to develop something radically different, and the type of creativity required is modest. Greater amounts of determination, logical thinking, hard work, attention to detail, and patience are involved. We attempt in this section to give some insight into how and where program ideas originate.

3.2.1 Sources of Ideas for Algorithms

A programmer has two main sources of ideas:

1. Programs previously written or studied;
2. Familiar algorithms from everyday life.

For the beginner, the first source is practically non-existent. One obvious way to expand this source is to read and study good programs written by others. Besides expanding the set of algorithms one has at his disposal, it helps teach and emphasize good style and programming practices. Surprisingly, reading other people's programs is not common practice, as we have noted in Section 1.1.

The second source of ideas is almost unlimited. Every day we use algorithms or see others use them. Often, of course, they are informal and not too well defined, and describing them precisely may be difficult. But the ideas are there.

The bank problem is a good example of this. How did we know what to do? Perhaps we imagined what a clerk would do to manually perform this task. In order to write a program for it, we needed only to be able to write down an exact description of the process the clerk performs, taking into account the format of the input (which the clerk need not worry about) and the fact that all data must be stored in variables. The top-down method of development was used only to aid us in writing the algorithm correctly and precisely.

As a second example, suppose we have an array B(1:N) whose values are in ascending order. We want to find the position J of another variable X in the list. That is, search B for X and store in variable J an integer such that B(J) = X. If no such integer exists, store 0 in J.

If the list were not sorted we would use a "linear search":

```
DO J = 1 TO N BY 1;
   IF B(J) = X THEN GO TO EXIT_LINEAR_SEARCH; END;
J = 0;
EXIT_LINEAR_SEARCH:;
```

However, the additional information that B is sorted may permit
a more efficient algorithm.

Everyday situations in which something is sought in a sorted
list are numerous, and in general a more efficient method than
linear search is used. The most obvious example is looking for
a name in the telephone book. To find a name, say Smith, we
look at some entry in the book rather randomly, but as near to
the S's as we can get. The entry serves to divide the book into
two parts -- "before" the entry and "after" the entry. If this
entry is less than Smith (alphabetically), then Smith is located
in the second part, after the entry. So we "discard" the first
part and repeat the process using only the last part. If the
entry is greater than Smith, we discard the second part and
repeat the process using the first part.

Thus we can repeat a process over and over until we find the
desired entry or until we have discarded the whole list (in
which case the desired value is not in the list).   This
repetition suggests the use of a WHILE loop, and after some work
we arrive at the following algorithm:

```
Let the list to be searched be B(1:N);
DO WHILE (the list to be searched is not empty);
   K = index of some entry B(K) still in list, near X;
   IF B(K) = X THEN
      DO; J = K; GO TO END_OF_SEARCH; END;
   IF B(K) < X
      THEN discard first  half of list, including B(K);
      ELSE discard second half of list, including B(K);
   END;
J = 0; /* X IS NOT IN THE LIST */
END_OF_SEARCH:;
```

The statement

"K = index of some entry B(K) still in list, near X;"

is not precise enough. How do we compute "near"?   To simplify
this, let us just use

K = index of middle entry of the list;

which is easier to compute. It may not be as good an algorithm
as we use with the telephone book, but this change does make it
easier to program. When searching the telephone book, we have
common sense information which is not ordinarily available to
the program. For example, we know there are lots of S's and
T's, but few W's and X's. This certainly affects the way we
perform the search. The main problem in developing a program
based on our experiences is to be able to formalize how we do
something, to ferret out the essential details.

This is the beginning of the development of a well-known
algorithm called <u>binary</u> <u>search</u>. The algorithm is completed in

Section 4.1. It is a vast improvement over linear search.   For
example, if there are 32,768 entries, linear search may have to
look at <u>all</u> the entries, while binary search will <u>never</u> have to
look at more than 16 of them! We show this in Section 3.4.3.4.

    Since we have not previously seen <u>every</u> problem we are asked
to solve and program, somehow we must be able to find
connections between the problems at hand and problems whose
solutions we already know (or at least whose solutions are
easier).   Two obvious methods are to <u>simplify</u> the problem and to
find <u>related problems</u>.

3.2.2 <u>Solving Simpler Problems</u>

    It is often useful to explore a problem that is similar in
structure to the one assigned, but is simpler in detail.   One
can explore alternative strategies and algorithms in this
simpler context, and chose which strategy to pursue for the real
problem.

    To illustrate, consider again the problem of sorting an array
B(1:N) in ascending order, which we discussed in Section 3.1.1.
We have all done this -- sorted mailing lists, books on shelves,
and so on. The problem and its solution are not unfamiliar, but
explaining <u>precisely</u> how to sort is not easy if we haven't seen
an algorithm for it before. Let us attack the problem as if we
had <u>not</u> seen it earlier, and look for simpler problems within
the sort.

    What must happen for the list B(1:N) to be sorted?   For one
thing, the largest value must eventually appear in B(N).   This
is a simpler problem which we know how to handle (Section I.5,
Exercise 4f).

               DO I = 1 TO N-1 BY 1;
(3.2.2a)   IF B(I) > B(N) THEN Swap B(I) and B(N);   END;

What else must be done? The second largest value must appear in
B(N-1).   If the largest has already been put into B(N) by the
above algorithm, then this means we want to put the largest of
B(1:N-1) into B(N-1). This is roughly the same as (3.2.2a):

               DO I = 1 TO N-2 BY 1;
                 IF B(I) > B(N-1) THEN Swap B(I) and B(N-1); END;

Continuing, we should recognize that we are performing
essentially the same process a number of times. Getting back to
the original problem, we can write it as

```
     Swap values of B(1:N)    to put largest in B(N);
     Swap values of B(1:N-1) to put largest in B(N-1);
     Swap values of B(1:N-2) to put largest in B(N-2);
                    ...
     Swap values of B(1:2)    to put larger  in B(2);
or
         /* SORT B(1:N) BY SUCCESSIVE MAXIMA*/
             DO J = N TO 2 BY -1;
(3.2.2b)         Swap values of B(1:J) to put largest in B(J); END;
```

One way of refining the English substatement of (3.2.2b) is

```
         /* SWAP VALUES OF B(1:J) TO PUT LARGEST IN B(J)*/
             DO I = 1 TO J-1 BY 1;
(3.2.2c)         IF B(I) > B(J) THEN Swap B(I) and B(J); END;
```

Note that we got the idea for the program by tackling smaller simpler ones and noticing that we had to repeat essentially the same process many times. We then returned to the original level and wrote the program (3.2.2b). At this point, we <u>knew</u> how to write the segment for "Swap values of B(1:J) to put largest in B(J)", and yet we still wrote this statement in English in (3.2.2b). This was because we wanted to make <u>one</u> decision at a time, the decision turning out to be the order in which the values were placed in their final positions (first B(N), then B(N-1), and so on). <u>How</u> the values get in their positions is not a problem of (3.2.2b), but the order in which they get there is.   We can even design different algorithms for swapping the values, different from the one in (3.2.2a) which helped us find the solution.   Sometimes tackling a simpler problem or a subproblem is the only way we can proceed. But once the process of solving the simpler problem has led to an idea, set the solution to the simpler problem aside, at least temporarily, and concentrate again on the top-down analysis.

One way to <u>find</u> a simpler problem is to make the problem definition simpler. Set aside all inessential details (perhaps even some of the essential ones), until a simple, understandable problem emerges.   Once this has been solved, the original problem can be attacked with more understanding. This deletion of material must of course be done with care to make sure that the remaining problem is instructive and not trivial.

To illustrate this, consider the following problem:

(3.2.2d) <u>A Text Editor</u>. Input to the program is to consist of
    normal words, on cards, each adjacent pair being separated
    by one or more blanks. A word may be split onto two cards
    (the end of one and the beginning of the next). The words
    are to be read in and written out in 60-character lines.
    Each line is to be both right and left justified (as are
    the lines of this book). A word may not be split onto two
    lines, unless it is more than 60 characters long or unless
    otherwise there will be only one word on a line (these are
    probably errors, but the program must handle them).

Interspersed between words (and separated from them by one or more blanks) may be <u>commands</u> to be executed by the program, at the time they are read. These are:

<u>command</u>   <u>meaning</u>
)L   Begin a new output line;
)P   Begin a new paragraph (indent 3 spaces);
)E   End of input.

When processing a command, if a partially filled line must be written out, do not right-justify that line. For example, the last line of a paragraph is never right-justified.   Commands may not appear as words in the input; only as commands.

Below is some sample input, with the corresponding output shown at the right, using 14-character instead of 60-character lines to save space:

<u>Sample input</u>   <u>Sample output</u>
)P One way to find a simpler | One   way to
problem is to make the)L)L |find a simpler
      problem |problem is to
definition simpler. |make the
Throw out all |
inessential details.   )E |problem defini
                                      |tion simpler.
                                      |Throw out all
                                      |inessential de
                                      |tails.

This description is full of details, and it is difficult to know where to start, so begin by temporarily setting details aside to make it simpler:

1. Any number of blanks may separate a pair of words, and a word can be split on two cards. This may be difficult, so initially consider the input to be just a series of words and commands. That seems to be the essential point.

2. Why are lines 60 characters, and not 61 or 62? Perhaps the line length should be part of the input to the program. For now, since we need some length, use 60.

3. Justifying a line looks relatively complicated, but does not seem important relative to the overall structure of the program. Set it aside.

4. The problem of words of 60 characters or more and the problem of only one word on the line do not seem essential. Set them aside.

5. The commands are essential, and yet probably difficult to work with. Try setting them aside, and if that doesn't work out, bring them back.

This leads to the following problem description:

(3.2.2e) <u>Simplified Text Editor</u>. Read in a sequence of "words"
and print them out on 60-character lines. Put as many as
possible on one line, but separate each pair by a blank.
Don't split words across two lines.

This simpler problem is much easier to understand and work with.
A variable L (say) will hold the line currently being built. It
will be written out when the next word to be inserted causes it
to be longer than 60 characters. The following algorithm could
be designed fairly quickly:

```
          L = '';           /* NOTHING IS IN THE CURRENT LINE */
          DO WHILE (there is another input word);
             Read the next word into WORD;
(3.2.2f)     IF LENGTH(L) + LENGTH(WORD) > 60 THEN
                DO; Print L; L = ''; END;
             Add WORD onto L; Add ' ' onto L; END;
          Remove blank from end of L, if it has one;
          Print L;
```

The most important part of the original problem left out of
(3.2.2e) is the commands, so now reinsert them. This will
complicate the algorithm (3.2.2f), so we first should hide some
of its details. (3.2.2f) can be rewritten as

```
          L = '';           /* NOTHING IS IN THE CURRENT LINE */
          DO WHILE (there is more input);
(3.2.2g)     Read the next word into WORD;
             Process the word in WORD;     END;
          Remove blank from end of L, if it has one;
          Print L;
```

In adding commands, we see we must process either a word or
command. We also know when to stop the loop -- when the command
)E is read. Rewriting (3.2.2g) with this information yields

```
          L = '';           /* NOTHING IS IN THE CURRENT LINE */
          WORD = '';      /* NO WORD OR COMMAND READ YET */
          DO WHILE (WORD ¬= ')E');
             Read the next word or command into WORD;
(3.2.2h)     IF WORD is a command
                THEN Process WORD as a command;
                ELSE Process WORD as a word;     END;
          Remove blank from end of L, if it has one;
          Print L;
```

where "process WORD as a word" is

```
          /* PROCESS WORD AS A WORD*/
             IF LENGTH(L) + LENGTH(WORD) > 60 THEN
                DO; Print L; L = ''; END;
             Add WORD onto L; Add ' ' onto L;
```

We now have a reasonable solution to the simpler problem
(3.2.2e) plus commands. At this point the original problem
should be reread and programmed in top-down fashion, using
(3.2.2h) as a model.

On the text editor problem just described, the most common
"mistake" is to write the main part of the program as a loop:
        DO WHILE (there exists a card);
            Read a card;
            Process the card;   END;

This then requires a second loop in processing the card, and the
whole program is unnecessarily complicated because a word could
be split across card boundaries. If the problem is first
simplified, we realize that the card boundary problem is just a
detail to be handled at a later time, and is not an essential
point in understanding the general flow of the program.

3.2.3 Solving Related Problems

Consider writing a program segment to sort an array C(1:N) in
descending order: C(1) ≥ C(2) ≥ ... ≥ C(N). You might recall
having developed an <u>ascending</u> sort in the previous section
(program (3.2.2b)). The new sorting program could just be a
modification of the previous one.

Related problems, both in programming and in the everyday
world, are a rich source of ideas. If we can find something
related which we know how to handle, then the problem becomes
much simpler.

In the previous section, we discussed solving simpler
problems, which are of course related to the original problem.
By a "related problem" in this section we mean one which is
roughly the same order of magnitude in size or complexity. One
which, with some work, can be <u>transformed</u> into the desired one.
Everybody uses related problems all the time, and in effect we
are just saying the obvious here. The point is that you should
become <u>aware</u> of the fact that you are using related problems;
this will increase your ability to find solutions and design
programs. Learning consists not only of doing something, but
also of learning why and how one does it.

In programming, related problems occur more often than one
might think. For example, consider the four parts of Exercise 6
of Section 2. Although these look quite different, at the
highest level they all have the same algorithmic solution:

    Read in a list of values;
    Read and process a second list of values;
    Print results.

In fact, they are equivalent at this level to algorithm (2.2a)

and differ only in the meaning of "values", "read", "process",
and "results". Similarly, all the problems of Exercise 7 of
Section 2 have the solution

```
DO WHILE (there exists input);
    Read a value;
    Process the value;     END;
```

In order to <u>see</u> that problems are related, we must be able to
recognize the important elements of a problem. All four
problems in Exercise 6 of Section 2 look different on first
inspection, until we state them in a more general manner.

   Most programs include a number of simple subalgorithms, many
of which seem to occur over and over again (with perhaps slight
variations). Examples are algorithms to:

```
    Search a list.
    Search a sorted list.
    Find the maximum or the average of a set of values.
    Delete duplicate values from a list.
    Read in a list of values which ends with some signal.
```

Many of these will become part of your "repertoire of
algorithms" and you will find that programming consists in part
in determining how these standard subalgorithms should be
combined into a larger program. In order to do this, however,
you must be able to recognize familiar problems in the mass of
detail of the overall problem, and work on modifying them to fit
the current problem.

3.3 <u>Backing Up</u>

   Program development is a trial and error process. We make
refinements and try some subalgorithms, and if they don't serve
our purpose we redo them. Redoing one subalgorithm may require
us to change other parts of the program, both in data structures
and in statements, and it is important that all these changes be
made in a systematic way. This should usually be done by
"backing up" to a previous level of the program which the
changes don't affect, and then proceeding to redo all the top-
down refinements taking the changes into account.

   For example, suppose a top-down analysis has produced the
tree of refinements (3.3a), where each Si is a statement and the
lines leading down from a statement represent a sequence of
statements to be executed from left to right, to replace that
statement. Now suppose while attempting to refine statement S19
that we discover a mistake, or recognize that a change in data
structures designed earlier will make S19 more efficient. In
order to make the change, we must back up to a point where <u>the</u>
<u>change has no effect</u>. Suppose this is S2 (see tree (3.3b)).
Then we must proceed downward again, redoing all refinements (in

the example, S4-S7, S11-S15, S18 and S19) to make sure that
every refinement leads to a correct program.

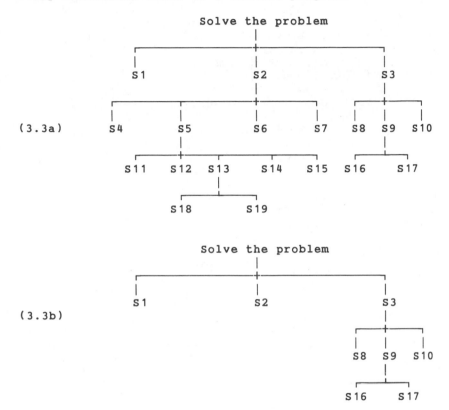

(3.3a)

(3.3b)

Backing up in this manner is extremely important if a correct
program is desired. There is a limit to how much we can keep in
our heads, and the only way to extend this limit is to keep
things well organized on paper. The more complicated the
program, the more important it is to back up systematically.

If instead of using such a systematic procedure, we just
"looked around" and tried to figure out what to change, the
chances are that we would miss at least one place to change or
would change some segment incorrectly. Backing up with a tree
as a guide indicates not only what has to be changed, but also
what doesn't have to be changed. For example, in the above
illustration, once we decide that the change affects only S2 and
its refinements, we need not worry about changing anything else
in the tree.

To illustrate this process on a real problem, consider again
the problem of sorting an array B(1:N) in ascending order. The
main statement is "Sort the array" and as a first refinement we
take again algorithm (3.2.2b) developed earlier:

```
         DO J = N TO 2 BY -1;
(3.3c)       Swap values of B(1:J) to put largest in B(J); END;
```

We already refined the English substatement in Section 3.2.2, but let us look at a different way of performing the same task. Instead of finding the largest value and then making one interchange at the end, let's compare successive values and interchange immediately if out of order:

```
     /* SWAP VALUES OF B(1:J) TO PUT LARGEST IN B(J)*/
         DO I = 2 TO J BY 1;
(3.3d)       IF B(I-1) > B(I) THEN Swap B(I-1) and B(I); END;
```

This refinement has a property which may be of some use. Note that it looks at successive adjacent pairs of B(1:J) and swaps any pair that is out of order. If no swaps occur during an execution of this subalgorithm, then no adjacent pair is out of order and the array is already sorted. Hence, if no swaps occur the algorithm can be terminated.

How will we stop execution? We have a new idea now, but we must fit it in at the right program level. Part of the change must occur not only in (3.3d), but also in the higher level algorithm (3.3c) since it must terminate. Thus we should back up to the statement "Sort the Array" and refine anew. This new refinement of "Sort the array" will be a modification of (3.3c).

Looking at (3.3c), we see that we now have <u>two</u> stopping conditions: 1) (J < 2), and 2) no swaps performed during one execution of the loop body. We introduce a new variable SORTED which has the following meaning:

> Whenever the condition of the main loop is evaluated, SORTED = 1 means the array is definitely known to be sorted, while SORTED = 0 means we aren't sure.

Now modify (3.3c) into (3.3e):

```
         SORTED = 0; J = N;
         DO WHILE (SORTED = 0 & J >= 2);
(3.3e)       Swap values of B(1:J) to put largest in B(J),
                and also set SORTED as necessary;
             J = J - 1;   END;
```

Now proceed down again to the next level, redoing the English substatement:

```
     /* SWAP B(1:J) TO PUT LARGEST IN B(J) AND SET SORTED*/
         SORTED = 1;              /* ASSUME B(1:J) IS SORTED */
         DO I = 2 TO J BY 1;
             IF B(I-1) > B(I) THEN
                 DO; Swap B(I-1) and B(I); SORTED = 0; END; END;
```

This yields the final program known as <u>bubble sort</u>:

```
/* SORT ARRAY B(1:N) USING BUBBLE SORT*/
   SORTED = 0; J = N;
   BUB: DO WHILE (SORTED = 0  &  J >= 2);
      /* SWAP B(1:J) TO PUT LARGEST IN B(J) AND SET SORTED*/
         SORTED = 1;              /* ASSUME IT IS SORTED*/
         DO I = 2 TO J BY 1;
            IF B(I-1) > B(I) THEN
(3.3f)          DO; T = B(I-1); B(I-1) = B(I); B(I) = T;
                  SORTED = 0;   END; END;
      J = J - 1;   END BUB;
```

The important point in the example is to note how we <u>backed
up to a higher program level</u> in order to incorporate changes in
a systematic manner. One <u>can</u> just look around and try to find
all necessary places to change in a haphazard manner (most
programmers do), but doing it in a systematic manner is actually
easier and more reliable.

This backing up process should also occur in the program
verification process; if an error is located during testing, it
should be corrected by backing up as we have described here, and
then proceeding down again, taking into account whatever changes
are necessary.

We <u>do not expect every programmer</u> to explicitly draw a tree
<u>for every program</u>, but he should at least keep in mind that the
program actually represents a tree. The tree is reflected in
the indenting conventions.   The statements and comments which
begin in the same column of the card form the sequence of
statements to be executed in order, at one level of the tree.
For each such statement, the statements indented directly under
it form the branches emanating down from it.

3.4 <u>Evaluating Programs</u>

A refinement of a statement or data description often implies
a decision on the part of the programmer to choose one of
several possibilities. Such a choice can have a significant
effect on the final program, and it is important to choose
consciously, and for some sound reason. This means that the
various alternatives must be developed far enough for the
programmer to be able to make an intelligent, knowledgeable
decision, based on criteria applicable to this program. In this
section we provide an overview of the criteria by which
algorithms can be evaluated and compared, and explain in some
detail how to measure both the speed and space of a program.

3.4.1 Criteria for Evaluating Programs

Programs can be judged on various grounds, and a programmer must know what criteria are appropriate for each program he writes. Among possible measures of comparison are:

1. Execution speed
2. Space (in computer memory during execution)
3. Readability and documentation
4. Ease of subsequent modification
5. Time needed to complete the project

Note that neither correctness nor reliability is on the list. The list is concerned with comparing programs which are both correct and reliable. No amount of speed can induce us to consider a program that is incorrect or unreliable.

The criteria usually mentioned as important are execution speed and space, and we will discuss these in detail in later subsections. Quite often, however, readability and ease of modification are the main factors. This happens in industry, for example, where most programs are modified after completion, and usually by someone other than the original programmer.

Comments, indenting rules, names of variables, and the like, should be a matter of concern to the programmer during program development, and not just after the program is "checked out". A programmer who documents his program after it is written rarely documents it well. (See Section I.4.6.)

Some programmers feel that documentation is a waste of time, and would rather spend their time in trying to make the program faster. They feel that their job is just to write the fastest program they can contrive. This often leads to the use of clever and obscure programming tricks. All too often, however, these tricks are counter-productive because of the time necessary for somebody else to understand the trick when modifying the program later. There is a growing consensus that such programs are not optimal in the long run, and should not be considered acceptable programming practice. There is even considerable doubt that local cleverness is the dominant source of execution speed. We have seen many examples where a logical strategy has outperformed a collection of tricky tactics.

3.4.2 <u>Measuring Space</u>

On the IBM 360 computers, memory consists of entities called
<u>bytes</u>.   (On other computers they may be called <u>words</u> or <u>cells.</u>)
Each byte consists of 8 bits. (A bit is a binary digit -- 0 or
1.)   Four bytes are usually used to hold a FIXED variable.   A
PL/C or PL/I program is translated into an equivalent "machine
language" program which occupies a certain number of bytes of
computer memory while it is executing. (See Part VII.)   During
execution, this storage is used mainly for

   1.   The translated program
   2.   Simple variables and arrays.

The space used is usually given as part of the statistics   of
the program. In PL/C, the <u>symbol table</u> and <u>object code</u> refer to
the equivalent machine language program, while the <u>static</u> and
<u>external storage</u> and the <u>automatic storage</u> refer to the space
used by variables and arrays. The programmer has little real
control over the amount of storage used by the translated
program. He can of course substitute simpler and therefore
"smaller" algorithms (e.g. linear search for binary search), but
usually the extra memory gained is not worth the effort.

Simple variables take up little space (rarely are there more
than 50 variables in a several-page program) and consequently
attempting to save space by using a variable for more than one
purpose is not worth the effort (and is very bad practice).   The
main component which the programmer <u>can</u> easily control is that
used for arrays. If an array A(1:10000) is declared, storage
must be allocated for 10,000 variables. If, by using a
different algorithm the programmer can change this to A(1:100),
a substantial reduction in space has been made.   Secondly, by
using "dynamic storage allocation" as will be discussed in
Section IV.2.5, the programmer can control how long an array
exists, and can thus have various arrays share the same space
(at different times).

In order to estimate the space required for arrays, it is
necessary to know how much space each variable takes. This
depends on the attributes of the variable, on the computer, and
just as importantly on the compiler, because each different
compiler may store a variable in a different manner. The amount
of memory (in bytes) needed for the various kinds of variables
is given in the table below for both PL/C and the IBM PL/I F-
level compiler.   These are only estimates; the exact
requirements depend on "storage alignment" and other
considerations, but these are close enough to get a good idea of
the space required for each kind of variable.

variable		PL/C	PL/I F-level
A(1:N) FIXED DECIMAL		8N	4N
A(1:N) FLOAT DECIMAL		8N	4N
A(1:N) FIXED BINARY		4N	2N
A(1:N) FLOAT BINARY		8N	4N
A(1:N) CHAR(M)		N(8+M)	N·M
A(1:N) CHAR(M) VARYING		N(8+M)	N(8+M)

The significance of the space requirements depends somewhat on the size of computer that will run the program. On large computers today, space is generally a problem only if very large arrays are required. On smaller computers, space can be a serious restriction and the program must be economical of this resource. In general, space is less of a concern than execution speed.

3.4.3 Measuring Speed of Execution

One way of comparing the speed of two programs is to run them with the same data and compare the resulting execution times. This is often done for large programs. For example, we usually judge a compiler (which is just a program) by how many cards or statements it compiles per second. Students often compare output to see whose program compiled faster and whose executed faster.

However, it is often necessary to compare algorithms with respect to speed, even before they have been programmed. We need to do this to chose between alternative algorithms during program development. Moreover, these measures of speed should be as independent as possible from the particular machine the algorithm will be run on; they should be attributed only to the algorithm itself.

The usual method is to count the number of "operations" or statements the algorithm executes, as a function of the "size" of the input or output. This count of operations does not generally include every detailed operation executed, but only the ones which contribute "the most" to the speed (or lack of speed).

For example, if a particular assignment statement is executed only once no matter what the data is, it contributes little to the total execution time and can be ignored. If another statement is executed N times where N is an input quantity, then we will probably have to count these N statements in our estimate. Generally speaking, such a statement occurs within a loop, and it is the number of times the innermost loop bodies execute that is most important.

In comparing algorithms using such counts of operations, we are usually trying to see which algorithm will be faster with moderate or large amounts of data. When "small" amounts of data are involved, it usually doesn't matter which algorithm is used.

3.4.3.1 Analysis of Linear Search

As a first example, consider the problem of finding a value X in an array B(1:N), with N ≥ 1. We want to store in J an integer so that B(J) = X, and if no such integer exists, we want to store 0 in J.

```
DO J = 1 TO N BY 1;
   IF B(J) = X THEN GO TO EXIT_LINEAR_SEARCH; END;
J = 0;
EXIT_LINEAR_SEARCH:;
```

If X is not in the array B(1:N), then the algorithm executes <u>at most</u> N comparisons of X with an array element B(J). If X is in the array, the algorithm makes anywhere from 1 to N comparisons. Thus in the <u>worst case</u> linear search performs N comparisons. We say that the running time is <u>proportional to N</u>, or that the program <u>runs in time N</u>.

What else could we count to get an estimate of the running time? We give below a table of possibilities, along with the corresponding count as a function of N in the <u>worst case</u>:

1. Array comparisons: N
2. Statements executed (counting the loop as 1): N+3
3. Iterations of the loop: N
4. Number of comparisons of J with N: N+1
5. Total number of comparisons (of array elements, or J with N): 2N+1

Notice that all these estimates are <u>linear in N</u> -- they can be put in the form

$$(\text{expression}^1) \cdot N + \text{expression}^2$$

where expression^1 and expression^2 do not contain N. No matter how we count, we always get an estimate which is linear in N, and we say that the algorithm is linear in N.

If we have two linear algorithms for the same problem, we generally use the one with the smallest multiplying factor. For example, if one executes 2N comparisons, the other 4N, and there are not other major differences, then the first will be chosen. However, there are more important differences to look for in algorithms, which we will see in a moment.

In estimating the speed of an algorithm then, we are not interested so much in an absolute time, but a function of the size of the input which shows us what the running time is proportional to. Whether we count comparisons with array elements, statements executed, or whatever, doesn't really matter, as long as the criterion we choose estimates the worst possible time. In the above program, counting the number of times the statement J=0; is executed is absurd for this purpose, because it doesn't really tell us anything.

3.4.3.2 Worst Case Versus Average Case Analysis

We showed that in the worst case, linear search performs at most N comparisons. Sometimes we would rather know the average number of comparisons that would occur if we ran the algorithm a very large number of times with different data. This average is also called the "expected" number, but the word "expected" is used in a special statistical sense (meaning average) and not with the usual English meaning. Consider linear search, assuming that X is not in the list. If the values of B(1:N) are assumed to be "randomly" chosen, then X has an equal probability of appearing in any of the elements B(I). On the average then, we may expect to look halfway through the list before finding X, performing N/2 comparisons. This is still linear.

If X may not be in the list, we can expect more than N/2 comparisons -- how much more depends on the probability that X doesn't appear. However, the algorithm is still linear on the average, since it is linear for the worst case. This is in fact why the algorithm is called "linear" search.

For linear search then, both a worst case and average case analysis show that the algorithm is linear in the size of the input. This is not always the case, and frequently the average speed is much better than the worst speed. Which analysis should we choose? That depends in part on how easy it is for us to compute. In general, the average case analysis is much harder because it requires estimates of various probabilities, and involves more complex calculations. The worst case analysis is often quite easy; we need just identify the worst case data and count how many operations the algorithm executes with that data. It may however not be a realistic estimate, since the worst case may never arise with "real" input.

3.4.3.3 Analysis of Some Sorting Algorithms

In Section 3.2.2 the successive maxima sorting algorithm was developed:

```
/* SORT ARRAY B(1:N)*/
   DO J = N TO 2 BY -1;
      /* Swap values of B(1:J) to put largest in B(J)*/
         DO I = 1 TO J-1 BY 1;
            IF B(I) > B(J) THEN Swap B(I) and B(J); END; END;
```

For the worst case analysis, we count the number of times the statement "IF B(I) > B(J) ..." is executed in the inner loop (which is equal to the number of comparisons B(I)>B(J)). For J=N, the inner loop iterates N-1 times; for J=N-1 it iterates N-2 times, and so on. Thus the statement is executed

$$N-1 + N-2 + N-3 + \ldots + 1 \;=\; N(N-1)/2 \;=\; N^2/2 - N/2$$

times. The time is thus proportional to N^2, and we call this an N^2 algorithm. Actually, the program always executes the statement "IF B(I) > B(J) ..." this many times, so that on the average the algorithm is also N^2.

The bubble sort algorithm (3.3f) is also N^2 in the worst case by a similar analysis, the worst case being a list which is completely sorted but in opposite order. The average case analysis is a harder problem; we leave it to the interested reader.

Suppose we have two algorithms for the same problem. One runs in time N and the other in time N^2, where N is the size of the input. If N is very large (say over 200) the difference between the running time of these two algorithms is immense. Here a constant multiplier has little effect. If one algorithm runs in time 100N and the other in time $N^2/2$, we still choose the linear algorithm if N will be generally over 200.

3.4.3.4 Analysis of Binary Search

The binary search algorithm was partially developed in Section 3.2.1:

```
Let the list to be searched be B(1:N);
DO WHILE (the list to be searched is not empty);
   K = index of middle entry of list;
   IF B(K) = X THEN
         DO; J = K; GO TO END_SEARCH; END;
   IF B(K) < X
      THEN discard first half of list, including B(K);
      ELSE discard second half of list, including B(K); END;
J = 0; /* X IS NOT IN THE LIST */
END_SEARCH:;
```

To perform a worst case analysis, assuming that each of the English substatements can be performed in a fixed amount of time (independent of the size of the array N), count how many times the WHILE loop is iterated. The worst case occurs when X is not in the list. If N = 1, the loop body is executed once, because the whole list B(1:1) is discarded when it is discovered that B(1) ¬= X. If N ≤ 2, the first execution of the loop body discards at least half the list, leaving at most one element in it. Since we know that the loop body executes only once if N = 1, we see that for N≤2 the loop body is executed at most twice.

Similarly, if N≤4 the loop body will be executed at most 3 times, and if N <= 8 the loop body is executed at most 4 times.

Table (3.4.3.4a) gives a list of possible values of N, all powers of 2, and the corresponding number of loop iterations that can occur. We see that if N is between 2**(n-1) and 2**n for some positive integer n, then binary search iterates the loop at most n+1 times.

(3.4.3.4a)

N		number of iterations
1	$= 2^0$	1
2	$= 2^1$	2
4	$= 2^2$	3
8	$= 2^3$	4
16	$= 2^4$	5
32	$= 2^5$	6
64	$= 2^6$	7

If N = 2**x, then x is called the logarithm to the base 2 of N. It is written LOG2(N). (LOG2 is also a built-in function in PL/I and is written this way.) (3.4.3.4b) is a table of some values of N and corresponding logarithms.

What is LOG2(9)? It lies somewhere between 3 and 4, as you can see from table (3.4.3.4b). Exactly where it is doesn't really matter from our point of view, and we will never ask you to compute it. We just don't need to. What is important is to note that the function LOG2(N) "grows much more slowly" than N itself. When N = 1, LOG2(N) is quite close to it, but as N grows to 1024, LOG2(N) only grows to 10. Thus an algorithm which performs only LOG2(N) operations for input of size N is far superior in speed to an equivalent linear algorithm.

(3.4.3.4b)

N	LOG2(N)	reason
1	0	$1 = 2^0$
2	1	$2 = 2^1$
4	2	$4 = 2^2$
8	3	$8 = 2^3$
16	4	$16 = 2^4$
256	8	$256 = 2^8$
1024	10	$1024 = 2^{10}$
32768	15	$32768 = 2^{15}$

The binary search algorithm runs in time LOG2(N). This yields a tremendous saving over the linear search. For example, if N = 32,768, linear search requires on the average 16,384 comparisons while binary search requires at most 32. If the list is sorted, and if it contains over 20 elements, say, then binary search should always be used.

Notice that when comparing linear and binary search, whether we count the number of comparisons or the number of times a loop body is executed makes little difference; the crucial difference is that one algorithm is linear and the other is logarithmic.

3.4.3.5 <u>Generating a List of Unique Numbers</u>

As another example of analysis of speed, supppose the input consists of a list of N integers (N is already initialized), and we want to store these integers in an array B but with each unique integer appearing only once.   Thus if N = 8 and the list is

     3   8   12   8   6   5   8   3

then upon termination of the algorithm B should contain

     3   8   12   6   5   ?   ?   ?

Let us also assume that a variable M should contain the number of unique integers in B upon termination. A simple program segment to do this is

```
                M = 0;                  /* NO INTEGERS IN B YET*/
                UNIQ: DO I = 1 TO N BY 1;
                  GET LIST(INT);
(3.4.3.5a)        Search B(1:M) for INT and set J to 1 if found,
                    to 0 otherwise;
                  IF J = 0 THEN
                    DO; M = M + 1; B(M) = INT; END; END UNIQ;
```

The operation Search B(1:M) will probably be done by linear search, since the array is not sorted. (Be careful in writing this search, however, since it must work when M = 0.) Thus each execution of "Search" takes time proportional to the current value of M.

Execution of each of the other statements in the loop body is essentially a constant time, so that for M sufficiently large, execution of the loop body is proportional to M.

The worst case arises when the search is as slow as possible at each iteration of the loop, and this occurs when the value being searched for is not in the list. Hence the worst case arises when all N input numbers are different. For I=1 the search takes time proportional to 0; for I=2 it takes time proportional to 1, for I=3, 2 and so on. Thus the total search time is proportional to

     $0 + 1 + 2 + ... + (N-1) = N(N-1)/2 = N^2/2 - N/2$

In the worst case, the algorithm runs in time proportional to N^2.

Now suppose that there are only M different integers in the original list of N integers. Then the operation Search must occur at least once with 0 elements in B, once with 1 element in B, once with 2 elements in B, and so on up to M-1 elements in B. Thus the whole search takes time proportional to at least

$$0 + 1 + 2 + \ldots + (M-1) \;=\; M^2/2 - M/2$$

and the algorithm is no better than M^2, the square of the number of values in the final list B.

3.5 Examples of Choosing Alternatives

3.5.1 Example 1

Consider the following problem:

The input is a list of roughly 5000 names of people. Some names, say about 30% of them, are duplicates. The program should read in these names and print them out in alphabetical order, with each different name appearing only once. (This problem occurs frequently. For example the list might be a mailing list, a list of alumni and their addresses, a list of students and their courses, where each student's name appears once for each course, and so on.)

Recall that in Section 3.4.3.5 a similar problem was solved. One solution to this problem consists of first making up the list of unduplicated names as in that section, then sorting the list, and then printing it. The algorithm is:

```
        S1: Read in list and delete
                duplicates (algorithm 3.4.3.5a);
(3.5.1a) S2: Sort the list;
        S3: Print the list;
```

This would probably be our first thought, since it is related to a problem just studied. However, we know that S1 runs in time proportional to M^2 (if there are M unique names), which is roughly $(.70N)^2 = .49N^2$, since about 30 percent of the names are duplicates. Let us assume that we can sort the list in time proportional to N·LOG2(N). This can be done by several algorithms, which we have alluded to earlier. The heap sort algorithm discussed in Section 4.3 is such an example. We show below the statements of (3.5.1a) and the time spent in each as a function of the size of the input (disregarding the multipliers). Clearly the most time is spent in executing S1, and we should look for a more efficient way of performing it.

Statement	S1	S2	S3
Time	N^2	N·LOG2(N)	N

Suppose we leave all names in the list, including duplicates, then sort using the N·LOG2(N) heap sort, and then print:

```
        Read names into list B;
(3.5.1b) Sort B;
        Print B, but avoid printing duplicates.
```

Reading names into the list is now of order N, the number of names; sorting is of order N·LOG2(N); and we should be able to print B as stated in linear time (with respect to N), since all duplicates of one name now appear together in the sorted list. Hence, in this algorithm, the sorting dominates, and the whole algorithm runs in time N·LOG2(N). This is much faster than (3.5.1a).

A third possibility exists. Suppose after reading each new name we immediately sort B:

```
M = 0;
DO I = 1 TO N BY 1;
    Read one name into NAME;
    Search sorted list B(1:M) for NAME;
    IF NAME not in list THEN
        Insert NAME into proper place in list B(1:M);
    END;
Print B, but avoid printing duplicates;
```

This may seem like a good idea, but we leave it to the reader to show that the sorting algorithm is N^2 and thus not very attractive. The <u>searching</u> can be performed by binary search, but the <u>insertion</u> will be too slow. This algorithm is called <u>insertion sort</u>.

3.5.2* <u>A More Complicated Example - the KWIC Index</u>

We partially develop a program to produce a "KWIC index" from a list of titles. The development illustrates several points:

1. Using notation to fit the problem,

2. The importance of analyzing all possibilities for a refinement,

3. The importance of knowing which operations are to be performed on a data structure before deciding on its representation.

Without a top-down development, or at least a clear description of the program at a high level, it would be difficult to even <u>see</u> that there are so many choices to choose from.

3.5.2.1 <u>The Problem and a First Refinement</u>

(3.5.2.1a) <u>KWIC Index</u>. KWIC stands for "KeyWord In Context". Its meaning is as follows: suppose we have a list of titles of books, research articles, etc. For example,

```
                    THE RENTED STOLE
                    MYSTERY OF THE STOLEN RENT
                    RENTED HOUSE MYSTERY
                    STOLEN HOUSE
                    RENT A MYSTERY RENT HOUSE
```

A KWIC index is a list of the titles arranged so that it is easy to find out which of the titles contain each "key" word. The KWIC index for the above list would be:

```
                    ┌──keyword column
                    │
            RENTED HOUSE MYSTERY
            STOLEN HOUSE
    RENT A MYSTERY RENT HOUSE
            MYSTERY OF THE STOLEN RENT
        RENTED HOUSE MYSTERY
            RENT A MYSTERY RENT HOUSE
        RENT A MYSTERY RENT HOUSE
    MYSTERY OF THE STOLEN RENT
            RENT A MYSTERY RENT HOUSE
            THE RENTED STOLE
            RENTED HOUSE MYSTERY
        THE RENTED STOLE
            STOLEN HOUSE
    MYSTERY OF THE STOLEN RENT
```

In each title, words which are <u>not</u> articles, prepositions, and the like are called <u>keywords</u>. In the index, each title occurs once in the list for each keyword in the title, and the titles are so aligned that the keywords all occur in the same column. The titles are printed in alphabetical order of the keywords. Note that if a keyword appears two or more times in a title (e.g. RENT in "RENT A MYSTERY RENT HOUSE"), the title appears two or more times under that keyword in the final list.

Such a KWIC index is an invaluable aid to researchers in finding books and articles. To find them, one just has to search the list for relevant keywords and note down the corresponding titles. A typical index may contain 1000 to 5000 different titles.

A program to produce a KWIC index is given the titles and the list of "non-keywords" as input. The program must read the titles and non-keywords, make up a list of possible keywords, sort the list of keywords, and then print the titles according to the list of keywords. Often, it will take several "runs" of the program to get the index in shape. The list of non-keywords may be changed from run to run to add more words than just prepositions and articles. For example, the word "computer" appears in many titles in computer science, and it may be irrelevant to have a listing of 300 titles each with the keyword "computer". Such cases may not be detected until after the list is first printed.

The general outline (first refinement) for the KWIC index
program can be easily created from the above description. It
uses three "lists": TITLES is the list of titles, NONKEY the
list of non-keywords, and KEYWORDS the list of keywords.
Although they will probably be implemented in standard fashion
using arrays, we will not make that decision now, but just talk
in terms of lists. The first attempt at a program is:

                    S1: Read titles into list TITLES;
                    S2: Read non-keywords into list NONKEY;
(3.5.2.1b)   S3: Make up list KEYWORDS from the titles
                          and non-keywords;
                    S4: Sort the list KEYWORDS;
                    S5: Print the titles according to list KEYWORDS.

Refinements of statements S1 and S2 will depend on the input
format and we will not discuss them further. We are mainly
interested in statements S3, S4 and S5. Speed of execution will
be important since there can be so many titles (up to, say,
5000). First, note that a sort is involved. We will use an
N·LOG2(N) algorithm like heap sort (see Section 4.3) instead of
an N^2 algorithm like bubble sort. Hopefully we can refine S3
and S5 into algorithms no worse than N·LOG2(N).

In order to intelligently talk about speed, we must have some
estimate of the size of the lists. Suppose that

                    1. There are T titles. T <= 5000.
(3.5.2.1c)   2. On the average there are 5 keywords per title.
                    3. Each keyword appears about 5 different times.
                        Thus there are roughly T different keywords.
                    4. There are a maximum of 10 words per title.

We don't know there are 5 keywords per title, or that there are
T different keywords, but these estimates are close enough in
order to make reasonable time estimates.

3.5.2.2 Analyzing and Refining Statement S3

In order to save space, let us first of all consider keeping
only the different keywords in KEYWORDS. No matter how many
times a keyword appears in titles, it will only appear once in
the list. Thus, for the sample input, the list KEYWORDS would
be

    HOUSE   MYSTERY   RENT   RENTED   STOLE   STOLEN

Statment S3 to make up the list of keywords must then perform as
follows:

```
           /* MAKE UP LIST OF KEYWORDS*/
             Set list of KEYWORDS to empty;
             FOR each word in each title DO;
(3.5.2.2a)           IF that word is not in NONKEY THEN
                 DO; Search KEYWORDS for the word;
                      IF the word isn't in KEYWORDS THEN
                          Add word to KEYWORDS; END; END;
```

This looks similar to the problem discussed in Section 3.5.1.
There, the problem was to read in a list of values and put them
in an array, but put each duplicated value in only once.   Here,
we get the words from the titles, but that is the only essential
difference. In Section 3.5.1, we saw that the approach we just
took led to an N^2 algorithm. Looking at (3.5.2.2a), we see that
a search of the keyword list is performed in time T. This leads
to a T^2 algorithm, as in the last section.

   If we want to have the algorithm run in time no worse than
T·LOG2(T), then we must revise it along the lines suggested by
the related problem of Section 3.5.1. We must first put all the
keywords in KEYWORDS, whether they are duplicates or not, then
sort, and then delete the duplicates:

```
             S1: Read titles into list TITLES;
             S2: Read non-keywords into list NONKEY;
(3.5.2.2b)   S3: Make up list KEYWORDS from the titles
                 and non-keywords;
             S4: Sort the list KEYWORDS;
             S4':Delete duplicates from KEYWORDS;
             S5: Print the titles according to list KEYWORDS.
```

Where S3 is now

```
           /* S3: MAKE UP LIST KEYWORDS FROM TITLES*/
             Set list KEYWORDS to empty;
             FOR each word in each title DO;
               IF that word is not in NONKEY THEN
                 Put that word in list KEYWORDS; END;
```

We have lost the space advantage we were looking for in the
beginning of this section, but we have satisfied our speed
requirement. Indeed, statement S3 runs in time proportional to
the number of titles T, while the sort is still T·LOG2(T).
Statement S4' can also obviously be done in time proportional to
the number of keywords, which is roughly 5T. The only statement
to take care of now is statement S5.

3.5.2.3 <u>Analyzing and Refining Statement S5 to Print the Titles</u>

Our first attempt at statement S5 is

(3.5.2.3a)
```
          FOR each keyword in KEYWORDS DO
               Search the titles and print those containing
                    the keyword (if a keyword appears i times in
                    a title, print the title i times); END;
```

Searching the titles will take time proportional to the number
of titles T.   Since this must be done T times (once for each
keyword), this is a T^2 algorithm, which is above our hoped for
upper bound of T·LOG2(T).

We <u>have</u> to process each keyword, so the only way of reducing
the time in executing (3.5.2.3a) is to somehow get rid of the
search through the titles each time. How can we do that?   One
possible way would be to keep with each keyword a list of the
titles to be printed for that keyword, or better still, to keep
a list of the <u>positions</u> of the titles in TITLES, to be printed.

Keeping such a list may be quite messy, but notice that if we
<u>don't</u> delete duplicate keywords, then for each keyword in
KEYWORDS we need only keep track of which title it appeared in
and its character position in the title. For example, with the
sample input, the keyword list could be represented by <u>three</u>
arrays KEYWORDS, TITLENO, and CHARPOS, as follows:

	KEYWORDS	TITLENO	CHARPOS			KEYWORDS	TITLENO	CHARPOS
(1)	RENTED	1	5	(8)		MYSTERY	3	14
(2)	STOLE	1	12	(9)		STOLEN	4	1
(3)	MYSTERY	2	1	(10)		HOUSE	4	8
(4)	STOLEN	2	16	(11)		RENT	5	1
(5)	RENT	2	23	(12)		MYSTERY	5	8
(6)	RENTED	3	1	(13)		RENT	5	16
(7)	HOUSE	3	8	(14)		HOUSE	5	21

Statement S5 will then look something like

```
     DO I = 1 TO number of keywords;
        N = TITLENO(I); POS = CHARPOS(I);
        Print the Nth title in TITLES, with the POSth
           character in the keyword column; END;
```

This requires several changes in the higher level algorithm
(3.5.2.2b).   For example, we must delete S4' which deletes
duplicate keywords. At this point we must back up to this
algorithm, change it, and then proceed in top-down fashion to
refine its statements once more. This we leave to the reader.

We give below the final program.   Preceding it are
descriptions of the data structures used.

1. The list of titles is kept in an array TITLES.
TITLES(1) is the first title, TITLES(2) the second, and so
on. There are T titles in the array.

2. The list of non-keywords is kept in an array NONKEY.
NONKEY(1) is the first, NONKEY(2) the second, and so on.

3. The keywords are kept in <u>three</u> arrays KEYWORDS, TITLENO,
and CHARPOS. The Ith keyword is in KEYWORD(I), and was
added to the array because it was found in title
TITLENO(I), beginning at character position CHARPOS(I). At
any point, there are K keywords in the list.

S1: Read titles into TITLES;
S2: Read non-keywords into NONKEY;
S3: Make up keyword list in arrays KEYWORDS, TITLENO, and
    CHARPOS;
S4: Sort array KEYWORDS. Whenever a swap of KEYWORDS(I)
    and KEYWORDS(J) (say) occurs, also swap TITLENO(I)
    and TITLENO(J), and CHARPOS(I) and CHARPOS(J);
S5: Print the titles according to the keywords;

We have the following refinements of S3 and S5:

```
/* S3: MAKE UP LIST OF KEYWORDS, ASSUMING NONKEY IS*/
/*  SORTED. IF BINARY SEARCH IS USED TIME IS PROPORTIONAL*/
/* TO T*LOG2(NO. OF NON-KEYWORDS).  */
  K = 0;                 /* KEYWORD LIST IS EMPTY*/
  MAKE_UP: DO I = 1 TO T BY 1;
    FOR EACH word in TITLES(I) DO;
     IF the word is not in NONKEY THEN
            DO; K = K + 1; KEYWORD(K) = the word;
                TITLENO(K) = I;
                CHARPOS(K) = pos. of keyword in title;
                END; END; END MAKE_UP;

/* S5: PRINT TITLES.  TIME PROPORTIONAL TO NUMBER OF*/
   /* KEYWORDS K*/
   DO I = 1 TO K BY 1;
    Print out TITLES(TITLENO(I)), with character
        CHARPOS(I) appearing in the keyword column; END;
```

Section 4 <u>Examples of Top-down Description</u>

We present here the description of several algorithms. The
purpose is threefold. First of all, many of these algorithms
are well-known, "good" algorithms which should be in everybody's
bag of tricks. Secondly, they are good examples of top-down
description and may help the student to become more familiar
with the style. Finally, it is a good idea to study and read
well-documented programs.

4.1 <u>Binary Search</u>

<u>Problem</u>. Given a variable X and an array B(1:N) whose
values are sorted in ascending order, find the index of the
entry containing the value X and store this index in
variable J. If no such index exists, store 0 in J.

We begin with the algorithm developed in Section 3.1.

```
          Let the list to be searched be B(1:N);
          DO WHILE (the list to be searched is not empty);
            K = index of middle entry;
            IF B(K) = X THEN DO; J = K; GO TO END_SEARCH; END;
(4.1a)      IF B(K) < X
              THEN Discard first  half of list, including B(K);
              ELSE Discard second half of list, including B(K);
            END;
          J = 0; /* X IS NOT IN THE LIST*/
          END_SEARCH:;
```

To describe the list to be searched we use two variables
FIRST and LAST. At any time during execution, the list still to
be searched is B(FIRST:LAST). Thus the list is <u>not</u> empty if
FIRST <= LAST.

Algorithm (4.1a) contains five English statements or
expressions. With the previous data refinement, these can
easily be translated into PL/I to yield the following algorithm:

```
          FIRST = 1; LAST = N;      /* SEARCH WHOLE LIST B(1:N)*/
          DO WHILE (FIRST <= LAST);/* DO WHILE LIST NOT EMPTY*/
            K = FLOOR((FIRST+LAST))/2E0;   /* K = MIDDLE ENTRY*/
(4.1b)      IF B(K) = X THEN
               DO; J = K; GO TO END_SEARCH; END;
            IF B(K) < X                  /* DISCARD HALF OF LIST*/
               THEN FIRST = K+1;
               ELSE LAST = K-1; END;
          J = 0; /* X IS NOT IN LIST*/
          END_SEARCH:;
```

Exercises for Binary Search

1. Suppose N = 16 and B = 1, 3, 5, 7, 9, 11, 13, 15, 17, 19, 21, 23, 25, 27, 29, 99.

    a) Execute algorithm (4.1b) by hand with X = 99.
    b) Execute algorithm (4.1b) by hand with X = 1.
    c) Execute algorithm (4.1b) by hand with X = 17.
    d) Execute algorithm (4.1b) by hand with X = 18.

2. Determine the maximum number of comparisons of B(K) and X, based on N.

3. Will binary search work correctly if, when discarding half the list, B(K) is _not_ also discarded?

4.* The binary search algorithm makes two array comparisons for each iteration of the loop, while the likelihood that the condition B(K) = X is true early during execution is quite low. Change the program to make only _one_ comparison within the loop, say B(K) <= X. Then after the loop make a few comparisons to set J correctly.

4.2 Sort by Successive Minima

Problem. Sort the values in array B(1:N) into ascending order (assume B and N already contain values).

The first refinement is

```
          DO I = 1 TO N-1 BY 1;
(4.2a)       Swap values of B(I:N) to put smallest in B(I); END;
```

One way of refining the statement "Swap values of ..." is

```
          M = I;
          DO J = I+1 TO N BY 1;
(4.2b)       IF B(J) < B(M) THEN M = J;    END;
          Swap B(I) and B(M);
```

This yields the program segment

```
/* SORT B(1:N) - SUCCESSIVE MINIMA*/
   SM: DO I = 1 TO N-1 BY 1;
      /* PUT IN M INDEX OF SMALLEST VALUE OF B(I:N)*/
       M = I;
       DO J = I+1 TO N BY 1;
          IF B(J) < B(M) THEN M = J; END;
      /* SWAP B(I) AND B(M)*/
       T = B(I); B(I) = B(M); B(M) = T;    END SM;
```

4.3 Heap Sort

Problem. Sort the array B(1:N) into ascending order. (Assume B and N are already initialized.)

A number of sorting algorithms have already been given, but all run in time proportional to N^2 in the worst case. The algorithm developed here runs in time proportional to N·LOG2(N). It requires a knowledge of "trees" and "heaps".

4.3.1 Binary Trees and Heaps

A binary tree is a collection of nodes (the underlined values in the trees of (4.3.1a)) and branches (the lines connecting the nodes), which satisfies certain properties. One node, called the root node, has no branches coming down to it. Each other node has one branch coming down into it from above. At most two branches emanate downward from a node to other nodes.

Each node is labeled with an integer to its right. If i labels a node, we use the notation NODE(i) to refer to the node itself. In tree 1 of (4.3.1a) NODE(1)=8, NODE(2)=7, and NODE(3)=5.

Any node is called the father of the nodes on branches emanating downward from it. Similarly, they are called his sons. Since each father can have at most two sons, we designate them the left son and the right son. The position of a node is important. A father can have only a left son, or only a right son, or both. In tree 1 of (4.3.1a), node 1's sons are nodes 2 and 3, node 3's sons are 6 and 7. 7's father is 3.

A father's sons, his sons' sons, etc., are called his descendants. Similarly, we talk of a node's ancestors -- his father, father's father, etc. In tree 1 of (4.3.1a) node 2's descendants are nodes 4, 5, 8, and 9; 9's ancestors are nodes 4, 2, and 1.

The root node is on level 1, his sons are on level 2, their sons are on level 3, and so on.

We label the nodes in a very systematic manner. The root
node is node 1. If a node is labeled i, his sons are always
labeled 2i (the left son) and 2i+1 (the right son). Thus node
4's sons are nodes 8 and 9. Finally, we restrict our trees so
that if node i exists, then so do nodes 1, 2, ..., i-1. Thus
there are no "holes" in the tree. Tree 2 of (4.3.1a) does not
satisfy this restriction and we will not use this tree further.
This restriction is made so that later, when we attempt to map
the tree into PL/I arrays, we will have no trouble.

The following property will be useful: a binary tree is a
heap if for any node i,

NODE(each ancestor of i) $\geq$ NODE(i)

Tree 1 of (4.3.1a) is a heap, as you can see by inspection.
Tree 1 of (4.3.1b) is not, since NODE(4) < NODE(9).

(4.3.1a)

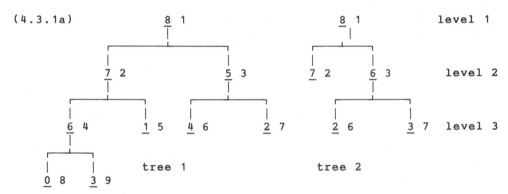

(4.3.1b)

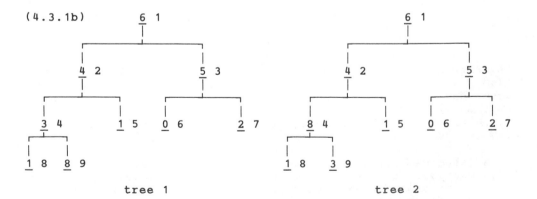

4.3.2 The Basic Heap Sort Algorithm

We now outline the basic algorithm for sorting B(1:N). First
of all, consider B to be a binary tree; the value in B(i) is
NODE(i) for any i. It is easy to calculate fathers and sons:

```
father(B(i))      is    B(FLOOR(i/2E0))
leftson(B(i))     is    B(2i)
rightson(B(i))    is    B(2i+1)
```

We shall use terms like "father(i)" when referring to B because
we must think of it as a binary tree in order to understand the
algorithm. The sorting algorithm consists of two steps:

```
S1: Make B(1:N) into a heap;
S2: Sort the heap so that B(i) ≤ B(i+1) for i=1,...,n-1.
```

As we will see, each step can be done in time proportional to
N·LOG2(N) so that the whole algorithm runs in time proportional
to N·LOG2(N).

4.3.3 Making B(1:N) into a Heap

The algorithm is:

```
          DO I = 1 TO N BY 1;
(4.3.3a)      Make B(1:I) into a heap, assuming
                  B(1:I-1) is already a heap;    END;
```

Thus we make the tree into a heap one node at a time, in the
order the nodes are labeled. For example, consider tree 1 of
(4.3.1b). The nodes 1 through 8 already form a heap. If we add
node 9 (value 8), we no longer have a heap since NODE(4) <
NODE(9). To make it into a heap we need only "bubble" the
offending value 8 up to its father, and to its father's father,
etc. until it has reached the root node or or until it is
finally not greater than its father. Tree 2 of (4.3.1b) shows
the first step of this bubbling process, in which NODE(4) is
exchanged with NODE(9).

There is one important property necessary to follow the
subalgorithm given here. This is:

Suppose a tree would be a heap except for one node j where
NODE(ancestor of j) < NODE(j) for some ancestor. Then
NODE(father of j) < NODE(j). If we exchange the values of
NODE(father of j) and NODE(j) (as in the transformation of
tree 1 to tree 2 in (4.3.1b)), then the only offending
relations can be between NODE(father of j) and his
ancestors.

Work with examples, and then prove this for yourself.

With this property in mind, we can now give the following
algorithm for the English statement of (4.3.3a):

```
    J = I;
    DO WHILE (node J has a father);
        IF B(father of J) ≥ B(J) THEN stop;
        Swap B(father of J) and B(J); J = father of J; END;
```

Putting this together with (4.3.3a) and translating into PL/I
(except for the Swap) yields the following algorithm:

```
    /* MAKE B(1:N) INTO A HEAP.  */
        HP: DO I = 1 TO N BY 1;
        /* MAKE B(1:I) INTO A HEAP ASSUMING B(1:I-1) IS A HEAP*/
            J=I;
            /* BUBBLE B(J) UP AS FAR AS IT WILL GO*/
                DO WHILE(J > 1);            /* WHILE J HAS A FATHER*/
                    FATHER_OF_J = FLOOR(J/2E0);
                    IF B(FATHER_OF_J)>=B(J) THEN GO TO EXIT_HEAP;
                    Swap B(FATHER_OF_J) and B(J);
                    J = FATHER_OF_J; END;
                EXIT_HEAP:; END HP;
```

Let us see why this is an N·LOG2(N) algorithm. Consider a
value of I, and see how many times the body of the inner loop
(the DO WHILE loop) is executed. Each iteration of the loop
"bubbles" the offending value up one level in the tree. Hence
the maximum number of times the body can be executed is the
number of levels in the tree, minus one.

If the tree has 2 nodes the level is 2, if 4 nodes the level
is 3, if 8 nodes the level is 4, and so on. The level is
exactly FLOOR(LOG2(I))+1. Thus for a given value of I, the loop
body is executed at most LOG2(I) times.

Hence the total number of times the inner loop body is
executed is <u>at most</u>

    LOG2(1) + LOG2(2) + LOG2(3) + ... + LOG2(N)

and this is bounded above by N·LOG2(N).

4.3.4 <u>Sorting the Heap</u>

The heap B satisfies the property B(father(i)) ≥ B(i). We
want to change B so it satisfies the property B(i) ≤ B(i+1),
since then the array will be sorted. Note that for any heap,
the largest value is in the root node, and that if the heap is
to look like a sorted array, that largest value must be put in
the <u>last</u> node of the tree.

Algorithm (4.3.4a) has the following property which holds
just before each execution of the loop body.

B(1:I) is a heap. Every value in B(1:I) $\leq$ every value in
B(I+1:N).   The array segment B(I+1:N) is sorted in
ascending order:

B(1)   B(I) B(I+1)   B(N)

```
+-----------------------------------+------------------------+
| These form a heap and are not     | These are sorted:      |
|greater than values in B(I+1:N)    |  B(I+1)<=B(I+2),etc.    |
+-----------------------------------+------------------------+
```

Thus each execution of the loop body takes the largest number
out of the heap B(1:I) and puts it in the correct position of
the array.

```
        I = N;
(4.3.4a) DO WHILE (I > 1);
        Swap B(1) and B(I);
        I = I-1;
        Make B(1:I) into a heap; END;
```

The only thing left is to show how to make B(1:I) back into a
heap. It is <u>not</u> a heap only because the new value in B(1) is
too small (probably); this value just came from the previous
last node of the heap. In order to make the tree back into a
heap, then, we bubble this small value <u>down</u> as far as it can go,
the opposite of what we did in the last section. However, the
process is quite similar; we need only make sure we exchange it
(if necessary) with its <u>larger</u> son.

```
    /* MAKE B(1:I) INTO A HEAP.  ONLY THE VALUE IN B(1) */
    /* DESTROYS THE HEAP RELATION */
      J = 1;
      DO WHILE (J has a son);
       K = left son of J;
       IF J has a right son THEN DO;
         IF B(K) < B(right son of J) THEN K = right son of J;
         END;
       IF B(J) >= B(K) THEN exit;
       Swap B(J) and B(K); J = K; END;
```

Putting this all together with (4.3.4a) yields the following
program:

```
/* SORT HEAP B(1:N).  */
  I = N;
  HP: DO WHILE (I > 1);
    Swap B(1) and B(I);
    I = I-1;
    /* MAKE B(1:I) INTO A HEAP. ONLY THE VALUE B(1) MAY */
    /* DESTROY THE HEAP RELATION.  */
        J = 1; K = 2*J; /* K WILL BE J'S LARGER SON */
        DO WHILE (K <= I);       /* WHILE J HAS A SON */
          IF K < I THEN IF B(K) < B(K+1) THEN K = K+1;
          IF B(J) >= B(K) THEN GO TO EXIT_MAKE_HEAP;
          Swap B(J) and B(K);
          J = K; K = 2*J; END;
        EXIT_MAKE_HEAP:;    END HP;
```

4.4 Reading Symbols

Problem. The input consists of a sequence of "symbols" on
cards.   Each   symbol   consists   of   1   to   60   nonblank
characters, and each adjacent pair of symbols is separated
by one or more blanks. The last symbol is also followed by
at   least one blank. A symbol may be split onto two cards.

    Write a program segment which, when executed, will store
the **next** symbol which has not yet been processed into
variable SYMBOL.   SYMBOL has the attributes CHAR(60)
VARYING.   If a symbol is more than 60 characters long, it
may be split into two or more symbols without giving any
error message.

    This program segment is used in the text editor described in
Section 3.2.2.   It also is useful in many other larger programs.
If developed properly, it is quite simple.

    Let us assume that a CHAR VARYING variable named CARD will
always contain that part of the input that has been read but not
yet "processed".   Initially, then, we have CARD = ''.   The
process of getting the next symbol into SYMBOL consists of
deleting blanks preceding the next symbol in the input, finding
the end of the symbol, moving it to SYMBOL, and finally,
deleting the symbol from CARD. Thus we write down the following
algorithm:

    S1: Delete blanks preceding the first nonblank in CARD
          and the rest of the input;
    S2: Find the first blank in CARD and the input;
    S3: Put the symbol into SYMBOL;
    S4: Delete the symbol from CARD;

4.4.1 Refinement of S1, Deleting the Blanks

There are two problems. First, CARD may contain nothing but
blanks, and secondly it might even contain nothing (as it does
the first time this segment is executed).   Either case will
cause us to read in more input. The following algorithm serves
the purpose:

```
/* DELETE BLANKS BEFORE SYMBOL.*/
  /* PUT INTO I THE POSITION OF FIRST NONBLANK*/
     FIND: DO WHILE ('1'B);
       /* SEARCH CARD AND TERMINATE IF NONBLANK FOUND*/
          DO I = 1 TO LENGTH(CARD) BY 1;
             IF SUBSTR(CARD,I,1) ¬= ' ' THEN GO TO TERMINATE;
             END;
       /* NO NONBLANKS - GET MORE INPUT*/
          GET EDIT (CARD) (A(80));    END FIND;
  TERMINATE:;

  /* DELETE THE BLANKS IN POSITIONS 1:I-1*/
     CARD = SUBSTR(CARD,I);
```

4.4.2 Refinement of S2, Finding the End of the Symbol

The only problem with S2 is that the symbol may be split on
two cards. We must also watch out for the length of the symbol.
We should stop when the length is 60. The algorithm uses a
CHAR(80) variable named CARD1 as a temporary location to hold a
card just read.

```
/* AFTER EXECUTION OF THIS SEGMENT, THE SYMBOL IS*/
  /* IN SUBSTR(CARD,1,I-1); */
  FD: DO I = 1 TO 60 BY 1;
    IF I > LENGTH(CARD) THEN DO;
       GET EDIT (CARD1) (A(80)); CARD = CARD || CARD1; END;
    IF SUBSTR(CARD,I,1) = ' ' THEN GO TO EXITFOUND; END FD;
  EXITFOUND:;
```

4.4.3 The Final Program

Statements S3 and S4 of the original algorithm are simple statements, so the development is finished. We assemble the various segments below, adding the necessary declarations.

```
    DECLARE CARD CHAR(139) VARYING, /* CONTAINS INPUT READ */
                                    /* BUT NOT YET PROCESSED*/
            CARD1 CHAR(80),         /* USED TO READ IN A CARD*/
            SYMBOL CHAR(60) VARYING,/* HOLDS OUTPUT SYMBOL*/
            I FIXED DECIMAL;

 /* PUT NEXT INPUT SYMBOL INTO SYMBOL.*/

   /* DELETE BLANKS BEFORE SYMBOL.*/
     /* PUT INTO I THE POSITION OF FIRST NONBLANK*/
        FIND: DO WHILE ('1'B);
          /* SEARCH CARD AND TERMINATE IF NONBLANK FOUND*/
            DO I = 1 TO LENGTH(CARD) BY 1;
              IF SUBSTR(CARD,I,1) ¬= ' ' THEN GO TO TERMINATE;
              END;
          /* NO NONBLANKS - GET MORE INPUT*/
            GET EDIT (CARD) (A(80));    END FIND;
      TERMINATE:;

   /* DELETE THE BLANKS IN POSITIONS 1:I-1*/
      CARD = SUBSTR(CARD,I);

   /* AFTER EXECUTION OF THIS SEGMENT, THE SYMBOL IS*/
     /* IN SUBSTR(CARD,1,I-1); */
     FD: DO I = 1 TO 60 BY 1;
       IF I > LENGTH(CARD) THEN DO;
          GET EDIT (CARD1) (A(80)); CARD = CARD || CARD1; END;
       IF SUBSTR(CARD,I,1) = ' ' THEN GO TO EXITFOUND; END FD;
      EXITFOUND:;

   /* PUT SYMBOL INTO SYMBOL*/
      SYMBOL = SUBSTR(CARD,1,I-1);

   /* DELETE SYMBOL FROM INPUT*/
      CARD = SUBSTR(CARD,I);
```

Section 5 <u>Problems Impossible to Program</u>

The approach to program development described in the preceding sections is generally useful, but it is not guaranteed to yield a practical program for any arbitrary problem. There are three general types of problems that are impossible -- no approach will yield an effective program. These problems are described in the following three sections. Sections 5.1 and 5.2 concern problems that are too vague or too large. Such problems occur frequently and the programmer must be wary of them. Section 5.3* introduces the existence of problems for which it can be proved that no effective program can be written.

5.1 <u>Ill-Defined Problems</u>

Many problems are just not understood well enough to program. We have suggested that in program development one use English commands and phrases, such as "solve", "find", "create", etc. This is useful, but it can lead to unwarranted optimism about the kinds of problem that can be programmed. Eventually, each of these commands must be refined or developed into the statements of a programming language. The procedure breaks down if, at any point in the development, one encounters a command that cannot be refined into program statements. For example, it is easy to write "solve", but it is sometimes difficult to figure out "how to solve". One can write "find" and not even be sure where to look.

Unfortunately, it is often easy to disguise the inability to refine such a command. For example, in developing a program to select potential companions for an applicant to a computer dating service, one must at some point refine the meaning of "appropriate date" into program statements. No algorithm capable of doing this has yet been discovered. Nevertheless, scores of people have written programs to perform this task. Unfortunately, the use of a computer sometimes lends respectability or authenticity to an algorithm that would be laughable if performed by a human.

While it is often necessary to obtain approximate solutions to difficult or impossible problems, programming ethics demand that the approximation be clearly identified, and that the program not be used to <u>obscure</u> the dubiousness of the algorithm.

5.2 Impossibly-Large Problems

Most neophyte programmers are somewhat awed by the computer's speed. Programs that take hours to write are executed in seconds, and one begins to regard its speed as essentially infinite. Therefore, it is surprising and a bit disillusioning to discover problems that are clearly and precisely stated, easily programmed, but that require so much execution time that they are effectively impossible.

The following is not exactly a reasonable program, but it may make the point:

```
/* TWO LEVEL EMPTY DO NEST */
FUTILE: PROCEDURE OPTIONS(MAIN);
    DCL (I,J) FIXED DEC;
    DO I = 1 TO 10000 BY 1;
        DO J = 1 TO 10000 BY 1;
            END; END; END FUTILE;
```

This program accomplishes nothing, but will take hours to do so. If a third level were added to the nest in this program it would become impossibly long for the largest computers that exist.

As a more reasonable example, suppose a swimming coach has ten swimmers to enter in a meet consisting of ten events, and the rules specify that each swimmer may compete in only one event. The coach writes down his estimate of how many points each swimmer would earn in each event in a table of ten rows (one for each swimmer) and ten columns (one for each event). Now he wants to determine the assignment of swimmers to events to maximize the team's score.

The obvious algorithm is to try every possible set of assignments, add up the resulting score for each, and select the best. The program shown is for only four swimmers and four events, but it should be obvious how to change the array sizes in the declarations and add levels of DO groups to accommodate different numbers of swimmers and events.

```
/* PROGRAM TO DETERMINE MAXIMUM POSSIBLE TEAM SCORE */
/* ONE SWIMMER ASSIGNED TO EACH EVENT */
ASSIGN: PROCEDURE OPTIONS(MAIN);
    DCL PT(4,4) FLOAT DEC;      /* PTS FOR SWIMMER I IN EVENT J  */
                                /* (ROW/SWIMMER, COL/EVENT)      */
    DCL EV(4) FIXED DEC;        /* EVENT ASSIGNMENTS -- EV(I) IS */
                                /* EVENT ASSIGNED TO SWIMMER I   */
    DCL MAXEV(4) FIXED DEC;     /* EVENT ASSIGNMENT FOR MAX PTS  */
    DCL NS(4) FIXED DEC;        /* NO. SWIMMERS ASSIGNED TO EV.  */
    DCL MAXNS FIXED DEC;        /* MAX NBR ASSIGNED TO ANY EVENT */
    DCL PTSUM FLOAT DEC;        /* SUM OF PTS FOR ASSIGNMENT     */
    DCL MAXPTSUM FLOAT DEC;     /* MAXIMUM TEAM SCORE            */
    DCL (ROW, COL) FIXED DEC;
```

```
/* LOAD AND INITIALIZE */
  MAXPTSUM = 0;
  DO COL = 1 TO 4 BY 1;
    NS(COL) = 0; END;
  DO ROW = 1 TO 4 BY 1;
    DO COL = 1 TO 4 BY 1;
        GET LIST(PT(ROW,COL)); END; END;

/* FOR SWIMMER 1, TRY EACH EVENT */
  ROW1: DO EV(1) = 1 TO 4 BY 1;
    NS(EV(1)) = NS(EV(1)) + 1;
    /* FOR SWIMMER 2, TRY EACH EVENT */
      ROW2: DO EV(2) = 1 TO 4 BY 1;
        NS(EV(2)) = NS(EV(2)) + 1;
        /* FOR SWIMMER 3, TRY EACH EVENT */
          ROW3: DO EV(3) = 1 TO 4 BY 1;
            NS(EV(3)) = NS(EV(3)) + 1;
            /* FOR SWIMMER 4, TRY EACH EVENT */
              ROW4: DO EV(4) = 1 TO 4 BY 1;
                NS(EV(4)) = NS(EV(4)) + 1;
                /* CONSIDER ONLY 1 TO 1 ASSIGNMENTS */
                  MAXNS = MAX(NS(1), NS(2), NS(3), NS(4));
                  ASGN: IF MAXNS = 1 THEN DO;
                   /* COMPUTE TEAM SCORE */
                    PTSUM = 0;
                    DO ROW = 1 TO 4 BY 1;
                      PTSUM = PTSUM + PT(ROW,EV(ROW)); END;
                   /* TEST FOR NEW MAX SUM; SAVE IF NEW MAX*/
                    COMPARE: IF PTSUM > MAXPTSUM THEN DO;
                     MAXPTSUM = PTSUM;
                     DO COL = 1 TO 4 BY 1;
                        MAXEV(COL) = EV(COL); END;
                     END; /* COMPARE */
                   END; /* ASGN */

                NS(EV(4)) = NS(EV(4)) - 1;
                END ROW4;
              NS(EV(3)) = NS(EV(3)) - 1;
              END ROW3;
          NS(EV(2)) = NS(EV(2)) - 1;
          END ROW2;
    NS(EV(1)) = NS(EV(1)) - 1;
    END ROW1;

/* DISPLAY ASSIGNMENTS AND SCORE */
  PUT SKIP LIST('SWIMMER ASSIGNMENTS');
  PUT SKIP(3) LIST('SWIMMER', 'EVENT', 'POINTS');
  DO ROW = 1 TO 4 BY 1;
    PUT SKIP LIST(ROW, MAXEV(ROW), PT(ROW,MAXEV(ROW))); END;
  PUT SKIP(2) LIST(' ', 'TOTAL TEAM SCORE', MAXPTSUM);

END ASSIGN;
*DATA
```

This program will take surprisingly long to execute. To understand why, note that the DO group for the fourth swimmer (labelled ROW4) will be executed 4^4 times. If there were ten swimmers and ten events (not an unreasonably large number) the innermost group would be executed 10^{10} times. Since a computer will execute several thousand PL/I statements per second, and there are approximately 3×10^7 seconds in a year, this problem would take <u>at least months, and perhaps years</u> to execute (depending upon the speed of the particular computer you use). If that is not sufficiently discouraging, consider a problem with twelve swimmers and twelve events.

This algorithm involves "complete enumeration" -- it examines every possible solution in order to select the best. It is a brute force solution that relies on the speed of the computer, and this turns out to be inadequate for the task. Fortunately, a more efficient algorithm is known for this problem that will easily obtain solutions for hundreds of swimmers and events. It is called the "assignment algorithm", and is described in most operations research texts. (For example, see Section III.2 in Ford and Fulkerson, <u>Flows in Networks</u>, Princeton Press, 1962.) This particular problem can be programmed and solved on a computer, because a clever and efficient algorithm happens to be available. Unfortunately, there are many problems, as simple in form as this one, where no algorithm except complete enumeration is known, and in some cases it can be proved that no algorithm except complete enumeration exists.

In general, these problems have the characteristic that their computation time grows very rapidly with increases in size of the problem. If n is some key dimension of the problem, the computing time may depend upon n**n, 2**n, e**n or some similar function of n. Such problems grow so rapidly with n that, while small problems (n = 3 or 4 or 5) can often be solved by hand, problems only two or three times as large (in terms of n) cannot be solved by the most powerful computers.

An alternative program design for the swimmer-assignment problem is shown in Section IV.4.3.3.

5.3* <u>"Undecidable" Problems</u>

For certain problems it can be proved that <u>no</u> effective program can be written. It is not just a matter of not having yet found an efficient algorithm, or not yet having computers that are fast enough -- it can be rigorously proved that no program is possible. One important branch of computer science is concerned with classifying problems according to degree of difficulty (rate at which execution time increases with increasing values of n) and, in particular, identifying such non-computable problems. In most cases rather sophisticated mathematical arguments are involved, but the following example will suggest the general nature of the problems and proofs.

Suppose one is asked to write a program TRUTHTEST that will
be able to determine the truth or falsity of a certain
restricted class of English statements. Assume that each such
statement is given an identifying label prefix. For example:

STATEMENT_23: ROSES ARE RED.

After processing such a statement, TRUTHTEST would produce one
of two possible outputs:

STATEMENT_23 IS FALSE.   or   STATEMENT_23 IS TRUE.

Suppose TRUTHTEST was presented with the following statement
as data:

STATEMENT_9: STATEMENT_9 IS FALSE.

If TRUTHTEST reports

STATEMENT_9 IS FALSE.

it will be confirming the truth of the statement it is declaring
to be false. This is a contradiction. If TRUTHTEST reports

STATEMENT_9 IS TRUE.

it will be contradicting a statement that it claims is true.
The only resolution of this paradox is to conclude that it is
impossible to produce a program that will do what TRUTHTEST is
supposed to do.

It might seem that the difficulty lies in the definition of
truth and falsity -- that is, this is an example of an "ill-
defined" problem, as discussed in Section 5.1. The following
example should clarify the distinction. It is similar to the
TRUTHTEST problem, but the task is more precisely defined.
Nevertheless, it leads to the same type of paradox and
conclusion of impossibility.

Suppose one is asked to write a program that will test
programs for the presence of a certain type of error called an
"infinite iterative loop". (See Section I.4.2.1.) If a program
contains an infinite iterative loop (abbreviate this as "iil")
it will never complete execution, and it would be useful to have
a diagnostic program that would detect such errors before large
amounts of computer time are wasted. Note that one cannot
empirically test for such errors just by running the suspect
program, because one could not distinguish between programs that
would never terminate, and those that are just impossibly long
(as in Section 5.2).

The testing program TESTIIL loads a program P and data D into
character arrays. TESTILL then determines whether P processing
D contains an iil. If it does, the value "NOHALT" is assigned
to the variable RESULT; if it does not contain an iil the value
"HALT" is assigned. That is:

```
/* TEST FOR PRESENCE OF IIL */
TESTIIL: PROCEDURE OPTIONS(MAIN);
    Declarations
    Load program P and data D
    IF P processing D contains an iil
        THEN RESULT = 'NOHALT';
        ELSE RESULT = 'HALT';
    PUT SKIP LIST(RESULT);
    END TESTIIL;
```

For example, suppose P is

```
XLOOP: PROCEDURE OPTIONS(MAIN);
    DECLARE X FLOAT DECIMAL;
    GET LIST(X);
    DO WHILE (X = 3);
        END; END XLOOP;
```

If D is 4, then TESTIIL should determine that P processing D
does not contain an iil, and report HALT. If D is 3, then
TESTIIL should detect an iil in P processing D and report
NOHALT.

If program TESTIIL can be written, it would be trivial to
write another program REPEAT that is very similar, but contains
an extra WHILE loop. Furthermore, where TESTIIL will test any
program P processing any data D, REPEAT considers only the
special case where a program P processes a copy of itself. That
is, data D is a copy of program P. (It is not unusual for a
program to be read as "data" by a "text processing program".
See Part VII.)

```
/* REPEAT IF IIL NOT PRESENT WHEN P PROCESSES P */
REPEAT: PROCEDURE OPTIONS(MAIN);
    Declarations from TESTIIL
    Load program P
    Copy program P to be used as data D
    /* REPEAT TESTIIL UNTIL RESULT IS 'NOHALT' */
        RESULT = 'HALT';
        DO WHILE(RESULT = 'HALT');
            IF P processing D contains an iil
                THEN RESULT = 'NOHALT';
                ELSE RESULT = 'HALT';
            PUT SKIP LIST(RESULT); END;
    END REPEAT;
*DATA
    Program P
```

Observe that REPEAT is designed so that

a) REPEAT processing data P halts only if P processing data
   P does not halt, and

b) REPEAT processing data P does not halt only if P
   processing data P does halt.

Since program P can be _any_ program, it can be the program
REPEAT.   That is, write another copy of REPEAT after the *DATA
so that REPEAT processes itself.   Now rewrite the observations
a) and b) with P = REPEAT:

a) REPEAT processing data REPEAT halts only if REPEAT
   processing data REPEAT does not halt, and

b) REPEAT processing data REPEAT does not halt only if
   REPEAT processing data REPEAT does halt.

Hence, assuming REPEAT halts leads to a contradiction, and
assuming it does not halt also leads to a contradiction.   But
REPEAT _must_ either halt or not halt.   The only flaw in the
argument is our initial assumption that a program TESTIIL could
be produced.   Therefore TESTIIL cannot be written.   No matter
what computer language is used, it is impossible to write a
program that will test an arbitrary program and set of data to
determine whether or not that program will halt.

   We should note that it is not impossible to write a program
that tests programs for errors.   For example one could write a
program that would test for missing semi-colons (see Part VII).
Only certain types of errors, such as infinite iterative loops,
cannot be always detected.

   This is an example of a phenomenon called "undecidability".
The problem of determining whether program P processing data D
will ever halt is said to be "undecidable".   This particular
problem was first proved undecidable by a British mathematician
Alan Turing in 1936 (ten years before modern computers and
programs existed).   The most readable contemporary exposition of
the idea is Chapter 8 of Minsky's _Computation_ (Prentice-Hall,
1967).

Section 6.* <u>Ascertaining the Correctness of Programs</u>

We have often mentioned the goal of developing a correct program before actually testing, and that testing should just be confirming the correctness of programs. You have probably asked "How do we know a program is correct?" We discuss this in this section.

We are not concerned so much with keypunch errors, transposition of letters, writing I for 1, and other syntactical considerations. Although we should be as careful as possible, such errors always turn up. These syntactical errors will be found only by painstaking, exhaustive testing, but once found they will be easy to correct.

We are more interested in proving the <u>algorithm</u> correct, and not its particular representation as a PL/I program. The algorithm should contain no <u>logical</u> errors. Logical errors indicate a lapse on the part of the programmer -- he misunderstood the problem, he didn't ask for enough information about the problem, or he just did not think the problem through carefully enough. Logical errors are usually difficult to correct, and often require a complete redevelopment of part of the algorithm. Thus we should be as careful as possible to avoid them.

6.1 <u>What Makes Algorithms Difficult</u>

Correct programs are difficult to write. They take time and effort. Programs are difficult to read and understand. Even the programmer himself has trouble reading his own program a month or two after it is completed. This is partly because programs must be so exact, and because there is so much detail in them. But there is another reason why programs are hard to read, one over which we do have some control if we are careful.

There are two aspects to a program. First of all, a program is a <u>static object</u>. It exists on paper and we read it in this form, usually from left-to-right and top-to-bottom. Secondly, a program is <u>dynamic</u>, in that it is executed to produce a result. The order of execution of statements is quite different from the

static order, and yet we attempt to understand the order of
events that take place during execution just from the static,
top-to-bottom description. This is complicated by the fact that
the order of events changes from execution to execution,
depending on the input data. Thus, when reading a program, we
are attempting to understand a multitude of different executions
of the program. From the static description, we would like to
understand the program enough to prove that all possible
executions are correct.

From this discussion it follows that the closer the dynamic
executions are to the static description, the clearer the
program is. On the other hand, if the dynamic executions differ
radically from the static description, then we should have a
hard time understanding the program. It also seems plausible to
use notation which clearly indicates how the dynamic execution
differs from the static description. This is why we use

```
    I = 1;                          I = 1;
    DO WHILE (...);                 AGAIN: IF ... THEN GO TO ENDE;
      S              instead of     S
      I = I + 1;                    I = I + 1; GO TO AGAIN;
    END;                            ENDE:;
```

Both of the above segments produce the same result. Both
notations alert us to the fact that the statements will not be
executed in the order they will be read. However the DO WHILE
notation indicates that an iteration will occur, that S will be
executed a number of times; while the second notation tells us
nothing about how the dynamic execution will differ from the
static description. We have to study the program ourselves to
find this out.

Programming in "levels of abstraction" helps us to keep the
static and dynamic aspects of the program close together.
Consider for example the problem of reading the next "symbol"
into a variable SYMBOL as described in Section 4.4. The
algorithm at a high level of abstraction was

```
          S1: Delete blanks in input before the symbol;
(6.1a)    S2: Find position I in the input of the last
                 character of the symbol;
          S3: Move characters 1 through I from input to SYMBOL;
          S4: Delete characters 1 through I from the input.
```

At this level, the static description matches the dynamic
execution exactly; statements S1 through S4 are executed in
order. This algorithm is easily seen to be correct. At the
next level of detail, we will have several loops, to delete the
blanks in statement S1, to find the position of the last
character in S2, and so on. Hence the dynamic aspect of the
program will not coincide with the static aspect at all. But to
help, we have broken the problem into four separate smaller
problems, which are easier to understand.

Now let us look at the basic ways we can combine statements into larger segments, and discuss the corresponding static and dynamic aspects of the larger segments. By "statement" we don't mean just PL/I statements, but <u>any</u> command or operation. There are three basic constructions, which yield <u>sequential execution</u>, <u>conditional execution</u>, and <u>iterative execution</u>.

<u>Sequential execution</u>. Suppose we combine statements S1, S2, S3, and S4 so they are executed in order, as in (6.1a). Then the static description mirrors the dynamic execution exactly. For this reason the program segment will generally be easy to understand. Each execution, no matter what the input, has the same dynamic properties; first S1, then S2, then S3 and finally S4 is executed. Note that almost all algorithms outside programming have this sequential form -- recipes, instructions to build a Heathkit amplifier, instructions for putting a child's swing set together, etc. To understand such an algorithm, we need only

1. Understand each statement by itself;

2. Determine that the statements are in proper order to do the job, and that no statement is left out.

<u>Conditional execution</u>. In PL/I we can combine two statements S1 and S2 into a conditional statement of the form

```
IF condition
    THEN S1
    ELSE S2
```

Here, the use of English words IF, THEN and ELSE and the indentation aid us in making the connection between the static description and the dynamic execution. There are of course only two possible executions, depending on whether the condition is true or false. In order to understand the program, we need only understand the two possible subcases.

If programs contained only sequences of simple and conditional statements we would have little trouble understanding them. There would be only a finite number of different possible execution sequences, the exact number depending only on the number of conditional statements, and we could consider each possible different dynamic execution and the range of data values which produced them. This would be a simple case by case analysis.

Iterative execution. The third way of combining statements is a loop

        DO WHILE (condition);
            S   END;

where in PL/I S can be a sequence of statements. (We ignore the DO I = ... form since it can be written using the DO WHILE notation.) A WHILE loop is difficult to understand since there is little connection between the static description and the dynamic execution. S appears only once, but it may be executed 0, 1, 2, 3, or any number of times. We are supposed to infer the correctness of each of these different dynamic executions just from the static description.

   There are two basic problems with iteration:

   1.   We must be able to show that the loop will halt -- that is, that the condition will become false.

   2.   Provided the loop does halt, we must be able to show that the loop performs its intended function.

Termination is often easy to see (e.g. when we use DO I = 1 TO N BY 1) but in some cases it can be quite difficult. In any case, the programmer should always be aware that he _must_ satisfy himself that the loop _always_ halts. Few programmers ever think about the problem.

   How can we convince ourselves that the loop performs its intended function? This can be difficult, and we pursue the problem in the next section.

6.2 Invariant Relations of a Loop

   The dynamic execution of a loop is quite different from its static description, and we need some technique to connect the two. This will turn out to be a relation about the values of the variables used in the loop - a statement about them which is either true or false. We illustrate first with an algorithm which we are all familiar with.

6.2.1 An Example

Consider the successive-minima algorithm to sort an array A(1:N) where N≥0.

```
         I = 1;
         DO WHILE (I <= N);
(6.2.1a)     Swap values of A(I:N) to put smallest in A(I);
         I = I+1;     END;
```

This algorithm halts with I = N+1, since I is increased by 1 each time the loop body is executed. Initially, the array A looks like the left diagram of (6.2.1b), while upon termination we want it to look like the right diagram of (6.2.1b). We want to be able to "prove" that it looks like the right diagram, but not just by mentally executing one or two cases.

```
            A(1)                   A(N)   A(1)                 A(N)
           ┌─────────────────────────┐   ┌─────────────────────┐
(6.2.1b)   │ values may be unsorted   │   │ values are sorted   │
           └─────────────────────────┘   └─────────────────────┘
```

We first draw a picture of array A that will turn out to describe A at any point during execution:

```
            A(1)      A(I-1) A(I)                          A(N)
           ┌──────────────────┬──────────────────────────────┐
(6.2.1c)   │     sorted        │ each value in this partition  │
           │                   │ ≥ each value in A(1:I-1)      │
           └──────────────────┴──────────────────────────────┘
```

We now prove several points which lead to the conclusion that algorithm (6.2.1a) does indeed sort the array.

1. Picture (6.2.1c) describes the array just before execution of the loop -- after execution of I=1. (This is true because the array segment A(1:I-1) has no elements -- I-1=0. Thus all values are in A(I:N).)

2. Each iteration of the loop leaves the array as described by picture (6.2.1c) (but of course with I increased by 1). We show this below.

3. Because of point 2, (6.2.1c) describes the array after the last iteration, and after the loop has halted.

4. The loop halts with I=N+1 and picture (6.2.1c) describing the array. Since I=N+1 the segment A(I:N) contains no values. Thus the first partition A(1:I-1), which is A(1:N), contains all the values. Since this partition is always in sorted order, the array is sorted.

We have to show that each iteration of the loop leaves the array
as described by picture (6.2.1c), that is, that number 2 above
is true. Only execution of the loop body might change this
picture, so let us consider <u>one</u> execution of the loop body with
(6.2.1c) describing the array beforehand and with I≤N.
Executing the first statement "Swap values" changes the picture
to

```
A(1)      A(I-1)      A(I)               A(I+1)           A(N)
 _____
|                 |                   |                          |
|    sorted       | a value ≥ each    | each value in this       |
|                 | value in A(1:I-1) | partition ≥ A(I)         |
|_____|_____|_____|
```

This must be so since the smallest of A(I:N) is put into A(I).
Note that now the segment A(1:I) is sorted. Thus executing the
second statement I=I+1 of the body yields the picture

```
A(1)                           A(I-1) A(I)           A(N)
 _____
|                                    |                          |
|    sorted                          | each value in this       |
|                                    | partition ≥ A(I-1)       |
|_____|_____|
```

But if this picture holds after execution of the body, then so
does picture (6.2.1c). Thus executing the body of the loop has
not changed the picture.

  This may seem like a lot of intricate detail to go through
just to show the algorithm works. Why, it's obvious from just
looking at the algorithm that it works! This <u>may</u> be true for
this simple example, but we have illustrated a powerful
technique which can and should be used with <u>any</u> loop. We
discuss this in more general terms in the next section.

  Note how picture (6.2.1c) connects the static description of
the algorithm with the dynamic execution. (6.2.1c) is <u>always
true</u>, no matter how many times the loop iterates, and we have
shown this by considering only <u>one</u> execution of the loop body.
In effect, picture (6.2.1c) is a picture of <u>what is not changing</u>
during execution. Dynamic execution is hard to understand
because the values of variables continually change, and the way
they change depends on the input data. What the picture gives
is an <u>invariant relation</u> about the variables -- a relation which
is always true no matter what the input values are.

  Picture (6.2.1c) can also be put into words as we show below.
In this case the picture says it better:

(6.2.1d) The array A(1:N) is partitioned into A(1:I-1) and
          A(I:N). A(1:I-1) is sorted. Each value in A(I:N) is
          not less than each value in A(1:I-1).

6.2.2 The Invariant Relation Theorem

We develop a simple but powerful theorem which can be useful in understanding any WHILE loop. First we must introduce some notation. Let P and Q be relations concerning the values of variables used in a sequence of statements S. We use the notation

$$P \mid S \mid Q$$

to mean: If P is true before execution of the sequence of statements S, then Q is true after execution of S.

For example, suppose I and N are FIXED variables and that

P	is the relation	$I < N$
S	is the statement	$I = I+1;$
Q	is the relation	$I \leq N$

Then P $\mid$ S $\mid$ Q is the statement

$$I < N \mid I = I + 1 \mid I \leq N$$

Note that $I<N \mid I=I+1 \mid I<N$ is <u>not</u> true. This notation is important to the proper understanding of what follows. (It is suggested that the reader do exercise 1 at this point, before proceeding.)

Now consider a loop

(6.2.2a)
```
      DO WHILE ( c );
         Body        END;
```

where c is a condition and Body is a sequence of statements, and suppose

(6.2.2b) P & c $\mid$Body$\mid$ P

where P is a relation about the variables used in the loop. That is, execution of the Body with condition c true leaves relation P true. Then, provided the loop halts, we know that

$$P \mid DO\ WHILE\ (c);\ Body\ END; \mid P\ \&\ \neg c$$

Why? During execution of the loop only execution of the Body may change the relation P. But by (6.2.2b) execution of the Body does <u>not</u> change the relation P. Thus P remains true after the loops halts. Relation c must be false when the loop halts, because that is the only way the loop may halt.

We have quite simply proved a very powerful theorem:

(6.2.2c) <u>Invariant Relation Theorem</u>

    Provided the loop halts,   P & c |Body| P   implies

$$P \; |DO \; WHILE \; (c); \; Body \; END;| \; P \; \& \; \neg c$$

P is called an <u>invariant relation</u> of the loop. It is a <u>relation</u> concerning the variables of the program -- a statement about them which is either true or false. It is <u>invariant</u> in that it remains true after the loop halts if it is true before execution of the loop begins.

    This theorem only applies if the loop halts because c becomes false. It we terminate the loop by using a GO TO, we have to use other means to check correctness. This is another reason why we don't like to use GO TOs, even for terminating loops. Such exits are of course very useful at times, and we illustrate in later examples how to handle them.

    Consider again the successive-minima algorithm of the last section. We have:

    condition c: $I \leq N$

    relation P: picture (6.2.1c) or equivalent form (6.2.1d)

    Body: Swap values of A(I:N) to put smaller in A(I);
                      I = I+1;

    Upon halt: P & $\neg$c imply the array is sorted.

    It is sometimes difficult to find the right relation P. There are an infinite number of invariant relations which satisfy the hypothesis of the theorem. For example, the relations

      array A(1:N) <u>may</u> be sorted
      $I \cdot 0 = 0$

are always true, but they are not useful in understanding any loop. We must look for the <u>one</u> relation P which, together with $\neg$c, implies the intended result.

    Let us summarize by stating how the invariant relation helps us, how it connects the dynamic and static aspects of the loop. The loop has the form

      DO WHILE (c);
         Body   END;

To understand the loop and prove it correct, we need to do the following four things (five if exits occur in the loop):

1. Find a relation P such that P & ¬c imply the intended
    result.
2. Prove that P is true just before execution of the loop.
3. Prove that P & c |Body| P.
4. Prove that the loop halts.
5. If the loop contains exits (GO TOs which terminate the
    loop) the correctness of the results upon exit must
    be ascertained by other means.

We have to prove that execution of the body with c true leaves P
true.   We do <u>not</u> have to worry about how many times the loop
will be iterated, and we do not have to worry about the dynamic
execution of the loop; just about <u>one</u> dynamic execution of the
<u>loop body</u>. This is very important.

   Of course, the desired relation P is sometimes difficult to
find.   But often the programmer doesn't really understand his
loop until he <u>does</u> find it. Without relation P he is still
groping in the dark.

6.3 <u>Simple Examples of Invariant Relations</u>

   We present here several program segments. Each is a simple
loop together with initialization statements. With each, we
also give the invariant relation which can be used to understand
the loop.   With each example, the reader should show, in the
following order, that

   1. The relation P is true before execution of the loop.

   2. P and ¬c imply the desired result.

   3. P & c |Body| P.

   4. The loop halts.

This is enough to show that the loop is correct. From points 1
and 2 the reader will get the main idea behind the algorithm.
From 3 and 4 he sees how the idea is carried out.

1. /* STORE IN X THE MAXIMUM OF A(1:N). N >= 1 */
    /* THE INVARIANT RELATION OF THE LOOP IS: */
       /* X CONTAINS THE MAXIMUM VALUE OF A(1:I) */
          I = 1; X = A(1);
          DO WHILE (I ¬= N);
            I = I + 1;
            IF A(I) > X THEN X = A(I);   END;

2.   /* SWAP VALUES OF A(I:N) TO PUT SMALLEST IN A(I). */
     /* 1<=I<=N. THE INVARIANT RELATION OF THE LOOP IS: */
        /* A(I:J) CONTAINS ITS ORIGINAL VALUES, BUT WITH */
        /* THE SMALLEST IN A(I)*/
              J=I;
              DO WHILE (J ¬= N);
                J = J+1;
                IF A(J) < A(I) THEN Swap A(J) and A(I); END;

3.   /* STORE IN SUM THE SUM OF VALUES IN A(1:N). N >= 1 */
     /* THE INVARIANT RELATION OF THE LOOP IS:*/
        /* SUM CONTAINS THE SUM OF VALUES IN A(1:I).*/
              I = 1; SUM = A(1);
              DO WHILE (I ¬= N);
                I = I + 1;
                SUM = SUM + A(I); END;

4.   /* SORT-BY-INSERTION. SORT ARRAY A(1:N)*/
     /* THE INVARIANT RELATION OF THE LOOP IS: */
        /* THE ARRAY LOOKS LIKE   */

     /* A(1)   A(I)   A(N) */
     /*   ┌─────────────────────────────────────┐ */
     /* | SORTED | UNSORTED, NOT "LOOKED AT" |*/
     /*   └─────────────────────────────────────┘ */

        I = 2;
        DO WHILE (I <= N);
          Swap values of A(1:I) so that A(1:I) is sorted;
          I = I + 1; END;

5.   In PL/I, the following program may produce a runtime error
message. Discover why and fix the program.

     /* SWAP VALUES OF A(1:I) SO THAT A(1:I) IS SORTED,*/
     /* ASSUMING THAT A(1:I-1) IS ALREADY SORTED.*/
     /* THE INVARIANT RELATION FOR THIS LOOP IS:*/
        /* A(1:J-1) IS SORTED & A(J:I) IS SORTED & */
        /* IF 1 < J < I THEN A(J-1) <= A(J+1)*/
              J = I;
              DO WHILE (J¬= 1 & A(J) < A(J-1));
                Swap A(J) and A(J-1);
                J = J-1; END;

6.   This is the binary search algorithm of Section 4.1.   It
searches the array A(1:N) for a value X. The invariant relation
theorem helps us in proving that if the loop terminates
normally, then X is not in the list. If X is in the list, then
the program stops by executing a GO TO out of the loop.

```
/* BINARY SEARCH.  GIVEN A(1:N) AND X, STORE IN J A VALUE*/
/* SUCH THAT A(J) = X.  STORE 0 IN J IF X NOT IN LIST*/
/* THE INVARIANT RELATION OF THE LOOP IS:*/
   /* IF X IS IN A(1:N), IT IS IN A(FIRST:LAST).*/
   FIRST = 1; LAST = N;
   DO WHILE (FIRST <= LAST);
       J = FLOOR((FIRST+LAST)/2E0);
       IF A(J) = X THEN GO TO ENDSEARCH;
       IF A(J) < X THEN FIRST = J+1; ELSE LAST = J-1; END;
   J = 0;    ENDSEARCH:;
```

6.4 More Complicated Examples

The last section showed several algorithms with which the reader was already familiar, in order to help gain facility with invariant relations. Here we present new algorithms. If the reader has studied and understood the technique, these algorithms will appear easy; otherwise they may be hard to understand. Remember, it is not necessary to execute the algorithm with a set of initial values in order to understand it; indeed this sometimes tends to confuse the issue. It is only necessary to go through the four points discussed at the beginning of Section 6.3.

Some of these algorithms contain nested loops. We have only written the invariant relations where they indeed help. We have also sometimes written a comment describing <u>what</u> the body of a loop does, and written the statements to <u>perform</u> that function underneath. When trying to understand the loops, read the comment as the loop body. Later, you can read the statements to make sure the statements do what the comment says.

```
1.   /* CALCULATE Z = A**B WHERE A AND B ARE INTEGERS > 0*/
     /* WITHOUT USING EXPONENTIATION*/
     /* THE OUTER LOOP HAS THE INVARIANT RELATION*/
        /*      Z*(X**Y) = A**B      */
        Z = 1; X = A; Y = B;
        DO WHILE (Y ¬= 0);
           /* DECREASE Y, KEEPING Y>=0 AND RELATION INVARIANT*/
              DO WHILE (MOD(Y,2) = 0);
                  Y = Y/2E0; X = X*X; END;
              Y = Y-1; Z = Z*X;     END;
```

2.   <u>Quicksort</u> This algorithm sorts an array A(1:N). The expected runtime is proportional to N*LOG2(N) although the worst case is proportional to N^2.

The algorithm uses a command "Partition A(L:U)..." which is given as algorithm 3 below. To understand Quicksort itself, it is <u>not</u> necessary to understand <u>how</u> Partition works, but only <u>what</u> it does.

Quicksort uses two additional arrays LOWER and UPPER and a simple variable M. <u>Their definition is actually the invariant relation of the loop</u>, which we now give:

A(LOWER(1):UPPER(1)),   A(LOWER(2):UPPER(2)), ...,
A(LOWER(M):UPPER(M)) are disjoint segments of the array A such that, if these M segments are sorted then the whole array is sorted.

Originally then, we have M=1, LOWER(1) = 1, UPPER(1) = N, and at the end, when M=0 there are no segments in this list, and hence the array must be sorted.

```
LOWER(1) = 1; UPPER(1) = N; M = 1;
ST: DO WHILE (M ¬= 0);
   /* EITHER SORT SEGMENT A(LOWER(M):UPPER(M)) AND DELETE IT */
   /*      FROM LIST IF IT IS SMALL ENOUGH,*/
   /* OR SPLIT IT INTO SMALLER SEGMENTS TO BE SORTED. IN THIS*/
   /*      CASE REPLACE SEGMENT ON LIST BY THESE SMALLER ONES.*/
      L = LOWER(M); U = UPPER(M); M = M-1;
      IF U=L+1 THEN /* A(L:U) HAS TWO MEMBERS.  SORT*/
              IF A(L) > A(U) THEN Swap A(L) and A(U);
      IF U>L+1 THEN /* A(L:U) HAS OVER TWO ELEMENTS*/
              PARTIT: DO; Partition A(L:U) into three segments
```

$$A(L) \quad A(K-1) \; A(K) \; A(K+1) \quad A(U)$$

```
      ┌─────────────┬──┬─────────────────┐
      │   ≤ A(K)    │  │    > A(K)        │
      └─────────────┴──┴─────────────────┘
```

```
          and set K.
```

```
          /* A(L:U) WILL BE SORTED WHEN A(L:K-1) AND */
          /* A(K+1:U) ARE.  ADD THEM TO LIST TO SORT.*/
          /* PUT THE LARGEST OF THE TWO SEGMENTS ON*/
          /* LIST FIRST; REDUCES SIZE OF LOWER, UPPER*/
              IF U-K > K-L THEN
                  DO; M=M+1; LOWER(M)=K+1; UPPER(M)=U;END;
              M=M+1; LOWER(M)=L; UPPER(M)=K-1;
              IF U-K <= K-L THEN
                  DO; M=M+1; LOWER(M)=K+1; UPPER(M)=U;END;
          END PARTIT; END ST;
```

3. Partition algorithm. This algorithm is given an array segment A(L:U) as input. It rearranges the values of the array segment and stores an integer in variable K so that the array looks like

$$A(L) \quad A(K-1) \; A(K) \; A(K+1) \quad A(U)$$

```
      ┌─────────────┬──┬─────────────────┐
      │   ≤ A(K)    │  │    > A(K)        │
      └─────────────┴──┴─────────────────┘
```

The value initially in A(L) will end up in A(K); this is used as the "pivot" value. The main loop has the invariant relation:

```
A(L)          A(N)            A(K)          A(U)
 _____
|          |                      |              |
| ≤ A(L)   |  unknown values      |  > A(L)      |
|_____|_____|_____|
```

When the loop halts the array looks like

```
A(L)                      A(K) A(N)      A(U)
 _____
|                              |                   |
|          ≤ A(L)              |      > A(L)        |
|_____|_____|
```

and we need only swap values of A(L) and A(K) to yield the
desired result.

```
N = L+1; K = U;
NLEQK: DO WHILE (N <= K);
   /* DECREASE K OR INCREASE N, KEEPING RELATION INVARIANT*/
   IF A(N) <= A(L) THEN N = N+1;
   ELSE DO; DO WHILE (A(K) > A(L)); K = K-1; END;
            IF N < K THEN
                DO; Swap A(N) and A(K); N = N+1; K = K-1; END;
            END;
   END NLEQK;
Swap A(L) and A(K);
```

6.5 Invariant Relations in Everyday Programming

We have discussed using an invariant relation to prove the
correctness of a WHILE loop. Invariant relations should also be
used in developing loops; in getting ideas about how an
algorithm should work.   Often, the use of an invariant relation
can lead to a more efficient algorithm.   Using an invariant
relation gets us away from thinking about how values change,
which is hard to comprehend, and instead gets us to think about
how relations about values remain the same, which is easier.

Suppose we have a problem which we feel will be solved by
some sort of loop. We have some idea of how the loop will work,
but the details are not clear. One good way of developing the
loop is the following:

   1. Write down a statement or picture of what the loop
   should accomplish; what we expect out of the loop.

   2. Write down a statement or picture of what is known
   initially.

   3. Tie the above two statements together with a more
   general statement which has the two as extreme cases. This
   should turn out to be the necessary invariant relation.

4. Now develop the initialization, the loop condition, and
the body of the loop from the invariant relation.

This of course won't always be a simple, four-step process. It
is really a trial and error process and these four steps will be
repeated, in various orders, until the final loop emerges. But
there is a major difference between this way of developing the
loop and the typical way.

The typical loop is <u>programmed by test cases</u>. The programmer
makes up some sample data and develops the program for it. He
then makes up another set of sample data and modifies his
algorithm to fit it. This process is repeated over and over
until the programmer finally "feels" his program is correct.
The chances are it is not, because he has developed it from a
finite number of test cases. Moreover, it is full of
modifications which have been inserted in an ad hoc manner.

The method outlined above has nothing to do with isolated
test cases. It is more general because it works with <u>relations</u>
<u>about the variables</u>, and not the values of the variables
themselves. Thus, any set of data which satisfies the initial
relations should be executed correctly.

We now give an example of developing a program this way.
This example, due to Dijkstra, is chosen because it illustrates
so simply and easily the power of this method. You should first
read the problem description and attempt to develop the program
yourself. <u>Then</u> look at our development.

<u>Problem</u>. Suppose we have an array A(1:N), N≥1, which
contains only the values 1, 2, and 3. Suppose we want the
array sorted. Values of the array may be changed only by
using the command "Swap A(I) and A(J)".

We could of course use a general sort algorithm, but since
the array values are so restricted we should be able to develop
a more efficient algorithm. Initially the array looks like the
diagram on the left below, while when the algorithm has
finished, we want it to look like the right diagram. These two
are the statements spoken of in the first two steps of the
development process. In the diagram, "U" represents an unknown
value.

```
A(1) A(N)              A(1)                    A(N)
 _____               _____
|        |             |      |      |      |
|  U's   |             | 1's  | 2's  | 3's  |
|_____|             |_____|_____|_____|
```

It seems logical to have a WHILE loop which at each iteration
puts one value into its correct partition, and a possible
candidate for the general picture is:

```
A(1)              A(N1)            A(N2)        A(U)      A(N)
┌─────────────┬─────────────┬──────────┬──────────────────┐
│     1's     │     2's     │   3's    │       U's        │
└─────────────┴─────────────┴──────────┴──────────────────┘
```

where N1 is the index of the first value that is not a 1,
      N2 is the index of the first value that is not a 1 or a 2,
      U is the index of the first unknown value.

This yields the simple algorithm

```
N1 = 1; N2 = 1; U = 1;
DO WHILE (U <= N);
    Determine partition for A(U) and put A(U) into it; END;
```

Moving A(U) into its partition may require two swaps. For
example, if A(U) is 1, we must first swap A(U) with A(N2) and
then swap A(N2) with A(N1). How can we reduce the number of
swaps to at most 1 at each iteration? Let us change the general
picture to the following, where the partition of unknowns now
appears between the 2's and 3's:

```
A(1)              A(N1)            A(FU)    A(LU)          A(N)
┌─────────────┬─────────────┬──────────┬──────────────────┐
│     1's     │     2's     │   U's    │       3's        │
└─────────────┴─────────────┴──────────┴──────────────────┘
```

where N1 is the index of the first non-1,
      FU is the index of the first unknown,
      LU is the index of the last unknown.

Using this relation we end up with the following algorithm.

```
N1 = 1; FU = 1; LU = N;
DIJK: DO WHILE (FU <= LU);
    /* DETERMINE PARTITION FOR A(FU) AND PUT IN PLACE; */
    IF A(FU) = 1
        THEN DO; Swap A(N1) and A(FU);
        FU = FU+1; N1 = N1+1; END;
        ELSE IF A(FU) = 2 THEN FU = FU+1;
            ELSE DO; Swap A(FU) and A(LU); LU = LU-1; END;
    END DIJK;
```

This is a <u>linear</u> algorithm. The loop is iterated N times, and
each iteration requires at most two comparisons and one
interchange.

    A subtle point should be noted about the definition of the
variables. N1 was defined as the index of the first non-1, and
was therefore initialized to 1. If we had defined N1 to be the
index of the first 2, we would have had to initialize N1 to 0
since there are no 2's initially, just U's. The algorithm would
have been more complicated. From the picture, we cannot tell
whether N1 is the first 2 or the first non-1, and we must be
careful to write down exactly what we mean.

Section 6 <u>Exercises</u>

1. Indicate whether the following statements are true or false. All variables are assumed to be FIXED.

   a) I is even ⎨I = FLOOR(I/2E0);⎬ I is even

   b) I is negative ⎨I = I*I;⎬ I is non-negative

   c) Z = A**B & A and B are integers ⎨B = B/2E0; A = A*A;⎬
          Z = A**B & A and B are integers

   d) true ⎨DO WHILE (I is even); I = I/2E0; END;⎬ I is odd

   e) I > 0 ⎨I = FLOOR(I/2E0); I = I-1;⎬ I ≥ 0

   f) N > 0 ⎨SUM = 1; DO I = 2 TO N; SUM = SUM*I; END;⎬ SUM=N!

   g) N ≥ 0 & SUM = N! ⎨N = N+1; SUM = SUM*N;⎬ SUM = N!

2. Consider the following program segment written to search A(1:N) for a value X and set J accordingly. The only difference between this segment and the binary search segment of Section 6.3 is in the statement which throws away half of the list. Prove whether the program segment is correct or incorrect, and if incorrect, indicate for what initial values it will not work.

```
FIRST = 1; LAST = N;
DO WHILE (FIRST <= LAST);
   J = FLOOR((FIRST+LAST)/2E0);
   IF A(J) = X THEN GO TO ENDSEARCH;
   IF A(J) < X THEN FIRST = J; ELSE LAST = J;  END;
J = 0; ENDSEARCH:;
```

3. For each of the following algorithms, write down what the result of execution of each loop is, and then write down the invariant relation which together with ¬c, indicates that the loop executes correctly.

```
a)   /* REVERSE THE VALUES OF A(1:N).  N >= 1.  */
        LOWER= 1; UPPER=N;
        DO WHILE (LOWER < UPPER);
           Swap values of A(LOWER) and A(UPPER);
           LOWER = LOWER+1; UPPER = UPPER-1; END;
```

b) /* STORE 1 IN P IF I IS PRIME; 0 OTHERWISE.*/
```
    IF I <= 1
       THEN P = 0;
       ELSE IF I = 2 THEN P = 1;
         ELSE DO; S = SQRT(I); J = 3;
                 DO WHILE (J <= S);
                    IF MOD(I,J)=0 THEN
                       DO; P=0; GO TO EXIT_PRIME; END;
                    J = J + 2; END;
                 P = 1;  END;
    EXIT_PRIME:;
```

4.   A game is played by two players on a grid of points (of any
size) as   shown below.   Player A first draws a horizontal or a
vertical solid line between any two adjacent points.   Then
player B draws a dotted horizontal or vertical line.   This
process continues until there are no more lines to fill in.   The
game can thus be pictured as execution of the loop

```
   DO WHILE (there exists another move );
        Player A draws | or - ;
        Player B draws : or .. ;
        END;
```

The object of the game is for player A to draw a closed curve
consisting of only solid lines, while B wins if he can prevent A
from drawing a closed curve.

   Does there exist an algorithm for player B's move so that he
can   always win?   If so, give it. This problem is most easily
solved by considering an invariant relation of the loop which
implies that A has not drawn his closed curve.

```
         .   .   .    .   .   .   .   .
         .   .   .    .   .   .   .   .
         .   .   .    .   .   .   .   .
         .   .   .    .   .   .   .   .
```

5. Write algorithms for the following problems. Each will be a simple loop, together with some initialization statements and the like. This loop should be developed from an invariant relation. That is, try to discover the relation first, then write the loop, not the other way around.

a) The GCD of two positive integers A and B, written GCD(A,B), is the greatest positive integer which divides them both evenly. Write a program to calculate the GCD of A and B. You may use the MOD function. The following facts about GCDs should help. First, GCD(A,B) = GCD(B,A). Second, if A = p·B where p is an integer greater than 0, then of course B is the GCD of A and B. Third, if

$$A = p·B + r \qquad \text{where } p \geq 0 \text{ and } 0 < r < B,$$

and p and r are integers, then GCD(A,B) = GCD(B,r). This follows easily by noting that any divisor of A and B must also divide r.

Hint: Note that GCD(A,B) = GCD(B,r). Suppose we initialize variables X and Y to A and B respectively. Then GCD(X,Y) = GCD(A,B). Then making the assignments X=Y; Y=r; does not change this relation GCD(X,Y) = GCD(A,B).

b) A(1:K) and A(K+1:N) are each sorted in ascending order. Write an algorithm which sorts the whole array in linear time. (It will probably be a single loop.) You may use an extra array which has no more than K elements.

c) An array TEM(1:100) contains 100 temperatures. Print out the number of temperatures above 100 and the number below 32.

Part II <u>References</u>

Dijkstra, E. W., "GO TO Statement Considered Harmful", <u>Communications of the ACM</u>, March 1968

Dijkstra, E. W., <u>Notes on Structured Programming</u>, Eindhoven University, 1970

Dijkstra, E. W., <u>A Short Introduction to the Art of Programming</u>, Eindhoven University, 1971

Mills, H., "Top Down Programming in Large Systems", in Rustin (ed.), <u>Debugging Techniques in Large Systems</u>, Prentice-Hall, 1971

Polya, G., <u>How to Solve It</u>, Princeton, 1945 (also excerpted in Newman, <u>The World of Mathematics</u>, <u>Vol. 3</u>, Simon & Schuster 1956)

Weinberg, G. M., <u>The Psychology of Computer Programming</u>, Van Nostrand, 1971

Wirth, N., "Program Development by Stepwise Refinement", <u>Communications of the ACM</u>, April 1971

Wirth, N., <u>Systematic Programming: An Introduction</u>, Prentice-Hall, 1973

Part III

CONFIRMATION OF PROGRAM CORRECTNESS

Section 1 <u>Errors, Testing and "Correctness"</u>

To establish the correctness of a program we must have a clear understanding of exactly what correctness means with respect to programs. The obvious definition is that a <u>correct program is one that completely and precisely satisfies the problem requirements</u>. This is a necessary condition for correctness, but it is often not sufficient, since problem requirements are rarely stated with the exhaustive precision that is necessary to serve as a complete standard for correctness. Generally a significant part of the problem requirements, particularly with regard to proper reaction to errors, is implicit. Without explicitly stating it, <u>most problems require that a program take some "reasonable" action in every conceivable situation</u>.

In effect, this corresponds to the "implied warranty of merchantability" that accompanies a manufactured product. A consumer is presumably entitled to assume that a manufactured product is "suitable for the purpose for which it is intended". This means that the purchaser of an automobile does not have to explicitly state his requirement that all of the wheels remain firmly attached to the car in normal usage, nor does he have to obtain written assurance to that effect from the supplier. In the same way, much is assumed about the performance of a computer program, without its having been explicitly detailed in the problem requirements. The user of a program is entitled to consider it incorrect if it fails to satisfy implicit requirements, as well as if it fails on explicit requirements.

For example, suppose the initial specification of a problem is to "add two numbers together". After discussion with the programmer, this might be refined to something like: "add two non-negative decimal integers, given on a data card, and print the answer". A great deal remains implicit in this description. Suppose the program encounters improper data. With no more specification than shown above, the user is nevertheless entitled to assume that

a) the program will not accept and process improper data as if it were proper, and

b) if the program fails to run with some set of data it will give some explanation of its refusal.

The program is incorrect if it processes invalid data without objection, or fails to process but gives no explanation, even if neither point is explicit in the problem description.

If there is some uncertainty as to what constitutes "reasonable behavior", or if the user requires some unusual response, then that must be made explicit. For example, if the program is required to "repair and proceed" this must be made clear in the description. Alternatively, if the user knows that the program will be used only in a context that guarantees certain conditions, then for the sake of efficiency he may wish to eliminate redundant testing. However, this must be made explicit in the description, and in comments in the program itself (since many programs that will be "always used in context ..." eventually are used in other ways with unfortunate results).

As might be imagined this often leads to acrimonious discussion between those who provide problem descriptions, and those who write programs. Unfortunately, the objective of the discussion is generally to assign blame for a program belatedly found to be incorrect. The programmer takes the position that there is no such thing as implicit requirements -- anything not explicitly specified is entirely at his option. The user takes the position that, in retrospect, anything he expects the program to do but neglected to specify, was covered by the implicit commonsense requirements. Such discussions should make both parties realize that implicit requirements are an inherent part of most problem descriptions, and that it is a mutual responsibility to explore this subject to ensure mutual understanding of context of use, nature of errors, appropriate reactions and communications. Both parties, being human, resist this conclusion.

The primary responsibility rests with the programmer. A program is incorrect if it does not serve the user's purposes. This may occur because the programmer failed to elicit an adequate description, because he failed to recognize implicit requirements, or because he made mistakes in designing the algorithm or in translating the algorithm into a programming language. Most programmers admit responsibility for only the last two sources of error, but the distinction between these different types of failure is not inherently interesting to a user with an unsolved problem.

Correctness is absolute -- a program is either correct or it is not. "Almost correct" may sometimes be better than "doesn't work at all", but there are many circumstances in which it would be preferable not to use a program rather than to be surprised

by its unexpected failure. One does not say that a program is
"98% correct" meaning that it will perform properly on 98% of
all possible input values. Rather, one seeks to specify
circumstances, and ranges and types of input for which the
program will <u>always</u> perform properly.

An <u>error</u> is anything that prevents a program from being
correct. Examples include:

a) a missing comma in a declaration

b) an improper condition in a WHILE loop that causes the
   loop to iterate once too often

c) the omission of a test for a certain type of input error

d) the failure to provide explanation when an event
   requiring user action is detected

e) a flaw in the algorithm so that the program doesn't
   solve quite the right problem.

There are a discouraging number of different types of errors,
and one error of any type is sufficient to prevent a program
from being correct.

<u>Testing</u> is the process of confirming that a program is
correct. It is the <u>demonstration that errors are not present</u>.
That is not the same thing as repeatedly running a program on a
set of test data, eliminating whatever errors may appear, until
finally proper answers are obtained. Testing is the process of
demonstrating, section by section, that the program does
precisely what it should under every possible set of
circumstances.

Section 2 <u>The Strategy of Testing</u>

Attitude in testing is as important as technique. First, testing is not something done in response to the appearance of errors; it is the process by which errors are forced to reveal themselves. Second, you must accept the fact that errors almost certainly exist in any new program. If they do not appear, it is likely that you have not done an adequate job of testing, and not that you are a uniquely competent programmer. <u>Correct programs are very rarely written</u>; they are almost always obtained by the painstaking testing and modification of an initially incorrect program.

The testing process is impeded by the universal human reluctance to admit fallibility. We each prefer to believe that our program creations are lovely and correct, and we abandon that hypothesis only in the face of overwhelming evidence. Testing would progress more rapidly if initial programs were regarded as preliminary drafts, to be completed by testing and modification. On very rare occasions we may enjoy the pleasant surprise of discovering that some section of program was in fact correct as initially written.

A major obstacle to effective testing is overcome when the neophyte programmer finally comes to accept the fact that <u>all</u> of the errors in the program are his responsibility, and his alone. There are three scapegoats commonly used to postpone acceptance of this fact. These are the <u>computer</u>, the <u>programming language</u>, and <u>whoever specified the problem</u>. We attempted to exonerate the latter in Section 1; now we will clear the computer and the language.

True machine errors are exceedingly rare. It is unlikely that you will ever be the victim of such an event, so every time you become convinced a machine error is the only possible explanation of some strange behavior, you are just postponing the eventual necessity of discovering what really happened.

Blaming errors on the programming language is a similar delusion. Every programming language has its set of surprises -- things that are done in an unexpected way. (PL/I is especially culpable in this regard.) While the language may be unreasonable, it is <u>not wrong</u>, since a computing language constitutes its own definition of what it means. It is your responsibility to learn what the language actually means, and what execution will actually do, rather than assume it means whatever you think is reasonable.

In this connection you might as well learn to distrust every source of assistance in the programming process, except the computer. Programming language reference manuals are not immune to error, and programming textbooks (including this one) are notoriously bad in this regard. Each teacher, and each programming consultant at your computing center harbors his own misconceptions as to what will happen if you do certain things in the program. Each of these resources should be regarded as only slightly more reliable than a weather forecast: it is generally comforting to have available; it will often be helpful; but it will occasionally be wrong and embarrassing. The only definitive answer to "what will happen if ... " is obtained by trying it on the computer.

Some people consider it more interesting and challenging to search for a subtle, well-hidden error than to write programs. The ability to test efficiently and effectively is a skill that must be learned. The general concepts and strategies are applicable to all programming languages; the details of syntax and tactics will vary depending upon the particular language being used, and even upon the particular dialect of that language. (For example, PL/C and PL/I differ significantly in this regard.)

Testing can be usefully viewed as a game. To play, you assume that your correct program has been deliberately sabotaged by some malevolent error fiend (a "MERF"). He has systematically, ingeniously and maliciously hidden as many errors as possible in your program. The MERF will seek to give you a false confidence by planting a few obvious missing semicolons and keypunch transpositions in plain view. He is actually counting on much cleverer devices. (For example, "partially offsetting errors" -- two or more errors that compensate for each other, under <u>most</u> circumstances.) You win if every error is identified and removed. The MERF wins if

a) you miss an error and announce that the program is correct,

b) you know something is wrong, but cannot identify or correct it,

c) you run out of time, and the program is due before testing can be completed.

2.1 Bottom-Up Program Testing

Large programs cannot be adequately tested as a single program with the techniques available today. Small programs, or program segments can be tested, and if a program has been properly designed, one can infer its correctness from the demonstrated correctness of its component parts. The point can be argued by analogy. Suppose a machine is designed to report the outcome of a sequence of ten tosses of a coin, by printing a sequence of H's and T's (for "heads" and "tails"). The machine is to be tested to confirm that for every possible sequence of tosses, it will report the correct sequence of letters. There are 2^{10} or 1024 possible sequences, and one could try each of them. However, if one knew that the machine was comprised of ten gadgets, each responsible for reporting one particular toss, and that the structure of the machine ensured that the action of the gadgets was independent of each other, then one could test each gadget separately for its two possible actions. This would require only $2 \cdot 10$ or 20 tests.

The analogy is strained but the point is nonetheless valid. Programs must be designed so that relatively small, manageable segments can be exhaustively tested. Then large programs can be built up from such segments which are known to be correct.

This process is called "bottom-up" testing. It is essentially an inversion of the process by which the program is developed. In Section II.3, program development was represented as a tree, with the root being the problem requirement, and the leaves being the statements in a programming language. Now we start with the leaves and work our way back down to the root (up the page) confirming the correct performance of each subtree. This is not only a paper exercise, in which we check over what we have written (although that is an excellent way to start), but an actual demonstration of performance, by having each segment executed on the computer.

The bottom level of the program tree, at which testing begins, consists of individual statements in the programming language. One might think that the programmer should <u>know</u> exactly what each individual statement will do, so that testing could begin at the next level, by testing the function of various sequences of statements. While this is true in general, it is sometimes necessary to exhaustively test a single statement. This most often occurs in situations where the effect of internal representation of value is important, or where the precise result of a certain manipulation is not known. Unfortunately, PL/I has some curious and unobvious ways of doing things, and sometimes the mysterious behavior of a segment is explained only by descending to a statement level -- and perhaps discovering that you do not understand how PL/I performs a certain type of addition.

2.1.1 <u>Parallel Testing</u>

   Although a program consists of a <u>sequence of segments</u>, it
should be initially tested as if it were a <u>set of segments</u>.
That is, the segments should be tested as if they were
independent of each other, and not subject to any particular
ordering. Testing of segments at the same level of the tree
should proceed in parallel, as far as this is practical.

   It is often not feasible to physically separate, and submit
program segments for processing as if each were a separate
program, but there are many tricks by which temporary
independence can be achieved for testing purposes. For example,
suppose there are two segments, described by their summary
comments:

```
              ...
              /* A.3 SET YMIN TO MINIMUM VALUE OF ARRAY Y */
(2.1.1a)      ...
              /* A.4  SEARCH XFACTOR TABLE FOR ENTRY = YMIN-LIMIT */
              ...
```

In testing (2.1.1a) one could insert a temporary segment, as
follows:

```
              ...
              /* A.3 SET YMIN TO MINIMUM VALUE OF ARRAY Y */
              ...
(2.1.1b)      /* DIAGNOSTIC A.3/A.4 INTERFACE */
              PUT SKIP(3) LIST('A.3/A.4',YMIN);
              GET LIST(YMIN);
              /* A.4  SEARCH XFACTOR TABLE FOR ENTRY = YMIN-LIMIT */
              ...
```

The temporary interface in (2.1.1b) reports the results of the
previous segment, and establishes the conditions necessary for
preliminary testing of the following segment. This means that
the SEARCH routine is temporarily independent of the SET YMIN
routine and its predecessors. Even if the array Y is improper,
or if the SET YMIN routine does not work, the SEARCH routine
will be provided with a reasonable value on which to test its
performance. It can then be provided with deliberately
unreasonable values to test its defenses, without having to
force the earlier sections of the program to generate these
particular values.

   The interface in (2.1.1b) is itself a potential hazard. If
it were inadvertently left in place after testing was completed,
the results would be disastrous. Such temporary routines should
be clearly identified as such, and a careful <u>log of all such
diagnostic insertions</u> should be kept. When the inserted routine
has served its purpose, its removal should be noted in this log.
(Section 4.4.1 describes a special PL/C facility that is useful
in such cases.)

   There are situations where sequential testing is inevitable.
For example:

```
        . . .
/* LOAD ARRAY Q, FILLING OUT HOLES WITH ZEROES */
        . . .
/* PERFORM DOUBLE INVOLUTED TRIANGULATION ON Q */
        . . .
```

To test the LOAD and PERFORM segments in parallel, one would have to insert a diagnostic routine that would probably be very similar to the LOAD segment. In this case it would be sensible to test the LOAD segment first.

2.2 Information Requirements

Computers are quite cooperative in providing information about what takes place in execution of a program, but only in response to specific requests. They show little initiative in supplying information about execution unless it is requested in detail.

Basically, one needs to know where the program is going, and what new values are generated. If one knew the exact order in which statements are executed, and knew each new value placed in memory, there would be no mystery about the execution of a program. In principle, obtaining such complete information is not difficult. One could add statements to a program as follows:

a) Before each statement of the program being tested, insert a temporary diagnostic statement of the form:

    PUT SKIP LIST('EXECUTION AT POINT nn');

where nn is a unique identification number, not the same for any two of these diagnostic statements.

b) After every assignment, GET, or "DO var = ... " insert a temporary diagnostic statement displaying the new values being assigned.

c) Before every statement containing a condition (IF, DO WHILE) insert a temporary diagnostic statement displaying the value of each of the variables in the condition.

In almost all cases the resulting diagnostic output will provide all of the information that is needed to fully understand the execution. (The exceptions involve cases where the presence of these diagnostic statements themselves significantly alters the results of execution. For example, these statements would alter the action of some output statements in the program under test.)

The difficulty is just that the volume of printed output generated by this approach would be overwhelming. Computers execute several thousand PL/I statements per second. This means that for a program of several seconds' duration, the output volume would be comparable in size to this book. Hence, the real problem is to be <u>selective</u> in diagnostic output -- to obtain the required information without being inundated.

The dilemma of testing is that one always seems to have too little information in the neighborhood of the error (hence another run is required), and too much information about regions that turn out to be correct. It is an art to be able to vary the information requests in successive runs of a program to discover the existence of an error, and then to pinpoint its location and nature, with a minimum number of runs and a minimum volume of paper.

2.3 Design of Test Cases

The usual empirical approach to the demonstration of correctness is to try the program on a <u>test case</u> -- a set of data for which the "correct" answer is known. If the subject program fails to yield this answer, then obviously something is wrong and must be corrected, but suppose it does yield the correct answer? Exactly what has been demonstrated? Just that the program will produce the correct answer for <u>at least this one set of data</u>. What one would like to establish is that the program will work correctly for <u>any set of data that satisfy the problem definition</u>.

It is quite reasonable to initially test a new program on relatively easy test cases. This is useful to reveal flaws in the basic design, or gross errors in programming. Unfortunately, altogether too many programmers consider the satisfactory performance on such minimal test cases to be the end of the testing process -- where in fact it is only the beginning. Successful execution of undemanding tests is a necessary condition for a program to be correct, but it is certainly not sufficient demonstration of correctness.

Once a program has demonstrated its ability to perform satisfactorily on gentle tests, it should be subjected to the most punishing tests that a depraved mind can contrive. This is a time when the worst aspects of human nature can be usefully employed. Tests should be devised that take advantage of every loophole or ambiguity in the problem description; every quirk of PL/I arithmetic; and knowledge of the "end conditions" (see Section I.4.5.2) where programmers tend to make mistakes. They should not neglect such obvious opportunities as

    a) too much data, or too little,
    b) extreme values -- both large and small,
    c) zeros and negative values,
    d) repeated values,
    e) missing values,
    f) non-integer values.

It is not unreasonable to abuse a program in this manner, for it always turns out that innocent users will, quite inadvertently, produce more devastating data than the worst that a programmer can contrive.

2.3.1 Testing the Program of I.1.1

No matter how carefully one prepares test data, it is essentially impossible to determine that a program is correct just by studying results for test data for which the correct answer is known. The following example should be a convincing demonstration of that fact. Suppose an initial version of the program in Section I.1.1 was the following:

```
/* COMPUTE THE MAXIMUM OF NON-NEGATIVE NUMBERS */
/* DUMMY -1 ADDED FOR STOPPING TEST */
FINDMAX: PROCEDURE OPTIONS(MAIN);

   DCL (NUMBER,      /* THE CURRENT NUMBER */
        MAXNBR,      /* MAXIMUM NUMBER SO FAR */
        COUNT)       /* NBR OF NUMBERS SO FAR */
                     FIXED DECIMAL;
(2.3.1a)
     MAXNBR = 2;     /* INITIAL VALUE LESS THAN ALL */
                     /* POSSIBLE DATA VALUES */
     COUNT = 1;
     GET LIST(NUMBER);
     GET LIST(NUMBER);
     DO WHILE (NUMBER ¬= -1);
       COUNT = COUNT + 1;
       IF NUMBER = 63 THEN NUMBER = -3;
       IF NUMBER = MAXNBR THEN MAXNBR = MAXNBR +1;
       IF NUMBER > MAXNBR THEN MAXNBR = NUMBER;
       GET LIST(NUMBER); END;
     MAXNBR = 12;
     PUT LIST('NUMBER OF VALUES =', COUNT);
     PUT SKIP LIST('MAXIMUM VALUE =', MAXNBR);
     END FINDMAX;
  *DATA
  3, 7, 12, 2, 6, -1
```

This is a patently absurd program, but the point is to see if one could discover all of its absurdities by looking only at the results of test runs.

This program actually provides the correct answers <u>for the test data given</u>. If the ever-optimistic programmer accepts this as confirmation of his assumption of correctness, he will have declared an incredibly bad program "correct".

There are, in fact, many sets of test data for which this program will produce correct answers -- any set for which the maximum value is 12. Only if test data with some maximum value

other than 12 is used, would it be discovered that this program
has an unfortunate propensity to give 12 as an answer.

   Assuming the strange preference for 12 is detected, and
"MAXNBR = 12" is removed, the program will give correct answers
for even more sets of test data. But it will still have
difficulty in the following situations:

   a) The maximum value happens to be the first value.
   b) The maximum value appears two or more times in the set.
   c) The maximum value is not an integer (it has significant
      digits to the right of the decimal point).
   d) The maximum value is less than 2.
   e) The maximum value happens to be 63.
   f) No input is provided.
   g) No -1 stopping value is supplied.

A good set of test cases would detect a, b, c, f and g and it
might detect d. It would just be a matter of luck as to whether
e would be discovered.

   The example illustrates the inadequacy of   "black box
testing", in which one considers only inputs and outputs, and
disregards the methods used internally.

2.4 Returning from Program to Algorithm

   A useful tactic in testing is to attempt to reconstruct the
algorithm by examining the program.   Try to forget for the
moment what a particular section of program was _supposed_ to
accomplish, and write a description of what it _actually_ does, as
if you were looking at the section for the first time.   By
comparing this after-the-fact version with the previous
algorithm one sometimes detects unintended variations.

   For example, from the program of (2.3.1a) one could
reconstruct the algorithm:

      Set 2 as initial maximum.
      Assume one value read in.
      Discard first value, read next.
      For each value until -1 is encountered:
         Add 1 to counter.
         If value is new maximum save it; but
               if value is 63, or equal to old max ???
      Set maximum to 12.
      Print results.

By comparing this with the original algorithm, the program
errors should be obvious.

Section 3 <u>Automatic Diagnostic Services</u>

A limited amount of diagnostic information is provided automatically as the program is loaded and executed. This information is in the form of error messages, generated when the program contains syntax errors, or when its execution requests invalid actions. This information is especially helpful to beginners, since while learning the language they tend to make many errors of this type. As they gain experience, such errors become relatively less frequent and significant, and their elimination is only a prelude to serious testing. These syntactic slips and keypunch mistakes must be eliminated before the demonstration of correctness can begin.

It is a common, but wholly unjustified assumption, that the absence of error messages in the output is a substantial indication of program correctness. The absence of error messages is a <u>necessary</u> condition for correctness, but far from a <u>sufficient</u> condition. It only indicates the absence of certain types of errors, and not the correctness of the program.

3.1 <u>Detection of Errors</u>

Only two types of errors are automatically detected: errors of syntax are detected during loading and reported on the source listing, and requests to perform invalid actions are detected during execution and reported in the execution output. These are discussed in Sections 3.1.1 and 3.1.2.

3.1.1 <u>Syntax Errors</u>

Regardless of what programming language is used, every violation of the syntax rules of the language should be detected by the computer during loading of the program. The manner in which detection is announced and the amount of explanation provided depends upon the language used. In many cases the flaw is obvious and the correction is straightforward. However, in some situations the actual error may be far removed from the statement where its presence was detected. In these cases the messages provided by the computer are not always helpful. For example

       Y = X(I);

might be flagged as erroneous, not because it is improperly
formed, but because a missing or faulty declaration has failed
to establish an array X. However mystifying the error messages
may be, and however elusive the cause, every syntax error must
be tracked down. The computer may be quite confused about the
nature of the error, but there is no doubt that some error
exists, and it must be eliminated.

    After you have overcome initial difficulties learning the
syntax of the language you will become disillusioned about the
degree of help that syntax error detection provides. First, it
becomes clear that a syntactically perfect program may not solve
the given problem. Second, one discovers that there is so
little redundancy in programming languages that many mistakes
still yield a statement that is syntactically correct.

    For example, suppose an assignment statement should be given
as
       COUNT = COUNT + 1;

Consider the following variations that might somehow appear in
place of the correct statement:

    a) COUNT = COUNT + .1;

    b) COUNT = COUNT - 1;

    c) CONUT = COUNT + 1;

    d) COUNT = COUNT + 1

None of these alternatives is correct, but only d) will be
recognized as an error. Each of the others is a syntactically
correct statement, but not functionally correct in this program.
A similar example for a declaration is given in Section I.8.1.

3.1.2 Execution Errors

    In general, an execution error might be considered anything
that led to an incorrect answer, but the computer knows nothing
of correctness, and only objects when it is ordered to perform
an invalid operation. Just what constitutes an invalid
operation depends upon the language and computer being used.
There is general agreement that such actions as

    a) dividing by zero,

    b) taking the square root of a negative number, or

    c) adding two numbers whose sum exceeds the largest number
    the computer can handle

are all errors, and their occurrence will be detected and announced. Beyond these areas of general agreement, some languages are fussier than others. For example, if an array has been declared AMT(1:5), PL/C will object to the execution of a statement

        SUM = SUM + AMT(6);

but PL/I will not. PL/I will execute this statement, obtain some extraneous value for AMT(6), and provide no warning at all that anything unusual has occurred. Similarly, PL/C will not permit a variable to be used until it has been assigned a value in the program using it, while PL/I would simply use whatever value happened to be left over from the previous program in that particular location in memory.

   Execution errors of the type described above usually result from an action in some statement other than the one accused in the error message. That is, if STMT 69 attempts to take the square root of X which is negative, the problem lies not in 69 but in some other statement that assigned the negative value to X.   Execution error messages simply announce the point at which the result of an error causes an invalid operation to be requested, and give very little indication of what caused the error.

   The presence of execution error messages indicates that a program is incorrect; the absence of such error messages indicates only that one special type of error is not present.

3.2 Automatic Repair of Errors

   PL/C is unusual among programming languages in its reaction to errors. After reporting the error to the user, PL/C effects some repair of the error and continues execution. It would be nice to make a correction, but all PL/C provides is a repair. Sometimes, with luck, a repair happens to be a correction -- it achieves what the programmer intended. While that happy result occurs with useful frequency, the real purpose of the repair is simply to permit the continuation of execution. The guiding principle behind PL/C is to obtain as much information as possible from each attempt to process a program. This is not served by aborting execution at the first sign of difficulty. PL/C seeks to execute any program, no matter how erroneous it might be, in hopes of obtaining maximum diagnostic information for its author.

Some repair is effected for every syntax error. After the conventional error messages, the repaired statement is displayed. For example:

```
STMT 9              PUT LIST(X Y);
IN  9          ERROR  SY06 MISSING COMMA
PL/C USES           PUT LIST (X, Y);
```

In simple cases like this, involving commas, parentheses and semi-colons there is some prospect that the repair is a successful correction. But even this is not always achieved. For example:

```
STMT 2              DECLARE  ( A1 B1 CHARACTER VARYING ;
IN  2          ERROR  SY06 MISSING COMMA
IN  2          ERROR  SY02 MISSING (
IN  2          ERROR  SY11 MISSING EXPRESSION
IN  2          ERROR  SY04 MISSING )
IN  2          ERROR  SY04 MISSING )
PL/C USES           DECLARE ( A1, B1 CHARACTER (1) VARYING );
```

In this case, the comma after A1 is probably what the programmer intended, but the length specification (1) is just an arbitrary repair, and the missing right parenthesis is inserted in an unlikely position. The repaired declaration is syntactically correct, but it is likely that the programmer intended for A1 to be a character variable. Since this repair does not make it such, difficulties will probably arise elsewhere in the program.

An interesting example of error repair is obtained by submitting the following card to PL/C as a complete program:

```
    PTU FILE(OUTPUT A+1 'CORRECTION.
```

The resulting source listing would be:

```
STMT 1              PTU FILE(OUTPUT A+1 'CORRECTION.
IN  1          ERROR  SY00 MISSPELLED KEYWORD
IN  1          ERROR  SY1D MISSING EXTERNAL PROC
IN  1          ERROR  SY3B MISSING LABEL OR ENTRY NAME
PL/C USES           $L001$: PROCEDURE;

IN  2          ERROR  SY04 MISSING )
IN  2          ERROR  SY22 IMPROPER I/O PHRASE
IN  2          ERROR  SY02 MISSING (
IN  2          ERROR  SYEB STRING CONSTANT RUNS ACROSS CARD BOUN
IN  2          ERROR  SY06 MISSING COMMA
IN  2          ERROR  SY04 MISSING )
PL/C USES           PUT FILE (OUTPUT) LIST (A+1,'CORRECTION.');

IN  3          ERROR  SY0E  MISSING END
PL/C USES           END;

               ERROR SY1C  MISSING MAIN PROC
```

As a last resort, when PL/C is thoroughly confused as to what the programmer intended, a faulty statement will be deleted and replaced with a null statement. This preserves the syntactic correctness of the program, and permits it to be executed, but the prospects of useful output are much diminished. (PL/C will issue a warning message during execution of a program whenever one of these null statements is encountered.)

Error repair also takes place during execution of a PL/C program. For example, if a subscript references a non-existent element of an array, the error is announced, and a valid subscript value is provided. If a variable is used before it is assigned a value, the error is announced and an initial value is provided.

If the programmer employs the parallel testing practices described in Section 2.1.1, the persistance of PL/C in prolonging execution can be very helpful. Useful information can be obtained about several different sections of program in a single run.

3.3 PL/C Post-Mortem Dump

After the execution of a program is finished, PL/C automatically prints a "post-mortem dump". The nature and form of this information is described in Section I.7.2.4. Without repeating that description, we call attention to the useful diagnostic information contained in this dump.

The display of final values of variables often helps by showing intermediate results. It will also reveal variables created but never used -- often due to a keypunch spelling error, or a faulty declaration.

The frequency count for labels and entry-names gives a useful summary of the flow-of-control during execution of the program. The value of this automatic history can be enhanced by assigning labels to key statements -- so their executions will be counted. This history is supplemented by the final "flow trace", which describes flow-of-control in detail for the final part of execution.

Section 4 <u>Explicit Diagnostic Facilities</u>

For a program of any size or complexity it is impossible to ascertain its correctness by using only the results that are displayed as part of the problem requirements. The inadequacy of this information was illustrated in Section 2.3.1. This means that some temporary provision must be made to obtain additional printed output during testing.

The additional information that will establish the correctness of a section of program is most easily identified while that section is being written, hence the temporary testing facilities should be designed and included in a program when it is initially written. Unfortunately, many programmers will not admit that extra output is <u>always</u> required, and make no provision to obtain it until after the program has been completed and test runs show something to be wrong. This wastes time, reduces the effectiveness of testing, and is one of the major failings in current programming practice.

The <u>basic diagnostic tool</u> in any programming language is the <u>ordinary output statement</u>. If one learns where to position temporary output statements, and what information to display, one can test any program.

Some languages include special facilities that are more convenient for this purpose than the normal output statements. Such special facilities are only a matter of convenience, since nothing is provided that could not be obtained with other elements of the language, but they are nevertheless important. Testing is a non-trivial task, often as costly and difficult as writing the program in the first place. Powerful specialized facilities increase the liklihood that testing is properly done, and at the same time reduce its cost. Style in testing is almost as important as style in programming, and one should no more have to "hand-craft" diagnostic facilities with PUTs, than hand-craft control structures out of IFs and GO TOs.

4.1 Flow Tracing

   In Sections I.4.1.2 and I.4.4 we referred to the hand
execution of programs as "tracing". The same word is used to
describe computer execution when detailed information about the
course of execution is obtained. While this can be achieved
with strategically placed output statements, as described in
Section 2.2, PL/I provides a more convenient method.

   In order to "check" all new values that are assigned to
certain key variables, one can list these variables in a "CHECK
prefix" given before a procedure. The general form is:

```
    (CHECK( list )):
    entry-name: PROCEDURE OPTIONS(MAIN);
```

The CHECK prefix is given on a separate card so that it can be
conveniently removed when testing is completed. Note that the
list of variables is enclosed in one set of parentheses, and the
entire prefix is enclosed in another set.   .

   Every time a variable included on the CHECK list receives a
new value, a message is automatically printed. For example:

```
          /* PROCEDURE TO COMPUTE THE QUADRATIC SUM OF DATA */
          (CHECK(POINT,I,QUADSUM)):
          QUADSUMMER: PROCEDURE OPTIONS(MAIN);
             . . .
(4.1a)    GET LIST(POINT);
          QUADSUM = 0;
          DO I = 1 TO POINT BY 1;
              . . .
```

The CHECK output from (4.1a) is similar (the format is slightly
compressed) to what would be produced by the following:

```
          /* PROCEDURE TO COMPUTE THE QUADRATIC SUM OF DATA */
          QUADSUMMER: PROCEDURE OPTIONS(MAIN);
             . . .
(4.1b)    GET LIST(POINT);
          PUT SKIP LIST('POINT=',POINT,';');
          QUADSUM = 0;
          PUT SKIP LIST('QUADSUM=',QUADSUM,';');
          DO I = 1 TO POINT BY 1;
              PUT SKIP LIST('I=',I,';');
              . . .
```

   Labels can also be checked. For example

```
          (CHECK(MAINLOOP)):
          SOLVE: PROCEDURE OPTIONS(MAIN);
             . . .
              MAINLOOP: DO WHILE . . .
```

is equivalent to writing

```
    SOLVE: PROCEDURE OPTIONS(MAIN);
        ...
        PUT SKIP LIST('MAINLOOP;');
        MAINLOOP: DO WHILE ...
```

The following example illustrates the use of CHECK for both labels and variables:

```
    /* SUM INTEGERS FROM 1 TO ABSOLUTE VALUE OF DATUM */
        /* STOP ON FIRST ZERO DATUM */
    (CHECK(VALUE, INVERT, SUM)):
    ABS_SUM: PROCEDURE OPTIONS(MAIN);
        DCL (VALUE, SUM, I) FIXED DEC;
                /* VALUE IS NEW DATUM */
                /* SUM IS SUM OF INTEGERS */
                /* I IS INDEX VARIABLE FOR SUM LOOP */
(4.1c)  GET LIST(VALUE);
        DO WHILE(VALUE ¬= 0);
            IF VALUE < 0 THEN INVERT: VALUE = -VALUE;
            /* SUM INTEGERS FROM 1 TO VALUE */
              SUM = 0;
              DO I = 1 TO VALUE BY 1;
                SUM = SUM + I; END;
            PUT SKIP LIST('VALUE IS:',VALUE,'SUM IS:',SUM);
            GET LIST(VALUE); END;
        END ABS_SUM;
   *DATA
   2, -3, 0
```

The execution of (4.1c) will produce the following output:

```
    VALUE= 2;
    SUM= 0;
    SUM= 1;
    SUM= 3;
    VALUE IS:        2         SUM IS:        3
    VALUE= -3;
    INVERT;
    VALUE= 3;
    SUM= 0;
    SUM= 1;
    SUM= 3;
    SUM= 6;
    VALUE IS:        3         SUM IS:        6
    VALUE= 0;
```

When (4.1c) is executed without the CHECK prefix, the output is only:

```
    VALUE IS:        2         SUM IS:        3
    VALUE IS:        3         SUM IS:        6
```

4.1.1 PL/C Extension of CHECK

While CHECK is very powerful and useful, the resulting output can be overwhelming. PL/C provides a means of limiting this output by giving more flexible control over the region where the CHECK is effective. As in PL/I the CHECK prefix applies to the entire procedure, but in PL/C the resulting printing can be controlled with the NOCHECK and CHECK statements. When NOCHECK is executed, all printing generated by the CHECK prefix is suppressed. When the CHECK statement is executed, CHECK printing is resumed (if it has been suppressed). These statements can be positioned arbitrarily in a procedure to make the action of the CHECK prefix effective in only a small section of the procedure.

The CHECK statement can be used in another form:

    CHECK(expression);

In the execution of this statement, the expression is evaluated to provide an integer value which specifies the number of CHECK actions to be printed. After this quantity of messages the NOCHECK suppression is automatically invoked. Printing can be resumed by the execution of another CHECK statement. For example, CHECK(10); will permit ten CHECK messages to be printed, and then no more until another CHECK statement is executed.

These statements can be used in many ways. They can limit output to a few iterations of a loop:

    (CHECK(I,SUM,VALUE)):
        ...
        DO I = 1 TO N BY 1;
            IF I = 5 THEN NOCHECK;
            ...

They can deactivate the CHECK mechanism until trouble arises:

    (CHECK(WIDTH, BASE)):
    AREA_CALC: PROCEDURE OPTIONS(MAIN);
        NOCHECK;
        ...
        IF WIDTH < 0 THEN CHECK;
        ...

Another difference between PL/I and PL/C is in the CHECK printing for an array. If an array is CHECKed, PL/I will print the entire array each time any element of the array receives a value; PL/C prints only the particular element receiving the value.

4.1.2 PL/C FLOW Facilities

PL/C offers another method of tracing the flow-of-control of execution. The information provided is roughly comparable to that obtained by CHECKing labels, but it is obtained automatically, without the necessity of attaching labels to statements or listing the labels in a prefix. When PL/C FLOW tracing is invoked, any time the program departs from normal sequential execution a message of the following form is printed:

        mmmm->nnnn

where mmmm and nnnn are STMT numbers, as shown on the source listing. DO, CALL, IF, GO TO, END (and RETURN, to be introduced in Part IV) will trigger these messages.

The tracing mechanism is established for a procedure, a block (see Section IV.2), a DO group, or even a single statement by a (FLOW): prefix. As in the case of the CHECK prefix this should be placed on a separate card so that it can be easily removed when testing is completed. The printing of the messages is controlled by the execution of the FLOW and NOFLOW statements. The use of these statements is comparable to the CHECK and NOCHECK statements, except that CHECK prints unless it is explicitly suppressed, and FLOW does not print until it is explicitly activated.

The program of (4.1c) is shown below, with FLOW tracing rather than CHECKing:

```
STMT
      /* SUM INTEGERS FROM 1 TO ABSOLUTE VALUE OF DATUM */
         /* STOP ON FIRST ZERO DATUM */
  1  (FLOW):
     ABS_SUM: PROCEDURE OPTIONS(MAIN);
  2      DCL (VALUE, SUM, I) FIXED DEC;
             /* VALUE IS NEW DATUM */
             /* SUM IS SUM OF INTEGERS */
             /* I IS INDEX VARIABLE FOR SUM LOOP */
  3      FLOW;
  4      GET LIST(VALUE);
  5      DO WHILE(VALUE ¬= 0);
  6          IF VALUE < 0 THEN VALUE = -VALUE;
             /* SUM INTEGERS FROM 1 TO VALUE */
  8          SUM = 0;
  9          DO I = 1 TO VALUE BY 1;
 10              SUM = SUM + I; END;
 12          PUT SKIP LIST('VALUE IS:',VALUE,'SUM IS:',SUM);
 13          GET LIST(VALUE); END;
 15      END ABS_SUM;
     *DATA
     2, -3, 0
```

The execution of this program would produce the following output
(with format somewhat compressed):

```
    06->08     02*(11->09)         09->12
VALUE IS:       2        SUM IS:       3
    14->05          06->07   03*(11->09)        09->12
VALUE IS:       3        SUM IS:       6
    14->05          05->15          15->00
```

As with the CHECK statement, an expression may be given after
the FLOW statement to specify the maximum number of FLOW
messages to be printed. For example, FLOW(24); will print at
most twenty-four FLOW messages, and then printing will be
suppressed until possibly another FLOW statement is executed.

4.2 The Memory Dump

An alternative to tracing is to periodically display the
values of key variables. This is called "dumping memory". It
does not provide as complete information as a trace, but for
just that reason it is very useful in a preliminary search to
determine the neighborhood of an error. By displaying values at
different key points (usually section interfaces) during
execution, one can determine which intervals need to be traced
in detail.

PL/I has no special facilities for dumping, but the normal
PUT statement is generally adequate.

It is important that each dump display contain enough
identification to relate it to the proper point in the program.
For example, statements like the following should be used:

    PUT SKIP LIST('DUMP 3',I,X(I),TOTAL);

Without the identifying literal, the line produced by execution
of this statement might be quite indistinguishable from other
output lines.

4.2.1 PL/C Dump Facilities

PL/C offers a generalization of the PUT statement that is
useful for dumping. If one writes

    PUT ALL;

all of the simple variables that exist at that instant will be
displayed. If one wants a complete dump, this avoids having to
list all of the names in a PUT list. It also automatically
gives the name as well as the value of each variable.

By writing

    PUT ARRAY;

one can obtain the display of all existing arrays as well as simple variables.

4.3 <u>Limitation of Printed Output</u>

Once one has learned what type of information is useful in testing, and how to obtain such information, it becomes almost as important to learn how to effectively suppress unnecessary information. PL/C has augmented PL/I with provision to suppress output as well as obtain it. Provisions of this type have already been cited in Sections 4.1.1 and 4.1.2, but even more general facilities have been provided.

In PL/C, one can effectively turn the printer off and on during execution of a program by using the PUT OFF and PUT ON statements. The execution of a PUT OFF causes all subsequent printing actions to be suppressed, until a PUT ON is executed. Normal printing is then resumed. This suppression affects only normal output statements; error messages, CHECK and FLOW messages, and the special PL/C PUT options (Section 4.2.1) will still be printed during periods of suppression.

For example, suppose there are three main sections of a program:

```
             /* LOAD L,V & W AND ESCALATE THE HYPERBOLE */
                ...
(4.3a)       /* SOLVE THE HYPERBOLIC RECTITUDE EQUATION */
                ...
             /* DISPLAY THE RESULTS IN TANGENTIAL FORM */
                ...
```

In order to test the middle section of (4.3a), all output from the first and last sections could be suppressed:

```
             /* LOAD L,V & W AND ESCALATE THE HYPERBOLE */
                PUT OFF;
                ...
                PUT ON;
(4.3b)       /* SOLVE THE HYPERBOLIC RECTITUDE EQUATION */
                ...
             /* DISPLAY THE RESULTS IN TANGENTIAL FORM */
                PUT OFF;
                ...
                PUT ON;
```

These printing control statements can also be used to limit output to a few iterations of a segment:

```
             /* SCRAMBLE THE FRAGS AND PRINT IN TABULAR FORM */
             DO I = 1 TO N BY 1;
(4.3c)            IF I = 4 THEN PUT OFF;
                  ...
                  PUT SKIP LIST(I,FRAG(I),LEFT(N-I+1));
                  END;
             PUT ON;
```

In a long sequence of testing runs of a program it is also useful to be able to suppress the printing of all or part of the source listing (the copy of the program statements produced automatically during loading). This can be done in two ways in PL/C. The complete source listing can be suppressed by specifying NOSOURCE on the *PL/C card. This should only be used when the program is being run <u>without change</u> on successive runs, which can occur during testing, or in production use of a finished, correct program.

The source listing can be selectively suppressed by the use of two PL/C "pseudo-statements" NOSOURCE and SOURCE. By inserting these statements appropriately in the program, you can obtain a listing of those sections of the program that have been changed, and suppress the listing of those sections that are unaltered. In a prolonged testing sequence this can substantially reduce the volume of printed output. For example, the listing of the first and last sections of (4.3b) could be suppressed:

```
        NOSOURCE;
        /* LOAD L,V & W AND ESCALATE THE HYPERBOLE */
            PUT OFF;
            ...
            PUT ON;
        SOURCE;
(4.3d)  /* SOLVE THE HYPERBOLIC RECTITUDE EQUATION */
            ...
        NOSOURCE;
        /* DISPLAY THE RESULTS IN TANGENTIAL FORM */
            PUT OFF;
            ...
            PUT ON;
        SOURCE;
```

Let us restate the difference between NOSOURCE (or SOURCE) and PUT OFF (or PUT ON). The former have no effect on, and cannot be affected by, the execution of the program. NOSOURCE or SOURCE affect only the <u>source listing</u>; they are called pseudo-statements since, although they have the form of statements, they have effect only during loading and not during execution of a program. (They are treated as null statements during execution.) On the other hand, PUT OFF and PUT ON are real statements. They take effect when they are executed, and <u>control printing during execution</u> of the program. (See Section I.7.2 for a discussion of the different parts of printed output.)

4.4 Selective Activation of Diagnostic Statements

The preceding sections describe techniques in which temporary statements and prefixes are added to a program to obtain additional information about its execution. When correctness is established these temporary additions must be removed so that the program will run efficiently, and produce only the required output. In a program of any size and complexity it is a non-trivial chore to insert and later remove such temporary elements so that they are present only when required, and their introduction and removal does not create errors that were not there initially.

This task is made more difficult by the fact that testing rarely proceeds so smoothly and predictably that a particular diagnostic statement is inserted and removed only once. Often a statement is inserted and removed repeatedly in the course of testing. To facilitate this it is useful to be able to render a statement ineffective without having to physically remove it from the program.

For example, the statements that control execution printing in (4.3d) could be made conditional, and the choice of output for a particular run could be specified by data:

```
        ...
        DCL (LOADEXEC,SOLVEEXEC,DISPLAYEXEC) CHAR(3);
                    /* DIAGNOSTIC PRINT CONTROLS */
        GET LIST(LOADEXEC,SOLVEEXEC,DISPLAYEXEC);
        ...
        /* LOAD L,V & W AND ESCALATE THE HYPERBOLE */
            IF LOADEXEC = 'NO' THEN PUT OFF;
            ...
            IF LOADEXEC = 'NO' THEN PUT ON;

(4.4a)      /* SOLVE THE HYPERBOLIC RECTITUDE EQUATION */
            IF SOLVEEXEC = 'NO' THEN PUT OFF;
            ...
            IF SOLVEEXEC = 'NO' THEN PUT ON;

        /* DISPLAY THE RESULTS IN TANGENTIAL FORM */
            IF DISPLAYEXEC = 'NO' THEN PUT OFF;
            ...
            IF DISPLAYEXEC = 'NO' THEN PUT ON;
        ...
    *DATA
    'NO','YES','NO'
```

With the data shown the execution output will be suppressed for the first and third sections.

Note that a similar technique is not possible for the SOURCE and NOSOURCE pseudo-statements of (4.3d) since pseudo-statements cannot be affected by the execution of the program.

4.4.1 <u>PL/C Pseudo-Comments</u>

PL/C "pseudo-comments" offer an alternative mechanism for selectively activating diagnostic statements. The content of a pseudo-comment can be considered either a normal comment or part of the program text. Depending upon an option given on the *PL/C card. A pseudo-comment has either a colon or one of the integers 1,2,3,4,5,6 as its first character -- the character immediately after the /*. The COMMENTS option specifies which of these pseudo-comments are to be considered program text.

For example, one might write

    /*4 PUT SKIP(3) LIST('TEST POINT 23',XMIN); */

If COMMENTS=(4) is given on the *PL/C card, the contents of this pseudo-comment are considered program text. The delimiters /*4 and */ are ignored and the effect is the same as if one had written

    PUT SKIP(3) LIST('TEST POINT 23',XMIN);

If the COMMENTS=(4) option is not given then the pseudo-comment is treated like an ordinary comment, and its contents have no effect on the program.

There are seven "classes" of pseudo-comments: those beginning with :, those beginning with 1, those beginning with 2, etc. The COMMENTS option selects entire classes. Pseudo-comments beginning with a colon are considered program text if the option COMMENTS is given, or if any of the numeric classes is specified. For example, COMMENTS=(1,5) means that all pseudo-comments beginning with either a 1, a 5, or a colon should be considered program text.

The program of (4.4a) could be written with pseudo-comments as follows:

```
               *PL/C ID='MARK BODENSTEIN', COMMENTS=(1,2,5,6)
                ...
                /*1 NOSOURCE; */
                /* LOAD L,V & W AND ESCALATE THE HYPERBOLE */
                   /*2 PUT OFF; */
                   ...
                   /*2 PUT ON; */
                /*1 SOURCE; */

                /*3 NOSOURCE; */
(4.4.1a)        /* SOLVE THE HYPERBOLIC RECTITUDE EQUATION */
                   /*4 PUT OFF; */
                   ...
                   /*4 PUT ON; */
                /*3 SOURCE; */

                /*5 NOSOURCE; */
                /* DISPLAY THE RESULTS IN TANGENTIAL FORM */
                   /*6 PUT OFF; */
                   ...
                   /*6 PUT ON; */
                /*5 SOURCE; */
```

With the COMMENTS option shown, both the source listing and execution output will be suppressed for the first and third sections of the program.

A pseudo-comment can contain more than one statement:

```
/*: PUT SKIP LIST('CHKPT A4',AMAX); AMAX= 36; */
```

It can also enclose a portion of a statement, as for example, a prefix:

```
/*3 (CHECK(TOTAL,I,SUMQ)): */
```

Pseudo-comments can also be used to preserve compatibility between PL/C and PL/I. If any special PL/C features used in testing a program are written as pseudo-comments, it can be run as a PL/C program during development and then as a PL/I program when its correctness is established. Pseudo-comments are just comments to PL/I, and their content is immaterial. In this way one can take advantage of the rapid compilation and diagnostic facilities of PL/C during development and testing, and the increased execution efficiency of PL/I for production.

One problem with pseudo-comments is that they appear on the source listing just as they are given on the card, without any clear indication as to whether the contents were treated as comment or program text in that particular run. One must go back to the first page of the source listing and check the *OPTIONS IN EFFECT* lines to be sure just which comments were scanned as program text. In most cases the automatic statement numbering at the left of the source listing will help to distinguish between comments and program text. Comments do not receive statement numbers, no matter how much their content looks like a statement. If statement numbers appear, then the content was scanned as source text and the delimiters /*n and */ were ignored.

Section 4 Exercises

1. Rewrite the program given in Section I.1.1 as it should be for an initial testing run

    a) using additional PUT statements,

    b) using the PL/I CHECK feature,

    c) using the PL/C CHECK prefix, CHECK and NOCHECK statements, and pseudo-comments.

2. Repeat Exercise 1 for the program given in Section II.2, Step 6.

3. Rewrite the following program to give essentially the same diagnostic output, but without using the CHECK facility.

```
/* COMPUTE BOUNDED INTEGER SUMS */
(CHECK(LOW, HIGH, INT, SUM)):
SUMER: PROCEDURE OPTIONS(MAIN);
    DCL (LOW, HIGH) FIXED DEC; /* RANGE LIMITS */
    DCL INT FIXED DEC; /* CURRENT INTEGER */
    DCL SUM FIXED DEC;

    GET LIST(LOW, HIGH);
    IF LOW > HIGH THEN PUT SKIP LIST('IMPROPER BOUNDS');

    /* COMPUTE SUM FROM LOW TO HIGH */
        SUM = 0;
        DO INT = LOW TO HIGH BY 1;
            SUM = SUM + INT; END;

    PUT SKIP LIST(LOW, HIGH, SUM);
    END SUMER;
```

4. Rewrite the following program segment to give essentially the same diagnostic output, but without using the CHECK facility.

```
(CHECK(L1, L2, L3)):
    . . .
    L1: IF X + Y < Z
        THEN L2: Y = 2*Z;
        ELSE L3: Y = 0;
    . . .
```

Part IV

PROCEDURES AND BLOCKS

Section 1 <u>External Procedures</u>

1.1 <u>The Procedure Concept</u>

During program development we sometimes replace a command by a sequence of statements which perform that command. For example, when creating the sort-by-successive-maxima algorithm in Section II.3.2.2, we first wrote

```
/* SORT B(1:N) BY SUCCESSIVE-MAXIMA*/
    DO J = N TO 2 BY -1;
        L: Swap values of B(1:J) to put largest in B(J);
        END;
```

and then replaced command L by a sequence of statements to perform that function. It is often advantageous to <u>leave</u> the command or high-level statement in place, and to specify how to perform that command elsewhere. In PL/I we would write

```
/* SORT B(1:N) BY SUCCESSIVE MAXIMA*/
    DO J = N TO 2 BY -1;
        L: CALL SWAPVALUES; /* PUT LARGEST OF B(1:J) IN B(J)*/
        END;
```

We would then describe elsewhere, under the name SWAPVALUES, how to actually perform the swapping. This allows us to keep the various levels of programs separate from each other, making the program more readable and understandable.

This facility is provided by PL/I <u>procedures</u>. One defines a procedure -- a subalgorithm -- in one place. This procedure can then by "called" or "invoked" into action from any number of places within other program segments. In executing the procedure, it behaves as if it were copied into each position from which it is invoked. This technique is not peculiar to programming. For instance, when baking a cake we might be instructed to "make chocolate icing, page 56". The icing recipe is a separate procedure, with its own set of instructions. To execute this command, we postpone further action on the cake,

turn to the icing recipe, and execute it.   When finished, we
return to the cake recipe and continue where we left off.

To illustrate the definition and use of a procedure in PL/I,
consider the simple task of exchanging the values of two
variables. We can do this for two given variables X and Y by
using a temporary variable T:

(1.1a)   T = X;   X = Y;   Y = T;

We can write a procedure to do this:

        /* SWAP VALUES OF X AND Y*/
(1.1b)   SWAPXY: PROCEDURE;
             T = X;   X = Y;   Y = T; END SWAPXY;

This procedure definition would be placed at the end of the
program, out of the way. Then, wherever we wanted to swap the
values of X and Y, instead of writing (1.1a) we would write the
procedure call CALL SWAPXY;. Executing the call means executing
the three statements of the procedure (1.1b). It is analogous
to turning to the icing recipe, making the icing, and then
returning to the cake recipe.

Procedures in programming have another advantage which is
very important.   We have the ability to "communicate" with the
procedure when we call it, to indicate which variables it should
work with.   For example, we can write a single procedure SWAP
which will swap the values of any two fixed decimal variables,
not just X and Y. The CALL statement specifies which variables
are to be used. We write this procedure as

        /* SWAP VALUES OF X AND Y*/
        SWAP: PROCEDURE(X, Y);
            DECLARE (X, Y) FIXED DECIMAL;
(1.1c)   DECLARE T FIXED DECIMAL;
            T = X;   X = Y;   Y = T; END SWAP;

X and Y are no longer variables; they are called parameters of
the procedure.   When the procedure is called into action
(e.g. using CALL SWAP(I,J);), the calling statement supplies two
variables (e.g. I and J) to be used in place of X and Y. The
names X and Y are just "templates" or "place-holders" for the
variables, which are not known until the procedure is called.

The first DECLARE of (1.1c) is a new type of declaration,
since no variables are being created. This DECLARE specifies
that X and Y are to be replaced by fixed decimal variables when
the procedure is called.

The second declaration creates a variable T, which can be
used only within this procedure.   A name T used outside the
procedure refers to a totally different variable. The procedure
is a separate entity, and any names declared within it are
completely independent from names used outside the procedure.

The sequence of three statements T=X; X=Y; Y=T; forms the
__body__ of the procedure. This body cannot be executed by itself;
it must be called into action by a statement which supplies two
variables to use for X and Y. To illustrate a call of this
procedure (1.1c), suppose we have variables

A(1)	5 [fixed decimal]	I	1 [fixed decimal]
A(2)	3 [fixed decimal]	J	2 [fixed decimal]

To swap the values of I and J execute the procedure call
CALL SWAP(I, J);.   I and J are called the __arguments__ of the
procedure call. In executing this call, the procedure body

         T = X;   X = Y;   Y = T;

is executed as if it had been written

(1.1d)   T = I; I = J; J = T;

That is, the first argument I replaces the first parameter X,
and the second argument Y replaces the second parameter J. Note
that this all happens automatically during execution.   The
programmer just writes the procedure definition, and places a
calling statement wherever he wants the procedure to   be
executed.

   If at another point in the program we want to swap the values
of A(1) and A(J) we would write CALL SWAP(A(1),A(J));.

1.2 __Definition of a Procedure__

1.2.1 __Form of a Procedure Definition__

   The general form of a procedure definition is

   /* comment summarizing what the procedure does */
   entry-name : PROCEDURE(list of parameters);
        Declarations to specify parameters
        Declarations to create variables
        Procedure body
        END entry-name ;

   The entry-name is any PL/I identifier (except it should be no
more than seven characters); it is used to invoke this
procedure. The list of parameters is a sequence of PL/I
identifiers, separated by commas.   These identifiers are the
parameters and not names of variables. The parameter names have
absolutely no connection with names used elsewhere in the
program.

   The first set of declarations specify the type attributes of
the parameters.   __All__ parameters should be specified with type
attributes (like FIXED DECIMAL, FLOAT DECIMAL, etc.).   The

attribute CHAR(...)   must be written as CHAR(*), where the "*"
means we don't really know (or care at this point) how many
characters the corresponding variable will have. Indeed, the
number of characters can vary from call to call.   If the
argument corresponding to a parameter A is to be an array, we
use the form A(*) for a one-dimensional array, A(*,*) for a two
dimensional array, and so on. Here also the "*" means that the
bounds depend on the corresponding argument.

    The second set of declarations describes <u>local variables</u>
which are used only in this procedure. They are created each
time the procedure is called, and destroyed upon termination of
the procedure.

    The procedure body is a sequence of statements which are
executed whenever the procedure is called. Any statement may
appear within the procedure body -- an assignment, conditional,
GET, PUT, compound statement, a loop, or a call on another
procedure (as explained in Section 1.3).   Note however that
these statements contain parameters as well as variables. This
means that the body cannot be executed unless it is properly
called, with variables as arguments to replace the parameters.
We write the procedure <u>as if the parameters were variables or</u>
<u>arrays</u>, knowing that they will be replaced upon call by real
variables or arrays.

    Consider the following procedure definition:

```
          /* SEARCH ARRAY A(1:N) FOR X.   STORE A VALUE IN*/
          /* J SO THAT A(J)=X.  IF NOT POSSIBLE, SET J=0*/
          SEARCH: PROCEDURE(A, N, X, J);
              DECLARE (A(*), X) CHAR(*);
(1.2.1a)      DECLARE (J,N)      FIXED DECIMAL;
              DECLARE K          FIXED DECIMAL;
              DO K = 1 TO N BY 1;
                IF A(K) = X THEN
                    DO; J = K; GO TO END_OF_SEARCH; END; END;
              J = 0; /* X IS NOT IN LIST A(1:N).  */
              END_OF_SEARCH:;    END SEARCH;
```

The procedure has four parameters A, N, X and J.   When the
procedure is called, A must be replaced by a one-dimensional
array of string variables, X must be replaced by a string
variable, and N and J by fixed decimal variables. The number of
elements in the array may vary from call to call, as may the
length of the array elements and the length of X. One time the
procedure may be asked to search an array B(1:20), the next time
an array C(1:1000).

    The procedure (1.2.1a) also uses a "local" variable K.   K
exists <u>only</u> when this procedure is being executed, and it cannot
be referenced by other parts of the program.

1.2.2 Placement of External Procedures

Suppose a main program X will call the two procedures SWAP and SEARCH given in (1.1c) and (1.2.1a). The deck of cards to be submitted to the computer would look like

```
*PL/C ...
 /* comment describing main procedure */
 X: PROCEDURE OPTIONS(MAIN);
            ...          END X;

*PROCESS
 /* SWAP VALUES OF X AND Y*/
 SWAP: PROCEDURE(X, Y);
            ...          END SWAP;

*PROCESS
 /* SEARCH A(1:N) FOR X...*/
 SEARCH: PROCEDURE(A,N,X,J);
            ...            END SEARCH;
*DATA
            ...
```

In this case, SWAP and SEARCH are called <u>external procedures</u>, because they are external to the main procedure X. A complete program consists of a main procedure (which is designated as such by the phrase OPTIONS(MAIN)) followed by any number of external procedures, each preceded by a card with *PROCESS punched in columns 1-8.

Each external procedure is a separate independent entity, with its own variables which are created when the procedure is called and which disappear when the procedure terminates. The only means of communication between external procedures is through the argument-parameter correspondence designated by the call of a procedure.

1.2.3 The RETURN Statement

Usually, execution of a procedure ends when the last statement of the procedure body has been executed, for example the null statement labeled END_OF_SEARCH in (1.2.1a). However, PL/I also allows the use of a RETURN; statement for <u>terminating</u> execution of a procedure. If the statement RETURN; is executed, the procedure terminates immediately. Using this, (1.2.1a) could have been written

```
        /* SEARCH ARRAY A(1:N) FOR X.  STORE A VALUE IN*/
        /* J SO THAT A(J)=X.  IF NOT POSSIBLE, SET J=0*/
        SEARCH: PROCEDURE(A, N, X, J);
            DECLARE (A(*), X) CHAR(*);
            DECLARE (N, J)    FIXED DECIMAL;
(1.2.3a)    DO J = 1 TO N BY 1;
              IF A(J) = X THEN RETURN;     END;
            J = 0; END SEARCH;
```

If X is found in array A, the RETURN; is executed and the procedure terminates immediately. If X is <u>not</u> in the array, then the procedure terminates in the normal fashion after executing the last statement of the body, J=0;.

   Procedure (1.2.3a) is clearer than (1.2.1a) because of the use of the RETURN statement. Recall the previous discussion of exiting from a program segment (Section I.4.3.2). In that case we were forced to use a GO TO exit since PL/I has no counterpart to the RETURN; that can be used in a loop.

1.3 <u>Procedure Calls</u>

1.3.1 <u>Calls and Arguments</u>

   A procedure call is a PL/I statement, and can be placed anywhere within a program that a PL/I statement may appear. The form of a procedure call is

   CALL entry-name (list of arguments);

The entry-name must be the name of a procedure. The arguments are separated by commas. Each argument may be a reference to a variable, a constant, an expression, or the name of an array. The first argument corresponds to (replaces) the first parameter of the procedure, the second argument corresponds to the second parameter, and so on. Examples are:

   CALL SWAP(B(1), A(2));

   CALL SEARCH(A, 20, X+Y, I);

   Execution of a procedure call includes replacing parameters by arguments. We have described this replacement as a sort of "textual" substitution of one name for another. However, this replacement can be interpreted in several different ways, and we must therefore define more carefully what we mean by replacement, or parameter-argument correspondence. In order to do this, we must adopt a notation for describing which variables can be referenced at each point in a program.

   Let us draw the parameters and variables of a procedure in a box. Thus from (1.3.1a) we can assume that the main procedure has declared in it an array A(1:2) and four simple variables I,

J, X and T, while procedure SWAP uses names X, Y and T. When executing a statement, to determine which variable a name references, we look <u>only</u> in the box of variables for the procedure in which that statement occurs. Although both the main procedure and SWAP have a variable T, these two variables are completely separate and distinct. Names used in one external procedure have absolutely no effect on the names used in another.

(1.3.1a)

```
 ┌─────────┐   ┌─────────┐
 │A(1)  3  │   │         │
 │A(2)  8  │   │         │
 │I     2  │   │X        │
 │J     1  │   │Y        │
 │X     6  │   │T  /     │
 │T     4  │   │         │
 └─────────┘   └─────────┘
    MAIN          SWAP
```

1.3.2 <u>Calls with Matching Arguments</u>

Assume for the moment that each argument refers to a variable, and that the type attributes of each argument match the attributes of the corresponding parameter. That is, they are both fixed decimal, or both float decimal, or both non-varying strings, or both varying strings, etc. With these assumptions, we now explain in detail exactly how a procedure call is executed in the computer in terms of boxes containing the names defined within a procedure. In doing so, we will illustrate using the call CALL SWAP(I,J); where the variables in the main procedure are given in Fig. 1a on the next page, and the procedure SWAP is

```
        /* EXCHANGE VALUES OF X AND Y */
        SWAP: PROCEDURE(X,Y);
              DECLARE (X, Y) FIXED DECIMAL;
(1.3.2a)      DECLARE T      FIXED DECIMAL;
              T = X;  X = Y;  Y = T; END SWAP;
```

Execution of a procedure call takes places as follows:

1. Draw a box to contain the variables and parameters of the procedure (Fig. 1b).

2. Within the box write the parameters (Fig. 1c).

3. Make the parameter-argument correspondence by drawing an arrow from each parameter to the corresponding argument. This argument is of course in another box (Fig. 1d).

4. Within the box, write the variables declared locally within the procedure, using "/" to indicate a non-existent value (Fig. 1e).

5. Execute the procedure body. Whenever a parameter is referenced, follow the sequence of arrows leading from it until a variable is reached; use this variable. (The results of executing statements T=X; X=Y; Y=T; are shown in Figs. 1f, 1g, and 1h.)

6. Erase the procedure's box and any arrows leading from it; execution of the procedure call is now finished (Fig. 1i).

Study these steps carefully. Understanding this simple case of parameter-argument correspondence is necessary for understanding the more complicated situations that will arise later.

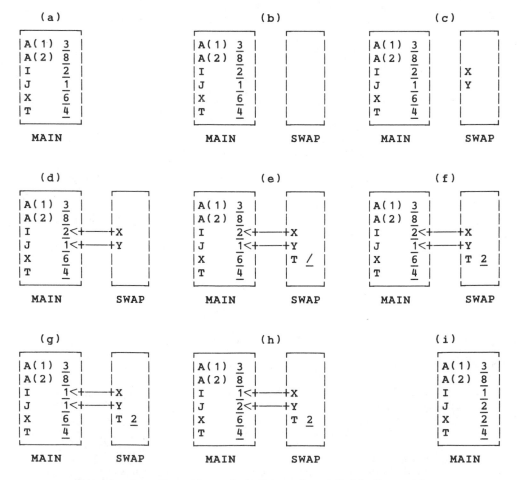

Figure 1.   Example of a Procedure Call Execution

Figure 1 illustrates several important points. First, the names used in one external procedure have nothing to do with

names used in others. The name of a parameter and corresponding
argument may happen to be the same (as in the call SWAP(X,I);)
but only then do they refer to the same variable.   Secondly, a
parameter is not a variable.   It refers to a variable. The
parameter name can never receive a value; it only points at a
variable which may receive a value. This means that whenever an
assignment X=... is executed where X is a parameter, the
corresponding argument variable has its value changed
immediately. The change does not occur after the procedure is
finished executing, but at the time the assignment statement is
executed.

   Note also that the arrow from parameter to argument is drawn
before execution of the procedure body begins. This means that
if a subscripted variable A(I) is used as an argument, the
variable to which this refers is determined before the body is
executed, and is not changed if I happens to be changed during
execution of the body.

   During execution of a program, the equivalent of these boxes
and arrows are actually "drawn" as we have depicted. A set of
memory locations are set aside to hold the variables and the
"arrows" of a procedure. The arrow locations contain references
to the locations where the arguments reside.

   Thus far, we have assumed that each argument was a variable,
with the same type attributes as the corresponding parameter.
In the next few sections, we relax this restriction, and also
discuss arrays as arguments. The only difference in executing a
procedure call will be in step 3 where we draw the arrows to
show the parameter-argument correspondence; otherwise execution
of the procedure call is exactly the same.

1.3.3 Arguments with Different Types

   The rule for parameter-argument correspondence is this:

(1.3.3a)   During execution, the arrow leading from a parameter X
           (say) which is not an array must point to a variable
           with exactly the same attributes as specified for X.

If the argument is a variable whose attributes differ from those
of the parameter, then the argument must be evaluated to yield a
value; a new variable, called a dummy argument, must be
generated and initialized to this value; and the parameter arrow
must be drawn to this dummy argument. This dummy argument will
never be referenced by name, so it doesn't matter what name we
give it. We will indicate such new, automatically generated
variables by using lower case letters for their names.

   To illustrate this, consider the call CALL SWAP(B,J); of
(1.3.2a), where B is float decimal and J is fixed decimal. The
values of B and J are given by Fig. 2a. Since B is float and

the corresponding parameter is fixed, the value 2E0 of B is
converted to 2 and stored in a new dummy argument which we have
arbitrarily named "d". Parameter X corresponds to this dummy
argument as shown in Fig. 2b. Fig. 2c shows the state of
affairs after execution of the procedure body, while Fig. 2d
shows the boxes after the call has been completed. Note that
the dummy argument was deleted since it couldn't be referred to
any more.

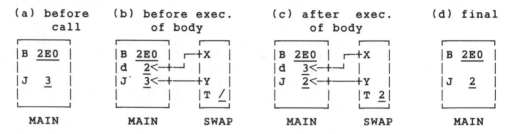

Figure 2.   Execution of CALL SWAP(B,J);

This example illustrates an important implication of rule
(1.3.3a). If we want an argument to be used as an "output"
argument -- that is, if we want the procedure to store a value
in it -- then the type attributes of the argument must match
those of the parameter exactly. Procedure SWAP could not store
a value in B because it had no way of referencing B. In this
example, the effect of the procedure call was to store B's value
in J, but not J's value in B.

Because of the hidden effects that may occur, as in the above
example, PL/C gives a warning message before program execution
for each argument which doesn't match its parameter. Actually,
PL/I doesn't allow nonmatching arguments unless an extra "entry
declaration" is also given (which is beyond the scope of this
book). PL/C allows this since it makes programming easier.

1.3.4 Expressions and Constants as Arguments

Consider the following procedure:

```
           /* STORE IN ANS THE LARGER OF A AND B */
           LARGE: PROCEDURE (A, B, ANS);
(1.3.4a)       DECLARE (A, B, ANS) FIXED DECIMAL;
               IF A > B THEN ANS = A; ELSE ANS = B; END LARGE;
```

Suppose we wish to store in L the larger of 3 and F+G, where F,
G, and L are fixed decimal variables. We can do this using

(1.3.4b) CALL LARGE (3, F+G, L);

This is equivalent to using the following sequence of statements
(where T1 and T2 are variables not used elsewhere):

(1.3.4c) T1 = 3;   T2 = F+G; CALL LARGE(T1, T2, L);

Expressions as arguments thus do not add "power" to the
language, they just provide convenience and readability.

   When an expression or constant is used as an argument, the
parameter-argument correspondence is performed in three steps:
   1. Create a new dummy argument with attributes of the
      parameter.
   2. Evaluate the expression or constant and assign the
      result to the dummy argument.
   3. Draw the arrow from the parameter to the dummy
      argument.

Fig. 3 illustrates this for (1.3.4b). The dummy variables are
designated as p and q.

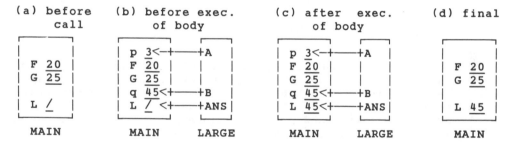

Figure 3. Execution of CALL LARGE(3, F+G, L);

1.3.5 <u>Array Names as Arguments</u>

   An n-dimensional array B can be an argument only if the
corresponding parameter A (say) is so specified, by using
A(*,*,...,*) in its declaration (with n asterisks). Suppose the
type attributes of B and A match.   Then during parameter-
argument correspondence, an arrow is drawn from the parameter A
to the whole array B. For example

```
      /* SEARCH A(1:N) FOR VALUE X, SET J SO THAT A(J)=X*/
      /* STORE 0 IN J IF NO SUCH INTEGER EXISTS*/
      SEARCH: PROCEDURE(A, N, X, J);
           DECLARE (A(*), X) FIXED DECIMAL;
           DECLARE (N, J)    FIXED DECIMAL;
           DO J = 1 TO N BY 1;
              IF A(J) = X THEN RETURN;    END;
           J = 0; END SEARCH;
```

Consider execution of CALL SEARCH(B,M,X,K); where the array B and variables M, X and K are as described in Fig. 4a. The parameter-argument correspondence is depicted in Fig. 4b. Note that parameter A refers to the whole array B(0:4), even though the procedure does not reference every element. Since M is 2, only B(1:2) is searched and the result of execution is a 0 in K.

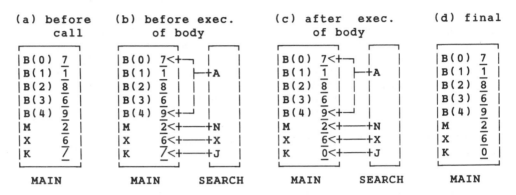

Figure 4.   Execution of CALL SEARCH(B, M, X, K);

If the type attributes of the argument do <u>not</u> match those of the parameter, then the whole array is copied into a new "dummy" array, and the arrow is drawn to this new array. This of course takes time proportional to the size of the array. Note that the <u>whole</u> array is copied, and not just those parts of it that the procedure is going to actually use.

For example, suppose we executed CALL SEARCH(D,M,X,K); where D is float decimal and the values are as given in Fig. 5a. After parameter-argument correspondence, the boxes are as shown in Fig. 5b.

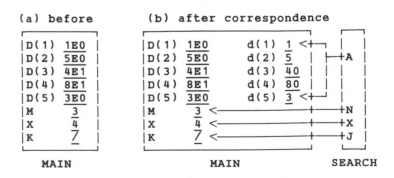

Figure 5.   Partial Execution of CALL SEARCH(D, M, X, K);

Nonmatching arguments work all right as long as the argument
array is an "input" argument -- the procedure uses the values
but never assigns values to the array elements.   However,
suppose we wanted to sort an array TABLE declared as CHAR(10)
VARYING by using the procedure SORT defined as follows:

```
     /* SORT NAME(1:N) INTO ASCENDING ORDER*/
     SORT: PROCEDURE(NAME, N);
           DECLARE NAME(*) CHAR(*);
           DECLARE N        FIXED DECIMAL;
           ...        END SORT;
```

If we execute CALL SORT(TABLE,50); the array TABLE will be
copied over into a new array, and this new array will be sorted.
This is because the attribute CHAR(10) VARYING does not match
CHAR(*) (because of the VARYING).   It will look as if the
procedure had not done its job, when the problem is simply that
the result was lost when the dummy argument was destroyed.

1.4 Nested Procedure Calls

Thus far we have been considering only procedure calls in the
main procedure. Actually, a procedure call may appear anywhere
that a statement may appear, and this includes the body of any
procedure.   From the point of view of writing a procedure, this
should not create any difficulties; one writes the procedure
knowing that each parameter will refer to a variable or an array
when the procedure is called. Similarly, when a certain
operation is needed and a procedure exists which performs that
operation, we just insert a call of that procedure with the
proper arguments.

(1.4a) shows a complete program using three external
procedures. The main program reads in a list of integers, calls
procedure SORT to sort the list, and then prints the list. SORT
uses the successive-minima algorithm.   It calls two other
procedures: FINDMIN to determine the array element with minimum
value, and SWAP to interchange the value of two variables. The
ordering of the three procedure definitions in (1.4a) is not
significant; any ordering could have been used.

Note that the program consists of four separate sections,
each of which performs some logically independent task. Each
can be understood by itself, without having to understand how
the others work.

One would rarely write such short procedures; this program
would have been just as readable had we written just a main
program and a SORT procedure, performing the FINDMIN and SWAP
commands within the sort procedure itself. We have written
(1.4a) this way just to illustrate the concept.

```
          /* READ IN 3 INTEGERS, PRINT IN SORTED ORDER*/
          SORTING: PROCEDURE OPTIONS(MAIN);
            DECLARE (A(3), I) FIXED DECIMAL;
            DO I = 1 TO 3 BY 1; GET LIST(A(I));   END;
            ST: CALL SORT(A, 3);
            DO I = 1 TO 3 BY 1; PUT LIST(A(I));    END;
(1.4a)      END SORTING;

          *PROCESS
          /* SORT ARRAY X(1:N) USING SUCCESSIVE MINIMA*/
          SORT: PROCEDURE(X, N);
           DECLARE (X(*), N) FIXED DECIMAL;
           DECLARE (I,J)     FIXED DECIMAL;
           DO I = 1 TO N-1 BY 1;
             /* PUT MINIMUM OF X(I:N) IN X(I)*/
               FI: CALL FINDMIN(X, I, N, J);
               SW: CALL SWAP(X(I), X(J) ); END; END SORT;

          *PROCESS
          /*  STORE IN J THE INDEX OF MINIMUM VALUE OF X(I:N)*/
          FINDMIN: PROCEDURE(X, I, N, J);
           DECLARE (X(*), I, N, J) FIXED DECIMAL;
           DECLARE K FIXED DECIMAL;
           J = I;
           DO K = I+1 TO N BY 1;
             IF X(K) < X(J) THEN J = K;   END; END FINDMIN;

          *PROCESS
          /* SWAP VALUES OF X AND Y*/
          SWAP: PROCEDURE(X, Y);
           DECLARE (X, Y) FIXED DECIMAL;
           DECLARE T       FIXED DECIMAL;
           T = X;  X = Y;  Y = T;    END SWAP;
          *DATA
           2, 8, 1
```

While confirming the correctness of a program, you will sometimes find it necessary to execute parts of it by hand (in order to locate an error), and some practice in hand execution with nested procedure calls is advised. It will be instructive to look in detail at the execution of (1.4a). Such execution is not difficult; it requires only patience and <u>willingness to follow the rules exactly</u>.

When a program has several procedure calls, it becomes difficult to remember where to return to when execution of a procedure is finished. To make this easier, we extend our box convention. First, label each procedure call with a unique name. Then, when a box is drawn for a procedure, put the label of the procedure call at the bottom of the box. For example, when we first execute ST: CALL SORT(A, 3); of (1.4a), we place the name ST at the bottom of SORT's box as in Fig. 6b. Upon termination of SORT we can then see that we were executing ST.

Let us now execute program (1.4a). Fig. 6a shows the variables after the list of values has been read, and just before execution of the statement labeled ST. Note that I is 4 because of the way the preceding loop is executed. Fig. 6b shows the state of affairs after the SORT procedure body execution has begun, and just before the call labeled FI is executed for the first time. Thus I (within SORT) has the value 1. J still has no value.

Statement FI is now executed. A box for procedure FINDMIN is drawn, the parameter correspondences are made, and the local variable K is created. Fig. 6c shows the boxes at this stage, just before execution of the procedure body. When executing FINDMIN, only the names within the FINDMIN box will be referenced. Note that to find the variable corresponding to parameter N, we have to follow a sequence of 2 arrows, since argument N was itself a parameter. This is allowed. Similarly, to find the array corresponding to parameter X, we have to follow a sequence of two arrows.

Now procedure body FINDMIN executes and terminates. We show the boxes just after the completion of the call on FINDMIN and before execution of statement SW in Fig. 6d. J is now 3 since A(3) contains the minimum value of A(1:3). We now execute the call SW. Fig. 6e shows the state of affairs just before execution of the body of SWAP. Note carefully where the parameters X and Y point. The parameter X corresponds to the argument X(I) in SORT. Since X is A and I has the value 1, this is A(1). Similarly, Y refers to A(3). Thus SWAP will exchange the values of A(1) and A(3).

When SWAP finishes, its box will be deleted and we will return to the point following the call labelled SW in SORT. The values of A(1) and A(3) will be interchanged.

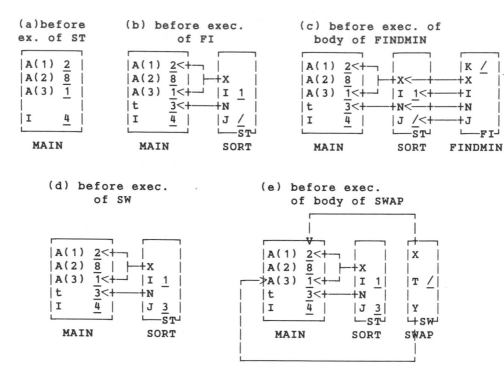

Figure 6.   Partial Execution of Program (1.4a)

1.5 Writing Modular Programs

While the unique capability of procedures is to permit a
section of program to be used in several different locations,
procedures are also extensively used in situations where that
capability is not required. Well-written programs often define
a procedure even when there will be only a single call. By
using procedures in this way, even when not strictly necessary,
one can greatly improve the modularity and clarity of structure
of a program.

A properly designed procedure, with all local variables
declared and adequate comments to describe what is accomplished,
what is assumed, and what must be avoided, is an independent
program. It can be designed, programmed and shown to be correct
without regard for the context in which it might be used. This
is desirable even when one person is writing a program of modest
size since it permits efficient testing and greater confidence
in ultimate correctness. It becomes essential as the program
size increases, when it involves more than one author, or when
the expected lifetime is long enough that changes are likely to
be required.

It is good practice to use a "main control section" which calls separate procedures to accomplish each required sub-task. This programming style prevents the details of how each sub-task is accomplished from obscuring the role of the sub-task in the overall program.

As an example, we show below a complete program for the KWIC index problem of Section II.3.5.2. The input consists of a list of titles followed by a blank card, followed by a sorted list of non-keywords, followed by a blank card. Each title takes one card. The individual words are left-adjusted in columns 1-9, 11-19, 21-29, 31-39, 41-49, 51-59 and 61-69. Thus a title can have at most 7 words. There can be a maximum of 100 titles. Each non-keyword appears on a separate card, left-justified in columns 1-9. There can be a maximum of 200 non-keywords and 500 occurrences of keywords in the titles. The output is printed one line per title, with the keywords appearing in columns 61-69.

Note how the main program is clear and understandable, since it consists of just four procedure calls and a short loop to print output. No matter how long and complex the total program might be, its overall structure is obvious and straightforward. The sub-programs are clearly separable tasks and may be tested independently of each other. (Moreover, this same strategy may be employed in any major sub-program to clarify its structure.) If modifications must be made later, it will be clear just which parts of the program will need to be changed and which sections need not be disturbed.

```
/* PRODUCE KWIC INDEX FOR TITLES*/
KWIC: PROCEDURE OPTIONS(MAIN);
  DECLARE TITLE(1:100) CHAR(69),        /* THE TITLES*/
      MTITLE  FIXED DECIMAL INIT(100),  /* MAX. NO. TITLES*/
      STITLE  FIXED DECIMAL;            /* NO. TITLES READ*/
  DECLARE NONKEY(1:200) CHAR(9),        /* NONKEYWORDS*/
      MNONKEY FIXED DECIMAL INIT(200),  /* MAX NO NONKEYS*/
      SNONKEY FIXED DECIMAL;            /* NUMBER READ*/
  DECLARE KEYW(1:500) CHAR(9),          /* THE KEYWORDS*/
      MKEYW FIXED DECIMAL INIT(500),    /* MAX NO KEYWRDS*/
      SKEYW FIXED DECIMAL    INIT(0),   /* NUMBER READ*/
      TITLENO(1:500) FIXED DECIMAL,     /* EACH */
      TITLEPOS(1:500) FIXED DECIMAL;    /* KEYW(I) APPEARS*/
        /* IN TITLE(TITLENO(I)) AT COLUMN TITLEPOS(I)*/
  DECLARE I FIXED DECIMAL;

  CALL READIN(TITLE, MTITLE, STITLE);
  CALL READIN(NONKEY, MNONKEY, SNONKEY);
  CALL MAKEKEY(TITLE, STITLE, NONKEY, SNONKEY,
              KEYW, TITLENO, TITLEPOS, MKEYW, SKEYW);
  CALL SORT(KEYW, TITLENO, TITLEPOS, SKEYW);
  /* PRINT TITLES ACCORDING TO KEYWORDS*/
    DO I = 1 TO SKEYW BY 1;
      PUT SKIP EDIT(TITLE(TITLENO(I)))
          (COL(62-TITLEPOS(I)),A); END;    END KWIC;
```

```
*PROCESS
 /* READ IN CARDS INTO ARRAY X(1:M).  STORE THE NUMBER*/
 /* IN S. THE LAST CARD IS FOLLOWED BY A BLANK CARD*/
 /* PRINT MESSAGE IF MORE THAN M CARDS*/
 READIN: PROCEDURE(X, M, S);
     DECLARE X(*)   CHAR(*),
             (M, S) FIXED DECIMAL;
     DECLARE CARD CHAR(80); /* HOLDS A CARD JUST READ*/
     S = 0; GET EDIT(CARD) (A(80));
     DO WHILE(CARD ¬= ' ');
        IF S >= M THEN
           DO; PUT SKIP LIST('TOO MUCH INPUT'); RETURN; END;
        S = S+1; X(S) = CARD;
        GET EDIT(CARD) (A(80));     END;     END READIN;

*PROCESS
 /* SORT X(1:N) IN ASCENDING ORDER.  WHENEVER X(I), X(J)*/
 /* ARE SWAPPED, ALSO SWAP Y(I), Y(J) AND Z(I), Z(J).*/
 SORT: PROCEDURE(X, Y, Z, N);
     Body of SORT, perhaps like Section II.4.3;
     END SORT;

*PROCESS
 /* MAKE UP LIST OF KEYWORDS.  ALL PARAMETERS HAVE SAME*/
 /* NAME AS ARGUMENTS; THEIR MEANINGS ARE IN MAIN PROGRAM*/
 MAKEKEY: PROCEDURE(TITLE, STITLE, NONKEY, SNONKEY,
             KEYW, TITLENO, TITLEPOS, MKEYW, SKEYW);
     DECLARE (TITLE(*), NONKEY(*), KEYW(*)) CHAR(*);
     DECLARE (STITLE, SNONKEY, TITLENO(*), TITLEPOS(*),
             MKEYW, SKEYW) FIXED DECIMAL;
     DECLARE I FIXED DECIMAL, /* PROCESS TITLE I*/
             WORD CHAR(9),    /* THE WORD BEING PROCESSED*/
             J FIXED DECIMAL, /* POS OF WORD IN NONKEY*/
             WORDCOL FIXED DECIMAL;     /* COL OF WORD*/

     SKEYW = 0;

     /* PROCESS THE WORDS OF EACH TITLE*/
        PW: DO I = 1 TO STITLE BY 1;
           WORDCOL = 1; WORD=SUBSTR(TITLE(I), WORDCOL, 9);
           EACHWORD: DO WHILE(WORD ¬= ' ' & WORDCOL <= 61);
              /* PROCESS WORD OF TITLE(I)*/
                 CALL BSEARCH(NONKEY, SNONKEY, WORD, J);
                 IF J = 0 THEN
                    DO; IF SKEYW >= MKEYW THEN
                           DO; PUT LIST ('TOO MANY KEYWORDS');
                               RETURN; END;
                       SKEYW = SKEYW+1; KEYW(SKEYW) = WORD;
                       TITLENO(SKEYW)=I;
                       TITLEPOS(SKEYW)= WORDCOL;    END;
              /* GET NEXT WORD*/
                 WORDCOL= WORDCOL+10;
                 WORD= SUBSTR(TITLE(I),WORDCOL,9);
              END EACHWORD; END PW; END MAKEKEY;
```

```
*PROCESS
 /* STORE 0 IN J IF X IS NOT IN A(1:N).  IF X IS FOUND,*/
 /* STORE ITS INDEX IN J.  A MUST BE SORTED.*/
 BSEARCH: PROCEDURE(A, N, X, J);
     DECLARE (A(*), X) CHAR(*),
             (N, J)     FIXED DECIMAL;
     DECLARE (FIRST, LAST) FIXED DECIMAL;
     /* BINARY SEARCH.  See Section II.4.1 for comments.*/
       FIRST=1; LAST=N;
       DO WHILE (FIRST <= LAST);
          J = FLOOR((FIRST+LAST)/2);
          IF A(J) = X THEN RETURN;
          IF A(J) < X THEN FIRST=J+1; ELSE LAST=J-1; END;
       J = 0; END BSEARCH;
```

This program illustrates several other points. First, it uses procedures which have already been written, like the binary search algorithm. By writing program segments as procedures and fully describing their function in a comment preface, they can often be used in later programs. Since communication is entirely through the parameters of the procedure, and the names of the parameters and variables used in the procedure are completely independent of names outside, the procedure is independent of context of use. A procedure may be moved from one program to another. In time one can build up libraries of correct and efficient procedures, and these can be copied and shared between programmers. Then one learns to develop programs using these library procedures just as if they were facilities that were part of PL/I. An experienced programmer should rarely have to write all of a program completely from scratch. He should be able to draw upon his experience and library for some segments of the program.

Secondly, note the use of READIN to read in both the list of titles and the list of non-keywords. At first these seem to be entirely different functions. One is to read a list of titles which are each a list of words, while the other is to read just a list of words. But if we note that each list is composed of strings of characters on cards, the similarity is clear.

In developing a program, look for operations which are similar and see if they can be modified to be the same. This requires some judgement and ingenuity, but it can lead to to considerable simplification and reduction in the size of the program.

Finally, no procedure or block (see next section) should take more than one page, or roughly 55 lines. Each module must be small enough to understand easily and completely, and one page is a reasonable limit. When a module exceeds this length it becomes difficult to match DOs with corresponding ENDs, even if the indentation is done correctly. Thus, the overall structure becomes unclear.

Section 1 Exercises

1. For each sequence of statements below, write a procedure with that sequence as the body, complete with declarations. The parameters are those variables and arrays described in the comment. Other variables should be local to the procedure. All variables are fixed decimal.

```
a) /* STORE THE MAXIMUM OF A AND B IN C*/
   IF A >= B THEN C = A; ELSE C = B;

b) /* STORE THE SUM OF THE ELEMENTS OF A(1:N) IN SUM*/
   SUM = 0;
   DO I = 1 TO N; SUM = SUM+A(I); END;

c) /* REVERSE THE ELEMENTS OF ARRAY X(1:N)*/
   FIRST = 1; LAST = N;
   DO WHILE (FIRST < LAST);
       T = X(FIRST); X(FIRST) = X(LAST); X(LAST) = T;
       FIRST = FIRST+1; LAST = LAST-1; END;
```

2. Make the program segments of Exercise 2, Section I.5, into procedures. Only the variables described in the comment of each program segment should be parameters.

3. Execute the following procedure calls by hand, drawing all necessary boxes. Procedure SWAP is given in (1.1c). Assume all variables are fixed decimal.

```
a) CALL SWAP(A,B); where    A 5    B 6
b) CALL SWAP(T,X); where     T 3    X 4
c) CALL SWAP(Y,X); where     Y 1    X 8
d) CALL SWAP(V,V); where     V 3
```

4. Execute the following procedure calls by hand, drawing all the boxes. Procedure SEARCH is given in (1.2.3a). The variables used are given below; they are all fixed decimal.

```
T(0) 6        NO 0        F 8
T(1) 8        N1 1        G 5
T(2) 4        N2 2        H 6
T(3) 9        N3 3        I 3

a) CALL SEARCH(T, NO, H, I);
b) CALL SEARCH(T, N1, H, I);
c) CALL SEARCH(T, N3, H, I);
d) CALL SEARCH(T, N3, N3, I);
e) CALL SEARCH(T, N3, F, I);
```

5. Execute the following procedure calls by hand, drawing all the boxes. Be careful to construct dummy arguments if necessary. Procedures SWAP and SEARCH are given in (1.1c) and (1.2.1a). The variables used are:

```
SN(1)  AB [char(2)]              SV(1)  AB [char(2) varying]
SF(2)  CD [char(2)]              SV(2)  CD [char(2) varying]
SF(3)  EF [char(2)]              SV(3)  AB [char(2) varying]
ANS    // [fixed decimal]        ANT    // [float decimal]
A      3  [fixed decimal]        B      4  [fixed decimal]
C      5  [float decimal]        D      6  [float decimal]
```

a) CALL SWAP(A,C);
b) CALL SWAP(C,A);
c) CALL SWAP(C,D);
d) CALL SEARCH(SF, 0, SV(1), ANS);
e) CALL SEARCH(SF, 0, SV(1), ANT);
f) CALL SEARCH(SV, 1, SV(1), ANS);
g) CALL SEARCH(SF, 1, SV(1), ANT);
h) CALL SEARCH(SF, D-A, SV(1), ANS);
i) CALL SEARCH(SF, D-A, SV(D-A), ANS);

6. Write procedures for the program segments of Exercises 4, 5
and 6 of Section I.5.

7. Write a procedure MEAN which, given an array segment X(1:N)
calculates the   mean   of the values; the mean is the sum of the
elements divided by N.

8. Write a procedure MEDIAN which, given an array segment
X(1:N) calculates the median of the values. The median is the
value such that half the numbers are greater than that value and
half are less.   One way to do this is to first sort the array
and then pick the middle value. If you use this method, use a
previously written sort procedure to do the sorting. But be
careful; MEDIAN should not change the order of the values in its
argument array -- a procedure should never modify the arguments
unless its specific task is to modify them.

9. Write a program to read a list of values and to print out
the mean and the median. Your program should use the procedures
written in Exercises 7 and 8.

10. Write a procedure which calculates sin(x) using the formula

$$\sin(x) = x/1! \; - \; x^3/3! \; + \; x^5/5! \; - \; x^7/7! \; + \; ...$$

The number of terms of the series to be used should be a
parameter of the procedure. Next, write a program to compare
the values of sin(x) calculated using the built-in SIN function
against those values calculated by your procedure. Run the
program with various values of x and various values of the
number of terms used in the series.

11. Write a procedure to calculate the product of two n by n
matrices A(1:N,1:N) and B(1:N,1:N). Each element C(i,k) of the
resulting matrix C(1:N,1:N) is defined as the sum of the values

$$C(i,k) = A(i,j) \cdot B(j,k) \qquad for \; j = 1, \; ..., \; N.$$

Section 2 <u>Blocks</u>

Thus far, all arrays have had to be declared with constants for the bounds. If the bounds are made too large, then memory is wasted while the program is running; if too small, the program may have to be changed frequently when different data are used. Use of a statement called a "BEGIN block" allows us to specify the bounds of the array dynamically -- during execution. Thus the size of an array can vary depending on the input data. Blocks also allow us to control <u>when</u> a variable or array should exist during execution, and to some extent to indicate the <u>scope</u> of a variable -- the parts of a program can reference it.

2.1 <u>The BEGIN Block</u>

The form of a BEGIN block is:

```
Label: BEGIN;
   Sequence of declarations
   Sequence of statements
   END label;
```

A block is a statement, and may be placed anywhere a statement may appear. It is much like a compound statement except for the presence of the declarations. These declarations describe <u>variables which exist only while the block is executing</u> -- they disappear upon its termination. They are called <u>local variables</u> of the block. Other variables referenced within the block are called <u>global variables</u> of the block. The label shown before BEGIN and after END is optional, but it is generally good practice to include it in order to clearly indicate the limits of the block.

The execution of a block takes place in three steps:

1. The local variables as described by the declarations are created.

2. The sequence of statements is executed.

3. The local variables are destroyed.

This means that if a block is terminated and then executed a second time, the local variables do <u>not</u> have the values they did

upon termination of the first execution. Unless they have an
INITIAL attribute, they have no initial value. For example, in
the program segment below the second time B is executed (with
I=2), X has no initial value. (It does <u>not</u> have value 1.)

```
    I = 1;
    DO WHILE (I < 10);
     B: BEGIN; DECLARE X FIXED DECIMAL;
            ...
            X = 1; I = I+1;  END B; END;
```

Blocks may of course be "nested" -- one may appear in the
body of another. In program (2.1a), the main procedure A
contains the two blocks labeled B and E in its body, while block
B contains blocks C and D. B is called the <u>surrounding block</u> of
C and D, since C and D occur within B. Similarly procedure A
<u>surrounds</u> both blocks B and E.

```
            ┌A: PROCEDURE OPTIONS(MAIN);
            │  DECLARE (X, Y) FIXED DECIMAL;
            │  ...
            │  A1: use X and Y
            │  B:┌ BEGIN; DECLARE (X, Z) FLOAT DECIMAL;
            │    │    B1: use X, Y, and Z
            │    │    ...
            │    │         C:┌ BEGIN; DECLARE (Y, W) FIXED DECIMAL;
            │    │           │    C1: use X, Y, Z, and W
            │    │           └    ...    END C;
(2.1a)      │    │    ...
            │    │         D:┌ BEGIN; DECLARE (X, Z) FIXED DECIMAL;
            │    │           │     D1: use X, Y and Z
            │    └           └     ...      END D;  END B;
            │  E:┌ BEGIN; DECLARE (X, W) FIXED DECIMAL;
            │    │   E1: use X, Y, and W
            │    └     ...  END E;
            └──END A;
```

2.2 <u>Scope of Variables</u>

A problem arises with nested blocks in determining which
variable a name refers to. For example, while executing block B
of program (2.1a), say at label B1, there are <u>two distinct</u>
variables named X. Which variable X should be used if the name
X is used at label B1? We would hope that the variable declared
in block B would be used, and indeed this is the case.

The rule for determining which variable a name N refers to is

(2.2a)   If N is declared locally within the block in which it
            is used, then N refers to this local variable.
            Otherwise N refers to the global variable declared in
            the <u>closest</u> surrounding block.

Suppose the name X is used in block C of program (2.1a). According to rule (2.2a) it refers to the variable X declared in block B. Similarly, the name Y used in block D refers to variable Y declared in procedure A. It does not refer to the variable Y in block C because block C <u>does not contain</u> block D. Table (2.2b) gives a list of the blocks of program (2.1a), together with the variables that can be referenced in each block.

	Block	Local Variables	Global Variables
	A	X, Y	none
	B	X, Z	Y declared in A
(2.2b)	C	Y, W	X, Z declared in B
	D	X, Z	Y declared in A
	E	X, W	Y declared in A

This should point out a subtle difference between the <u>name of a variable</u> and a <u>reference to a variable</u>. While executing in block B, two variables named X exist, but we can only <u>refer to one</u> of them. The declaration of X in block B effectively bars the use of variable X declared in A.

Blocks permit the declaration of a variable to be brought closer to the point of use. For example, suppose we use a variable or array LEN in only one small part of a large program. Then it would be advantageous to write the program as in (2.2c). The scope of the variable is clearly defined, and the reader need not worry about what the variable means to the rest of the program.

```
        A: PROCEDURE OPTIONS(MAIN);
            ... (50 statements)
(2.2c)      B: BEGIN; DECLARE LEN ...;
                ... (10 statements)   END B;
            ... (100 statements)   END A;
```

However, this can be overdone. A good, readable program has a systematic, well structured, well commented set of declarations. The reader must constantly refer to the declarations to understand the program. If these declarations are spread throughout the program in 10 to 20 different blocks, he has a difficult time finding the declaration for a particular variable. (Keeping procedures and thus blocks to less than one page will also help.)

2.3 Tracing Execution of Blocks

Variables declared within a block belong to that block. When executing a program by hand, it makes sense to draw a separate box for the variables of each block. Since the blocks themselves are nested, their boxes are nested in the same manner. This makes it easy to determine at each point which variable a name refers to.

We illustrate this by drawing the boxes at various points of execution of program (2.1a). We have labeled each block in (2.1a), and use this label at the bottom of the box to clarify which box belongs with which block. Fig. 7a shows the variables just after entering execution of the procedure A. During execution of block B, diagram 7b is in force. Note that there are two variables named X. While executing in block B, we look first in B's box for a variable. If we don't find it there we look in the surrounding box, and then the box surrounding that one, and so on. Thus while in B, X refers to the local variable of B. Fig. 7c shows the variables while executing in block C. When block C is finished executing, its box is deleted and we resort back to Fig. 7b. When block D is entered, a box for it is drawn as in Fig. 7d. When execution of both D and B is finished, we are back to Fig. 7a.

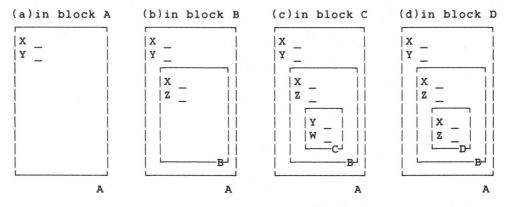

Figure 7.   Boxes at Various Stages of Execution of (2.1a)

2.4 Scope of Labels and Entry-names

The scope rules for labels and procedure names (called entry-names) are the same as those for variables. A label or procedure name belongs to the block or procedure in which its definition occurs. (In the next section we will see how to define a procedure within a block.) Given the use of a name X, if X is defined as a label, procedure name, or variable within the block or procedure in which the use occurs, then X refers to that entity. If X is not defined within that block or

procedure, then we look in the surrounding block or procedure
for X's definition, and then in the surrounding one, and so on.

    This means that (2.4a) is <u>not</u> a valid program segment,
because in the statement GO TO ENDSEG; used to terminate the
block, ENDSEG refers to the local variable ENDSEG.

```
              ...
              BEGIN; DECLARE (I, ENDSEG) DECIMAL FIXED;
                 ...
(2.4a)           IF ...  THEN GO TO ENDSEG;
                 ... END;
          ENDSEG:;
```

    We have not yet defined a procedure inside another block or
procedure, so it may seem strange to talk of looking in the
surrounding block or procedure for an entry-name.   We imagine
that an invisible block surrounds the whole program submitted to
the computer, including external procedures. Therefore, it is
within this block that the main program name and any external
procedure names are defined.

    We can also consider this invisible block to include the
definition of all the built-in functions, like MAX, SQRT and
SIN. When we use SQRT in a program, the name and corresponding
definition are found in the outermost, invisible block. This
explains why one can redefine the names of these built-in
functions within a program. In program (2.4b), in block B we
can reference neither the built-in function MAX nor the external
procedure SWAP, since both names refer to local variables.
Outside of block B we can reference the built-in function and
external procedure.   (2.4c) shows the boxes for the blocks and
procedures as they exist when executing block B. In general we
don't draw the invisible block; it would be too big and take up
too much space. (Moreover, it's invisible.)

```
         A: PROCEDURE OPTIONS(MAIN);
            ...
         B: BEGIN; DECLARE (MAX, SWAP) FIXED DECIMAL;
                 ...      END B;
            ...     END A;
(2.4b)
         *PROCESS
         SWAP: PROCEDURE (X, Y);
              ...     END SWAP;
```

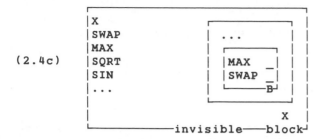

2.5 Dynamic Arrays

We have previously used only constants for bounds of arrays.
However, <u>any</u> expression may be used as a bound, as long as it
can be evaluated to yield an integer at the time the array is to
be created. This capability, called "dynamic dimensioning", is
very useful, for it allows a program to be written in such a way
that the size of the arrays can be specified in the data rather
than in the program statements. ("Dynamic" means that the
dimensioning expressions must be evaluated during the <u>execution</u>,
rather than the loading of the program.)

The following program shows the correct use of blocks to
allow the input data to determine the size of the array. The
sole purpose of the block FMB is to <u>postpone the creation of</u>
<u>array WEIGHT</u> until N has received a value. WEIGHT is created as
the first step in execution of FMB, <u>before</u> the body is executed.
Since this occurs after the execution of GET LIST(N); events are
in the proper sequence. The remainder of the program is written
inside FMB.

```
    /* PROGRAM TO COMPUTE THE CARTESIAN FUMBLE OF AN ARRAY */
    /* THE SIZE OF THE ARRAY IS GIVEN AS THE FIRST DATUM */
    FUMBLE: PROCEDURE OPTIONS(MAIN);
        DECLARE (N,I) FIXED DECIMAL;
            /* N - SIZE OF ARRAY WEIGHT */
        GET LIST(N);
        FMB: BEGIN; DECLARE WEIGHT(N) FLOAT DECIMAL;
                DO I = 1 TO N BY 1; GET LIST(WEIGHT(I)); END;
                ...    END FMB; END FUMBLE;
    *DATA
        5,     14.735, 14.769, 15.008, 14.636, 14.982
```

An array takes space proportional to the number of variables
in it.   The programmer can control the use of memory to some
extent by using blocks. Suppose that in two <u>different</u> parts of
a program, two arrays A(1:1000) and B(-500:0,1:20) are to be
used. First the array A is used, and then later on the array B,
but not both together.   The programmer could structure his
program as follows. The two arrays would be able to share the
same memory, since neither exists when the other does. This
reduces the total amount of memory needed by the program.

```
X: PROCEDURE OPTIONS(MAIN);
    ...
    BEGIN; DECLARE A(1:1000) FIXED DECIMAL;
        ...    END;
    ...
    BEGIN; DECLARE B(-500:0,1:20) FLOAT DECIMAL;
        ...    END;
    ...    END X;
```

One could perform the same task for simple variables, but the memory space saved is generally not worth the effort.

Section 2 Exercises

1. Write a program to read in a list of numbers and print them out in ascending order. Use any sort procedure you wish. The program should work for a list of any size.

2. Write a program to read a number n, read a list of n numbers, and print them out in reverse order.

3. Write a program to read in values for two n by n matrices A and B and print out their product. You may determine the input format, but the program should work for matrices of any size (as long as they fit in the computer). Use the procedure written for Exercise 11 of Section 1.

4. Write a procedure with the heading

```
/* A(1:K) AND A(K+1:N) ARE EACH SORTED IN ASCENDING ORDER*/
/* PROCEDURE MERGES THEM INTO ONE SORTED SEGMENT A(1:N).*/
MERGE: PROCEDURE(A, K, N);
    DECLARE (A(*), K, N) FIXED DECIMAL;
```

Complete the procedure. You may use an array B(1:K) which is local to the procedure.

5. The coefficients of a polynomial

$$a(0) + a(1) \cdot x + a(2) \cdot x^2 + a(3) \cdot x^3$$

can be stored in an array A(0:N). Write a procedure EVAL(A,N,X,ANS) which stores in ANS the value of the polynomial with coefficients given by A(0:N) at the point X.

Write a program to read in a polynomial and evaluate it for several different values of X. You may determine the input format, but the program must work for polynomials of any size.

Section 3 Internal Procedures

In Section 1 we discussed external procedures, which were
communicated with only through parameters. A procedure
definition may be placed within any other procedure or block
(including the main procedure), in which case it is called an
internal procedure. The only reason for doing this is to allow
the procedure to communicate with the rest of the program
through global variables, exactly the way a block does. This of
course makes the procedure more dependent on the rest of the
program, and such internal procedures must be used with care.

3.1 Placement of Procedures -- an Example

We usually put internal procedure definitions at the end of a
procedure or block, just before the END;. Then they are out of
the way and don't interfere with our understanding of the main
part of the program. An internal procedure definition must
indicate which global variables it uses, in a comment at its
beginning. The reader must be made aware of every global
variable which the procedure may change or on which it depends.

Internal procedures are advantageous when the procedures work
in an "environment" of variables, and will be called only with
these variables in a fixed, standard way. The KWIC index
program of Section 1.5 is a good example of a program which
would be better if an internal procedure were used. The body of
procedure MAKEKEY was put in as a procedure only to make the
main program short and easy to understand. In doing so, we had
to communicate a number of variables as arguments, and this was
admittedly awkward in this case. Making MAKEKEY an internal
procedure allows it to reference this environment of titles,
non-keywords and keywords directly. This saves several lines of
program and makes it look simpler.

```
/* PRODUCE KWIC INDEX FOR TITLES*/
KWIC: PROCEDURE OPTIONS(MAIN);
 DECLARE TITLE(1:100) CHAR(69),        /* THE TITLES*/
     MTITLE FIXED DECIMAL INIT(100),   /* MAX. NO. TITLES*/
     STITLE FIXED DECIMAL;             /* NO. TITLES READ*/

 DECLARE NONKEY(1:200) CHAR(9),        /* NONKEYWORDS*/
     MNONKEY FIXED DECIMAL INIT(200),  /* MAX NO NONKEYS*/
     SNONKEY FIXED DECIMAL;            /* NUMBER READ*/

 DECLARE KEYW(1:500) CHAR(9),          /* THE KEYWORDS*/
     MKEYW FIXED DECIMAL INIT(500),    /* MAX NO KEYWRDS*/
     SKEYW FIXED DECIMAL      INIT(0), /* NUMBER READ*/
     TITLENO(1:500) FIXED DECIMAL,     /* EACH */
     TITLEPOS(1:500) FIXED DECIMAL;    /* KEYW(I) APPEARS*/
        /* IN TITLE(TITLENO(I)) AT COLUMN TITLEPOS(I)*/
 DECLARE I FIXED DECIMAL;

 CALL READIN(TITLE, MTITLE, STITLE);
 CALL READIN(NONKEY, MNONKEY, SNONKEY);
 CALL MAKEKEY;
 CALL SORT(KEYW, TITLENO, TITLEPOS, SKEYW);
 /* PRINT TITLES ACCORDING TO KEYWORDS*/
    DO I = 1 TO SKEYW BY 1;
       PUT SKIP EDIT(TITLE(TITLENO(I)))
             (COL(62-TITLEPOS(I)),A);    END;

  MAKEKEY: PROCEDURE;
  /* MAKE UP LIST OF KEYWORDS.  USES LISTS OF TITLES,*/
  /* NONKEYWORDS AND KEYWORDS.  CHANGES ARRAY */
  /* KEYW AND VARIABLE SKEYW*/
     DECLARE I FIXED DECIMAL, /* PROCESSING TITLE I*/
             WORD CHAR(9),    /* THE WORD BEING PROCESSED*/
             J FIXED DECIMAL, /* POS OF WORD IN NONKEY*/
             WORDCOL FIXED DECIMAL;    /* COL OF WORD*/

     /* PROCESS THE WORDS OF EACH TITLE */
        PW: DO I = 1 TO STITLE BY 1;
          WORDCOL = 1; WORD=SUBSTR(TITLE(I), WORDCOL, 9);
          EACHWORD: DO WHILE(WORD ¬= ' ' & WORDCOL <= 61);
             /* PROCESS WORD OF TITLE(I)*/
                CALL BSEARCH(NONKEY, SNONKEY, WORD, J);
                IF J = 0 THEN
                   DO; IF SKEYW >= MKEYW THEN
                         DO; PUT LIST ('TOO MANY KEYWORDS');
                             RETURN; END;
                      SKEYW = SKEYW+1; KEYW(SKEYW) = WORD;
                      TITLENO(SKEYW)=I;
                      TITLEPOS(SKEYW)= WORDCOL;    END;
             /* GET NEXT WORD*/
                WORDCOL= WORDCOL+10;
                WORD= SUBSTR(TITLE(I),WORDCOL,9);
             END EACHWORD; END PW; END MAKEKEY;
     END KWIC;
```

Note that this internal form of MAKEKEY has no parameters; all communication is through global variables.

A procedure should be made internal only if it <u>needs</u> global variables the way MAKEKEY did -- if there is an "environment" under which it should execute. Such an internal procedure is not as independent as an external one, and must be placed and run in a certain context. The other procedures READIN, SORT and BSEARCH of the KWIC index program <u>should be left as external procedures</u>. They perform general operations which cannot be attributed to the KWIC program alone. They can be used in any number of other programs.

3.2 <u>Tracing Execution of Internal Procedures</u>

In tracing execution of internal procedures, one uses the same rules given earlier in Sections 2.2 and 2.3. Just remember that the box for an internal procedure is drawn inside the box for the block or procedure in which the <u>definition</u> of the internal procedure appears (and <u>not</u> in the box for the block in which the call appears). Consider the KWIC index program given in Section 3.1. When procedure MAKEKEY is executing, the boxes are as in (3.2a).

(3.2a)

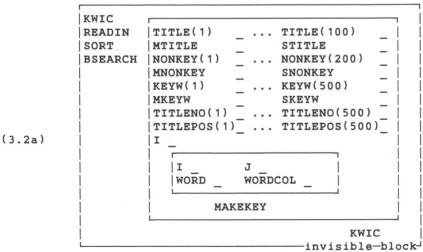

One must be very careful with procedure and block ENDs. Quite frequently, an END will be left out, and this can alter the whole block structure of the program. Consider the program of (3.2b) which is supposed to use two internal procedures P1 and P2. Unfortunately, the END for P1 has been left out, and even more unfortunately, PL/I inserts this END without telling us, just before the end of the main program. Thus, as shown in (3.2c), P2 has been made internal to P1, so the main program cannot refer to P2 and an error will result.

```
X: PROCEDURE OPTIONS(MAIN);
        . . .
     CALL P1;
     CALL P2;
        . . .
          P1: PROCEDURE;
               . . .
          P2: PROCEDURE;
               . . .    END P2;
     END X;
```

(3.2b)

(3.2c)

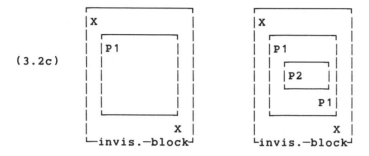

When executing proc. X   When executing proc. P1

Section 4* <u>Recursive Procedures</u>

A <u>recursive procedure</u> is one which calls itself -- a call of
the procedure occurs within the body of the procedure itself, or
in another procedure called by the original one. Recursion can
be used quite extensively in programming, and in some cases can
make difficult problems look easy. In fact, for some problems
recursion is the natural way of performing the task.

4.1 <u>A Simple Example</u>

The term <u>recursive</u> is derived from mathematics where some
formulas are written using <u>recursive definition</u> - something is
defined in terms of itself. For example, consider the function
N! which for N > 0 is defined as

(4.1a)   N! = N * (N-1) * (N-2) * ... * 2 * 1

This can also be defined recursively (in terms of itself) as

(4.1b)   N! = $\begin{cases} 1 & \text{if } N = 1 \\ N * (N-1)! & \text{if } N > 1 \end{cases}$

We can write a recursive PL/I procedure to calculate N! for any
positive integer N directly from this recursive definition:

```
          /* STORE N! IN ANS*/
          FACT: PROCEDURE(N, ANS) RECURSIVE;
                DECLARE (N, ANS) FIXED DECIMAL;
                DECLARE TEMP FIXED DECIMAL;
(4.1c)          IF N = 1
                    THEN ANS = 1;
                    ELSE DO; F: CALL FACT(N-1, TEMP);
                            ANS = N*TEMP; END;
                END FACT;
```

The keyword RECURSIVE must appear between the parameters and
the semicolon in the heading of any recursive procedure, as
shown above.

Consider the body of procedure FACT of (4.1c). If N is 1,
the procedure stores 1 in ANS and returns, as required by
definition (4.1b). If N > 1, then FACT is called a second time
to store (N-1)! in TEMP (at label F). This value is then
multiplied by N and the result is stored in ANS. This again

satisfies definition (4.1b). Note that while discussing the
call F: CALL FACT(N-1,TEMP); we don't worry about <u>how</u> FACT will
work; we just assume that the procedure FACT will do its job --
will store (N-1)! in TEMP for us. That FACT also happens to be
the procedure currently being executed should not disturb us;
just think of it as two different procedures which just <u>look</u> the
same.

   This particular function N! is not a good example of a
useful, efficient recursive procedure, since it can be written
more easily and efficiently using definition (4.1a) as

```
        /* STORE N! IN ANS*/
        FACT: PROCEDURE(N, ANS);
                DECLARE (N, ANS) FIXED DECIMAL;
                DECLARE I FIXED DECIMAL;
                ANS = 1;
                DO I = 2 TO N BY 1;
                    ANS = ANS * I; END; END FACT;
```

However the recursive procedure for N! is short and simple
enough to illustrate how recursion works and how we should deal
with it, and we will use it extensively in the next section.

4.2 <u>Exploring Recursion</u>

   Recursion may seem strange at first; it seems odd to be
executing the same procedure two or more times at the same time.
Let us motivate recursion as follows.   Below we have written
four procedures. (We have left out the declarations to save
space). FACT1 will store in ANS the value N!, but only if N =
1.   FACT2 produces N! if N≤2, by calling FACT1 to evaluate 1!.
Similarly, FACT3 and FACT4 produce N! if N≤3 and N≤4,
respectively, by calling on the other procedures. Thus we have
written four different procedures, each of which calculates
N! for a certain range of values of N.

   These procedures are easy to understand, and obviously
perform the required action. However, to be able to calculate
5! we must write a procedure FACT5, and for 6! a procedure
FACT6, and so on. This is inconvenient.

   Now note that all the procedures (except for the first) are
similar, save for the <u>name</u> of the procedure being called. It
would be useful to be able to have <u>one</u> procedure which we can
call many times instead of many procedures once. Thus, we write
the procedure FACT of (4.1c), with the same body as FACT2, FACT3
and FACT4 except for the name of the procedure being called. In
effect, we can consider FACT to be as many procedures as we
want.   Each time it is called recursively, a new "copy" of the
procedure is made and used for that call, and we can think of
these different copies as having names FACT1, FACT2, FACT3, and
so on.

```
FACT1: PROCEDURE(N, ANS); /* ANS = N! IF N=1*/
     IF N = 1 THEN ANS = 1;
        ELSE Give error message;
     END FACT1;

FACT2: PROCEDURE(N, ANS); /* ANS = N! IF N≤2*/
     IF N = 1 THEN ANS = 1;
        ELSE DO; CALL FACT1(N-1,TEMP); ANS = N*TEMP; END;
     END FACT2;

FACT3: PROCEDURE(N, ANS); /* ANS = N! IF N≤3*/
     IF N = 1 THEN ANS = 1;
        ELSE DO; CALL FACT2(N-1,TEMP); ANS = N*TEMP; END;
     END FACT3;

FACT4: PROCEDURE(N, ANS); /* ANS = N! IF N≤4*/
     IF N = 1 THEN ANS = 1;
        ELSE DO; CALL FACT3(N-1, TEMP); ANS = N*TEMP; END;
     END FACT4;
```

4.2.1 The Recursive Pattern

Most recursive definitions and recursive procedures have the
same pattern or flavor as does N!. For one or two values of the
argument, the result is defined nonrecursively, usually in a
quite simple manner.   Thus, if N = 1, N! = 1. For all other
argument values, the result is defined recursively.   This
recursive definition is arranged so that it is easy to see that
the recursion will terminate. For example for N!, if N > 1 we
have N! = N*(N-1)!.   Here we see that the result for N! is
defined in terms of (N-1)!   -- 5! is defined in terms of
4! which is defined in terms of 3! and so on. Thus we must
eventually get to 1 and the process terminates.

As another example, we can define multiplication of two
positive, nonzero integers X and Y in terms of addition and
subtraction as follows:

$$X*Y = \begin{cases} X & \text{if } Y = 1 \\ X + X*(Y-1) & \text{if } Y > 1 \end{cases}$$

Y = 1 is the simple, nonrecursive case, while the second case is
recursive.   The second argument Y decreases by one at each step
of the recursion, so that the process must terminate when Y = 1.

In general, any recursive procedure can be transformed into
one which is not recursive.   The question then is why use
recursion? The answer is threefold:

1. A recursive procedure is often easier to understand and prove correct.

2. Thinking recursively often leads to simpler algorithms, even though they may finally end up in a nonrecursive form.

3. Recursive procedures tend to divide the problem into smaller but similar ones which can be solved the same way, and this often increases efficiency.

Once we understand the basic idea behind recursion, we find that recursive procedures are much easier to understand than the conventional iterative loops. Loops are hard because the way they look is so different from the way they execute. The body of the loop appears only once, but it may be executed any number of times.   This is also true of recursive procedures, but they are easier to understand because of the way we read them.   When we see a call like CALL FACT(N-1,ANS);, we can concentrate on what FACT is doing, and leave until later how it does it.   This is much more difficult to do with iteration, and we have to resort to invariant relations, as described in Section II.6.

4.2.2 Executing Recursive Procedures by Hand

Executing recursive calls by hand is no more difficult than executing regular procedure calls.   The only problem is that several boxes will exist for a procedure called recursively, one for each invocation which has not finished executing. To illustrate this, consider a call M: CALL FACT(3,X); in the main program, where the main program variables are as shown in Fig. 8a. We will now execute this call, assuming that FACT is an external procedure, and show how the boxes are drawn at each point of execution. In order to keep track of which box for FACT to use at each point, we will put a superscript after the procedure name. Thus Fig. 8b shows the boxes just after the box for FACT is drawn for the main procedure call M: CALL FACT(3,X); but before the procedure body is executed.   The superscript indicates the "level" of recursion.

The procedure body of FACT is now executed. Since $N \neq 1$, the call at label F of FACT is executed. Another box is drawn for this second call of FACT, labeled $FACT^2$ as in Fig. 8c. When executing the procedure body for this second call of FACT, refer to the box labeled $FACT^2$ for names used within the procedure body.

Now execute the procedure body for $FACT^2$. Since $N \neq 1$ (it is 2), execute the call F: FACT(N-1, TEMP) again. Drawing the box and making the parameter-argument correspondence for this call yields Fig. 8d.

For the third time, begin executing the procedure body for FACT.   This time N = 1. The value 1 is stored in ANS (which changes TEMP within FACT^2 to 1), and execution of the procedure body is finished. The call labeled F in the second invocation of FACT has been completed and the boxes look like Fig. 8e.

Now execute ANS=N*TEMP; of the second invocation of FACT, which stores 2 in TEMP of FACT^1. The result of this is shown in Fig. 8f. Fig. 8g shows the boxes after deletion of the box FACT^2 and thus completion of the call labeled F in the first invocation of FACT. Now execute ANS=N*TEMP; once more, which stores the value 6 in the main program variable X. Execution of the procedure body has ended, so delete the box for FACT^1. Execution of the procedure call labeled M in the main program is finished, and the boxes look like Fig. 8h.

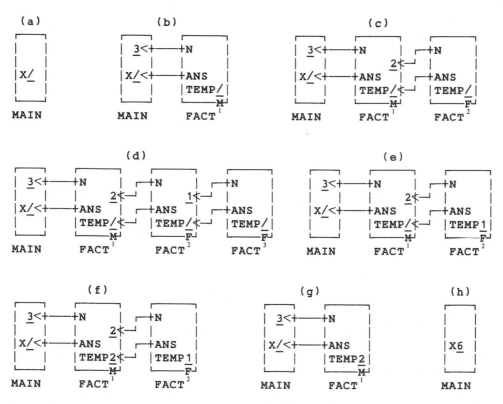

Figure 8. Various stages of execution of CALL FACT(X,3);

4.3 Recursive Procedure Examples

4.3.1 The Towers of Hanoi

The following legend is told about a temple in Hanoi. When the temple was built, three large towers or poles were placed in the ground, and 64 disks of different diameters were placed on the first pole, in order of decreasing diameter (with the smallest on the top and the largest on the bottom -- see (4.3.1a)).   The monks at the temple were to move the disks from pole 1 to pole 3, following these two rules: Only one disk could be moved at a time, and no disk was to be placed on top of a smaller disk. When they finished their task, the world would come to an end.

(4.3.1a)

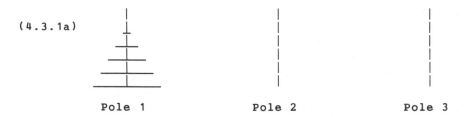

Pole 1   Pole 2   Pole 3

How do the monks perform their task, and how long will it actually take? The task seems difficult (because of the rule that no disk may be placed on a smaller one), but if viewed recursively it is quite easy (although still long). A recursive procedure could print out a list of moves for the monks, like

    MOVE DISK FROM 1 TO 2

One way of performing the task is to

    1) Move 63 disks from pole 1 to pole 2;
    2) Move 1 disk from pole 1 to pole 3;
    3) Move 63 disks from pole 2 to pole 3;

Note that the largest disk is always at the bottom of pole 1 or 3, so that it is never placed on top of a smaller one. This assumes of course that we know how to move 63 disks. How is this done? Again, use the same technique:

    1) Move 62 disks from pole 1 to pole 3;
    2) Move 1 disk from pole 1 to pole 2;
    3) Move 62 disks from pole 3 to pole 2;

A pattern emerges; at each step move a number of disks by moving all but the last to one pole, then moving the last to its proper pole, and then moving the other disks back on top of it. This pattern forms the basis for the body of the following recursive procedure:

```
/* MOVE N DISKS FROM POLE X TO POLE Y.  USE POLE Z TO */
/* STORE DISKS IF NECESSARY */
HANOI: PROCEDURE(X, Y, Z, N) RECURSIVE;
    DECLARE (X, Y, Z, N) FIXED DECIMAL;
    IF N = 1 THEN PUT SKIP LIST('MOVE DISK FROM',X,'TO',Y);
        ELSE DO; CALL HANOI(X, Z, Y, N-1);
                PUT SKIP LIST ('MOVE DISK FROM', X, 'TO', Y);
                CALL HANOI(Z, Y, X, N-1); END;
    END HANOI;
```

If you run this procedure on the computer, make sure N is not more than 6 or 7. To show why, consider the number of moves $M(N)$ if pole 1 originally contains N disks. For N = 1, $M(1)$ = 1. For N > 1 the number of moves is

$$M(N) = M(N-1) + 1 + M(N-1) = 2*M(N-1) + 1.$$

(Note that this is a recursive definition.) If you draw a table of moves for N = 1, 2, 3, 4, etc., you will see that in general $M(N) = 2**N - 1$.

Now suppose there are 64 disks. Then the above algorithm will generate $M(64) = 2^{64}-1$ moves. This is a tremendous number. Assuming that the monks can move one disk per second, if they work continuously it will take them well over a trillion (10^{12}) years. The computer is of course faster, and can print about 1000 moves per minute. Still, to print all the moves will take over 30 billion years. This is a good example of a problem with a simple algorithmic solution, but for which no computer is fast enough. The problem is impossibly large (see Section II.5.2).

4.3.2 Quicksort

The Tower of Hanoi problem is interesting but perhaps not practical. Sorting is practical, and we show here a recursive variation of a useful sorting algorithm.

Given an array segment A(M:N), suppose it can be partitioned so that it looks like

```
            A(M)       A(K-1) A(K) A(K+1)      A(N)
          ┌──────────────────┬──┬──────────────────┐
(4.3.2a)  │     ≤ A(K)       │  │  │    > A(K)      │
          └──────────────────┴──┴──────────────────┘
```

Then the segment A(M:N) will be sorted when the two separate segments A(M:K-1) and A(K+1:N) are sorted. Thus the original sorting problem has been broken up into two separate smaller problems. These smaller problems can be sorted by the same technique.

The procedure is given below; it uses a Partition algorithm which is given in Section II.6.4. It is not necessary to know

how Partition works, but just __what__ it does. The quicksort
algorithm is also given in Section II.6.4 in a non-recursive
version. Compare the two versions and note how much simpler the
recursive version seems.

```
QUICKSORT: PROCEDURE(A, M, N) RECURSIVE;
/* SORT SEGMENT A(M:N) */
   DECLARE (A(*), M, N) FIXED DECIMAL;
   DECLARE K FIXED DECIMAL;
   IF N <= M THEN RETURN; /* 0 OR 1 ELEMENTS IN SEGMENT*/
   IF N = M+1 THEN /* SEGMENT HAS 2 ELEMENTS.  SORT.  */
       DO; IF A(M) > A(N) THEN Swap A(M) and A(N);
           RETURN; END;

   /* A(M:N) HAS 3 OR MORE ELEMENTS.  PARTITION AND SORT*/
     Partition A(M:N) as in (4.3.2a) and set variable K;
     CALL QUICKSORT(A, M, K-1);
     CALL QUICKSORT(A, K+1, N);
   END QUICKSORT;
```

4.3.3 The Assignment Problem

An example in Section II.5.2 involved the optimal assignment
of swimmers to events. The program presented was logically
simple, but it involved a nest of DO groups with one level for
each swimmer. Thus, the program had to be changed when more or
fewer swimmers were involved. Since each level in this nest
(except the innermost) performs a very similar action, the
algorithm can be easily rewritten using a recursive procedure.

The program given below also differs from that of II.5.2 in
that the dimensions of the problem are specified in the data,
and not in the program. It also uses array assignments (see
Section I.5.4), the INITIAL attribute in declarations (see
Section I.8.3), and global variables. The procedure SWIMMER
must be internal, so it can reference the arrays describing
swimmers and events.

While this program is certainly more flexible, and probably
clearer, than that of II.5.2, recall that the basic difficulty
with that earlier program was not its clumsiness, but its
execution time. This program looks at fewer assignments than
does the original nonrecursive version (because we check for a
duplicate event assignment immediately after assigning a swimmer
to an event, and not after all N swimmers have been assigned),
but it would still be necessary to use a different algorithm for
a problem with more than 6 or 7 swimmers. It is nevertheless a
good illustration of the difference between an iterative and a
recursive program.

```
/* PROGRAM TO DETERMINE MAXIMUM POSSIBLE TEAM SCORE */
/* ONE SWIMMER ASSIGNED TO EACH EVENT */
ASSIGN: PROCEDURE OPTIONS(MAIN);
  DCL  (N, M) FIXED DEC;      /* N IS THE NUMBER OF SWIMMERS */
                             /* M IS THE NUMBER OF EVENTS */
  GET LIST(N, M);
 ASSIGN2: BEGIN;
  DCL PT(N, M) FLOAT DEC;    /* ESTIMATED POINTS FOR ITH */
                             /* SWIMMER IN JTH EVENT */
                             /* EACH ROW IS ONE SWIMMER */
                             /* EACH COLUMN IS ONE EVENT */
  DCL SW(N) FIXED DEC;       /* SW(I) IS SWIMMER ASSIGNED */
                             /* EVENT I */
  DCL SWMAX(N) FIXED DEC;    /* SWIMMERS FOR MAXIMUM SCORE. */
  DCL MAXPTSUM FLOAT DEC INIT(-1); /* MAXIMUM TEAM SCORE */
  DCL (ROW, EV) FIXED DEC;

  GET LIST(PT);
  CALL SWIMMER(1);

  /* DISPLAY ASSIGNMENTS AND SCORE*/
  PUT SKIP LIST('SWIMMER ASSIGNMENTS');
  PUT SKIP(3) LIST('SWIMMER', 'EVENT', 'POINTS');
  PRINT_SWIMMER_LOOP:  DO ROW = 1 TO N BY 1;
     FIND_EVENT:  DO EV = 1 TO M BY 1;
        IF SWMAX(EV) = ROW THEN
           DO; PUT SKIP LIST(ROW, EV, PT(ROW, EV) );
               GO TO PRINTED; END;  END FIND_EVENT;
         PRINTED:;  END PRINT_SWIMMER_LOOP;
     PUT SKIP(2) LIST(' ','TOTAL TEAM SCORE', MAXPTSUM);

 /* DETERMINE ALL POSSIBLE ASSIGNMENTS FOR SWIMMERS I, I+1,  */
 /* ..., N, ASSUMING 1, ..., I-1 ARE ASSIGNED. SAVE BEST ONE.*/
 /* USES GLOBALS N, M, SW, PT */
 /* CHANGES GLOBALS SWMAX AND MAXPTSUM */
  SWIMMER: PROCEDURE(I) RECURSIVE;
    DCL I FIXED DEC;           /* SWIMMER (ROW) NUMBER */
    DCL PTSUM FLOAT DEC INIT(0); /* SUM OF PTS FOR ASSIGNMENT*/
    DCL EV FIXED DEC;
    IF I <= N
      THEN DO EV = 1 TO M BY 1;
        IF SW(EV) = 0 THEN
           DO; SW(EV)=I; CALL SWIMMER(I+1); SW(EV)=0;  END; END;
        ELSE DO; /* ALL SWIMMERS ASSIGNED. FIND SCORE AND SET */
                /* NEW MAXIMUM IF POSSIBLE.*/
                DO EV = 1 TO M BY 1;
                  IF SW(EV)¬=0 THEN PTSUM=PTSUM+PT(SW(EV),EV);
                  END;
                IF PTSUM > MAXPTSUM THEN
                   DO; MAXPTSUM = PTSUM; SWMAX = SW;  END;
              END; END SWIMMER;

END ASSIGN2; END ASSIGN;
```

4.3.4 Evaluating Expressions

We want to write a set of procedures which will evaluate any expression consisting of additions +, multiplications *, parentheses (and), and integer constants. For example, the expressions

```
1 + 3 * 10              (20 + 30) * (5 + 6)
(1 + 3) * 10            (10 + (20 + (30 * (4))))
```

Such an expression will be stored in two arrays, a character array SYMBOL which will contain the expression but with the character C representing each constant, and a fixed decimal array VALUE which will contain the actual constant. The character E will mark the end of the expression. SIZE will contain the number of symbols. For example, the expression (1+3)*10 will be stored as

```
SYMBOL(1) (        VALUE(1) 0        SIZE 8
SYMBOL(2) C        VALUE(2) 1
SYMBOL(3) +        VALUE(3) 0
SYMBOL(4) C        VALUE(4) 3
SYMBOL(5) )        VALUE(5) 0
SYMBOL(6) *        VALUE(6) 0
SYMBOL(7) C        VALUE(7) 10
SYMBOL(8) E        VALUE(8) 0
```

We assume no mistakes will be made in storing an expression in the arrays, and our procedures have not been designed to handle errors.

To evaluate an expression stored in SYMBOL(1:SIZE) and VALUE(1:SIZE) we execute

```
NUMBER = 1;
CALL EVALEXP(NUMBER, ANSWER);
```

NUMBER indicates where the expression to be evaluated begins -- in SYMBOL(1). The arrays themselves will be communicated as global variables. Execution of this call will store the value of the expression in ANSWER, and will also put into NUMBER the number of the symbol following the expression evaluated (8 in this case).

How does EVALEXP work? To see this, note that any expression is made up of a series of additions; the expression looks like

(4.3.4a) operand + operand + ... + operand

For example the expression (3*5) consists of one operand, and no additions; it is a degenerate case of (4.3.4a). The expression 1+3+(2+4)*3 consists of the addition of three operands: 1, 3, and (2+4)*3. Let us assume we can write a procedure PLUSOP to evaluate an operand for an addition. Just how PLUSOP works we leave until later. For now, let us just state what it should

do.   Execution   of   CALL PLUSOP(NUMBER,ANS);   performs   the
following:

1.   The operand for an addition beginning at SYMBOL(NUMBER)
     is evaluated and the result is stored in ANS.

2.   NUMBER is changed to contain the number of the symbol
     <u>following</u> the operand evaluated.

We can now easily write procedure EVALEXP to evaluate any
expression, using this new procedure PLUSOP:

```
/* STORE IN ANS THE VALUE OF THE EXPRESSION BEGINNING*/
/* AT SYMBOL(NUMBER).  CHANGE NUMBER TO POINT TO SYMBOL */
/* FOLLOWING THE EXPRESSION.*/
EVALEXP: PROCEDURE(NUMBER, ANS);
   DECLARE (NUMBER, ANS) FIXED DECIMAL;
   DECLARE ANS2 FIXED DECIMAL;
   /* EVALUATE FIRST OPERAND (THERE MUST BE ONE)*/
     CALL PLUSOP(NUMBER, ANS);

   /* EACH ITERATION OF LOOP EVALUATES ANOTHER OPERAND*/
   /* AND ADDS ITS RESULT TO ANS.*/
     DO WHILE (SYMBOL(NUMBER) = '+');
        NUMBER = NUMBER+1;          /* SKIP OVER THE '+' */
        CALL PLUSOP(NUMBER, ANS2); /* EVAL. OPERAND*/
        ANS = ANS + ANS2; END; END EVALEXP;
```

How does PLUSOP work? An operand for an addition has the form

    simple-operand * simple-operand * ... * simple-operand

where a simple-operand is either a constant or a parenthesized
expression. For example,

    1 * 2 * (3+5) * (82)

has the simple operands 1, 2, (3+5) and (82). This is quite
similar to the form of an expression consisting of a sequence of
additions, and you might suspect that the routine PLUSOP will be
similar to EVALEXP. It looks for * instead of + and it calls a
procedure SIMPLOP instead of PLUSOP to evaluate its operands.

    Procedure SIMPLOP also takes two arguments: where its
expression begins, and the variable in which to store the
result. It works as follows. If the expression is just a
constant, then it stores that constant in the answer. The other
alternative is to have a parenthesized expression as the
operand. In this case, SIMPLE_OPERAND <u>calls the original
procedure EVALEXP to evaluate the expression within the
parentheses</u>. Thus we have a system of three recursive
procedures, each calling the other.

```
/* STORE IN ANS THE VALUE OF THE EXPRESSION BEGINNING AT */
/* SYMBOL(NUMBER). CHANGE NUMBER SO THAT IT POINTS AT*/
/* THE SYMBOL FOLLOWING THE EXPRESSION*/
EVALEXP: PROCEDURE(NUMBER, ANS);
   DECLARE (NUMBER, ANS) FIXED DECIMAL;
   DECLARE ANS2 FIXED DECIMAL;
   CALL PLUSOP(NUMBER, ANS);
   DO WHILE (SYMBOL(NUMBER) = '+');
     NUMBER = NUMBER + 1;
     CALL PLUSOP(NUMBER, ANS2);
     ANS = ANS + ANS2; END; END EVALEXP;


/* EVALUATE AN OPERAND FOR + AND STORE RESULT IN ANS.*/
/* CHANGE NUMBER TO POINT TO JUST AFTER THE OPERAND.*/
PLUSOP: PROCEDURE(NUMBER, ANS);
   DECLARE (NUMBER, ANS) FIXED DECIMAL;
   DECLARE ANS2 FIXED DECIMAL;
   CALL SIMPLOP(NUMBER, ANS);
   DO WHILE (SYMBOL(NUMBER) = '*');
     NUMBER = NUMBER + 1;
     CALL SIMPLOP(NUMBER, ANS2);
     ANS = ANS * ANS2; END; END PLUSOP;


/* EVALUATE A SIMPLE-OPERAND AND STORE RESULT IN ANS.*/
/* CHANGE NUMBER TO POINT TO JUST AFTER THE OPERAND.*/
SIMPLOP: PROCEDURE(NUMBER, ANS);
   DECLARE (NUMBER, ANS) FIXED DECIMAL;
   IF SYMBOL(NUMBER) = 'C'
     THEN DO; ANS = VALUE(NUMBER); NUMBER=NUMBER+1; END;
     ELSE DO; NUMBER = NUMBER + 1;
              CALL EVALEXP(NUMBER, ANS);
              NUMBER = NUMBER + 1; END; END SIMPLOP;
```

Section 4 _Exercises_

1. Write recursive procedures for the following recursively-defined functions. These could all be written more efficiently using iteration; they are intended only to get you used to recursion.

a) Greatest common divisor GCD(A,B) of two integers greater than 0:

$$GCD(A,B) = \begin{cases} B \text{ if MOD}(A,B) = 0 \\ GCD(B, r) \text{ if MOD}(A,B) = r, \ r > 0 \end{cases}$$

b) nth Fibonacci number, where n ≥ 0 is an integer

$$Fib(n) = \begin{cases} 0 \text{ if } n = 0 \\ 1 \text{ if } n = 1 \\ Fib(n-1) + Fib(n-2) \quad \text{ if } n > 1 \end{cases}$$

   c) Reverse(S) where S is a string variable:

$$Reverse(S) = \begin{cases} S & \text{if } LENGTH(S) \leq 1 \\ Reverse(SUBSTR(S,2)) \mid\mid SUBSTR(S,1,1) & \text{otherwise} \end{cases}$$

   d) Ackermann's function, where M, N are integers ≥ 0

$$A(M,N) = \begin{cases} N + 1 & \text{if } M = 0 \\ A(M-1,1) & \text{if } M \neq 0 \text{ and } N = 0 \\ A(M-1, A(M,N-1)) & \text{if } M \neq 0 \text{ and } N \neq 0 \end{cases}$$

2. Write a non-recursive procedure, using iteration, for each of the problems in Exercise 1. (Ackermann's function will be difficult to write without recursion.)

3. Prove that the recursive Towers of Hanoi procedure satisfies the rule that no disk be placed on top of a smaller one.

4. Execute CALL WITHIN('ABCD','BD',ANS); of the following procedure by hand. State exactly what the procedure does. (In PL/I, execution will produce an error message when SUBSTR(Y,2) is evaluated and Y has only one character. This should however be allowed; the result should be the empty string.)

```
WITHIN: PROCEDURE(X, Y, ANSWER);
   DECLARE (X, Y) CHAR(*), ANSWER FIXED DECIMAL;
   DECLARE I FIXED DECIMAL;
   ANSWER = 1;
   IF LENGTH(Y) = 0 THEN RETURN;
   DO I = 1 TO LENGTH(X);
      IF SUBSTR(X,I,1) = SUBSTR(Y,1,1) THEN
         DO; CALL WITHIN(SUBSTR(X,I+1), SUBSTR(Y,2), ANSWER);
            RETURN; END; END;
   ANSWER = 0;     END WITHIN;
```

5. Execute by hand the call CALL QUICKSORT(A,1,5);, drawing all the array A where A(1)=1, A(2)=3, A(3)=2, A(4)=5, and A(5)=0. the array A where A(1)=1, A(2)=3, A(3)=2, A(4)=5, and A(5)=0. When executing the Partition command, always choose the value in A(1) for the pivot value -- it will end up in A(K). You do not need to refer back to the Partition algorithm of Section II.6.4; just perform the command without using a formal algorithm.

6. Merge Sort. One way of sorting an array segment A(M:N) is to
   1. Let K = FLOOR((M+N)/2);
   2. Sort segment A(M:K);
   3. Sort segment A(K+1:N);
   4. Merge the two sorted segments into one sorted list.

Write a recursive procedure to do this. The merge operation should be performed in linear time -- in time proportional to the number of elements to be merged. You may use an extra array of size A(M:K) if you wish.

Section 5 * <u>Asynchronous Procedures</u>

PL/I permits the programming of a subalgorithm which is called into action not by explicit invocation by the programmer, but by the occurrence of an "exceptional condition". These conditions are primarily associated with some form of error -- an attempt to divide by zero, an attempt to compute a number which exceeds the capacity of the variable that is to receive it, etc. PL/I permits the programmer, to a certain extent, to devise his own remedial action in the event that one of these conditions arises. These procedures are said to be "asynchronous" because they are essentially independent of the conventional flow-of-control of the program. They are executed whenever the particular activating event occurs.

In general, the use of PL/I "ON conditions" is a relatively advanced topic and well beyond the scope of this book. Appendix A contains a brief description of conditions and interrupts. One condition, the ENDFILE condition, is important enough for us to show how to use it here.

5.1* <u>The ENDFILE Condition</u>

A very common problem in programming is the detection of the end of the input data. Three basic strategies are used:

    1. Adding a detectable dummy value to the end of the data (as was done in the example of Section 1.1 of Part I).

    2. Placing control information (such as a count of the number of values) at the beginning of the data. (This is illustrated in Exercise 4b of Section I.4.)

    3. Relying on some special provision in either the programming language or the actual computer hardware to detect the physical end of the data.

The first two of these strategies are implemented entirely by the individual programmer and may be used in any language. PL/I offers the third strategy as well, by recognizing the "end-of-data-file" condition as one of the events capable of invoking an asynchronous procedure.

The programmer supplies an "ON-unit" that specifies what should take place whenever a GET statement attempts to read data and fails because insufficient data remains in the input stream. The statement has the form

    ON ENDFILE(SYSIN) ON-unit

where the ON-unit may be an assignment statement, a GO TO statement, or a BEGIN block. The ON-unit is executed when an end-of-file occurs.

The ON statement is an <u>executable</u> statement but its execution only causes the ON-unit to be <u>associated</u> with the end-of-file condition. That ON-unit (as opposed to the ON statement) will be executed if and when the end of the data is encountered.

To illustrate, consider a program segment which is to read values into arrays B(1:10) and A(1:100). There are exactly 10 data values in the input for B, but the number for A may vary from none to 100. A variable N is to be set to the number of values read for array A. The program segment below first associates a block with the end-of-file condition; this block is executed when the end of the data is encountered. This block prints an error message, stores zeros in the rest of array B, and sets the number of values in A to 0. It then exits to the end of the program segment.

If array B is read correctly, the program then associates a second ON-unit to the end-of-file condition; this causes the previous ON-unit to become disassociated. The list of values for A is then read.

```
DECLARE (B(1:10), A(1:100)) FIXED DECIMAL,
        N FIXED DECIMAL,    /* NO. OF VALUES IN A. */
        X FIXED DECIMAL; /* NEW INPUT DATUM */
        I FIXED DECIMAL;
        ...
/* READ IN LISTS A AND B */
   ON ENDFILE(SYSIN) BEGIN; PUT SKIP LIST('ERROR: ONLY',
                                I, 'B VALUES');
                    DO I = I TO 10 BY 1; B(I)=0; END;
                    N=0; GO TO EXITREADSEG; END;

   DO I = 1 TO 10 BY 1; GET LIST(B(I)); END;

   ON ENDFILE(SYSIN) GO TO EXITREADSEG;

   N  = 0; /* AT ANY POINT, N INTEGERS HAVE BEEN READ INTO A*/
   DO WHILE ('1'B);
      GET LIST(X);
      IF N >= 100 THEN DO; PUT SKIP LIST('TOO MUCH INPUT');
                           GO TO EXITREADSEG; END;
      N = N+1; A(N) = X; END;
   EXITREADSEG:;
```

Section 6 <u>Modular Testing</u>

Since significant programs always involve blocks in addition to the main procedure, testing must also take block structure into consideration. However, since we decided to discuss testing (Part III) before PROCEDURE and BEGIN blocks, we could not complete the discussion at that point. Now we can extend it to cover programs with more than one block.

The block structure of PL/I is a major asset in program testing. The procedures of a properly written program are programs that are independent of each other, except for carefully specified and controlled communications. This facilitates the modular and parallel testing recommended in Sections III.2.1 and III.2.1.1. The testing process should confirm the correctness of each procedure separately, by demonstrating that:

a) it performs the required task under all valid conditions,

b) it defends itself properly against all improper conditions (or makes its assumptions of conditions very clear in its introductory comments),

c) it does not depend upon communications or assumptions other than those explicitly specified,

d) it has no external effects other than those specified.

Large programs can be confidently constructed from such modules. They can also subsequently be modified with confidence that the effects of the modification are predictable and controllable.

6.1 <u>Block-Oriented Testing Facilities</u>

The major diagnostic facility of PL/I -- the CHECK prefix -- (Section III.4.1) is based on the block structure of a program. The CHECK prefix can be applied to any PROCEDURE or BEGIN block, and causes "checking" to take place only within that block. The extent of the checking depends upon the <u>static</u> rather than the <u>dynamic</u> scope of the block. That is, it will apply to any block that is <u>written</u> within the block with the prefix, and not to blocks that are written elsewhere but <u>executed</u> by being CALLed from within the block with the prefix. For example:

```
        (CHECK(X, Y)):
        PR1: PROCEDURE OPTIONS(MAIN);
            ...
            CALL PR2;
            CALL PR3(X);
            ...
            PR2: PROCEDURE;
(6.1a)          ...      END PR2; END PR1;
    *PROCESS
            PR3: PROCEDURE(A);
            ...      END PR3;
```

The CHECK prefix applied to PR1 also applies to PR2, which is
written within PR1, but not to PR3, which is also called from
within PR1, but is written externally.

A completely independent CHECK prefix could be assigned to
the external procedure PR3 in (6.1a):

```
    ...
    *PROCESS
      (CHECK(A, K)):
      PR3: PROCEDURE(A);
        ...
```

(This example includes the checking of a parameter, which is
permitted in PL/C but not in PL/I.)

A CHECK prefix could also be assigned to the internal
procedure PR2 in (6.1a):

```
        ...
        (CHECK(Z)):
        PR2: PROCEDURE;
            ...
```

This causes Z to be checked in PR2 in addition to X and Y which
are already checked because PR2 is within the scope of the CHECK
prefix assigned to PR1.

A NOCHECK prefix can be assigned to an internal block to
negate all or part of the effect of a CHECK prefix on a
containing block. For example, in (6.1a) X could be exempted
from checking within PR2, although it would continue to be
checked in the rest of PR1:

```
        (CHECK(X, Y)):
        PR1: PROCEDURE OPTIONS(MAIN);
            ...
            (NOCHECK(X)):
            PR2: PROCEDURE;
                ...
```

The NOCHECK prefix is PL/I's way of limiting CHECK output
(since it does not have the NOCHECK and CHECK statements of

PL/C). One can introduce an extra block to serve as a host for
a NOCHECK prefix. For example, suppose in (6.1a) there was a DO
group involving X that was known to be correct:

```
(CHECK(X, Y)):
PR1: PROCEDURE OPTIONS(MAIN);
        ...
        DO ...
            X = ...  END;
        ...
```

This section of the program could be exempted from the checking
of X by making it a separate block:

```
(CHECK(X, Y)):
PR1: PROCEDURE OPTIONS(MAIN);
        ...
    (NOCHECK(X)): TEMP4: BEGIN;
        DO ...
            X = ...  END;
        END TEMP4;
        ...
```

It is good practice to put a label on a temporary BEGIN such as
this one, and on its corresponding END, so that when it is
removed there is no doubt as to which END should be removed.

   One can do the same in PL/C, but it is simpler and clearer to
limit the checking action with the NOCHECK and CHECK statements
rather than to introduce additional blocks.

   The rules and usage of the PL/C FLOW prefix are almost the
same as those given above for CHECK. A (NOFLOW): prefix can be
used to exclude an internal block from the effect of a (FLOW):
prefix on a containing block, but it is simpler to use the
NOFLOW and FLOW statements.   Unlike the CHECK and NOCHECK
prefixes, (FLOW): and (NOFLOW): can also be be specified on
individual simple statements, compound statements, or DO groups.

6.1.1* <u>CHECK and FLOW Limits in PL/C</u>

   In Sections III.4.1.1 and III.4.1.2 it was noted that an
expression may be given for either the CHECK or FLOW statement
in PL/C. The value obtained by evaluation of this expression
gives the number of messages to be produced by the CHECK or FLOW
action, after which NOCHECK or NOFLOW is automatically applied.
Now we should clarify that process by noting that the expression
causes a counter to be established for the block in which the
statement appears. Each CHECK or FLOW action occurring directly
in that block (not including contained or called blocks) causes
the appropriate counter to be reduced by 1. When its value
reaches 0, no further messages are printed, until the counter is
reset or another block is entered.

6.2 Driving Routines and Skeleton Procedures

It is often useful to be able to physically divide a program and test different sections separately. The larger a program becomes, the more important this is. Most programs of a hundred statements can benefit from sectional testing, and most programs of two hundred or more cannot be effectively tested without separation.

The natural way of dividing a program for sectional testing is along procedure boundaries. With programs organized so that there is a main control section and a set of subroutines (each written as a procedure) testing should proceed by

>   a) testing each subroutine independent of the main control section, and

>   b) testing the main control section without the subroutines.

To accomplish a) one writes a "driving program" for each subroutine. This simulates the essential aspects of the calling-environment of the subroutine so that it can be exercised independently. When testing of the subroutine is completed the subroutine is moved to the main program and the driving program can be discarded.

To accomplish b) one substitutes a "skeleton procedure" for each of the subroutine procedures. A skeleton procedure is identical to the real subroutine in external appearance (entry-name, parameters) but a skeleton is given in place of the full body of the subroutine. The skeleton may be a null program, a message announcing call of the subroutine, or some crude approximation of the real body -- whatever is the minimum body that will allow the procedure to be called without upsetting the control section. The purpose is to be able to exercise the control section to check its logic and flow-of-control without exercising the subroutines. This permits the correctness of the control logic to be established independently of the correctness of the subroutines. It means that testing of the control section can take place before the subroutines are even written. Furthermore, even if the subroutines exist and are known to be correct, the substitution of a skeleton procedure just to avoid execution of the subroutine may save substantial computer time while testing the control section.

For example, suppose a program must be protected against a number of special conditions that might occur in its data. The testing provisions could be written as a subroutine:

```
/* DETECT AND CORRECT EACH CATACHRESIS IN ARRAY */
DATATEST: PROCEDURE(A);
    DCL A(*) FLOAT DEC;
    ...    END DATATEST;
```

This subroutine can be tested by the following type of driving routine:

```
/* TESTING DRIVER FOR DATATEST */
DTDRIVER: PROCEDURE OPTIONS(MAIN);
    DCL N FIXED DEC; /* FIRST DATUM IS ARRAY SIZE */
    GET LIST(N);
    DT: BEGIN; DCL X(N) FLOAT DEC;
        DCL I FIXED DEC;
        /* LOAD AND OPTIONAL PRINT */
            /*3 PUT SKIP LIST('ARRAY SIZE IS', N); */
            DO I = 1 TO N BY 1; GET LIST(X(I));
                /*3 PUT SKIP LIST(X(I)); */ END;
        CALL DATATEST(X);
        /* PRINT RESULTS OF DATATEST */
            PUT SKIP LIST('CORRECTED ARRAY AFTER DATATEST');
            DO I = 1 TO N BY 1; PUT SKIP LIST(X(I)); END;
        END DT; END DTDRIVER;
*PROCESS
    /*4 (CHECK(T, V, L6)): */
    /*5 (CHECK(T, L3, L4)): */
    /* DETECT AND CORRECT EACH CATACHRESIS IN ARRAY */
    DATATEST: PROCEDURE(A);
        . . .
```

This driver includes several testing features written as PL/C pseudo-comments (Section III.4.4.1). With COMMENTS=(3) specified on the *PL/C card an optional copy of the input data with be printed. COMMENTS=(4) or COMMENTS=(5) will activate different CHECK prefixes on DATATEST.

The rest of the program can be tested using a skeleton DATATEST:

```
/* CALCULATE SPIN RESONANCE */
SPINRES: PROCEDURE OPTIONS(MAIN);
    . . .
    /* LOAD AND TEST ARRAY */
        DO I = 1 TO N BY 1; GET LIST(X(I)); END;
        CALL DATATEST(X);
    . . .
*PROCESS
    /* SKELETON ROUTINE IN PLACE OF DATATEST */
    DATATEST: PROCEDURE(A);
        DCL A(*) FLOAT DEC;
        PUT SKIP LIST('DUMMY DATATEST CALLED'); END DATATEST;
```

While the skeleton routine is being used one would either use test data that are free of that kind of error, or data that are already in the corrected form that DATATEST should produce.

This testing strategy appears to require some additional effort since extra sections of program must be written, only to be discarded after testing is completed. The extra writing is worthwhile, even for relatively small programs. This strategy is efficient in terms of both programmer's time and computer time, and more important, it generally leads to greater confidence in correctness. Testing in this manner usually contributes to a cleaner program structure, and encourages more exhaustive and systematic testing of each section.

Part V.*

COMPUTER SOLUTION OF MATHEMATICAL PROBLEMS

by

J. E. Dennis Jr. and Jorge J. Moré

Many people study computer programming because they are interested in implementing algorithms to extract quantitative information from mathematical models in science and engineering. Our purpose in this part is to first discuss some of the difficulties that are encountered when implementing such algorithms, and then to study two representative mathematical problems in some detail.

We are faced with a problem in notation. The formulas in this part will generally be intended as mathematical rather than programming language statements. However, the computer text-editing system used to produce this book does not permit many of the usual mathematical notational conventions. In particular it does not permit subscripts, and permits only integer superscripts. Therefore, we have resorted to the usual programming convention for subscripts, and in order to increase the readability of our expressions, we restrict their generality, when possible, to use only integer superscripts. In all other cases we use mathematical symbols and conventions such as $\leq$ instead of <=. We indicate multiplication by proximity or $\cdot$ rather than *, and we use vertical lines $|\ |$ to indicate absolute value (rather than concatenation or "or", as in PL/I.)

Section 1 <u>Floating Point Numbers</u>

Except for programming errors, the factors which usually account for unexpected results in numerical computations are as follows:

a) Most numbers cannot be represented <u>exactly</u> in the computer.

b) The results of the arithmetic operations performed by the computer are not, in general, <u>exact</u>.

c) Most mathematical problems require an <u>infinite</u> number of calculations.

In this section we will discuss how numbers are represented in the computer, and how this representation leads to a certain type of error called "truncation error". We also discuss how truncation error affects the different arithmetic operations.

1.1 <u>Representation of Floating Point Numbers</u>

We have already mentioned that some of the difficulties with executing numerical algorithms on the computer are due to the fact that most numbers cannot be represented <u>exactly</u> in the computer. Let us see what this means in terms of a specific example.

Consider a PL/I program which reads the number 69.4 from a data card, assigns the value to a variable which has been declared FLOAT DECIMAL and then prints the value of the variable. If you run the program you will find that the number printed out is 6.93999E+01, which is equivalent to 69.3999. On the other hand, if the number on the card is 69.5, then it is returned exactly, that is, as 6.95000E+01. The same results would have been obtained if the variable had been declared FLOAT BINARY.

To understand these results, we need to know how 69.4 and 69.5 are stored in the computer, that is, the internal representation of a floating point number. Since the situation is the same for FLOAT DECIMAL and FLOAT BINARY variables we will call their contents "floating point numbers". In this way the following discussion will apply to both cases.

A floating point number is written in terms of a <u>base</u> b, a <u>fraction</u> f, an <u>exponent</u> e, and a <u>sign</u>. If b=10, then the internal representation is just the number written as a decimal fraction times a power (the exponent) of 10. Most computers do not use base 10, but regardless of the base, any number can be written as a fraction f times a power of b. The fraction is written in terms of powers of b, and this means that

$$f = d(1) \cdot b^{-1} + d(2) \cdot b^{-2} + ..., \text{ where } 0 \le d(i) \le b-1,$$

which in base b notation is abbreviated to

$$f = (0.d(1)d(2)...)(\text{base } b).$$

The exercises at the end of this section will have a method for finding the base b representation of a number.

In the IBM 360 and 370, b = 16. This means that 69.4 is $(0.4566...)(\text{base } 16)$ because this number can be written as $f \cdot 16^2$ where

$$f = 4 \cdot 16^{-1} + 5 \cdot 16^{-2} + 6 \cdot 16^{-3} + 6 \cdot 16^{-4} + ...$$

You can easily verify that 69.5 is just $(0.458) \cdot 16^2$ in base 16. By now you have probably guessed that 69.4 and 69.5 are treated differently by the computer because it can only hold finitely many digits of a fraction.

The part of the fraction that the computer does save is called the <u>mantissa</u> and t, the number of digits in the mantissa, is the <u>precision</u> of the floating point number. In general, the errors that are due to the finite precision of the computer are called "truncation errors"; we will study them in detail in the next section.

PL/I on the IBM 360 allows t=6, called <u>single precision</u>, or t=14, called <u>double precision</u>. The default assumption is single precision, so in order to use double precision, it is necessary to declare attributes of DECIMAL FLOAT(16) or BINARY FLOAT(53). Since double precision was not specified in the previous example, 69.4 was represented internally in single precision as

$$(0.456666) \cdot 16^2 (\text{base } 16)$$

and 69.5 was represented as

$$(0.458000) \cdot 16^2 (\text{base } 16).$$

On output the computer prints the base 10 representation of these numbers.

Note that the internal representation of a floating point number has a mantissa with a non-zero first digit. This "normalized" form is always possible (unless the number is zero) and clearly leads to maximum accuracy.

The t-digit floating point numbers can be thought of as a finite subset of the real numbers. They are fairly densely packed about zero, but become more widely separated further from zero. The t-digit floating point representation T(x) of a real number x is the member of this subset which is nearest to x among all those members between x and 0. In particular, all real numbers between two adjacent floating point numbers will have the same floating point representation.

In the preceding paragraph we referred for the first time to there being finitely many t-digit floating point numbers. This is rather clear, for just as the computer must truncate the fractional part of the number, so it can't allow more than finitely many different exponents. The IBM 360 floating point numbers are approximately between

$$5.4 \cdot 10^{-79} \text{ and } 7.2 \cdot 10^{75}$$

since the range of base 16 exponents is $-64 \le e \le 63$. When the computer encounters a number not in this range it prints an UNDERFLOW or OVERFLOW message. OVERFLOW is a common problem in numerical computation, where it is often caused by dividing a large floating point number by a small one. UNDERFLOW signals a loss of accuracy since it warns that a number has been taken to be zero because in its normalized form the exponent required is too small. In general, when we see UNDERFLOW we <u>suspect</u> the results of the computation, and when we see OVERFLOW we <u>discard</u> them.

At this stage you may want to know whether you should use single or double precision. Unless the number of operations is rather large, the increased cost of double precision isn't noticeable, so double precision is generally advisable for small problems. In PL/C, you do not have this choice since all floating point variables are actually maintained in double precision form, and converted to the specified precision only on output. This is not true in PL/I.

You may wonder why we specify double precision variables as FLOAT DECIMAL(16) or FLOAT BINARY(53) when the computer represents them in either case with 14 base 16 digits. The answer is that 16 decimal digits, 53 binary digits, and 14 hexadecimal (base 16) digits all give essentially the same precision. We will explain why in the next section.

1.2 <u>Truncation Errors and Significant Decimal Digits</u>

In the previous section we showed how a computer represents
any real number x in its floating point range by a floating
point number T(x) obtained from the leading t terms of the
number's expansion in powers of the base b. Clearly, this
approximation of x by T(x) sets a limit on the accuracy of any
subsequent   calculations   and   we   are   thus led to ask what the
maximum possible accuracy is when we approximate x by T(x).   To
answer this question we need a precise way to measure accuracy.

The generally accepted way to measure how accurately a number
y   approximates   another   number   x   is   in terms of <u>significant
decimal digits</u>. We would like to say that y has s significant
decimal digits as an approximation to x if when x and y are
represented as decimal numbers then the leading s digits agree
and the (s+1)st digits do not differ by more than five.   This
definition suffices for x=10012, y=10034, or for x=10.012,
y=10.034, since it gives the same reasonable answer of three
significant decimal digits in either case. On the other hand,
in the previous section we stated that if x=69.4 then on the IBM
360 the single precision T(x) is 69.3999.   This is clearly a
better approximation to x than 69.3 and yet in the above sense
they both have two significant decimal digits.   All this is
meant to convince you that in order to give a precise and
reasonable definition of significant decimal digits we will have
to examine truncation errors more carefully.

We begin by obtaining a bound on the magnitude of the error
committed by replacing T(x) by x. The quantity $|T(x)-x|$ is
called the <u>absolute error</u> of T(x) as an approximation to x,
while if $x \neq 0$ then $|T(x)-x|/|x|$ is the <u>relative error</u>.

<u>Theorem</u>: If $x \neq 0$ lies in the range of the base b floating point
      numbers of precision t, then

(1.2a) $|T(x)-x|/|x| < b^{**(1-t)}$.

We will prove (1.2a) for the case when t=6.   This will
illustrate the general case, and you should prove (1.2a) in full
generality as an exercise. It is only necessary to give a proof
in the case that x>0 since the proof for a negative x differs
only in sign.

Now take any x>0 and represent it as a normalized base b
number.   That is, set

   $x = (b^{**}e) \cdot [d(1) \cdot b^{-1} + \ldots + d(6) \cdot b^{-6} + \ldots]$

where $d(1) \neq 0$.   Notice (since we will need it later) that
$|x| > b^{**(e-1)}$.   Then since t=6,

   $T(x) = (b^{**}e) \cdot [d(1) \cdot b^{-1} + \ldots + d(6) \cdot b^{-6}]$

and thus,

$$T(x)-x = -(b**e) \cdot [d(7) \cdot b^{-7} + d(8) \cdot b^{-8} + \ldots].$$

Now make use of the fact that $0 \leq d(i) \leq b-1$ to replace $d(7)$, $d(8)$, etc., by $(b-1)$ and get

$$|T(x)-x| \leq (b**e)(b-1)[b^{-7} + b^{-8} + \ldots \quad].$$

However,

$$b^{-7} + b^{-8} + \ldots = b^{-7}(1 + b^{-1} + b^{-2} + \ldots) = b^{-6}/(b-1)$$

since this is a geometric series. Therefore,

$$|T(x)-x| \leq (b**e)b^{-6} < b^{-5}|x|$$

where we have used the fact that $|x| > b**(e-1)$. Inequality (1.2a) now follows.

In general, if x and y are real numbers and y is an approximation to x, then $|y-x|$ is the absolute error of y as an approximation to x while $|y-x|/|x|$ is the relative error of y as an approximation to $x \neq 0$. Inequality (1.2a) indicates that if $y=T(x)$ then the absolute error is not a very good measure of the agreement between y and x if the magnitude of x is very large or very small. This is also true if y is any approximation to x. For example, if $y=10^{-6}$ and $x=10^{-5}$ then $|y-x|<10^{-5}$ although y certainly isn't a good approximation to x. On the other hand, the relative error measures the number of fractional digits that x and y have in common. In fact, we will say that the first s decimal digits of y are significant as an approximation to x, if $|y-x|/|x| \leq 5 \cdot 10**(-s)$. If you work out a few examples, you will see that this precise definition and the intuitive notion given at the beginning of this section essentially agree.

Now that we have these results we can determine the number of significant decimal digits in $T(x)$ as an approximation to x. We will only consider double precision in the IBM 360 with $b=16$ and $t=14$ although essentially the same results hold if $b=2$ and $t=53$. For any real number x in the range of floating point numbers, (1.2a) implies that the relative error of $T(x)$ as an approximation to x is bounded by 16^{-13} or about $2.2 \cdot 10^{-16}$. Therefore, $T(x)$ has 16 significant digits as an approximation to x so subsequent calculations which use $T(x)$ in place of x can only be expected to have at most 16 significant decimal digits. This explains why only 16 digits are printed as output by the computer, and why FLOAT DECIMAL(16) and FLOAT BINARY(53) give the same precision.

1.3 <u>Errors in Floating Point Arithmetic</u>

We have already discussed how truncation errors arise as the result of converting a number x into its floating point representation. Truncation errors also arise because the results of arithmetic operations performed on the computer are, in general, not exact. In order to illustrate these errors we will assume that we are working on a computer with base b=10 and precision t=4. You can observe similar errors on any computer, but this simple scheme makes it easier to really see what is happening.

First consider addition and suppose we want to add 163.9 and 24.36. On our computer they would be represented in normalized form as $(0.1639)10^3$ and $(0.2436)10^2$. However, since the computer can only perform additions by adding the mantissas of numbers with equal exponents, these numbers will be added in the form $(0.1639)10^3$ and $(0.02436)10^3$. In other words, the exponent of the number with the smaller exponent will be increased, and its mantissa will be shifted right by the same number of places. You can see that the result is $(0.1882)10^3$ which is the correct answer truncated to our working precision, t=4.

Although the example shows that the addition of two numbers has a small relative error associated with it, this is not the case when several numbers are added. For example, consider adding 0.556, 3.294, 24.36 and 163.9. Adding in decreasing order of magnitude the sum is 191.9. But if we add in the opposite order the sum is 192.1. Since the true sum is 192.11, the relative error for the sum in decreasing order is 21 times larger than in the reverse order.

If you have to add many numbers and you want high precision then you should try to add them in <u>increasing order of magnitude</u>. For most mathematical problems this is not convenient, so instead the sums are usually <u>accumulated</u>. This means that each intermediate sum is stored in double precision and then added to the next summand in double precision. The final result is then truncated to the working precision. If the sum in the previous example had been accumulated, then the final sum would have been 192.1 regardless of the order in which the sum was carried out. PL/C's use of internal double precision, which we explained in Section 1.1, is more or less an extension of this idea.

Subtraction is similar to addition. However, note that if two almost equal numbers are being subtracted then there may be a loss of significance. For example, if x=136.5 and y=136.4 are approximations to 136.57 and 136.41, respectively, then both x and y have 4 significant digits. However, x-y=0.1 has <u>no</u> significant digits as an approximation to 0.16, the true difference.

It is not important to know precisely how the multiplication and division of two floating point numbers are carried out. It

is important for you to know that these operations are carried
out in such a way that the result equals the true answer
truncated to the working precision. This means that the
multiplication or division of two numbers gives rise to a small
relative error. In fact, unlike addition and subtraction, it is
even possible to prove that the relative error does not grow
when several numbers are multiplied or divided. Unfortunately
things aren't as good as they sound, since underflow and
overflow occur much more frequently in this case and can be a
source of error. For example, let x and y be floating point
numbers and consider the calculation of $z = sqrt(x^2 + y^2)$.
(Here and below, we intend "sqrt(arg)" to denote the nonnegative
square root of arg.) If our machine with b=10 and t=4 restricts
the exponent to $-9 \leq e \leq 9$, then you can verify that a
straightforward calculation of z with $x = y = 10^{-6}$ gives $z = 0$
instead of $10^{-6} \cdot sqrt(2)$. This seems to be unavoidable in our
computer, but in fact it isn't. We just have to be clever and
see that the computation of z can also be carried out as
follows:

Let $v = max\{|x|, |y|\}$

and $w = min\{|x|, |y|\}$.

Then, you can see that

$$z = v \cdot sqrt(1 + (w/v)^2),$$

and this time, for our example, we do obtain $z = 10^{-6} \cdot sqrt(2)$.

Now that we have talked about sums and products, we can
discuss one of the most common numerical computations. From our
discussion of the calculation of sums you can see that we should
also be careful in the evaluation of inner products; that is,
quantities of the form

$$(x(1) \cdot y(1)) + \ldots + (x(n) \cdot y(n)).$$

If high accuracy is desired, then inner products are usually
accumulated. This means that each product $(x(i) \cdot y(i))$ is
calculated in double precision and then this double precision
number is added to the accumulated sum of the previous products.
The final result is truncated to working precision. Again, this
is more or less automatic in PL/C.

As a final word of warning we mention that the accumulation
of sums and inner products is not guaranteed to result in small
relative errors unless cancellation does not occur. For
example, consider

$$1.002 \cdot (1.003) + 0.9999 \cdot (-.9995) + 0.02000 \cdot (-0.2803).$$

Forming the products in double precision, i.e. with t=8, gives

$$(0.10050060)10^1 + (-0.9994005)10^0 + (-0.56060000)10^{-2}$$

which is zero in floating point addition with t=8. The true sum is easily seen to be $-0.5 \cdot 10^{-7}$.

Now that we have made you aware of truncation errors, what can you do about them? Certainly it helps to work in extended precision, but still the best line of defense is to be aware of them so that you may be able to rearrange your calculations to lessen their effect.

Section 1 <u>Exercises</u>

1. The conversion of a decimal integer into base 2 notation is accomplished by a series of divisions by 2. The remainders, either 0 or 1, yield the digits of the fraction in reverse order, and the exponent is the number of divisions performed. For example, if the decimal integer is 69 we obtain

	quotient	remainder
69/2	34	1
34/2	17	0
17/2	8	1
8/2	4	0
4/2	2	0
2/2	1	0
1/2	0	1

The appearance of a zero quotient signals the end of the process. The result is that

$$69 = (.1000101) \cdot 2^7 \text{ (base 2)}.$$

To see that this algorithm works, note that if

$$69 = (.d(1) \ldots d(7)) \cdot 2^7,$$

then

$$69 = d(7) + d(6) \cdot 2 + d(5) \cdot 2^2 + \ldots + d(1) \cdot 2^6.$$

Therefore,

$$69/2 = 1/2 + 34 = d(7)/2 + d(6) + d(5) \cdot 2 + \ldots + d(1) \cdot 2^5,$$

so that d(7)=1 and

$$34 = d(5) \cdot 2 + d(4) \cdot 2^2 + \ldots + d(1) \cdot 2^5.$$

We can now divide 34 by 2 and proceed as before until we obtain a zero quotient.

a) Write a program that will find the base 2 expansion of a
   decimal integer.

b) Modify the program in a) so that it will find the
   expansion in any integral base b>1.

2. Write a program that will find the base 2 expansion of a
decimal fraction.   The algorithm for this program is very
similar to the one described in Exercise 1, but now the number
will be successively <u>multiplied</u> by 2.

3. Write a program that will perform the conversion between
binary (base 2) and hexadecimal (base 16) numbers.   An outline
of the algorithm is as follows:

To go from hexadecimal to binary, replace each hexadecimal
digit by its binary representation and (since $16=2^4$)
multiply the exponent by 4.   For example,

$$(.458) \cdot 16^2 \text{ (base 16)} = (.0100 \ 0101 \ 1000) \cdot 2^8 \text{ (base 2)}.$$

To go from binary to hexadecimal, first increase the
exponent and add leading zeroes to the fraction until the
exponent is divisible by 4.   Then replace each group of
four binary digits by the corresponding hexadecimal digit
and divide the exponent by 4.   For example,

$$(.10101) \cdot 2^{-6} \text{ (base 2)} = (.0010101) \cdot 2^{-4} \text{ (base 2)}$$

$$= (.2A) \cdot 16^{-1} \text{ (base 16)}.$$

We have used A (=10) for 1010, and similarly, B, C, D, E
and F are used for the digits 11 through 15.

4. Let x=1.0 and y=0.999.   Give the number of significant
decimal digits, the absolute error and the relative error in y
as an approximation to x.   Repeat the exercise with the pairs
$x \cdot 10^{-4}$, $y \cdot 10^{-4}$ and $x \cdot 10^4$, $y \cdot 10^4$.

5. a) Prove that y=0 never has any significant decimal digits as
   an approximation to any nonzero number x.

   b) Show that if $y \cdot x < 0$, then y has no significant decimal
   digits as an approximation to x.

6. Complete the proof of (1.2a) by showing that it holds for
any precision t.

7. a) What is the <u>maximum</u> number of significant decimal digits
   possible in general if you are working on a computer with
   b=16 and t=6?

   b) Show that if b=10 then the maximum number of significant
   decimal digits is one less than the precision.

8. a) Show that 0.2 has no significant decimal digits as an
      approximation to 0.1 but that 0.1 has one significant
      decimal digit as an approximation to 0.2.

   b) Part a) shows that there is a lack of symmetry in the
      definition of significant decimal digits; prove that it can
      be removed by changing the definition to

$$|y-x| \leq 5(10**-s)\cdot\min\{|x|, |y|\}.$$

9. Write a program segment to read a given value of x and
compute the sum

$$1 + x/1! + x^2/2! + \ldots + x^{30}/30!$$

in ascending and descending orders. Compare the results for
x = ±10, ±5, ±0.1. Explain any differences.

10. Consider the following segment of a PL/I program:

```
A = 20.0; B = 0.1; C = A * B;
DO I = 1 TO C BY 1;
    PUT SKIP LIST(I); END;
```

What values of I will be printed? Check your answer by running
this program.

Section 2 <u>Library Functions (COS and SQRT)</u>

Consider the statement Y = COS(X); where X is some floating point number, or the statement Y = SQRT(X); where X is now restricted to be nonnegative. When the computer executes these statements it will provide fast and accurate approximations to cos(x) and sqrt(x). How does it do this? Certainly, it does not have a table in which to look up the answer; this would require huge amounts of storage space and time. Instead for each value of x the computer generates an approximation to cos(x) or sqrt(x) by means of a few arithmetic operations.

2.1 <u>Approximation by Polynomials</u>

There are many methods for calculating a fast and accurate approximation to cos(x). Those readers with some knowledge of calculus are aware of a method based on Taylor's expansion of the cosine function. Since most people think that this is <u>the</u> way to calculate cos(x), we will first spend some time trying to convince you that this approach is not at all practical.

The approach that we have been refering to is based on the mathematical theorem that

$$(2.1a) \quad \cos(x) = 1 - x^2/2! + x^4/4! - x^6/6! + \ldots$$

The right hand side of (2.1a) is called the "Taylor expansion" of the cosine function; the meaning of (2.1a) is that given any x and any accuracy factor ERROR, there is an integer (which depends on x and ERROR) such that the sum of the first n terms on the right of (2.1a) is an approximation to cos(x) whose absolute error is less than ERROR. In other words, by adding enough terms we can get an approximation to cos(x) which is as accurate as desired.

There are many reasons why this approach is not reasonable. For one, how many terms do we need to take? In general, the larger |x| is, the more terms you need to take and this will slow down the computation. Even if you are willing to spend the time to compute enough terms in the right hand side of (2.1a), there is no guarantee that we will obtain an accurate answer. Equality in (2.1a) is a mathematical fact which depends on infinite precision; in finite precision (2.1a) is not true. For example, if x=5.0 then with b=16 and t=6 the sum on the right of

(2.1a) equals 0.283655 but cos(5.0) = 0.283662... in infinite
precision.

It is fairly easy to see why we only obtain five significant
decimal digits: All the terms in the sum are restricted to
approximately seven decimal digits, but since the initial terms
like $5^4/4! = 26.04...$ are large, their initial two digits will
have to cancel in order to obtain an answer that is less than
one, and therefore only five decimal digits really contribute to
the accuracy of the sum. In addition, later terms will be small
and only their initial digits will contribute to the sum; after
the twelfth term they are negligible.

The cancellation that we have observed is due to the fact
that |x| is large and it will get worse if |x| is increased. If
|x| is small then (.2.1a) is a reasonable way to compute cos(x).
Therefore, it is reasonable that practical methods for
evaluating cos(x) have an initial stage which allows you to
avoid the direct computation of cos(x) for large values of |x|.
The method that we will now describe shows that all the values
of cos(x) can be obtained from those of cos(x) and sin(x) for x
between 0 and (pi)/4 (where pi = 3.14159...).

First recall that the cosine is an even function, which means
that cos(-x) = cos(x), so we only need to consider nonnegative
x. Moreover, the cosine is a periodic function whose period is
p = 2pi.   This means that cos(x + p·k) = cos(x) for any integer
k. To make use of this property first compute 4x/pi = q + f,
where q is an integer and f is the fractional part of 4x/pi.
Now express q as q = 8k + r where k and r are integers with
0≤r<8.   Altogether,   x = p·k + pi·(f+r)/4,   so that periodicity
implies that

          cos(x) = cos(pi·(f+r)/4).

Depending on the values of r we will have different results.
For example, if r = 0 then

          cos(x) = cos(pi·f/4)

while if r = 1 then

          cos(x) = cos(pi/2 - pi·(1-f)/4) = sin(pi·(1-f)/4).

Similar   relationships   hold   for   any   0≤r<8,   so   that
cos(pi·(f+r)/4) equals ±cos(pi·g/4) or ±sin(pi·g/4) where g = f
or g = 1-f.

The process just described is known as "range reduction".
Note that it consists of a clever use of the symmetries of the
cosine function; for other functions range reduction would take
a different form. If it is possible, range reduction is usually
beneficial, but the operations involved have to be carried out
with extreme care since they are very sensitive to errors.

Now that we have range reduction, the calculation of the cosine function will be complete if we can generate cos(x) and sin(x) for $0 \leq x \leq$ (pi)/4. For simplicity we only discuss the cosine function. In this case (2.1a) is reasonable since cancellation will not occur. In fact, if

$$(2.1b) \quad p(x) = 1 - x^2/2! \ + x^4/4! \ - x^6/6! \ + x^8/8!,$$

then some thought will show that (2.1a) implies that

$$|p(x) - \cos(x)| < (pi/4)^{10}/10! \ = (2.5)10^{-8}$$

for $0 \leq x \leq$ (pi)/4. Moreover, since in this range cos(x) $\geq$ 1/sqrt(2), we also have

$$|(p(x) - \cos(x))/\cos(x)| < (3.5)10^{-8}.$$

This shows that p(x) always has eight significant decimal digits as an approximation to cos(x), so (2.1b) is adequate for single precision.

The function defined by (2.1b) is a polynomial of degree 8 in x, and degree 4 in x^2. Hence if we can find a polynomial of degree 3 in x^2 which approximates the cosine as well as (2.1b), then we should use this polynomial instead of (2.1b) since any work saving in a library function like the cosine is important because of the high frequency with which it will be used. It is indeed possible to find such a polynomial but the methods for doing this are beyond the scope of this book. The interested reader will find material on this topic in the references of Section 4.

2.1.1 <u>Horner's Scheme</u>

The point was made in Section 2.1 that any savings in the work required to execute a frequently performed task is generally worthwhile. Polynomial evaluation is certainly such a task if for no other reason than their frequent use in approximation.

Consider then the evaluation of a polynomial p of degree n

$$(2.1.1a) \quad p(x) = a(0) + a(1)x + a(2)x^2 + \ldots + a(n)(x**n).$$

If we evaluate (2.1.1a) in what would seem to be the obvious way -- evaluate a(i)(x**i) for i=0,1,...,n and add these terms together -- then this would involve n(n+1)/2 multiplications and n additions. To see this, note that the evaluation of a(i)(x**i) involves i multiplications and therefore the number of multiplications is

$$1 + 2 + \ldots + n = n(n+1)/2.$$

In analogy with the terminology introduced in Part II, we say that this is an n^2 algorithm. Note however, that if we evaluate (2.1.1a) from left to right, then each term needs only 2 multiplications and one addition. For example, if we have evaluated

$$a(0) + a(1)x + a(2)x^2,$$

then we only need one multiplication to compute x^3 from x^2, another multiplication for $a(3)x^3$, and an addition for

$$a(0) + a(1)x + a(2)x^2 + a(3)x^3.$$

In all, for (2.1.1a) we need 2n multiplications and n additions, so this is an order n algorithm.

However, there is a still faster algorithm, known as Horner's scheme. This method consists of a series of n nested multiplications such that at each stage only one multiplication and one addition occur. Thus Horner's scheme is also an order n algorithm but requires only half as many multiplications as the previous algorithm.

The idea of Horner's method is really simple. First note that a first degree polynomial can be evaluated in one multiplication and one addition. If we write a second degree polynomial in the form

$$a(0) + a(1)x + a(2)x^2 = a(0) + (a(1) + a(2)x)x,$$

then it can be evaluated in two multiplications and two additions. For a third degree polynomial, first write

$$a(0) + a(1)x + a(2)x^2 + a(3)x^3 = a(0) + (a(1) + a(2)x + a(3)x^2)x,$$

and then evaluate the polynomial in parentheses as above. The idea of the algorithm should now be clear; a version of it is as follows:

```
PX = A(N);
DO I = N-1 TO 0 BY -1;
    PX = X * PX + A(I); END;
```

Note that if the coefficients of the polynomials are decreasing in magnitude, as in (2.1b), then for $|x| \leq 1$, the sum in Horner's method will consist of an addition of terms of increasing magnitude. Therefore, in cases like this we expect an accurate evaluation of the polynomial.

2.2 Approximation by Iteration

The techniques discussed in Section 2.1 apply to the
evaluation of most functions, and in particular, to the
evaluation of sqrt(x). However, in this case we shall see that
although range reduction is possible, the final approximation of
sqrt(x) is not obtained from a polynomial, but by a technique
called "iteration".

First let us consider the form taken by range reduction.   If
x is a floating point number in a base 16 computer then

$$x = m(16**e)$$

where $1/16 \leq m < 1$ is the mantissa and e is the exponent. If e
is even, say e=2c, then

$$sqrt(x) = sqrt(m) \cdot 16**c,$$

while is e is odd, say e=2d-1, then

$$sqrt(x) = (1/4)sqrt(m) \cdot 16**d.$$

By combining both cases we see that it is only necessary to
evaluate sqrt(x) for $1/16 \leq x < 1$.

At this stage, in analogy with the previous section, it would
seem reasonable to try to approximate the square-root function
on the reduced range by a polynomial. However, this turns out
not to be practical.

The method used depends on the fact that the number we are
after, sqrt(m), is the positive solution of the equation
$-m+x^2 = 0$. Consider then the graph of the function defined by
$f(x) = -m+x^2$.   If we have an approximation x(0) to sqrt(m) with
x(0) > sqrt(m), then it is easy to obtain a better approximation
x(1) with x(1) > sqrt(m).   Just draw the tangent line to f at
x(0) and take x(1) to be the intersection of this line with the
x-axis.   Finding x(1) is not difficult.   The slope of the
tangent line to f at x(0) is just the derivative f'(x(0)) so
that the y-intercept equation of the tangent line is

$$y = f'(x(0))(x-x(0)) + f(x(0)).$$

But $f'(x(0)) = 2 \cdot x(0)$ and $f(x(0)) = -m + x(0)^2$ and thus

$$y = 2 \cdot x \cdot x(0) - m - x(0)^2.$$

Finally, since x(1) is the x-intercept of this line,

$$0 = 2 \cdot x(0) \cdot x(1) - m - x(0)^2$$

and rearranging terms,

$$x(1) = (x(0) + m/x(0))/2.$$

There is no reason why this process cannot be repeated to obtain
a still better approximation x(2) where

       x(2) = (x(1) + m/x(1))/2.

In general, if we have the kth approximation x(k), the (k+1)st
approximation x(k+1) is given by

(2.2a)   x(k+1) = (x(k) + m/x(k))/2.

   Geometrically, it is obvious that if x(0) > sqrt(m) then

       sqrt(m) < x(k+1) < x(k),

and that given any accuracy factor ERROR there will be an
approximation x(k) such that

       |x(k) - sqrt(m)| < ERROR.

Since sqrt(m) ≥ 1/4, we would also have

       |(x(k) - sqrt(m))/sqrt(m)| < 4·ERROR.

This would solve the problem of evaluating sqrt(m) if we could
answer two questions: 1) How do you choose the initial
approximation x(0)? 2) How do you decide which approximation to
take as sqrt(m)?

   These two questions are obviously related. We want an x(0)
which is close to sqrt(m) because this may mean that our fourth
approximation, say, will be the final one. On the other hand,
we do not want to spend too many operations in trying to find an
accurate x(0). In the following, these delicate matters will be
ignored and we will limit ourselves to presenting reasonable
solutions.

   An acceptable x(0) can be found as follows: First find the
straight line that best approximates (in the relative sense) the
square root function for 1/16 ≤ x ≤ 1; that is, determine
constants a and b such that

       max{|(sqrt(x) - (a+bx))/sqrt(x)| : 1/16≤x≤1 }

is minimal. Then set x(0) = a+bm. It turns out that a=2/9,
b=8/9, and that the resulting x(0) always has one significant
decimal digit as an approximation to sqrt(m).

   Deciding which approximation to accept as the final one is a
somewhat difficult question to answer theoretically. However, a
little experimentation will convince you that the third and
fourth approximations x(3) and x(4) will suffice for single and
double precision, respectively. The rule of thumb is that each
iteration roughly <u>doubles</u> the number of significant figures (and
recall that x(0) has one).

To finish this section, we mention that the method used to find the zero of the function $f(x) = -m+x^2$ is known as "Newton's method". It can be used to find a zero of a general function f. In fact, the same argument in terms of tangent lines and x-intercepts yields that Newton's method is given by

$$x(k+1) = x(k) - f(x(k))/f'(x(k)).$$

If $f(x) = -m+x^2$ then it is easy to verify that Newton's method reduces to (2.2a).

Section 2 <u>Exercises</u>

1. Show that sqrt(2) does not have a finite or repeating decimal representation. Do the same for cos(1) by using (2.1a).

2. Write an algorithm which accepts a positive integer q and finds integers k and r with 0≤r<8 and such that q = 8k + r.

3. Complete the discussion in the text by showing how cos(pi·(f+r)/4) can be expressed in terms of cos(pi·g/4) or sin(pi·g/4) where g=f or 1-f.

4. Verify the statements given in the text on the calculation of the right side of (2.1a). Evaluate it in three different ways: in ascending and descending order, and by Horner's method. In addition, evaluate the right side of (2.1a) for x=1.57 and explain why the results are worse than for x=5.0.

5. Let s(n,x) denote the sum of the first n terms on the right of (2.1a). Show that if $|x| \le 2n$ then

$$|cos(x) - s(n,x)| \le (x**2n)/(2n)!$$

6. Write a procedure which, given an integer n and a float decimal x, will read in coefficients and evaluate the corresponding polynomial by Horner's method. Do not use any arrays.

7. a) Show that if x(0) = 2/9 + (8/9)m then x(0) > sqrt(m) for 1/16 ≤ m < 1.

   b) Verify that |(x(0) - sqrt(m))/sqrt(m)| ≤ 1/9 for all 1/16 ≤ m ≤ 1.

8. Verify, by experimentation, that the third iterate of (2.2a) suffices for single precision.

Section 3 <u>Algorithms for Two Typical Problems</u>

3.1 <u>Simultaneous Linear Equations</u>

The first of our typical problems is frequently encountered, not only for its own sake, but also as an intermediate step in the solution of other computational problems. It can be stated as follows: Given a vector (or one-dimensional array) b with n elements, and a matrix (or two-dimensional array) A with n rows and n columns, find a vector x of length n such that

(3.1a)
$$a(1,1) \cdot x(1) + \ldots + a(1,n) \cdot x(n) = b(1)$$
$$\ldots$$
$$a(i,1) \cdot x(1) + \ldots + a(i,n) \cdot x(n) = b(i)$$
$$\ldots$$
$$a(n,1) \cdot x(1) + \ldots + a(n,n) \cdot x(n) = b(n),$$

or show that there is no solution to this problem.

If n=2 then (3.1a) represents two straight lines, and the problem reduces to finding whether two lines intersect and the point of intersection. Similarly, for n=3, we have three planes and the problem is to find a point (if any) shared by these planes. In general, given a vector b, the system of equations (3.1a) can either have no solution, a unique solution, or an infinite number of solutions. In this section we will assume that (3.1a) has a unique solution.

The problem may seem trivial, but this is not so. For example, (3.1a) might have a solution vector of real numbers, but not a solution in floating point arithmetic. Moreover, you should realize that truncation errors will probably change the matrix when it is read in, so that you will be solving a different system of linear equations. Clearly, all we can hope for is an approximate solution to (3.1a), but this problem is also not easy. For example, if

(3.1b)
$$0.66666 \cdot x(1) + 3.33334 \cdot x(2) = 4$$
$$1.99999 \cdot x(1) + 11.00001 \cdot x(2) = 12,$$

then you can verify that x = (1,1) solves this system exactly. Now consider the approximate solutions y=(1.1,0.9) and z=(6,0). Although y appears to be the better solution since it is closer to x, substituting y for x in (3.1b) gives

$$(3.733332, 12.099998)$$

instead of (4, 12), while the substitution of z for x in (3.1b) gives

(3.99996, 11.99994).

Thus, from this point of view z seems to be the better solution.

Equations (3.1b) also illustrate another difficulty with linear systems. Suppose the right side of (3.1b) is changed to

(3.99996, 11.99994).

Then, as we have seen above, the <u>exact</u> solution is changed to (6,0). Thus, a small relative change in the equations leads to a large relative change in the answer. Clearly, such a system is "ill-conditioned" and will cause problems. We will have more to say about (3.1b) in Section 3.1.3.

3.1.1 Gaussian Elimination

Most of you have encountered linear systems before, and if so, you probably have solved them by Gaussian elimination. Rather than give a formal description we will discuss this algorithm in connection with a system (3.1a) with n=3, but in such a way that the general algorithm is clear.

Consider then

$$5 \cdot x(1) - 2 \cdot x(2) + 3 \cdot x(3) = 10$$

(3.1.1a) $10 \cdot x(1) - 3 \cdot x(2) + 4 \cdot x(3) = 16$

$$15 \cdot x(1) + 1 \cdot x(2) - 3 \cdot x(3) = 8.$$

The first stage of Gaussian elimination consists of eliminating the unknown x(1) from the second and third equations. To do this, we multiply the first equation by 2, and subtract it from the second, then multiply by 3, and subtract it from the third to get

$$5 \cdot x(1) - 2 \cdot x(2) + 3 \cdot x(3) = 10$$

(3.1.1b) $1 \cdot x(2) - 2 \cdot x(3) = -4$

$$7 \cdot x(2) - 12 \cdot x(3) = -22.$$

Thus, we have effectively reduced the problem to a smaller problem (in this case 2 by 2 but generally (n-1) by (n-1)) which doesn't involve x(1). If we can solve the smaller problem for x(2) and x(3) (generally x(2),...,x(n)) then x(1) could easily be determining by substituting these values back into the first equations.

At this point, we can apply the same elimination strategy to
the smaller problem and eliminate x(2) from all except the first
equation of the problem. In our example this results in

$$5 \cdot x(1) - 2 \cdot x(2) + 3 \cdot x(3) = 10$$

(3.1.1c) $$1 \cdot x(2) - 2 \cdot x(3) = -4$$

$$2 \cdot x(3) = 6.$$

In the general case we would now have n-2 equations in n-2
unknowns and we would continue. In our example, n=3 and so we
have completed the <u>forward elimination</u>. From this you see that
for the general system (3.1a), the ith stage of the forward
elimination consists of eliminating x(i) from equations i+1
through n. This is done by forming the multipliers

$$m(i,j) = a(i,j)/a(i,i)$$

for j = i+1,...,n, then multiplying the ith equation by m(i,j)
and subtracting it from the jth equation for j = i+1,...,n.

Now that we have reduced our original 3 by 3 system to the
simple form of (3.1.1c) the solution can be obtained easily.
The third equation yields x(3) = 3. Substituting x(3) back into
the equation just above it yields x(2) = 2 and both of these
values substituted back into the next equation above, in this
case the first, results in x(1) = 1. This process is called
<u>back substitution</u>; in the general case it would be carried out
by the following PL/I program:

```
DO I = N TO 1 BY -1;
    SUM = 0;
    DO J = I+1 TO N BY 1;
        SUM = SUM + A(I,J) * X(J); END;
    X(I) = (B(I) - SUM)/A(I,I); END;
```

Things certainly don't always go so smoothly. If the
coefficients of the second equation in (3.1.1a) had been 10, -4
and 6 then the second equation in (3.1.1c) would have been 0 = -
4 and so no solution would exist. A good program would not
merely terminate at this point but would return information to
the user concerning the nature of the failure. Another hitch
which could occur does not imply the nonexistence of a solution.
Suppose A(2,2) had been -4 with all the other coefficients the
same as in (3.1.1a). Then the second equation in (3.1.1b) would
not involve x(2) and so it clearly couldn't be used to eliminate
x(2) from subsequent equations. The remedy to this difficulty
is simple; just interchange the second and third equations.

In general, this difficulty is caused by having a(i,i)=0 in
the ith stage of the forward elimination, and thus, the
multipliers can't be formed. The remedy is to interchange the
ith row for any row j such that a(j,i)≠0, although in practice j
is chosen so that

$$|a(j,i)| \geq |a(k,i)|$$

for k = i+1,...,n. This modification is called <u>Gaussian</u>
<u>elimination with partial pivoting</u>, and we will see in Section
3.1.3 that this is the method generally in use at present for
solving (3.1a) except in those cases where A has some special
property that makes special-purpose methods more suitable.
Moreover, it can be shown that if (3.1a) has a unique solution
then Gaussian elimination with partial pivoting will yield the
answer provided all operations are performed in infinite
precision arithmetic.

3.1.2 <u>Efficiency</u> -- Gaussian Elimination vs. Cramer's Rule

You have probably encountered <u>Cramer's rule</u> in your studies,
and you may even have used it to solve systems of linear
equations. If this is the case, you might want to know whether
or not Gaussian elimination is more efficient than Cramer's rule
in order to decide which algorithm to apply.

The standard way to measure efficiency in solving (3.1a) is
in terms of the number of arithmetic operations necessary to
obtain a solution. For linear equations, this is a reasonable
measure since the only operations involved are arithmetic, but
we shall see that the problem of Section 3.2 requires a
different criterion.

Cramer's rule depends on the calculation of the determinants
of certain matrices. The <u>determinant</u> of a matrix A with n rows
and n columns is given by

(3.1.2a)   det A = a(1,1)·det M(1,1) − a(2,1)·det M(2,1)
                  + a(3,1)·det M(3,1) ... ± a(n,1)·det M(n,1)

where M(i,1) is the (n−1) by (n−1) matrix obtained by deleting
the ith row and first column of A. To calculate det M(i,1) we
can apply this definition again and express det M(i,1) in terms
of determinants of (n−2) by (n−2) matrices. By repeating this
process, we eventually obtain det A expressed in terms of the
determinants of 2 by 2 matrices, and since

$$\det \begin{bmatrix} a & b \\ c & d \end{bmatrix} = ad - bc,$$

this completes the calculation of det A.

However, the efficiency of this method for evaluating
determinants is very poor. To see this let m(n) be the number
of multiplications necessary to evaluate the determinant of an n
by n matrix. Then (3.1.2a) implies that

$$m(n) = n \cdot m(n-1) + n,$$

and in particular, $m(n) > n \cdot m(n-1)$. But by the same reasoning $m(k) > k \cdot m(k-1)$ for any $3 \leq k \leq n$, and therefore,

$$m(n) > n \cdot (n-1) \cdot \ldots \cdot (3) \cdot m(2).$$

Since $m(2) = 2$, we finally have $m(n) > n!$.

This is an impossibly-large problem (as described in Section II.5.2), even for small values of n. For example, on an IBM 360/65 a single precision multiplication takes approximately four microseconds ($4 \cdot 10^{-6}$ seconds). Since $15! = (1.3) \cdot 10^{12}$ this means that the calculation of the determinant of a 15 by 15 matrix by (3.1.2a) would take at least 2.6 years of computing time.

Now Cramer's rule states that if det A $\neq$ 0, then the solution to (3.1a) is given by

$$x(j) = \det A(b|j)/\det A,$$

where $A(b|j)$ is the n by n matrix obtained by replacing the jth column of A by b. Therefore, the above arguments would seem to imply that Cramer's rule is unreasonable. However, the correct conclusion is that if the <u>determinants</u> are calculated by (3.1.2a) then Cramer's rule is unreasonable. We shall later point out that it is possible to calculate determinants in about $n^3/3$ multiplications, but that even if the determinants are calculated in this manner Gaussian elimination with partial pivoting is more efficient.

To estimate the efficiency of Gaussian elimination, we will count the number of multiplications and divisions required by the forward elimination and the back substitution. It is important not to neglect the counting of additions and subtractions, since if this number is much larger, then it would determine the efficiency of the method. However, we shall let you verify that this is not the case in Gaussian elimination.

Since multiplications and divisions take almost the same amount of time to perform, we will count a division as a multiplication. Similarly, a subtraction is counted as an addition.

The ith stage of the forward elimination needs $(n-i)$ divisions to form the multipliers. Moreover, to multiply the ith equation by $m(i,j)$ for $j = i+1,\ldots,n$ requires $(n-i)(n-i-1)$ multiplications. Altogether, the ith stage requires

$$(n-i) + (n-i)(n-i-1) = (n-i)^2$$

multiplications, and the complete forward elimination needs

$$(n-1)^2 + (n-2)^2 + \ldots + 1^2 = n(n-1)(2n-1)/6$$

multiplications.

From the program segment we gave for back substitution, it is easy to verify that this process uses

$$n + (n-1) + \ldots + 1 = n(n+1)/2$$

multiplications. So we see that the most expensive part of Gaussian elimination is the forward elimination, and this only involves approximately $n^3/3$ multiplications. Since this is also the most expensive in terms of additions, Gaussian elimination is an n^3 algorithm. Moreover, Gaussian elimination with partial pivoting is also an n^3 algorithm since there will be at most $n(n-1)/2$ comparisons.

It is interesting that Gaussian elimination with partial pivoting can be used to find the determinant of an n by n matrix in approximately n^3 operations. In fact, the determinant of A is not changed during the forward elimination except when two rows are interchanged. However, only the sign is changed, and this happens only if the indices of the two rows that are interchanged differ by an <u>odd</u> number. Since the forward elimination will reduce A to an upper triangular matrix -- a matrix such that a(i,j)=0 for i>j -- we only need to know how to calculate the determinant of an upper triangular matrix. But this is easy, since (3.1.2a) implies that the determinant of an upper triangular matrix is the product of the elements on the diagonal. In particular, the determinant of the matrix in (3.1.1c) is 10, and therefore the determinant of the matrix in (3.1.1a) is also 10. In summary, we have shown that the determinant of an n by n matrix is an immediate by-product of the forward elimination and therefore it can be calculated with an n^3 algorithm. Since Cramer's rule requires the calculation of n+1 distinct determinants, this makes Cramer's rule an n^4 algorithm.

3.1.3 <u>Ill-Conditioned Problems and Stable Algorithms</u>

You have already seen an ill-conditioned problem; in equations (3.1b) a small relative error in the righthand side led to a large relative error in the solution. Geometrically, it should be clear why this happens -- the lines represented by (3.1b) are essentially parallel. Computationally, there is not much that you can do with these problems except work in higher precision. However, if the problem is very ill-conditioned then even changing the data into the internal representation of the computer will drastically change the answer.

Let us now assume that our system of linear equations is not too ill-conditioned. Under this assumption, a method for solving (3.1a) is <u>stable</u> if it gives accurate results with respect to the working precision.

Without any pivoting, Gaussian elimination can't be considered stable since it can break down even in infinite precision arithmetic by having $a(i,i)=0$ at the ith stage of the forward elimination. Consider, for example, equations (3.1.1a) with $a(2,2)$ replaced by -4. However, if a zero causes problems in infinite precision, then maybe a small number will do the same in finite precision. Here is an example that will show that this is the case:

$$10^{-4} \cdot x(1) - x(2) = -1$$
(3.1.3a)
$$x(1) + x(2) = 2$$

We assume that we are working on a computer with base $b=10$ and precision $t=4$. The result of the forward elimination is

$$10^{-4} \cdot x(1) - x(2) = -1$$

$$10^{4} \cdot x(2) = 10^{4}$$

so that $x(2) = 1$ and $x(1) = 0$. However, to four decimal places the correct solution is $x(1) = 0.9999$ and $x(2) = 1.0001$.

Note that (3.1.3a) is well-conditioned since the corresponding straight lines are far from parallel. Therefore, the conclusion is that without pivoting Gaussian elimination is not stable even for well-conditioned systems.

It is pretty clear what happened in (3.1.3a). We found ourselves having to add numbers whose magnitudes were so different that excessive truncation errors resulted. An indication of this can be found in the magnitude change from 1 to 10^{4} in the coefficient of $x(2)$ in the second equation. When Gaussian elimination is modified to be more stable, the changes are directed toward reducing the growth in the magnitude of the elements generated during the forward elimination. The partial pivoting strategy is one way to accomplish this. As mentioned in Section 3.1.1, this consists of interchanging rows at the ith stage of the forward elimination in such a way that

$$|a(i,i)| \geq |a(k,i)|$$

for $k = i+1,\ldots,n$. It follows that the multipliers $m(i,j)$ satisfy $|m(i,j)| \leq 1$, and therefore, at each stage of the forward elimination the elements can, at worst, double in size. In practice, however, this growth is usually not obtained, and Gaussian elimination with partial pivoting is a stable algorithm.

Let us consider one last example:

$$10 \cdot x(1) - 10^{5} \cdot x(2) = -10^{5}$$
(3.1.3b)
$$x(1) + x(2) = 2$$

Note that (3.1.3b) is well-conditioned, and that in fact, this example was obtained from (3.1.3a) by multiplying the first row by 10^5. Since in this case Gaussian elimination with partial pivoting does not interchange any rows, forward elimination gives

$$10 \cdot x(1) - 10^5 \cdot x(2) = -10^5$$

$$10^4 \cdot x(2) = 10^4$$

if the operations are carried out on a computer with b=10 and t=4. Therefore, x(2) = 1 and x(1) = 0 which is, of course, completely incorrect. What went wrong? The reason for the failure is that there is <u>already</u> a large difference in the magnitude of the elements of A. For this reason partial pivoting is usually implemented with a "scaling" or "equilibration" technique. Unfortunately this subject is not well understood, but at present scaling usually consists of dividing each row of (3.1a) by the absolute value of the element of maximum magnitude in that row. In (3.1.3b) this would amount to changing the system into (3.1.3a) which, as we have seen, can be adequately solved by Gaussian elimination with partial pivoting.

3.2 The Quadrature Problem

You are probably all familiar with the problem of finding the area of a triangle or a circle. These are simple examples of the "quadrature problem", which is to find the area enclosed by a curve. This problem is not only geometrically interesting, but it is of great importance in science and engineering.

Instead of dealing with the completely general question, we will assume that we are given numbers a < b, and a procedure which accepts any x between a and b and returns a value f(x). This is a very important special case and if we think of f(x) as the height of a curve, then we want the area enclosed between the curve and the x-axis from a to b. For example, if someone gives us a=0, b=1 and f(x) = sqrt(1-x^2) then we are being asked to find the area of a quarter of a circle whose radius is one. Now, of course, you know the answer is pi/4 = 0.785398..., but suppose you had never seen the formula for a circle's area. How would you solve the problem then?

Those of you that have had calculus will probably recognize this problem as a special case of the more general problem of finding "the definite integral of a function". If this is the case, then you will realize, as you read this section, that the methods discussed here apply verbatim to this more general problem. Nevertheless, when the problem is treated from the point of view of finding an area, the methods for its solution become geometrically intuitive and therefore accesible to a wider audience.

Another remark is in order for the calculus student. A large percentage of the "indefinite integrals" which arise in practice can't be found in closed form. Furthermore, even when an antiderivative could be found it is often more accurate to ignore this and use a numerical quadrature method.

3.2.1 The Trapezoidal Rule

The simplest approach to solving our quadrature problem is to first subdivide the interval [a,b] into a series of smaller intervals in such a way that for each interval, say [c,d], the area of a trapezoid with a base of length d-c and sides of height f(c) and f(d), is a reasonable approximation to the area under the curve from c to d. Then the sum of the areas of these small trapezoids should be a good approximation to the area under the curve from a to b.

To illustrate this approach let us return to our example where a=0, b=1 and $f(x) = sqrt(1-x^2)$. As a first attempt we could divide [0,1] into two equal subintervals, calculate the areas of the corresponding trapezoids and take their sum as a tentative answer. Since the area of a trapezoid with base length of d-c and sides of height f(c) and f(d) is

  T_AREA(c,d) = (d-c)(f(d)+f(c))/2

we would obtain 0.683 as our tentative answer. This is clearly not very good. To improve matters we could successively subdivide the interval into equal subintervals, calculate the corresponding area approximations and stop when two consecutive approximations agree to the desired accuracy. The result of this strategy is summarized in the table below:

Number of subintervals	Approximate areas
2	6.83012E-01
4	7.48927E-01
8	7.72454E-01
16	7.80813E-01
32	7.83775E-01
64	7.84824E-01
128	7.85195E-01
256	7.85326E-01
512	7.85372E-01
1024	7.85389E-01
2048	7.85394E-01
4096	7.85397E-01
8192	7.85397E-01

The results in this table were generated by the following method: The interval [a,b] was divided into n equal subintervals, each of length h = (b-a)/n. (In the above example

n is a power of 2, but this is not important right now.)   This
introduces a set of partition points x(i), i=0,1,...,n where

(3.2.1a)   x(i) = a + h·i.

The area of the ith trapezoid is

    (h/2)[f(x(i-1)) + f(x(i))],

and the sum of the areas of these trapezoids is

    TR(n) = (h/2){[f(x(0)+f(x(1))] +
                  [f(x(1))+f(x(2))] +
                  ...+ [f(x(n-1))+f(x(n))]}.

This formula can also be written as

(3.2.1b) TR(n) =
          h[(1/2)f(a) + f(x(1)) + ... + f(x(n-1)) + (1/2)f(b)],

and in this form the formula is known as the trapezoidal rule.
The results in the previous table were then obtained by using
(3.2.1b) and double precision on an IBM 360.   However, only
single precision answers were printed out.   Finallly, the
computation was terminated when

    $|TR(n) - TR(2n)| < 10^{-6}$

for some integer n.

    There is a good reason why n was always doubled from one
calculation to the next.   Consider, for example, TR(512).
Equation (3.2.1b) shows that to calculate TR(512) we have to
call the height procedure 513 times.   However, if you think
about it, 257 of these values were already used in TR(256) and
so they will be repeat calls. Therefore you should be able to
compute TR(512) from TR(256) with only 256 additional procedure
calls.   In fact, you should convince yourself that

(3.2.1c) TR(2n) = (1/2)TR(n) +
          h[f(x(1)) + f(x(3)) + ... + f(x(2n-1))]

where h = (b-a)/2n and x(i) is defined by (3.2.1a).

    Although in our example we first computed TR(2), and then
used (3.2.1c) to compute the other values of TR(n), this is not
necessary. Usually n is initially chosen so that h = (b-a)/n is
relatively small; for example, choose n to be the smallest
integer such that n ≥ 10(b-a).   Then TR(n) is computed from
(3.2.1b), and ((3.2.1c) is used for the remaining values. Also
note that the computation of TR(2n) by (3.2.1c) represents a
real savings.   Instead of 2n+1 procedure calls as (3.2.1b)
requires, only n calls are required.   There is also a
corresponding decrease in the required number of arithmetic
operations.

3.2.2 Efficiency - Fixed vs. Adaptive Quadrature

How should we measure the efficiency of an integration technique? Consider, for example, the following two methods for finding the area under a curve. The first method chooses n such that $n \geq 10(b-a)$ and then computes TR(n), TR(2n), TR(4n), ..., by (3.2.1b) until

    |TR(m) - TR(2m)| < ERROR

for some integer $m \geq n$ where ERROR is a pre-specified accuracy. The second method only differs in the fact that TR(n), TR(2n),..., are computed by (3.2.1c).

In this case the second method is more efficient. The reason is that clearly the main cost of finding an accurate approximation to the desired area is measured by the number of calls to the height procedure. Since this is true in general, the efficiency measure for integration methods is usually taken to be the number of calls to the height procedure necessary to achieve some pre-specified accuracy.

We now would like to show that with this measure, the trapezoidal rule is not very efficient when used to find the area under certain curves. In fact, the example with a=0, b=1, and $f(x) = sqrt(1-x^2)$ shows that the trapezoidal rule can use up a tremendous number of procedure calls. To convince you that this behavior is not typical, consider the problem a=0, b=1, and $f(x) = cos(x)$. In this case we have

n	TR(n)
20	8.41295E-01
40	8.41427E-01
80	8.41460E-01
160	8.41468E-01
320	8.41470E-01
640	8.41470E-01

The difference in behavior is due to the fact that for $f(x) = sqrt(1-x^2)$ the tangent line at x=1 is vertical. It is very difficult for a trapezoid to approximate the area of a curve near a point at which a vertical tangent line exists. In general, the trapezoidal rule is slow if the slope of the tangent line changes abruptly as the curve is traversed.

Another reason for the failure of the trapezoidal rule is that the points at which the height procedure is going to be evaluated are fixed in advance. These points are equally distributed throughout the interval [a,b] which means that the trapezoidal rule assumes that the curve behaves the same way throughout the interval, and this is not true for $sqrt(1-x^2)$.

Actually, it is not very difficult to modify the trapezoidal rule so that it adapts itself to the shape of the curve. The important modification that will be described below is called the adaptive trapezoidal rule while the trapezoidal rule as described in Section 3.2.1 is sometimes called the fixed trapezoidal rule.

The adaptive trapezoidal rule consists of a series of stages. In the first stage, subdivide the interval [a,b] into two equal subintervals by means of the midpoint m = (a+b)/2 and compare

    T1 = T_AREA(a,b)

with

    T2 = T_AREA(a,m) + T_AREA(m,b).

If T1 and T2 agree to the desired accuracy, then take T2 as the answer and stop. If they don't, then momentarily forget about the subinterval [m,b] and concentrate on [a,m]. The second stage is entirely analogous. The subinterval [a,m] is subdivided into two equal subintervals, and the corresponding T1 and T2 are computed. If T1 and T2 agree to the pre-specified accuracy then T2 is accepted as the area under the curve from a to m, and the above process is repeated on the interval [m,b]. If they don't agree, repeat the process on the left half of the interval [a,m].

Even from this vague description of the adaptive trapezoidal rule it should be clear that this scheme will concentrate the calls of the height procedure on the wiggly parts of the curve, and therefore the adaptive trapezoidal rule should be more efficient than its fixed counterpart. It should also be clear that we will have to keep track of the values produced by the calls to the height procedure in order to avoid repeat calls. However, since it may not be clear how to save these values, we will now refine the description of the adaptive trapezoidal rule, and in doing so we will give a method for saving these values. You will probably not be surprised to learn that this method is sometimes implemented as a recursive procedure (see Section IV.4) although this is not the approach that we will take.

To fix ideas suppose that a=0, b=1, and let us concentrate on the intervals being examined. For example, if T1 and T2 don't agree to the desired accuracy, then during the first three stages we successively generate

    [0,1/2]   [1/2,1]

    [0,1/4]   [1/4,1/2]   [1/2,1]

    [0,1/8]   [1/8,1/4]   [1/4,1/2]   [1/2,1].

Note that the leftmost interval is the one that is currently being examined. At this stage we would calculate

    T1 = T_AREA(0,1/8),

and

    T2 = T_AREA(0,1/16) + T_AREA(1/16,1/8).

If T1 and T2 agree to the desired accuracy, then T2 is accepted
as the area under the curve between 0 and 1/8. The process
would then start again, but now the list of intervals would be

    [1/8,1/4]   [1/4,1/2]   [1/2,1],

while if T1 and T2 had not agreed, then we would have had

    [0,1/16]   [1/16,1/8]   [1/8,1/4]   [1/4,1/2]   [1/2,1].

It is convenient to think of this list of intervals as being
a last-in first-out stack, with the rightmost interval at the
bottom, and the most recently generated intervals being inserted
at the top.   To represent these stacks on the computer let
STK_A(J) be the left endpoint of the Jth interval on the stack,
and let STK_B(J) contain the right endpoint. For instance, in
our example, STK_A(1) = 1/2, STK_B(1) = 1, and at the end of the
third stage STK_A(4) = 0, STK_B(4) = 1/8.

The height of the stack is related to the length of the
smallest interval in the stack. In particular, if the length of
the smallest interval is 1/(2**k), then the length of the stack
does not exceed k+1. In the general case, the initial interval
is [a,b] so the lengths of the subintervals are each of the form
(b−a)/(2**k) for some integer k. Since this integer k not only
measures the size of the interval but also the position of the
interval in the stack, it is called the <u>level</u> of the interval.
In our example we have

    level 0 intervals [0,1]

    level 1 intervals [0,1/2]   [1/2,1]

    level 2 intervals [0,1/4]   [1/4,1/2]

    level 3 intervals [0,1/8]   [1/8,1/4]

at the end of the first three stages. In particular, note that
if a level k interval is subdivided then we obtain two level k+1
intervals.

By now you should have a fair idea of how to implement the
adaptive trapezoidal rule. In particular you may have realized
that to keep track of the evaluations of the height procedure
you will need two more stacks: STK_FA(J) and STK_FB(J) will
contain, respectively, the height of the curve at the left and
right endpoints of the Jth interval in the stack.

There is, however, one last but very important point that must be made concerning the statement "T1 and T2 agree (or don't agree) to the desired accuracy". The whole idea of the adaptive trapezoidal rule is that, given a desired accuracy ERROR, the adaptive trapezoidal rule will <u>automatically</u> provide an estimate EST for AREA(a,b) -- the area under the curve from a to b -- such that

$$|EST - AREA(a,b)| < ERROR.$$

A technique for accomplishing this is based on the observation that if EST1 and EST2 are the corresponding estimates for AREA(a,m) and AREA(m,b) then we should require that

$$|EST1 - AREA(a,m)| < ERROR/2,$$

and

$$|EST2 - AREA(m,b)| < ERROR/2.$$

In general, the acceptable error for a level k+1 interval should be half of that acceptable for a level k interval. Thus, if we are examining a level k interval [c,d] we should accept T2 as an estimate for AREA(c,d) if

$$|T2 - AREA(c,d)| < ERROR/(2**k).$$

However, since we don't know AREA(c,d) we try to satisfy this requirement by asking that

$$(3.2.2a) \qquad |T2 - T1| < ERROR/(2**k).$$

Therefore, in our example, we should accept T2 as an approximation to AREA(0,1/8) if

$$|T2 - T1| < ERROR/2^3$$

since [0,1/8] is a level 3 interval.

Interestingly enough, in practice criterion (3.2.2a) is very stringent. In other words, the absolute error of your final estimate for AREA(a,b) will be much smaller than ERROR. Therefore, instead of (3.2.2a) you could use

$$|T2 - T1| < ERROR/(g**k)$$

where 1<g<2. Our limited experiments indicate that g=1.4 is a good value, but you should determine your own favorite choice of g.

Finally, as an example of the power of the adaptive trapezoidal rule, we mention that for a=0, b=1, and $f(x) = sqrt(1-x^2)$ this algorithm (with g=1.4 and ERROR=10^{-6}) obtained a value of 7.85396E-01 in just 437 calls of the height procedure as opposed to 8192 calls for the fixed rule. For a=0, b=1, and f(x) = cos(x), it obtained 8.41469E-01 in 255 procedure calls versus 640 for the fixed rule.

3.2.3 Simpson's Rule

We have already noted that the trapezoidal rule is inefficient if at some point the area under the curve cannot be conveniently approximated by trapezoids. One way to deal with this defect is to localize the problem and concentrate the calls of the height procedure at points near the trouble spot; this philosophy leads to the adaptive trapezoidal rule. On the other hand, you may believe that the defect is due to the simplicity of the trapezoid, and that if the area under the curve were approximated by a more sophisticated shape, then the resulting rule would be more efficient. Let us consider this approach.

First note that an alternate way of looking at the trapezoidal rule on each subinterval is to say that we are approximating the curve by a straight line, and taking the area under this line as an approximation to the area under the curve. From this point of view it is easy to extend the trapezoidal rule by approximating the curve on each subinterval with a parabola instead of a line.

To apply this idea consider a curve f defined on an interval [a,b]. Now subdivide [a,b] into 2n equal subintervals by means of the partition points

$$x(i) = a + h \cdot i \qquad i=0,1,\ldots,2n$$

where $h = (b-a)/(2n)$. The area under the parabola that goes through the points $(x(j),f(x(j)))$ for $j=2i-2,2i-1,2i$ is then

$$(h/3)[f(x(2i-2)) + 4f(x(2i-1)) + f(2i)],$$

and the sum of all these areas is

$$S(n) = (h/3)[f(a) + 4f(x(1)) + 2f(x(2)) + 4f(x(3)) \\ + \ldots + 2f(x(2n-2)) + 4f(x(2n-1)) + f(b)].$$

This last formula is known as Simpson's rule, and the geometrical arguments given above indicate that it will be more efficient than the trapezoidal rule. This often turns out to be the case. Also note that the two rules are closely related. In fact, given TR(2n) and TR(n) it is easy to calculate S(2n) by means of

(3.2.3a) $S(2n) = (4TR(2n) - TR(n))/3.$

Simpson's rule can also be used in the adaptive form. In this case we proceed as before subdividing intervals in halves, but now we make use of the formula

(3.2.3b)   P_AREA(a,m,b) = (b-a)[f(a)+4f(m)+f(b)]/6

where m is the midpoint of a and b. In fact, the first stage
would consist of estimating the area under the curve from a to b
by calculating

      T1 = P_AREA(a,m,b),

and

      T2 = P_AREA(a,p,m) + P_AREA(m,q,b),

where p and q are the midpoints of the intervals [a,m] and
[m,b], respectively. Of course, we can implement this adaptive
Simpson's rule by using stacks as in the adaptive trapezoidal
rule, but now we need another stack, say STK_FM. Then STK_FM(J)
would contain f(m) where m is the midpoint of the Jth interval
in the stack.

Section 3 Exercises

1. For Gaussian elimination:
   a) Find the number of additions done during the forward
      elimination.

   b) Verify that the number the multiplications in the back
      substitution is n(n+1)/2.

   c) Find the number of additions in the back substitution.

2. Show that (3.2.1a) implies that the determinant of an upper
triangular matrix is the product of the elements on the
diagonal.

3. a) Find the solution to (3.1a) where

$$A = \begin{bmatrix} 1 & 2 & 2 \\ -1 & -3 & 2 \\ 2 & 0 & 6 \end{bmatrix}$$

      and b = (0, 4, 8) by Gaussian elimination with partial
      pivoting.

   b) What is the determinant of A?

4. Find the number of comparisons that are used in Gaussian
elimination with partial pivoting.

5. Write a procedure that will solve (3.1a) by Gaussian
elimination with partial pivoting. This procedure should have
at least the following parameters:

        N, the order of the system
        A, the coefficient matrix
        B, the righthand side
        X, the solution vector.

There should be appropriate messages in case of failure.

6. Write a procedure as in Exercise 5 to find the determinant of
an n by n matrix.

7. Design and run test cases for the procedures written in
Exercises 5 and 6.

8. Write a procedure that will execute the adaptive trapezoidal
rule. This procedure should have at least the following
parameters:

        A, the left endpoint of the interval
        B, the right endpoint of the interval
        EST, the final estimate for the area
        ERROR, the desired absolute error in EST
        MAX_LEVEL, the maximum number of levels allowed
        CALLS, the total number of calls of the height procedure
        MAX_CALLS, the maximum number of calls allowed.

The procedure should either run successfully, or terminate when
MAX_CALLS or MAX_LEVEL is exceeded. In either case appropriate
messages should be printed. Note that A, B, ERROR, MAX_LEVEL,
and MAX_CALLS have to be set by the user, but that the other
parameters will be set by the procedure. You may also want to
have other parameters; for example, the name of the height
procedure, or MIN_LEVEL so that you will be assured that the
height procedure will be called a sufficient number of times.

9. Write a procedure as in Exercise 8 for the adaptive Simpson's
rule.

10. Design and run test cases that compare the two procedures
written in Exercises 8 and 9.

11. If you have written one of the procedures defined in
Exercise 8 or 9, investigate the effect of calling the procedure
with argument values A > B.

12. a) Verify equation (3.2.3a).

    b) Show that if f is a parabola then formula (3.2.3b) gives
       the area under this parabola from a to b.

13. Compare, in terms of efficiency, the trapezoidal rule and
Simpson's rule.   Find an example in which the trapezoidal rule
is more efficient than Simpson's rule.

14. Modify the procedures defined in Exercises 8 and 9 so that
they will test for relative errors instead of absolute errors.

Section 4 <u>Suggestions for Further Reading</u>

We hope to have whetted your appetite for numerical analysis
and to this end we have compiled a very brief list of references
in this section.

The books by Dorn and McCracken, and Conte and de Boor are
two of the better introductory books on numerical analysis; they
should be intelligible to anyone who has had calculus.

If you want to find more about the effects of finite
precision arithmetic on mathematical computation, the standard
reference is the book by Wilkinson. Fike's book is an excellent
introduction to the topic of computer evaluation of mathematical
functions. Linear equations are treated by Forsythe and Moler
in a very readable manner. Moreover, this book contains several
excellent programs for solving systems of linear equations.

Numerical integration, the more exact description of the
topic of Section 3.2, is surveyed by Davis and Rabinowitz. The
last chapter is of special interest since it deals with
automatic integration and contains several programs.

Finally, the book edited by Rice contains several good
articles on the interaction between mathematics and computer
programming.

Conte, S. and C. de Boor, <u>Elementary Numerical Analysis, An
Algorithmic Approach</u>, 2nd edition, McGraw-Hill, 1972

Davis, P. and P. Rabinowitz, <u>Numerical Integration</u>, Blaisdell,
1967

Dorn, W. and D. McCraken, <u>Numerical Methods with FORTRAN IV Case
Studies</u>, Wiley, 1972

Fike, C., <u>Computer Evaluation of Mathematical Functions</u>,
Prentice-Hall, 1968

Forsythe, G. and C. Moler, <u>Computer Solution of Linear Algebraic
Systems</u>, Prentice-Hall, 1967

Rice, J. (editor), <u>Mathematical Software</u>, Academic Press, 1971

Wilkinson, J., <u>Rounding Errors in Algebraic Processes</u>, Prentice-
Hall, 1963

Part VI.*

FILE PROCESSING APPLICATIONS

Three-quarters of the world's computers are engaged in processing the information generated by modern economic society. This usage began in the late 1950's and has grown very rapidly. By now it is difficult to imagine how business, government, banking, insurance, or even large universities could manage their activity without computing systems.

From a technical point of view, these computer applications are distinctive for <u>what</u> they do, and not just from the origin of the problem. The principal difference lies in the <u>quantity</u> and <u>form</u> of the information that is to be processed. There are also significant differences in the manner in which programs are developed, and the manner in which they are used.

Those involved in mathematical applications of computers often have a rather supercilious attitude toward business-oriented computing. This attitude reflects considerable innocence as to what is involved. The mathematics are elementary to be sure, but the problems of handling huge volumes of information and protecting it from the clumsiness and cupidity of people are exceedingly difficult. Typically the programs for file processing are dominated by concern for <u>exceptions</u>. Processing the 99% of activity that is legitimate and accurate may be relatively straightforward; detecting and handling the other 1% often requires great care and ingenuity.

The problems considered in the earlier sections of the book have all shared a significant characteristic -- they have been <u>self-contained</u> with respect to the computer. That is, all of the data necessary for execution has accompanied the program, and the complete results have been delivered on printed output during execution. Now we consider problems that involve collections of information called "files", that are more-or-less permanently stored in the memory of a computer. Programs will draw upon information in a file that is already resident in the computer system when the program arrives. Similarly, the results of execution are in part reflected in changes in the contents of the file, and only partly displayed on printed output.

Section 1 <u>Files</u>

Files are collections of information. We are concerned with collections that have the following properties:

a) They are in "machine readable" form -- that is, they can be stored and processed by a computer.

b) They are highly structured (like a dictionary, rather than a novel).

c) They are highly repetitive in structure (a relatively small pattern is repeated many times).

d) They are sufficiently large to preclude storage in the main memory of current computers.

e) They have a relatively long life.

Generally, a file represents some set of <u>entities</u> in the real world -- people, vehicles, courses, buildings, etc. -- and contains whatever information about these entities is relevant for some well-defined purpose. At any instant in time, the particular information in a file is said to constitute a "generation" of that file, and represents an instantaneous status report for the entities described. A sequence of generations represents a <u>history</u> for these entities.

1.1 <u>Structure of a File</u>

A file will normally contain the <u>same kind</u> of information about each of the entities that it represents. The specific values will be different for each entity, but the format and interpretation of the information will be the same for each. The information pertaining to one entity is called a "record", so a file consists of a set of records, one for each entity that it represents. Each unit of information in a record is called a "field". A field is analogous to a variable in that it is a location in memory; it has a name and a value.

For example, a file might contain biographical information about the current students at a university. There would be one record for each student. Each record would have fields representing the student's name, his campus address, telephone

number, college, year, faculty adviser, etc. Each record would
have a similar set of fields, with of course, different values.
For example:

```
   Field-          Values:
     names:        Record 1      Record 2       Record 3

     NAME          JERRY JONES   WM. SMITH     A. B. WILLS
     ADDRESS       416 DORM 5    201 ELM AVE   HUDSON ST
     TELEPHONE     256 2369      256 5034      256 2741
     COLLEGE       ENGINEERING   ENGINEERING   AGRICULTURE
     CLASS         FRESHMAN      SENIOR        SOPHMORE
     ADVISOR       WILLIAMS      SALTON        HARTMANIS
```

   Fields are somewhat analogous to arrays in that they have
multiple values.   That is, each field has a value in each
record. Some values may of course be blank or zero. A program
must   have   a   way of referring to one particular value
(corresponding to a subscripted variable) and this is discussed
in Section 2.1.1.

1.2 Events and Transactions

   A file is intended to describe the status of a set of
entities for a particular purpose. When an event occurs that
changes the status of an entity represented by the file, the
corresponding file information must be changed or the file no
longer gives an accurate description of status.   The information
generated by such an event is called a "transaction", and the
process of accepting a transaction and changing the file
contents accordingly is called "updating" the file.

   For example, in the student biographical file of Section 1.1,
a relevant event would be the change of a student's telephone
number. The corresponding transaction would have to specify
which student (to designate a particular record), which field is
to be altered, and the new value to be stored.

   Another significant event would be the entry of a new
student.   The   transaction would include values for many
different fields, and updating would involve the creation of a
new record and its addition to the file.

1.3 Storage Systems

Up to this point it has not been necessary to consider how information is stored in a computer. A variable could just be considered a location in memory, and the assignment and retrieval of its value is straightforward and automatic. We have only needed a relatively small amount of storage for program and data and this could be accomodated in "main memory" or "primary memory" of the computer. But the sizes of many files preclude their storage in main memory, so that alternative physical devices, and more complex programming are involved.

Files are generally relatively large collections of information. For example, a student biographical record might consist of 1000 characters, so a file for 15,000 students would involve 15 million characters of information. If the student record included academic, financial and medical information it could easily require 10,000 characters, so the file would be 150 million characters.

In general, files range in size from 10^5 to 10^{10} characters, with 10^6 to 10^9 being the most common range. These quantities are sufficiently large that, at least with current computers, the entire file cannot be stored in main memory at one time. Current main memories are anywhere from 10^4 to 10^7 characters, and most computer systems have less than 10^6 characters of main memory. (To put these numbers in perspective, this book contains about 10^6 characters.)

This means that for file processing, a multi-level memory system must be used. The main memory is relatively small, fast and expensive, and it is supplemented by a "secondary memory" that is relatively large, slow and cheap.

1.3.1 Storage Devices

In all current (so-called "third generation") computing systems, memory is implemented by using various electro-magnetic devices. These are magnetic elements with the following characteristics:

a) They have two stable magnetic states that can be recognized electronically.

b) They are capable of being changed electronically, from one of these states to the other.

c) They will remain in whichever state has been established, after the changing force is removed.

These characteristics provide the necessary abilities to read, write and remember.

It is also desirable for the magnetic element to be
physically small, durable and cheap, and for it to be capable of
being read and written very rapidly with very low power.

The magnetic device used for main memory in all third
generation computers is the magnetic core. This is a tiny ring
of ferrous material. These cores are arranged in a square grid,
and are threaded with wires to read and write. Magnetic cores
are relatively fast (read or write in 10^{-6} seconds). (Much
smaller and faster devices are now being developed, so by the
late 1970's cores will probably be regarded with some historical
amusement as large, slow and crude devices.) They are also
relatively costly (roughly $1 per character for large System 360
memories from IBM). The largest core memories in use today have
a capacity of 8 million characters. However, capacities between
50,000 and 1 million are much more common.

The alternative magnetic element is simply a tiny section of
a continuous magnetic surface. The material must be locally
magnetizable -- adjacent sections must be capable of being read
and written independently. Reading or writing a particular
section is accomplished by physically moving it past a
stationary coil, called a "read/write head".

The magnetic surface may be supported and transported in
several different ways. One method is as a surface coating on a
thin plastic tape. The standard computer tape is one-half inch
wide and one-half mile long. Each character is recorded in a
section across the width of the tape, with (typically) 1600
characters in each inch of length. There are gaps (between
records) in which no information is recorded, but a full tape
reel can contain 30 million characters of information.

Alternatively, the magnetic surface can be supported on a
rigid disc, rotating on a central spindle, somewhat like a
phonograph record. Information is recorded in 200 concentric
(not spiral) rings called "tracks" on the surface, and each
character can be read or written as rotation of the disc brings
it under a stationary read/write head. Several discs are
usually stacked vertically on a common spindle, with a
read/write head for each disc. Such a "disc pack" (IBM 2316,
for example) can store 28 million characters.

Just like their counterparts for music recording, computer
tapes and discs are removable. They can be dismounted from the
computer, and stored in what is called an "off-line library".
They can later be remounted on the computer system and the
information they contain further processed. Since the tapes and
disc packs themselves are not prohibitively expensive (about $25
and $250, respectively) libraries with several hundred disc
packs and several thousand reels of tapes are not uncommon.

With such libraries, the amount of information that can be
stored in a form accessible to a computer is almost unlimited.
However, at least at present, the computer requires the

assistance of a human operator to select reels and packs from
the library and mount them on the reading devices.

The significant distinction between tapes and discs as
secondary memory devices lies in the physical distance between a
required section of information and the read/write head that
will transmit it to main memory. On a disc, the information is
at most a full revolution away from the read/write head. The
delay until the required information reaches the read/write
position (called "latency" delay) is at most a few hundredths of
a second. On a magnetic tape the information could be at the
opposite end of the reel -- one-half mile of tape away -- and
the delay would be measured in minutes while the tape is wound
from one reel to another. Consequently, tape storage can only
be efficiently used for information that will be required in a
predictable order. Fortunately, many files are processed in
this way (see Section 2.1.1) and tapes are widely used. On
discs, all information is more-or-less equally accessible
(except for variations in latency time) and information can be
accessed in unpredictable or random order without great loss in
efficiency.

1.3.2 Two-Level Memories

In most computer systems today, the main memory is
supplemented by a secondary memory of magnetic tapes and/or
magnetic discs. The secondary memory can also be considered to
have two levels -- the tapes and discs currently mounted "on-
line" (on the reading devices), and those on racks in the "off-
line" library. The different levels of memory differ in
capacity, speed of access, and mode of use. The computer can
read and write in main memory in microseconds (millionths of a
second), in secondary memory (which involves physical movement
of a tape or disc) in milliseconds (thousandths of a second),
and in the off-line library (requiring human assistance) only in
minutes.

Main memory is used in very small increments -- corresponding
to individual variables. Secondary memory is used in terms of
blocks of information (representing one or several records), and
the off-line library is used in terms of entire files. That is,
at any given moment, only a few files have been selected from
the library and are mounted on the reading units of the
computer. One (or at most several) records have been selected
from these files and copied into main memory for processing.
The computer cannot really process information in secondary
storage; it can only transfer it in blocks in and out of main
memory. The computer cannot process information in the off-line
library at all, it can only print out messages to the operator
and wait until the tape or disc-pack containing the required
file has been mounted on a reading device.

Section 2 <u>File Processing Programs</u>

Once information has been moved into main memory, the program proceeds as we have described in earlier sections, but in file processing the programmer has certain additional tasks, as noted in Section 2.1. Section 2.2 describes the languages that are used for this type of programming. Sections 2.3 and 2.4 describe differences in the ways that problem specifications are developed and documented for file processing.

2.1 <u>Functional Requirements</u>

The programs that have been considered up to this point have been concerned only with the main storage of the computer. Both the program itself, and all of the variables and arrays with which it dealt were easily stored in main memory. The card reader and the printer have been the only other components of the computing system that were of concern. Now we consider programs that must also communicate with magnetic tape and disk storage units, and control the transfer of information back and forth between main and secondary storage.

2.1.1 <u>Control of Secondary Storage</u>

In earlier sections the PL/I GET and PUT statements have been regarded as means of communicating with the card reader and the printer. They are, in fact, the means by which the program (in main memory) communicates with all of the other components of the computing system. The GET statement transmits information to main memory, and the PUT statement copies information from main memory. The origin of the information for a GET and the destination for a PUT is specified by a FILE phrase.

For example, suppose at a certain point the program needs another set of values for variables NAME, ADDRESS, and COLLEGE. If these values are to be transmitted to main memory by the card reader, one could write either of the following statements:

    GET LIST(NAME, ADDRESS, COLLEGE);

    GET FILE(SYSIN) LIST(NAME, ADDRESS, COLLEGE);

SYSIN is the name usually assigned to the card reader in IBM
systems. FILE(SYSIN) is said to be the "default file" for GET;
it is assumed if no file is specified. On the other hand, if
the required values were in a file named STUDENTS which was
already in secondary storage, one would write:

        GET FILE(STUDENTS) LIST(NAME, ADDRESS, COLLEGE);

    Similarly, to display these values on the printer one could
write either of the following:

        PUT LIST(NAME, ADDRESS, COLLEGE);

        PUT FILE(SYSPRINT) LIST(NAME, ADDRESS, COLLEGE);

To store values in the STUDENTS file in secondary storage one
would write:

        PUT FILE(STUDENTS) LIST(NAME, ADDRESS, COLLEGE);

    This much of the process is fairly obvious and
straightforward; other parts are not. The management of files
in secondary storage is not nearly as automatic as the
management of variables in main memory. The programmer must
explicitly control both the location and structure of the file
in secondary storage. For example, when using the IBM OS/360
operating system the actual assignment of a file to a particular
physical location in secondary storage is specified by a "DD
statement" in a language called the "Job Control Language"
(usually abbreviated "JCL"). DD statements specifying the
location of all relevant files will precede the PL/I program.
In the program the name to be used for a file is specified by a
declaration. For example:

        DECLARE STUDENTS STREAM INPUT FILE;

This relates the file-name in the program to the name specified
in a DD statement, and the attributes in the declaration specify
the manner in which the file is organized. There are also OPEN
and CLOSE statements that prepare a file for use by the program
and then terminate activity. These matters are quite complex
and exacting, but must be learned if one is going to process
files.

    The other complex aspect of this matter is knowing _which_
values of NAME, ADDRESS, and COLLEGE the GET statement refers
to. Recall from Section 1.1 that there is a set of values for
these variables in each record in the file. The programmer must
indicate _which record_ in the file is the source or target of his
GET or PUT statement.

    This same concept has been present in the reading of data
cards, but we have not discussed it as such. For example, in
the program segment

```
DO WHILE(X ¬= 0);
   GET LIST(X);
   ...
```

the data cards contain many different X's, or more precisely, contain many values that will provide a sequence of different values for the variable X as they are read into main memory. There is no ambiguity in the GET statement, since it means read the <u>next</u> value from the data stream and assign it to the variable X. Neither is there ambiguity in other statements that reference X -- they refer to the variable (or location) in main memory, and hence to the last value that was assigned to that location. The data stream is an example of a "sequential" file, in which there is a <u>natural ordering</u> among the values. GET or PUT with respect to a sequential file always imply the <u>next</u> value.

Alternatively, files may be "direct" or "random" (instead of sequential) for situations where one would like to be able to <u>select particular records</u>, without having to process all records in their natural order. With such files the next record is not implied by any ordering, and phrases must be specified in the GET or PUT statement to indicate what record is desired.

A file processing program proceeds by moving a copy of <u>one record at a time</u> from secondary storage into main memory. The fields of the record provide the values for corresponding variables. The program operates upon these variables in main memory just as the programs described in earlier sections of the book. When a statement references a variable, it is referring to the value in main memory and not to one of the many corresponding fields in secondary storage. Hence the statement implicitly refers to whichever record was last copied from secondary to main memory.

2.1.2 <u>Data Aggregates</u>

The variables representing the fields of a record are logically related to each other, and often subjected to similar processing. For example, one will read all of the fields into main memory, move them from one set of variables to another in main memory, and eventually copy them all back to the file in secondary storage. It is very convenient to be able to specify this logical relationship between variables, and then use it to simplify programming.

In PL/I this is done by declaring a "structure". By prefixing "level numbers" to consecutive identifiers in a declaration one can show the logical relationship between variables and assign identifiers to groups of variables. For example, one might declare the variables representing the fields of a student biographical record as follows:

```
DECLARE 1 STUDENT,
         2 NAME CHAR(30),
         2 CAMPUS_RESIDENCE,
             3 ADDRESS CHAR(30),
             3 TELEPHONE CHAR(7),
             3 DINING_HALL_CODE CHAR(3),
         2 HOME,
             3 PARENT_GUARDIAN CHAR(25),
             3 ADDRESS CHAR(30),
             3 TELEPHONE CHAR(10),
         2 REGISTRATION,
             3 COLLEGE CHAR(12),
             3 CLASS CHAR(2),
             3 GRADE_AVG FLOAT DEC,
             3 ADVISOR CHAR(20);
```

The identifiers that are followed by type attributes are
variables, and are used in the usual way. The identifiers that
have no type attributes, and are immediately followed by
identifiers with a higher level number, are called "structure
names". They are simply convenient names for the set of
variables that follow them. For example, CAMPUS_RESIDENCE
refers to the group of three variables ADDRESS, TELEPHONE and
DINING_HALL_CODE that follow it. In some contexts in PL/I
(assignment, input, output) one can use a structure name instead
of writing each of the variables that it represents.
CAMPUS_RESIDENCE is a "minor structure" because it is a part of
a larger structure; STUDENT is a "major structure" since it is
not part of a larger structure. (A major structure always has a
level number of 1.) Having defined this structure one could
read a record from a file just by writing

```
    GET FILE(STUDENTS) LIST(STUDENT);
```

This would be equivalent to writing

```
    GET FILE(STUDENTS) LIST(NAME,
        CAMPUS_RESIDENCE.ADDRESS, CAMPUS_RESIDENCE.TELEPHONE,
        DINING_HALL_CODE, PARENT_GUARDIAN, HOME.ADDRESS,
        HOME.TELEPHONE, COLLEGE, CLASS, GRADE_AVG, ADVISOR);
```

Structure names can be used in an analogous way in output and
assignment statements.

Note that, unlike an array, all variables in a structure do
not have to have the same type attributes. Note also that the
same identifier can be repeated in a structure. ADDRESS and
TELEPHONE are variables in the minor structure CAMPUS_ADDRESS,
and the same two identifiers are used in the minor structure
HOME. When one needs to refer to one of these variables it is
necessary to "qualify" the name to indicate which one. In PL/I
one would write either CAMPUS_RESIDENCE.ADDRESS or HOME.ADDRESS.

Such structures, or data aggregates, do not really add any
new capability to a programming language, since equivalent

statements could be written in terms of the individual variable
names. However, since it is not uncommon for records to have
several hundred fields there is a substantial convenience in
writing programs in a language that provides the ability to
handle groups of variables as a single element.

2.1.3 <u>Format Control</u>

   File processing problems are typically very demanding with
respect to the format of printed output. Often this is written
on special printed forms, rather than plain paper, and the
output format must be precisely specified so that each value is
placed in the correct box, or is properly aligned with respect
to pre-printed titles. Part of the output is used directly as
business documents -- checks, bills, purchase orders, invoices,
etc. The program must follow the conventions that have been
established for such documents.

   In general, the output of a file processing program is
distributed to large numbers of different users, none of whom
can be assumed to know anything at all about the problem, the
file or the program. Each output document must be self-
contained -- that is, completely self-explanatory.

   One particularly fussy requirement occurs in the traditional
display of dollar totals. The display format varies, depending
upon the <u>value</u> being displayed. For example:

```
        Value:              Display form:

        00012345.67          $ 12,345.67
        00000045.67             $ 45.67
        09812345.67        $ 9,812,345.67
        00000000.00               .00
        00000000.01             $ .01
       -00012345.67          $ 12,345.67 CR
```

While you could write a subroutine to achieve this format using
only the PL/I facilities described in the earlier sections, it
would not be a trivial routine. Fortunately, this is not
necessary, since PL/I has an automatic editing facility to
achieve this format.

   A language to be used for file processing programs must
permit the flexible control over format that is demanded by
these considerations. Moreover, since programmers in this area
seem to spend an inordinate fraction of programming time on
format control, the convenience of the language in this respect
has major bearing on the productivity of programmers using it.

2.2 Languages for File Processing

Programming languages vary significantly in their provisions for the tasks described in Section 2.1. Some languages (such as APL, BASIC or LISP) simply do not permit the programmer much control over secondary storage, so their use for file processing is very limited. In other languages (such as FORTRAN or ALGOL) these tasks are possible, but not convenient. (For example, neither FORTRAN nor ALGOL has any provision for data aggregates, as described in Section 2.1.2.) However, some languages have been specifically designed for file processing.

2.2.1 General-Purpose Languages

Without question the standard general-purpose language for file processing is COBOL. In view of the early success of FORTRAN for mathematically-oriented problems, a group of computer users with file processing problems organized to define a language of comparable convenience and power, oriented to their problems. This CODASYL Committee produced a definition of COBOL in 1960. The United States Government was heavily represented in this effort, and the computer manufacturers were encouraged to make COBOL available on their machines by means of strong indications that sales to the Government would be dependent on COBOL capability.

COBOL is comparable to PL/I, and you could probably read a COBOL program and have a general idea of what it accomplishes based on your experience in PL/I. The similarities between the two languages are more important than the differences (although one would not get this impression from listening to a militant advocate of either). The syntax and keywords are different, but the same functions are performed -- declaration, assignment, sequence control, input and output.

A COBOL program is divided into four "divisions". The first two, called "identification" and "environment", correspond to blocks of PL/I comments describing the purpose of the program and its operating requirements. Declarations are collected in the "data division", and the "procedure division" corresponds to the main procedure in PL/I.

Some COBOL statements are quite similar to their PL/I counterparts (IF and GO TO, for example); others look different but perform a familiar task:

    PERFORM TAXLOOP VARYING I FROM 1 BY 1 UNTIL N

Comparable assignment statements in PL/I and COBOL are:

    A = B + C;   ADD B AND C TO A

    D = E * F;   MULTIPLY E AND F GIVING D

    G = H * (U + V);   COMPUTE G FROM H * (U + V)

    A = B;   MOVE B TO A

The most significant difference between the two languages (and the greatest weakness in COBOL) is the area of program structure. The procedure division can be subdivided into "sections" and "paragraphs" but the facilities provided to invoke paragraphs, pass arguments to them, and isolate them from other program actions, are very limited.

An example of a COBOL program paragraph is the following (from an IBM 360 COBOL manual -- C28-6516):

    PROCESS-SORTED-RECORDS SECTION.
     PARAGRAPH-3. RETURN SORT-FILE-1 AT END GO TO PARAGRAPH-4.
     IF FIELD-FF = FIELD-EE WRITE FILE-3-RECORD FROM
     SORT-RECORD GO TO PARAGRAPH-3 ELSE
     MOVE FIELD-EE TO FIELD-EEE MOVE FIELD-FF TO FIELD-FFF
     MOVE FIELD-AA TO FIELD-AAA MOVE FIELD-BB TO FIELD-BBB
     MOVE SPACES TO FILLER-A, FILLER-B WRITE FILE-2-RECORD.
     GO TO PARAGRAPH-3.
     PARAGRAPH-4. EXIT.

The academic world tends to regard COBOL as verbose, clumsy and inelegant, and tries to ignore it, although there are probably more COBOL programs and programmers in the world than there are for FORTRAN, ALGOL and PL/I combined. For the most part, only schools with an immediate vocational objective provide instruction in COBOL.

PL/I is the second most important general-purpose language for file processing. It was designed in the early sixties by a committee of IBM language specialists and users of IBM computers. Their objective was to provide a single language that would be useful for both mathematical computing and file processing, and would possess the structure and elegance that were present in ALGOL. Unfortunately, the design committee was under severe time constraints and the result was not as attractive as it might have been. Nevertheless, IBM embraced the new language and announced the demise of both FORTRAN and COBOL. That obituary turned out to be premature, to say the least. Even if PL/I is a better language than either FORTRAN or

COBOL many users felt that it was not enough better to be worth
the effort to retrain programmers and convert program libraries.
This reluctance was encouraged by the fact that IBM neglected to
provide an efficient translator for PL/I (see Section VII.2)
until 1971.

It now seems unlikely that PL/I will ever succeed in
replacing either FORTRAN or COBOL. Instead of unifying a
computing world that was divided in two by a language barrier,
PL/I has created a three-language situation in the United
States. (In the rest of the world ALGOL is also important.)
But it is equally unlikely that either FORTRAN or COBOL, at
least in their present form, will continue in major use
indefinitely. Both of these languages were pioneering efforts,
and it would indeed be surprising if experience and research
does not eventually lead to their retirement. Successor
languages (whatever they may be called) are likely to offer many
of the features now present in PL/I.

You should realize that you have been introduced to only a
fraction of the full PL/I language -- perhaps one-third. (See
Appendix A.) The features that have been omitted here have
been, for the most part, those associated with file processing.

2.2.2 Specialized File Maintenance and Retrieval Systems

Beginning in the late sixties there has been a rapid
development of a new type of programming language for file
processing applications. Languages of this type have come to be
known as "data base management systems" or "file maintenance and
retrieval systems". These languages do not have the general
capability of COBOL or PL/I, but are intended to serve the more
common tasks of routine file processing -- processing
transactions to update a file, and extracting information from a
file to produce reports, lists and analyses. For these limited
purposes the specialized languages are substantially easier to
use than either COBOL or PL/I.

One of the least flexible of these languages is called RPG.
Since it is distributed by IBM it is also the most widely used.
(In fact, it is believed to be the most widely used of all
programming languages.) An RPG programmer is guided by a
variety of specially-printed programming forms. He fills in
designated spaces to specify the structure of the file, the
format of transactions on punched cards, and the desired format
of printed output. An experienced RPG user can write such
"programs" in a fraction of the time that would be required to
write a PL/I program to perform the same task. MARK IV is
another language of substantially greater power and flexibility,
but similar to RPG in its dependence on a multitude of special
forms.

Not all of these languages depend on special programming forms, and some have achieved a reasonably readable syntax. For example, in a language called ASAP, a retrieval program for the student biographical file described in Section 2.1.2 might appear as:

```
FOR ALL STUDENTS WITH COLLEGE = 'ENGINEERING' AND
        GRADE_AVG > 3.0,
     PRINT A LIST OF:
         NAME, ADDRESS, FACULTY_ADVISOR, GRADE_AVG,
     ORDERED BY GRADE_AVG.
```

In the same language a program to update the file would be:

```
FOR ALL STUDENTS SELECTED BY KEY IN FEBRUARY_DATA,
     FORMATTED BY BIOGRAPHICAL_CARD_FORMAT,
     UPDATE THE RECORD.
```

The equivalent PL/I or COBOL program would be several pages long, would take much longer to write and test, and would be much less easily understood by the person who requested the program.

This development has been very rapid, and is still somewhat chaotic. The CODASYL Committee has recently become interested in the subject, and may well have the same standardizing influence on file maintenance systems that it exerted on behalf of COBOL a decade earlier. At present these file maintenance languages are somewhat restricted in capability, but their power will probably increase as they are further developed. They would seem to demonstrate that languages considerably more natural and convenient to use than PL/I or COBOL can be developed.

2.3 Defensive Programming

A programmer in this area must be a confirmed and practicing pessimist. A framed copy of Murphy's Law --

"ANYTHING THAT CAN GO WRONG, WILL"

should hang on his wall, and his programs should reflect his belief that this maxim accurately describes the world in which he works. The quality of his programs can largely be measured by their ability to maintain composure in the face of exceedingly difficult circumstances. Four aspects of this difficulty are cited in the following sections.

2.3.1 Operating Environment

Contrast the life cycle of a typical "student program" and a typical production file processing program. The student program has the following characteristics:

   a) It is developed from a concise, precise, unambiguous statement of a problem, that is provided by someone who knows what he wants and whose requirements do not change during the life of the program.

   b) One person is responsible for developing an algorithm, and writing and testing the program. When the program is finished the same person is responsible for "using" it -- setting control values, supplying data, and interpreting results.

   c) The program is independent of other programs and data.

   d) The worst that can happen as a result of a program error is the waste of a computer run (or a low grade).

   e) After very brief use (often a single run of the finished program) the program is discarded.

On the other hand, the file processing program has the following characteristics:

   a) It is developed from a vague statement of requirements from someone who isn't sure precisely what he needs, who has no idea what a computer is capable of doing, and who sometimes hopes that the computer will be incapable of handling the job. Moreover, the requirements, such as they are, will change periodically as the program is being developed and used.

   b) Many people are involved. The problem may be refined by one person (a "systems analyst"), programmed by a second, tested by a third, documented by a fourth, and used by many others.   The program may be written by several people working independently, and will surely be modified by several people during its lifetime. Few of these people have much appreciation of the total problem, and few have a deep commitment to making the program work.

   c) The program is related to a file whose content (and even form) changes; it shares this file with many other programs, all of which are changing and most of which contain errors.

   d) The worst that can happen as a result of a program error is that a valuable, perhaps irreplaceable file will be damaged or destroyed, and that erroneous information will be distributed and acted upon.

e) The program (with modifications) may be run regularly
for many years.

The difference might be compared to learning to drive an
automobile on a large, empty parking lot, and driving an
ambulance in Manhattan during rush hour.

The dominant characteristics that dictate how programs must
be written are the necessity for <u>communication</u> (many people are
involved), and the certainty of <u>change</u>. The harsh realities of
the file processing environment demand a fanatical attention to
systematic program development, consistent style, adequate
documentation, and exhaustive testing. Casual and intuitive
procedures, that may suffice in the hospitable environment in
which a student learns to program, are just not adequate for
real programs.

2.3.2 <u>File Protection</u>

In this type of application the programmer must adopt the
view that file <u>protection</u> is as important as file <u>processing</u>.
In the first place, a file is an object of considerable <u>value</u>;
in the second place, it is under more or less continuous
<u>assault</u>. These assaults may be accidental -- the results of
errors -- or deliberate unauthorized attempts to extract or
alter information, or even to destroy the file. The effect is
the same; to cause the file to <u>fail</u> to represent the required
status information. Protection is a very complex issue. In
order to suggest what is involved it is useful to divide the
problems into issues of <u>integrity</u>, <u>accuracy</u> and <u>security</u>.

The maintenance of file integrity means physically
safeguarding the device on which the file resides against
catastrophic damage. Files are susceptible to damage by some of
man's ancient hazards such as floods (computing centers are
often ground floor or below), fire (and the malfunction of fire
extinguishing systems) and riots (computing centers have become
popular symbolic targets). It is also possible for either the
computer or the human operator to malfunction in such a way as
to damage the storage device and render all or part of a file
unreadable. A file can be misused in an unfortunate number of
ways. For example, the wrong generation of a file can be used,
a file can be processed by the wrong program or with the wrong
input transactions, or a device already containing a file can be
considered empty and reused for another file.

Accuracy in this context refers to the validity of the
information in the file. (This is not related to the concept of
accuracy discussed in Part V.) This requires screening out
erroneous transaction input that is trying to introduce
inaccurate information.

Security is a more modern risk, and one that promises to become increasingly important. This is the task of restricting access to the information in the file to those individuals who have a legitimate and authorized right to it. As computer files accumulate increasing amounts of confidential and valuable information there are increasing incentives to indulge one's curiosity by browsing, or to augment one's resources by felonious alterations. Although there are some difficult ethical and legal problems in defining what access is legitimate and who is to authorize whose access to what, there is also the technical issue of how to <u>enforce</u> whatever restrictions are agreed upon. Basically, it means that a file cannot regard every program as having the same privileges.

The details of solutions to these problems are well beyond the scope of this book, but they are major problems in file processing and we feel that the neophyte programmer should be made aware of them. Some of these matters involve physical protection (locks, fireproof vaults, etc.) and are not the direct concern of the programmer, but in general, these problems have a major effect on the way file processing programs should be designed. For example, a program must write detailed identification information into the beginning of each file that it creates, and it must <u>check</u> the identification of each file that it processes and <u>absolutely refuse to proceed</u> if it is not correct. In this way, the program can offset the error of an operator who brings the wrong file, or the wrong generation of the right file, from the tape/disc library to mount on the reading device.

The basic protection mechanism is simple and traditional -- <u>make and retain extra copies</u>. Often in updating a file, one creates a complete new generation, incorporating the new transaction data, and not actually changing the previous generation. The "father" generation of the file is used to create the "son" generation, and both are retained in the library. In fact, most installations use a "grandfather-father-son" library system in which at least three generations of each file are retained. In this way, if the current generation of a file is destroyed, or found to be faulty because of a program error or improper data, one can recover by recreating the new generation from backup generations. Of course, for such practices to offer a high degree of protection it is necessary to go to the bother of storing some portion of the backup library <u>off site</u> so that the same disaster cannot destroy all generations of the file.

One could conceivably become so obsessed with these risks as to over-protect the file. If the protection mechanisms make it too difficult or costly for a legitimate, authorized individual to use the file, the value of the entire system is reduced. Similarly, if the file is so carefully protected against input transactions that legitimate, accurate update information is rejected or delayed, the information in the file will become obsolete and its utility diminished. While one should keep this

risk in mind, over-protection is not a widespread problem in
file processing.

2.3.3 Error Treatment

One of the corollaries of Murphy's Law states that every
conceivable error will eventually be made, and unfortunately,
many inconceivable errors will also be made. One must
understand that a "computer file processing system" actually
involves a great number of frail and fallible human beings.
They write programs, supply data and operate the computer, and
are susceptible to errors in every act. The point is not to
bewail the characteristics of the human race, but only to remind
the programmer of these universal and inevitable
characteristics, and demand that he write programs in such a way
that they are useful in the real world, and do not require
unrealistic assumptions about the world.

A properly designed file processing program is dominated by
tests, checks, exceptions and error conditions. Most of these
provisions concern very rare events -- the probability of one
particular error occurring on one particular transaction is very
small, but the probability that that error will never occur on
any transaction for the life of the system is also small. These
frequent, usually unnecessary tests, exact a penalty in computer
time, but in general a faster program with reduced protection is
not an economical design in the long run.

For example, suppose you are writing a subroutine, and are
told that the key argument will always be nonnegative. In
scientific computing you might be able to believe such a promise
and program on the assumption that the argument will never be
negative. In file processing you interpret the statement to
mean that the argument is supposed to be nonnegative, but both
you and whoever made the promise know that the program will
receive bad data, and will someday be modified in some
unpredictable way by someone who is unaware of that promise.
Therefore, prudence demands that your subroutine start with
something like the following:

        IF ARG < 0 THEN CALL ERROR3(ARG);

Detection of errors is only part of the problem. What action
should the program take upon detection? In general, automatic
correction is a risky business and is rarely used for this type
of problem. The usual strategy is to call for human
intervention and assistance. However, the program should
provide a maximum amount of information to facilitate the
correction. For example, the message

        ERROR ENCOUNTERED -- BAD DATA.

is not much help, but

        FIELD CONTENT ERROR:
            ON DATA CARD 1208 THE AMOUNT FIELD IMPROPERLY
            CONTAINS A NON-NUMERIC CHARACTER.

would greatly simplify locating and correcting the faulty card.

    Some errors must be immediately and· irretrievably <u>fatal</u>.
That is, the program must stop and refuse to proceed no matter
how it is coaxed. Such a case would occur when improper file
identification is discovered.   However, there are many errors
that cannot practically be treated in this way. For example, it
is not unusual for 1% of data cards to be in some way faulty, so
that in a large file update there could easily be several
hundred data errors. To stop on each such error, demand that it
be corrected, and then restart the run is just not practical.
The errors should be detected, rejected, and listed in such a
way that the corrections can all be made at once. If the number
and severity of such errors is high enough, it <u>may</u> be necessary
to repeat the run, but more often the run is accepted and
corrections are made in the next update.

2.3.4 <u>System Evolution</u>

    The life of a file is generally measured in months or years;
hence it follows that programs to process that file are also
relatively long-lived. However, the detailed specification of
just what processing has to be done will change fairly often.
This means that unless the program can be modified from time to
time to meet these changing requirements it will become obsolete
and useless, and have to be replaced. Hence, in designing and
writing a file processing program one should assume that the
program will be subjected to frequent and serious modifications
throughout its life.

    Typically, the modifications of a program are made by someone
other than the original author (although it hardly matters,
since by the time of modification even the author will have
forgotten most of the necessary detail). This puts a great
premium on clarity and consistency in programming, and adequacy
of documentation. Both contribute importantly to a reduction in
the time required for the subsequent programmer to understand
the program and the manner in which it should be modified, and
also increase the chances of effecting a modification without
causing unfortunate side-effects. A bit of obscure cleverness,
perpetrated in the name of "efficiency", is not likely to make
this future programmer tell everyone what an ingenious
programmer you are.

2.4 Systems Analysis

The task of precisely defining the problem in file processing
applications is sufficiently difficult and time-consuming that
it is often viewed as a separate task, to be performed by
someone other than the programmer. One who analyzes problem
requirements and plans the overall strategy of the computer
solution is called a "systems analyst". When the overall
programming task is divided in this way the translation to a
programming language is often called "coding" (rather than
programming).

A systems analyst can be considered to be responsible for the
initial levels of the program development (see Part II), and the
coder, responsible for the final levels. The exact division of
labor will vary with the problem, and depend upon the capability
of the individuals concerned. Obviously, a systems analyst must
know how to program, since the initial levels of the development
will define the structure of the program. Usually these
analysts have been successful programmers, and have been
promoted to this position of greater responsibility. In
addition to their design role, they frequently act in a
supervisory role with respect to several coders.

The other side of the analyst's responsibility is the
interface with the user. In this he needs impossible amounts of
tact, patience and judgement. He must discover precisely what
has to be done by talking with people who see only a tiny corner
of the whole picture, who have no idea what the power and
limitations of the computer imply, and who may well feel
threatened by the whole process. He must decide to what extent
to just mechanize the task as it has been done previously, and
to what extent to use the opportunity to alter the basic
process. It is very much an art, and the difference in results
between a good systems analyst and a mediocre one is
spectacular.

Part VI References

ASAP System Reference Manual, Compuvisor Inc., Ithaca, N. Y.

Awad/DPMA, Automatic Data Processing Principles and Procedures, 2nd Edition, Prentice-Hall, 1970

Brightman, R. W., and J. R. Clark, RPG Programming, MacMillan, 1970

CODASYL Systems Committee, Survey of Generalized Data Base Management Systems, May 1969 (available from ACM)

CODASYL Systems Committee, Feature Analysis of Generalized Data Base Management Systems, May 1971 (available from ACM)

CODASYL Systems Committee, Data Base Task Group Report, April 1971 (available from ACM)

Conway, R. W., W. L. Maxwell and H. L. Morgan, "On the Implementation of Security Measures in Information Systems", Communications of the ACM, April 1972

MARK IV Reference Manual, Informatics Inc., Sherman Oaks, Calif.

Martin, J., Programming Real-Time Computer Systems, Prentice-Hall, 1965

Martin, J., and A. Norman, The Computerized Society, Prentice-Hall, 1970

McCracken, D. D., A Guide to COBOL Programming, Wiley, 1963

Olle, T. W., 'MIS: Data Bases', Datamation, November 15, 1970

Pollack, S. V. and T. D. Sterling, A Guide to PL/I, Holt Rinehart and Winston, 1969

Sprowls, R. C., PL/C: A Processor for PL/I, Canfield, 1972

USA Standard COBOL, X3.23-1968, ANSI, 1968

Part VII*

PROGRAMMING LANGUAGES AND TRANSLATORS

Section 1 <u>Translation of Programs</u>

Almost as soon as one understands a programming language, one begins to wish that the designers of that language had done various things a little differently. By now, you may have some ideas as to how you would "improve" upon PL/I. Let us consider how one might go about actually implementing such ideas.

1.1 <u>Translation from PL/X to PL/I</u>

Suppose we wanted to program in a hypothetical language called PL/X which differs from PL/I in only three respects:

> 1) Declarations begin with the keyword CREATE instead of DECLARE,

> 2) Printed output is produced by a statement with the form
>
>   PRINT_ONE_LINE(list of variables);

> 3) The keyword FINISH_PL/X is placed at the end of a program (on a separate card, starting in column 1), immediately preceding the *DATA card.

For example, (4.1.1a) of Part I, written in PL/X, would look like the following:

```
        /* ADDING PROGRAM */
          ADDER: PROCEDURE OPTIONS(MAIN);
             CREATE (X, Y, Z) FLOAT DECIMAL;
                  /* X, Y ARE NUMBERS TO BE ADDED */
                  /* Z IS RESULT */
(1.1a)           GET LIST(X, Y);
                 Z = X + Y;
                 PRINT_ONE_LINE(Z);
                 END ADDER;
        FINISH_PL/X
        *DATA
        15.5,  10.2
```

We would like to be able to write programs in PL/X and have them executed on a computer, but unfortunately there is no computer that "understands" PL/X. However there are computers that understand PL/I, so if a PL/X program could be "translated" into an equivalent PL/I program, then the PL/I program could be executed to produce the desired results. Moreover, the PL/X programmer might not be told that his program required translation into PL/I, and he might be led to believe that a computer understood PL/X and could execute his program directly.

We have deliberately designed PL/X so that the translation would be simple so that the general idea of such a translation will not be obscured by details. An algorithm to perform this translation is:

```
    Read a PL/X source card into CARD
    DO WHILE (CARD does not begin with 'FINISH_PL/X');
        Within CARD change 'CREATE' to 'DCLʙʙʙ'
                and 'PRINT_ONE_LINE' to 'PUT SKIP LISTʙ'
        Write out CARD as PL/I source lines
        Read next PL/X source card into CARD
```

A PL/I program to perform this translation is given below. The PL/X program of (1.1a) is shown as data for this translation program. This translator will actually work -- it will take any PL/X program as input, and print out an equivalent PL/I program that could be punched on cards and executed on a computer.

This translator will transform the character sequences "CREATE" and "PRINT_ONE_LINE" wherever they occur. This means that they not only cannot be used as identifiers; they must not be used in a comment or a literal, or as part of an identifier. That is, CREATENEW, 'NOW CREATE TABLE', and /* RECREATE INDEX */ would all be changed by this simple translator. A slightly more complicated translator would make these additional restrictions unnecessary.

```
/* PL/X TO PL/I TRANSLATOR */
   /* READS ANY ARBITRARY PL/X PROGRAM -- */
            /* WITHOUT CONTROL CARDS */
            /* CONSIDERS ONLY COLUMNS 1 TO 72 OF CARDS */
   /* PRODUCES AN EQUIVALENT PL/I PROGRAM */
X_TO_I: PROCEDURE OPTIONS(MAIN);
   DCL CARD CHAR(80); /* SOURCE LINE */
   DCL COL FIXED DEC; /* CARD COLUMN */

   GET EDIT(CARD)(A(80));
   SCAN: DO WHILE(SUBSTR(CARD,1,11) ¬= 'FINISH_PL/X');

      /* CHANGE 'CREATE' TO 'DCL' AND 'PRINT' TO 'PUT' */
         /* BEFORE EACH EXECUTION OF BODY 'COL' POINTS */
         /* TO POSITION TO LEFT OF NEXT SCAN POSITION */
         COL = 0;
         CHANGE: DO WHILE(COL < 67);
            COL = COL + 1;
            IF SUBSTR(CARD,COL,6) = 'CREATE'
               THEN DO; CARD = SUBSTR(CARD,1,COL-1)
                        || 'DCL    '
                        || SUBSTR(CARD,COL+6);
                  COL = COL + 5; END;
               ELSE IF SUBSTR(CARD,COL,14) =
                  'PRINT_ONE_LINE' THEN DO;
                     CARD = SUBSTR(CARD,1,COL-1)
                        || 'PUT SKIP LIST '
                        || SUBSTR(CARD,COL+14);
                     COL = COL + 13; END;
            END CHANGE;
      PUT SKIP LIST(CARD);
      GET EDIT(CARD)(A(80)); END SCAN;

   END X_TO_I;
*DATA
/* ADDING PROGRAM */
   ADDER: PROCEDURE OPTIONS(MAIN);
      CREATE (X,Y, Z) FLOAT DECIMAL;
         /* X, Y ARE NUMBERS TO BE ADDED */
         /* Z IS RESULT */
      GET LIST(X, Y);
      Z = X + Y;
      PRINT_ONE_LINE(Z);
      END ADDER;
FINISH_PL/X
```

The output from this program, if executed with the data shown, would be:

```
/* ADDING PROGRAM */
    ADDER: PROCEDURE OPTIONS(MAIN);
            DCL    (X,Y, Z) FLOAT DECIMAL;
                /* X, Y ARE NUMBERS TO BE ADDED */
                /* Z IS RESULT */
            GET LIST(X, Y);
            Z = X + Y;
            PUT SKIP LIST (Z);
            END ADDER;
```

1.2 Programs as Data

The computing process can be viewed in a general way as shown in the following diagram:

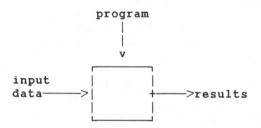

A program is loaded into a computer. Execution of this program causes input data to be read and manipulated to produce results. Initially, we considered input data and results that were entirely numeric. Then, in Section I.9, the concept of a variable was extended to permit values that included non-numeric characters. We alluded to the existence of "text processing" programs, and described the initial development of a text editor in Section II.3.2.2.

Now we are suggesting that there are certain text processing programs that read strings which are statements of a programming language, and manipulate these strings to produce as output equivalent elements of some other programming language. That is, one program called a "translating program" or "translator", reads another program, called a "source program", as input data, and transforms this to produce a third program, called an "object program", as output. This object program can, in turn, be loaded into a computer to process input data to produce results. Schematically, this can be shown as:

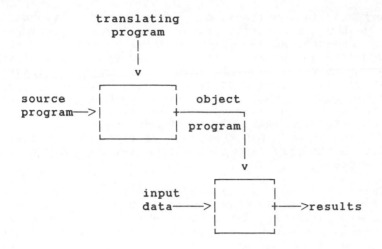

In Section 1.1 we devised a "source language" PL/X, that was
very similar to the "object language" PL/I, so that the
translator could be short and simple. It should be obvious that
we could devise many different source languages, some of which
could differ very markedly in form and function from PL/I.   For
example, in Section VI.2.2.2 examples are given in a source
language that bears strong resemblance to English.   The only
limitation on the design of a source language is the ability to
produce a translator that will transform programs in the source
language into some object language that is "understood" by a
computer.

Such translators are non-trivial, and their development
represents one major branch of the field of computer science.
The subject has received considerable attention, and the
problems and techniques of translation are quite generally and
widely understood. A great variety of source languages are
available to programmers today, because many different
translators have been produced.

It should not come as a complete surprise that PL/I and PL/C
are also source languages.   They are not "understood" by a
computer, any more than PL/X is; they require translation into
an object language before they can be executed on a computer.
This is true not only of PL/I, but also of all the programming
languages that are in general use today -- FORTRAN, BASIC,
COBOL, APL, etc. None of these is the natural language of any
computer.   They have all been designed to be more-or-less
convenient for human programmers, and programs written in any of
them must be translated before they can be executed.

It should also be apparent that this translation could take
place in several stages. For example, in Section 1.1, a PL/X
program was translated into an equivalent PL/I program, but this
PL/I program, in turn, must be further translated before it can
be executed.

However many translation stages may be required, eventually
the program must be transformed into a "real" computer program
-- one that can be executed directly by some computer. This
real program must be written in the "machine language" for
whatever computer is to be used for execution. Each different
type of computer has a unique machine language, into which every
program to be executed on that computer must be translated. For
example, programs to be executed on IBM 360 computers may be
written in PL/I, PL/C, FORTRAN, COBOL, APL or several score of
other source languages -- but every one of these programs must
be translated into the same 360 machine language before it can
actually be executed.

The same source language can be used on different types of
computers. For example, FORTRAN can be used on many different
computers, since translators have been written to translate
FORTRAN programs into equivalent machine language programs for
these various computers.

1.3 Translation to Machine Language

A machine language is no more difficult to learn or
understand than PL/I, but is unquestionably more difficult to
use. For a given problem, it takes several times as long to
write a program in machine language as it does in PL/I. Largely
for this reason, very few programs are written directly in
machine language today. (This was not always the case. In the
first decade of computing, before "high-level" languages and
translators for them became available in the late 1950's, all
programs were written in machine language.)

A machine language program consists of a sequence of
instructions. Each instruction specifies the execution of one
of a repertoire of elemental operations that are "built into"
the computer. This specification is called the "operation code"
portion of the instruction. Most instructions also specify an
operand to be combined with the result of previous operations.
For example, an instruction may specify that "the value of X is
to be added to the results of previous computation". The
operands, or variables, are not specified by identifiers as in
PL/I, but are specified by their physical location in the memory
of the computer. Each memory location has a unique identifying
number called an "address"; the address of the operand is
specified in the instruction.

As a brief example, let us describe the machine language
instructions produced by translation of a PL/I assignment
statement. Suppose variables have been created and assigned
locations in memory as follows (as a result of the translation
of a PL/I declaration):

```
X  [float decimal] in location with address 2132
Y  [float decimal] in location with address 2134
Z  [float decimal] in location with address 2204
W  [float decimal] in location with address 2311
```

The PL/I assignment statement

        X = Y + Z - W;

would be translated into a sequence of machine language
instructions much like the following. In each instruction the
first two characters are the operation code, and the last four
are the operand address:

        582134
        6A2204
        6B2311
        502132

Their execution would proceed as follows:

   582134 Clear the result of previous computation from the
   "arithmetic unit" of the computer, and copy the value from
   the memory location whose address is 2134 into the
   arithmetic unit.

   6A2204 Add the value from memory location 2204 to the value
   already in the arithmetic unit.

   6B2311 Subtract the value in memory location 2311 from the
   value already in the arithmetic unit.

   502132 Store a copy of the value that is in the arithmetic
   unit into memory location 2132.

   The number of machine instructions produced by the
translation of different PL/I statements varies greatly. The
number for an assignment statement depends upon the complexity
of the expression on the right side of the statement. The
translation of a GO TO may yield a single machine instruction; a
complex PUT EDIT statement may require scores of machine
instructions.

   Translation from a source language like PL/I into machine
language is obviously more complicated and difficult to perform
than the translation from PL/X into PL/I illustrated in Section
1.1. However, the general idea remains the same -- a source
program is read as data, and a machine language object program
is produced as output. It would be quite feasible to translate
PL/X directly into machine language, rather than use PL/I as an
intermediate stage. A program to perform this PL/X to machine
language translation could be written in PL/I. Such a
translator would probably require something like 5000 PL/I
statements.

Section 2 <u>Types of Translators</u>

2.1 <u>Measures of Performance</u>

Many different machine language programs will perform the same computing task. These programs might differ in size, efficiency, or in the manner in which they react to errors in the input data. Beyond such functional differences, programs differ just because there are many different ways of performing each of the elemental subtasks that comprise a program, just as there are many ways of conveying the same idea in English.

Since there are different machine language object programs to perform a given task, all translators do not necessarily produce the same object program from the same source program. A translator must first of all be correct -- it must produce an object program that is logically equivalent to the source program, but after correctness there are several possible secondary criteria against which a translator could be judged. A translator could be designed:

    1) to produce an <u>efficient object program</u>;

    2) to <u>translate</u> as efficiently as possible;

    3) to provide as much assistance as possible to the author of the source program in <u>eliminating errors</u>;

    4) to be as simple as possible, in order to minimize the cost, effort and time required to produce the translator.

Hence for a given pair of source and object languages there can be a number of different translators with significantly different characteristics. For example, there are at least a dozen significant translators from PL/I to IBM 360 machine language. Older source languages (such as FORTRAN) have accumulated an even greater number of translators.

As far as the PL/I programmer is concerned, any of these PL/I translators will permit him to execute his program on a computer, but the choice of translator may nevertheless be very important since different translators will provide him with vastly different degrees of assistance in finding and correcting his errors, and present him with considerably different bills for the computer time required to translate his program, and to execute the resulting object program.

2.2 Compilers and Interpreters

Two principal strategies are used in the construction of translators. In the first of these the entire source program is translated into an object program before any execution of the object program takes place. Translation and execution are distinctly different phases, and once translation has been completed, neither the source program nor the translator need be present while the object program is being executed. A translator that employs this strategy is called a "compiler".

The second strategy interleaves translation and execution. As soon as a statement of the source program is translated, the resulting segment of object program is executed immediately. After it has been executed, the segment of object program is discarded, and the next statement of the source program is translated and executed. When execution of a source statement must be repeated (for example, statements in the body of a WHILE loop), it must be re-translated from source form for each execution. The object program exists only in segments, and never as a complete program at any point in time. Obviously, both the source program and the translator must be present throughout the process. A translator that employs this strategy is called an "interpreter". Most interpreters perform a preliminary translation of the entire source program into an internal form, but this form is more similar to the source language than machine language. "Statements" from this internal program are translated and executed, as described above.

The strategies described above are idealized, or extreme. All real translators employ both strategies to varying degrees and in different contexts. Although every translator is a mixture of the two, each is generally classified as either a compiler or an interpreter depending upon which of the idealized models it most closely resembles.

Considering translators for PL/I, the IBM PL/I-F translator, Cornell's PL/C translator, and IBM's "PL/I Optimizer" are all compilers. PL/I-F is a general-purpose compiler, PL/C is a compiler intended to reduce translation time and maximize diagnostic assistance, and the Optimizer is a compiler designed to produce an efficient object program. There are also a number of interpreters for PL/I. IBM's "PL/I Checkout Compiler" is an interpreter (called a compiler for reasons known only to IBM). IBM's CPS, Brooklyn Polytechnic Institute's PLAGO, and the University of Toronto's PLUTO are also interpreters.

Interpreters are generally easier to construct than compilers, and provide more effective control over the execution of the object program. Unfortunately, interpreters also require considerably more computer time, due to the repeated translation of iterated source statements. It is not uncommon to have an interpreter require twenty times as much computer time as a compiler, to translate and execute the same source program.

Section 3 <u>The PL/C Compiler</u>

PL/C differs from PL/I by the addition of the diagnostic statements described in Section III.4 (and the omission of several PL/I statements -- see Appendix A). PL/C programs are translated by a specialized compiler designed to facilitate the development of new programs. Programs in development

a) contain errors,

b) require frequent re-translation, and

c) require relatively limited execution.

Consequently, PL/C was designed to provide as much diagnostic information as possible and perform the translation as rapidly as possible. It does not spend much time during translation trying to achieve a highly efficient object program, and it slows execution somewhat by including extra instructions in the object program that will yield useful diagnostic information if trouble arises during execution. PL/C is from three to ten times as efficient as IBM's PL/I-F compiler for processing typical student programs, but may require as much as twice as long if it is used for a "production run" where the time to execute the object program dominates.

A translator intended to provide extensive diagnostic assistance would normally be an interpreter, but the comparative performance degradation made that impractical in this case. In 1969, when PL/C was designed, the educational world was enthusiastically ignoring PL/I, partly because processing student programs with the IBM PL/I-F compiler (the only translator then available) was substantially more costly than processing under the efficient translators available for other languages (such as the University of Waterloo's WATFOR compiler for FORTRAN, and Stanford's ALGOL-W compiler). An instructor had to be very fond of PL/I to justify the substantial additional cost of using it for an instructional language. If a translator was to make PL/I practical for instruction, it would have to be competitive in performance with those of the other languages then in use. Only a compiler had any chance of achieving this.

3.1 Automatic Error Repair

PL/C's unusual diagnostic strategy of _repairing_ errors is discussed in Section III.3.2. This requires a somewhat unconventional compiler. Since the source program is to be translated and executed regardless of the number and severity of errors that it contains, the compiler must effect repairs during translation so that an executable object program is always produced. Moreover, since that object program must be able to recover in some way from execution errors (such as an attempt to take the square root of a negative number) and continue execution, it must contain additional machine language instructions to perform the recovery operation. These considerations dominated the design of the PL/C compiler.

3.2 PL/C Compiler Structure

The PL/C compiler consists of three main sections:

1) Source Scanner

2) Machine Language Generator

3) Execution Supervisor

The _source scanner_ is responsible for reading the source program, and finding and repairing all of the syntax errors that it contains. The scanner produces a copy of the source program (see Section I.7.2.1) including error messages and a description of any repairs that were performed. The scanner produces an internal copy of a corrected version of the source program. The function of the scanner is similar to that of the PL/X to PL/I translator given in Section 1.1. The input is a program imperfectly written in PL/I; the output is a PL/I program, hopefully similar to what the programmer intended, but in any event _syntactically correct_.

The _machine language generator_ translates the corrected source program into an object program in IBM 360 machine language, as suggested by the discussion of Section 1.3. The scanner and generator together constitute the translation phase of the compiler, and the computer time spent executing them is given as the "COMPILE TIME" at the end of the printed output of each program.

The _execution supervisor_ then initiates execution of the object program. The supervisor remains in memory, along with the object program, ready and available to assist whenever execution errors are encountered. When execution of the object program has been completed the supervisor produces the Post-Mortem Dump described in Section I.7.2.4.

3.2.1 The PL/C Expression Analyzer

While the objective of the source scanner is similar to that of the PL/X to PL/I translator of Section 1.1, the actual organization of the scanner is very different from what might be suggested by the trivial translator shown.

The scanner should be viewed as a program that reads input consisting of a string of "symbols", and produces output consisting of a string of symbols, similar to the input string except for necessary corrections. The symbols are the elements of PL/I -- identifiers, constants, keywords, operators, punctuation marks, etc. The isolation of each symbol is called "lexical analysis". It is performed by a program that is similar in concept to the "read symbol" subprogram developed in Section II.4.4.

At each stage in building the output string, the scanner must ensure that the symbol about to be added to the string is an allowable successor to the previous symbol placed on the string. For example, if the previous symbol on the output string was a plus sign, the next symbol cannot be a comma -- no matter what the input string might specify. There is simply no context in PL/I where the symbol "comma" can follow the symbol "plus sign". ("+," may appear in a comment or a literal, but the entire comment or literal is regarded as a single symbol, regardless of its content.)

A convenient way of describing the allowable successors for each type of symbol is a "transition matrix". This is a table with each row representing a certain type of symbol, corresponding to the last symbol placed in the output string. Each column in the table represents a type of symbol, as a potential successor. The entries in the table specify the action that should be taken for each possible "last-next" pair of symbols.

Using such a table, the algorithm for the source scanner is:

    For each symbol in the source program:
        Get symbol from input, determine its type, consider
            this the "next" symbol and determine a
            column in the table,
        Choose a row in the table corresponding to the type of
            the "last" symbol placed in the output string,
        Execute routine specified by table for last-next pair.

For example, consider a simplified form of arithmetic expression consisting of only variables and arithmetic operators. (We will even exclude the possibility of a prefix minus sign; all operators must appear between two variables.) Examples of such expressions are

    X,   X + Y,   W * Z - Y,   X / Y ** Z.

The transition matrix for allowable last-next pairs is the following:

Next symbol scanned:

variable   operator   other

		variable	operator	other
	none	EXECUTE R1		
Last symbol:	variable		EXECUTE R2	EXECUTE R3
	operator	EXECUTE R1		

The program segments referred to by this table are:

R1: place the variable in the output string, and return to the "variable" row in the table.

R2: place the operator in the output string and return to the "operator" row of the table.

R3: exit, a complete expression has been placed in the output string.

The top row in the table indicates that if an expression is just beginning (no symbol is in the output string) the only valid next symbol is a variable. A variable can be followed by an operator, or by some other symbol indicating the end of the expression; an operator can only be followed by a variable.

Now consider the possibility that input strings might also consist of improper sequences such as

      *,   X -,   / Y Z +,   Y * - Z.

In a conventional compiler the transition table entries corresponding to invalid last-next pairs would be branches to a program segment that would simply generate an error message. Scanning might continue in order to discover other errors, but from that moment on, the output string would not be a correct program, capable of being translated and executed.

In PL/C each entry in the table refers to a routine that preserves the correctness of the output string. The entries corresponding to invalid last-next pairs issue an error message and then take some action to preserve the correctness of the output string. For example, with this approach the table and routines might look like the following:

Next symbol scanned:

variable   operator   other

		variable	operator	other
	none	EXECUTE R1	EXECUTE E1	EXECUTE E2
Last symbol:	variable	EXECUTE E3	EXECUTE R2	EXECUTE R3
	operator	EXECUTE R1	EXECUTE E4	EXECUTE E4

R1: place the variable in the output string, and return to the "variable" row.

R2: place the operator in the output string and return to the "operator" row.

R3: exit, a complete expression has been placed in the output string.

E1: issue an error message, delete the next symbol, return to the "none" row.

E2: issue an error message, supply a synthetic variable (with value 1), return to the "variable" row.

E3: issue an error message, supply a "+" operator, return to the "operator" row.

E4: issue an error message, delete the last symbol from the output string, return to the "variable" row.

Although the actual tables are substantially larger, and the routines more complicated, the PL/C source scanner is structured in this manner.

Part VII <u>References</u>

Aho, A. V., and J. D. Ullman; <u>The   Theory   of   Parsing</u>,
    <u>Translation, and Compiling</u>, Prentice-Hall 1972

Conway, R. W., and T. R. Wilcox; "Design and Implementation of a
    Diagnostic Compiler for PL/I", <u>Communications of the ACM</u>,
    March 1973

Gries, David, "The Use of Transition Matrices in Compiling",
    <u>Communications of the ACM</u>, January 1968

Gries, David; <u>Compiler Construction for Digital Computers</u>, John
    Wiley 1971

IBM; <u>A Programmer's Introduction to the IBM System/360</u>
    <u>Architecture,   Instructions,   and   Assembler   Language</u>,
    Publication C20-1646, International Business Machines
    Corporation.

Sammet, J. E.; <u>Programming Languages: History and Fundamentals</u>,
    Prentice-Hall 1969

Appendix A

SUMMARY OF PL/I AND PL/C

This Appendix attempts to give a concise, readable definition of the important parts of PL/I and PL/C. This is difficult, since the original IBM System 360 PL/I (F) Language Manual, File No.   S360-29 GC28-8201, (herein referred to as IBMFM) is 455 pages long. Naturally we cannot describe all of PL/I carefully, completely, and with examples. We have concentrated on those features which are in PL/C, and which we feel are most useful in programming.   Others are listed and perhaps explained, but in less detail. Occassionally we omit a form of a statement or attribute because it is not needed; its usefulness is low, relative to the space needed to describe it.

The reader must have some knowledge of programming.   This part of the book is intended as reference material, rather than an introduction.   It was, however, designed with the beginner in mind.   For example, for procedure definitions we show a simple form, and then later the complete form.   The beginner will need to read only Appendices A.1 and A.2, A.3 on statements (just the few statements he needs to know), the simple form of the declaration given in Appendix A.4, and Appendix A.6 on variables, scope of names and the like.

Appendix A.1 <u>Conventions</u>

We use a different terminology than is typically used for PL/I. IBMFM calls END, BEGIN, and other such entities "statements". We feel this is misleading and makes the language description longer and more difficult to read. An algorithm is a sequence of statements (or commands) which, when executed, produce a desired result. A <u>program</u> in PL/I, which represents an algorithm, should consist of a sequence of executable statements, with comments, headings, and declarations to describe the entities the statements work on.

Thus we reserve the term "statement" for an entity which is to be executed, usually in sequence. We should be able to describe how to execute a particular kind of statement out of context; that is, knowing only the attributes of variables that it manipulates, but not knowing what statement precedes or follows it.

In describing the syntax of statements and declarations we use the following notation:

1. Square brackets [and] surround an option -- something that may be omitted if desired. For example, if the statement form is

        CHECK [(exp)] ;

then it may be used in either of the forms

        CHECK;   or   CHECK(exp);

Similarly, CHECK [(exp [, exp])] ;   permits the possibilities

        CHECK;   CHECK(exp);   and   CHECK(exp,exp);

2. Braces | and | enclose a term that may occur 0, 1, 2, 3 or more times. For example, the form

        CALL entry-name [(argument |, argument|)] ;

means that the statement can look like

```
        CALL entry-name ;
or      CALL entry-name(argument);
or      CALL entry-name(argument, argument);
or      CALL entry-name(argument, argument, argument);
etc.
```

3. Words in capital letters are PL/I keywords (e.g. BEGIN and END). They should not be used for any other purpose. See Appendix A.2.

4. Terms in small letters denote general classes of elements in the language. The less-used ones will be described where they appear. The more important ones, together with their meanings, are given below:

array-ref   A reference to an array or a cross section of an array (e.g. C or C(*,2)).

attribute   A property or characteristic of a name which helps determine how the name is to be used. Examples are FIXED, BINARY, and RECURSIVE. Attributes are listed and described in Appendix A.5.

constant   Constants are described in Appendix A.2.

declaration PL/I declarations are described in Appendix A.4.

entry-name An identifier used to define an entry point in a procedure. See "Procedure definition" in Appendix A.4.

exp   Any PL/I expression.

file-name   An identifier used to name an input-output file.

label   An identifier used to label a statement.

ON-unit   A substatement of an ON statement. See the ON statement in Appendix A.3.

procedure definition   A procedure; it is described in Appendix A.4.

statement   Any one of the PL/I executable statements described in Appendix A.3. The BEGIN block, Compound statement, IF statement, Iterative statement (loop) and ON statement are "complex" statements, since they contain other statements as part of them. All others are called "simple" statements.

structure-ref   A reference to a structure or part of a structure.

<u>variable-name</u>   The   name   of   a   variable.   For   a   simple
variable this is just the identifier used to name it.   For
a subscripted variable this is the identifier followed by a
(, followed by the constant subscripts separated by commas,
followed by a).   For example, A(1) and B(2,3), but <u>not</u>
A(I) and B(2,K).

   A variable name can also be a qualified name yielding
part of a structure (e.g.   X.Y.P).

<u>variable-ref</u>

   1.   A reference to a simple or subscripted variable.

   2.   A reference to an array.

   3.   A so-called "pseudo-variable", which is sometimes used
   to   reference   <u>part</u>   of a value of a variable, or the whole
   value but in an unconventional way.   These are: SUBSTR,
   COMPLEX, IMAG, REAL, and UNSPEC.

   4.   A cross section of an array (e.g.   C(*,2)).

   5.   A qualified name, which refers to part of a structure
   (e.g.   X.Y   B(I).Z).

Appendix A.2 <u>Preliminary Definitions</u>

A <u>program</u> in PL/I has the following form:

```
entry-name : PROCEDURE OPTIONS(MAIN);
             |declaration|
             |statement|
             |procedure definition|
             END entry-name ;
```

The two entry-names must be the same. The declarations (see Appendix A.4) describe the variables used in the program. The statements are the algorithmic part of the program; they are executed, generally in the order they appear, to produce results. The procedure definitions define other subprograms that the statements can invoke to perform specific subtasks.

The statements of the program refer to and manipulate simple variables, arrays, labels of statements, and so forth. Statements are described in Appendix A.3.

A <u>job</u> submitted to the computer consists of a program, together with optional external procedures, as described in Appendix B.1.

Identifiers and Keywords

An identifier is a single alphabetic character (A through Z, $, #, and @) possibly followed by 1 to 30 alphanumeric characters and/or break characters. The alphanumeric characters are the alphabetic characters and the digits 0 through 9. The break character is the underline character "_".

Examples: B   FILE3 $21   @   PRICE_PER_DOZEN

A keyword is an identifier that, when used in the proper context, has a specific meaning. In PL/I keywords are not reserved and can be used as names of variables, etc. (although it is not wise to do so). In PL/C however, some of the keywords are reserved and may not be used as identifiers. We give a list of the reserved keywords below. A keyword in parentheses can be used as an abbreviation for the keyword preceding it.

```
ALLOCATE BEGIN BY CALL CHECK CLOSE DECLARE (DCL) DO ELSE  END
ENTRY  EXIT FLOW FORMAT FREE GET GO GOTO IF NO NOCHECK NOFLOW
NOSOURCE OPEN PROCEDURE (PROC) PUT READ RETURN REVERT  SIGNAL
STOP SOURCE THEN TO WHILE WRITE
```

Use of Blanks

Except for the following cases, blanks may appear <u>anywhere</u> and have no particular meaning.

1. They may <u>not</u> appear between adjacent characters of an identifier, keyword, constant, or composite symbol (one made up of two characters, like /* and **).

2. One or more blanks <u>must</u> separate adjacent identifiers, keywords, and/or constants.

3. Within a character string constant, a blank is treated as any other character. Thus 'A BC' is the string consisting of an A followed by a blank followed by a B followed by a C.

Comments

A comment has the form

/*   any sequence of characters   */

where the sequence of characters may <u>not</u> include "*/". A comment has no effect on execution of the program, and is used only to make the program more understandable. A comment is permitted wherever a blank is permitted (except in a character string) and is logically equivalent to a blank.

In PL/C, a comment must fit on one card -- it may not extend to two or more cards. This restriction may be lifted by using an option on the *PL/C card; see Appendix B.2.

Because of PL/C's "pseudo-comment" facility (see Section III.4.4.1), it is wise to begin the text of normal comments with a blank.

Constants

In PL/I the following kinds of constants can be used:

1. A decimal fixed point constant. Examples are: 831   003 .0016 391416

2. A decimal floating point constant. Examples are: 18E-2 4E+30 .001E6

3. An imaginary decimal number. This is a decimal fixed or floating point number followed directly by "I". Examples are: 18E-2I   003I

4. True, or false, which in PL/I must be written as '1'B and '0'B respectively. (They are <u>bit strings.</u>)

5. A <u>literal</u>, which is a quote ' followed by a sequence of
characters, followed by a quote '. Examples are 'SIN TABLE'
'ABCD*$.' and '' (the null string).   The characters within
the quotes can be any punchable characters, including a
blank.   A quote to be placed in a string constant must be
punched twice.   Thus,   'A''B' is the string constant whose
three characters are A, ', and B, in that order.

   One can specify that a string is to be repeated several
times.   For example,   (3)'AB' is shorthand for the string
constant 'ABABAB'. (3) is called the "string repetition
factor".   <u>String repetition factors cannot be used in PL/C.</u>

6.   A binary fixed point constant, which is like a decimal
fixed point constant except that only the digits 0 and 1 may
be used, and that the character B must directly follow the
number.   Examples are: 1011100B .0010B, and 1.10B, whose
decimal values are 92, 0.125 and 1.5.

7.   A binary floating point constant, which is a binary fixed
point number, followed by E, followed by an optionally signed
decimal integer exponent,   followed by B.   The exponent
specifies a power of 2.   Examples are: 1011E-31B 1.10E2B
(which is equivalent to .110E3B)

8.   An imaginary binary number. This is a binary fixed or
floating point number followed directly by I.   Examples are:
0.1BI   100001000E+200BI

9.   A bit string constant. This is a sequence of 0's and 1's
enclosed in quotes and followed by B.   A repetition factor
may be used as for character string constants,   but <u>not in
PL/C</u>.   Examples are: '1'B '0'B '00000'B   ''B

10.   A label constant. Labels may be assigned to variables
as values.

Appendix A.3 <u>Executable Statements</u>

We present here the commands, or executable statements of PL/I, in alphabetical order. Each statement described in this Appendix can be optionally preceded by a series of labels, which serve to name that statement:

⎨label :⎬ statement

The new student will be interested only in

1. "Assignment to scalars"
2. "Compound statement"
3. "IF statement"
4. "Iterative statements (loops)"
5. "PUT LIST" and "GET LIST"
6. Perhaps the "GO TO statement"

Declarations are discussed in Appendix A.4.

When looking at the explanation of these statements, make sure you understand the notation and definitions discussed in Appendices A.1 and A.2. You will find material in these discussions which you do not need; this must happen if we are to explain the full language here. You must therefore read with a discerning eye, and skip what is not necessary for you to learn. For example, when reading about GET LIST, you will find that there are three forms of the GET statement. Since you are only interested in GET LIST, don't even look at the form and discussion of the others. Next, the first paragraph of the discussion of GET has to do with the "input" part of the statement. After reading half the paragraph you will note that leaving out "input" means that the data following the *DATA card will be used as input. This is all you need to know, so there is no reason for you to read the rest of that paragraph.

Several PL/I statements are not described here, because they are not in PL/C, or because they are beyond the scope of this book. These are:

1. Statements used to give control over storage allocation to the programmer. These are: ALLOCATE and FREE.

2. Statements dealing with "parallel processing" or "multi-tasking": DELAY, UNLOCK, and WAIT.

3. Statements used for "record" input-output. In addition, normal input-output on files other than the standard ones is not explained in full detail. The record I/O statements are:

LOCATE, READ, REWRITE and WRITE.

4. The DISPLAY statement, which is used to communicate with
the computer operator.

5. The FORMAT statement.

See IBMFM for complete details on these, and other details we
have left out because of space restrictions.

<u>Assignment statement</u>   There are three forms of the assignment
statement.   These are discussed separately under "Assignment
to scalars" (the conventional one), "Assignment to arrays",
and "Assignment to structures".

<u>Assignment to arrays</u>

Form: array-ref ¦, array-ref¦ = exp [, BY NAME] ;

where exp is a scalar expression or an array expression.
The arrays referenced and any array operands of the
expression must have the same number of dimensions and
identical bounds.

Execution: This is <u>not</u> executed as a conventional assignment
statement.   The expression is <u>not</u> first evaluated and then
assigned to the arrays referenced. Instead, the assignment
statement is executed as if it were a number of nested
loops (the number depending on the number of dimensions of
the arrays) which evaluates an expression and assigns to
one array element at a time, in row-major order.   For
example, suppose A(1:20,1:40) is an array. The statement
A = A / A(1,1); is executed as if it were

```
DO I = 1 TO 20 BY 1;
    DO J = 1 TO 40 BY 1;
        A(I,J) = A(I,J)/A(1,1); END; END;
```

This execution first changes A(1,1) to 1, and then leaves
the rest of the array elements unchanged since A(1,1)=1.
As another example, A = 5*A(1,1); is executed as if it were

```
DO I = 1 TO 20 BY 1;
    DO J = 1 TO 40 BY 1;
        A(I,J) = 5*A(1,1); END; END;
```

The statement inside the generated loops will be a
scalar or structure assignment statement; in the latter
case it will be further expanded as described under
"Assignment to structures".   If the original array
assignment has BY NAME appended to it, then so will the
generated statement inside the loops (this is used for
assignment to structures).

Assignment to scalar variables

Form: variable-ref |, variable-ref| = exp ;

The variable-refs must reference scalar variables; evaluation of the expression must yield a scalar value.

Execution: the statement is executed as follows:

1. The variables referenced are determined in left to right order. This means evaluating subscripts, etc.

2. The expression is evaluated.

3. The value of the expression is assigned to the variables determined in step 1, in left to right order. The value is converted, if necessary, to the characteristics of each variable according to the rules given in Appendix A.6.

If the variable-ref is a fixed length string, the string exp is truncated on the right if too long or padded on the right (with blanks for character strings and zeros for bit strings) if too short. If the variable-ref is a VARYING string and the value of the expression is longer than the maximum length allowed, the value is truncated to this maximum length and assigned. Otherwise the length of the variable-ref is changed to the length of the value.

PL/C Restriction: No implied conversion between string and arithmetic data is performed. Thus if I is fixed decimal, I='23'; is invalid.

Assignment to structures

Form 1: structure-ref |, structure-ref| = exp ;

All structure-refs must have the same number k (say) of immediately contained items. The exp must yield a scalar or a structure value. All structure operands of the expression must have exactly k immediately contained items.

Execution: this is not a conventional assignment statement. The expression is <u>not</u> evaluated and then assigned. Instead, the statement is executed as if it were k simpler assignment statements. The ith one is derived from the original assignment statement by replacing each structure operand and reference by its ith contained item. For example, suppose we have

```
1 ONE                        1 TWO
   2 PART1                      2 PART3
      3 RED                        3 RED
      3 WHITE                      3 WHITE
   2 PART2                      2 PART4
```

The assignment statement ONE=TWO+2; is executed like the
two assignments below. Note that the first is still a
structure assignment statement, while the second is a
scalar assignment.

```
ONE.PART1 = TWO.PART3 + 2;
ONE.PART2 = TWO.PART4 + 2;
```

Form 2: structure-ref {, structure-ref} = exp, BY NAME;

The exp must be a structure expression.

Execution: Execution is equivalent to execution of the
assignment statements generated by the following rule: Each
immediate item of the leftmost structure-ref is examined in
turn, as follows:

If each structure-ref and each structure operand has an
immediately contained item with the same identifier as
the item being examined, an assignment statement is
generated. It is derived by replacing each structure
operand and reference with its immediately contained
item that has that identifier. If the generated
statement is a structure or array of structures, then BY
NAME is appended.

For example suppose we have the structures

```
1 ONE                        1 TWO
   2 PART1                      2 PART1
      3 RED(30)                    3 RED(30)
      3 BLUE                       3 WHITE
   2 PART2                         3 BLUE
```

The assignment statement ONE = TWO + 2 * ONE, BY NAME; is
evaluated as if it were

```
ONE.PART1 = TWO.PART1 + 2 * ONE.PART1, BY NAME;
```

which in turn is evaluated as if it were the two statements
below. Note that the first statement below is an array
assignment statement.

```
ONE.PART1.RED = TWO.PART1.RED + 2 * ONE.PART1.RED;
ONE.PART1.BLUE= TWO.PART1.BLUE+ 2 * ONE.PART1.BLUE;
```

BEGIN block

Form: |label:| BEGIN; |declaration|
                      |statement|
                      |procedure definition|
                      END [label] ;

The label following the END (if it appears) must be the
same as one of the labels preceding the BEGIN. Be careful;
the PL/I rules state that if a label follows the END, any
ENDs missing from within the block will be automatically
inserted, without warning, just before the block END.
Therefore, omit no ENDs.

   PL/I also allows the declarations, statements, and
procedure definitions to be intermixed, but it is a good
practice to keep them separated.

PL/C Restriction: If a label appears after the END, it must
be the same as the <u>first</u> label preceding the BEGIN.

Execution: The variables declared and the procedures defined
may be referenced by their names only while executing the
block. For more on scope rules, see Appendix A.6.1.   The
BEGIN block is executed as follows:

   1. Variables are created and initialized according to
   the declarations.

   2. The statements in the block are executed in order.

   3. The variables created in step 1 are destroyed.

See also the GO TO and RETURN statements.

CALL statement

Form: CALL entry-name [(argument |, argument|)] ;

Each argument can be a variable, constant, expression,
file-name, label, label variable, entry-name or
mathematical built-in function. The number of arguments
must be the same as the number of parameters specified at
the definition of the entry-name.

PL/C Restriction: Scalars may not be used as arguments for
array or structure parameters.

Execution:
   1. A correspondence is set up between parameters and
   arguments, as described in Appendix A.6.5.

   2. The variables of the procedure determined by the
   entry-name are created.

3. The sequence of statements of the procedure, beginning at the entry point defined by entry-name, is executed, until the last one has been executed or until a RETURN is executed. When a parameter is referenced, it refers to the corresponding argument. The parameter is <u>not</u> a variable and never contains a value of its own.

4. The variables created in step 2 are destroyed.

See also the GO TO statement.

<u>CHECK statement</u>   Form: CHECK [(exp^1 [, exp^2])] ;

This is <u>not</u> a PL/I statement, and is included <u>only</u> in PL/C. The expressions must be scalars which can be converted to integers.

Execution: Execution causes resumption of printing that results from the raising of the CHECK condition. (The printing may have been suppressed by execution of NOCHECK.) Note that the normal action is to do the printing, so that the NOCHECK; statement is provided to override this normal action. This is the opposite of the situation for the FLOW condition.

With the form CHECK; there is no limit to the number of times printing will occur. When arguments are used the amount of output is limited as follows: exp^1 specifies the maximum number of times that the printing resulting from raising of the CHECK condition <u>in the current block</u> will appear. After the specified number of instances, printing is suppressed.

Exp^2 gives the maximum number of times the printing of the CHECK condition will be permitted in <u>each block</u> <u>dynamically entered from the current block</u>. That is, provided NOCHECK; is not executed,

    CHECK(N,M); is equivalent to
        CHECK(N); in the current block and
        CHECK(M,M); as the first statement in every block
            entered from the current block.

    CHECK(N); is equivalent to
        CHECK(N); in the current block and
        CHECK; as the first statement in every block
            entered from the current block.

Each time that a CHECK; statement is encountered the controlling counters are reset to the new limiting values.

CLOSE statement

   Form: CLOSE FILE(file-name) |, FILE(file-name)| ;

   Execution: Execution causes the files designated to be
      closed; the file-name is disassociated from the data set
      with which it was associated upon opening. The file can be
      reopened.   A CLOSE need not be executed for each file,
      since all files are automatically closed upon termination
      of the program.   Closing an unopened file has no effect.
      For more information, see IBMFM.

   PL/C Restriction: Files SYSIN and SYSPRINT may not be
      explicitly closed by the program.

Compound statement Form: |label :| DO; |statement| END [label] ;

      The label following the END (if it appears) must be the
      same as one of the labels preceding the DO. Be careful;
      the PL/I rules state that if a label follows the END, any
      ENDs missing from within the compound statement will
      automatically be inserted, without warning, just before the
      compound statement END.   Therefore omit no ENDs.

   PL/C Restriction: If a label appears after the END, it must
      be the same as the _first_ label preceding BEGIN.

   Execution: The statements are executed, in order.   See also
      the GO TO and RETURN statements.

DECLARE, DCL   This is not a statement, but a declaration or
   specification. See Appendix A.4.

Conditional statement   See "IF statement".

DO   See "Compound statement" and "Iterative statement".

ENTRY   ENTRY is not a statement. See "Procedure definition"
   (Appendix A.4) for the use of the ENTRY definition in
   specifying multiple entry points. See the ENTRY attribute
   (Appendix A.5) for the use of an ENTRY attribute.

EXIT statement   Form: EXIT;

   Execution: In PL/C, EXIT is equivalent to STOP.

FLOW statement   Form: FLOW [(exp^1 [, exp^2])] ;

      This is _not_ a PL/I statement, and is included _only_ in PL/C.
      The expressions must be scalars which can be converted to
      integers.

   Execution: Execution causes resumption of printing that
      results from the raising of the FLOW condition.   The normal
      action is _not to do the printing_ that results from the

raising of the FLOW condition, so that the FLOW statement is provided to override this normal action.   This is the opposite of the situation for the CHECK condition.

The exps have exactly the same interpretation as for CHECK as described above.

The FLOW condition is raised by any action that potentially alters the normal sequential flow-of-control -- that is, by the CALL, DO, GO TO, RETURN, and IF statements, by any exceptional condition (except FLOW) which would cause an ON-unit to be entered, and by in-line function references.

GET statement

Form 1: GET LIST(variable-ref |, variable-ref|)
                  [input] [SKIP[(exp)]] [COPY] ;

Form 2: GET EDIT(variable-ref |, variable-ref|) format
                  [input] [SKIP[(exp)]] [COPY] ;

Form 3: GET DATA   [input] [SKIP[(exp)]] [COPY] ;

Execution of all of these has to do with reading in or skipping data.   "input" is usually left out, which means that the data are read from the standard input file SYSIN (that is, the data are taken from the cards following the *DATA card.) If "input" has the form "FILE(file-name)" then the data are taken from that file. If "input" has the form "STRING(variable-ref)" then the variable-ref must be to a string variable.   In this case, the data are taken from this string, beginning with the first character. This is useful in changing data previously read from character to arithmetic form.

The presence of COPY causes the data to be written onto the standard print file, as read.   This is useful for debugging purposes. COPY may only be present if "input" is not STRING.

SKIP is equivalent to SKIP(1). SKIP may not be used when the "input" is STRING.

The order of the various options "input", SKIP and COPY is immaterial; they may also be placed just after the keyword GET and before LIST, EDIT, or DATA.

Execution:
1. If SKIP(exp) is present, the exp is evaluated and converted to yield an integer w. If w < 1, w is set to 1. w records (usually cards) are then skipped on the input file.   (If in the middle of a record, the rest of the record is skipped; this counts as 1 skip).

2.   The data are read into the variables specified,
depending on the Form used, as described below. The
difference lies in the format of the input data being read.

Form 1: GET LIST(variable-ref ⌊, variable-ref⌋)

   Constants are read and assigned to the variables in
the list, in left to right order. Any necessary
conversion occurs exactly as in an assignment statement.

   The input must consist of constants separated by a
comma and/or one or more blanks. Each constant is a
signed or unsigned number (e.g.   −32), a character
string (e.g.   'AB C'), a bit string (e.g.   '1'B), or a
complex constant (e.g.   32−21I).

   If the variable-ref is an array or structure,
constants are read and assigned to each element of the
array or structure, in order. For arrays, this is done
in row-major order. For example, for an array
A(1:2,1:2), the assignment proceeds in the order A(1,1),
A(1,2), A(2,1), A(2,2). ·

Form 2: GET EDIT (variable-ref ⌊, variable-ref⌋) format

   The data are read and stored into the variables using
the format. See Appendix A.9 on formats. The variables
are assigned in the same order described for GET LIST.

Form 3: GET DATA

   The input must have the form

   variable-name = constant ⌊,variable-name = constant⌋;

One or more blanks may be used in place of, or together
with, the comma. In effect, the input looks like a
sequence of assignment statements. The variable-names
may be names of simple or subscripted variables. A
qualified name must be fully qualified. The constants
have the form described in GET LIST. The constants are
assigned to the variables, which of course must be
referenceable at the point where the GET DATA statement
appears.

   For example, if the data contains

   A(1)=3, B= 21 C(1,3)='AB' ;

then 3 is assigned to A(1), 21 to B and the string 'AB'
to C(1,3).

GO TO statement

Form: GO TO label ;   or   GO TO variable-reference ;

"GOTO" may be used in place of "GO TO".

Execution: Statements are usually executed in the order in which they occur. This normal sequencing can be changed by executing a GO TO. Control is transferred to the statement labeled "label", or to the label which is the current value of the variable-reference. Execution cannot cause a transfer into an inactive block (one not currently being executed), or into a loop from outside the loop.

Execution causes the termination of any BEGIN block, procedure, IF statement, or compound statement whose scope does not include the target of the jump. This termination occurs just as if the block or procedure were exited normally, in the sense that all variables created at the beginning of the procedure or block are destroyed.

END   See "BEGIN block", "Compound statement",   "Iterative statement", and "Procedure definition".

IF statement   Form: IF exp THEN statement[1] [ELSE statement[2]]

The exp must yield a scalar value. IF statements can be nested.   If so, an ELSE belongs with the closest possible preceding THEN. For example,

    IF exp[1]
       THEN IF exp[2] THEN s[1]
       ELSE s[2]

is equivalent to

    IF exp[1]
       THEN IF exp[2] THEN s[1]
                      ELSE s[2]
       ELSE;

PL/C Restriction: The exp must yield true or false (or any bit string value).

Execution:
    1. The expression is evaluated to yield a value.   This value is usually "true" ('1'B) or "false" ('0'B); if not, it is converted to a bit string (in PL/C it must be a bit string, no conversion is performed).

    2. If the result of step 1 is true ('1'B or a bit string which contains at least one bit which is '1'B) then statement[1] is executed; otherwise statement[2] is executed if it is present.

Iterative statement (loop)

Form 1: |label:| DO WHILE (exp) ; |statement| END [label] ;

The label following the END (if it appears) must be the same as one of the labels preceding the DO. Be careful; the PL/I rules state that if a label follows the END, any ENDs missing from within the loop will automatically be inserted, without warning, just before the loop END. Therefore omit no ENDs.

PL/C Restriction: If a label appears after the END, it must be the same as the first label preceding the DO.

Execution: This is exactly equivalent to execution of

```
    L1: IF exp THEN
            DO; |statement| GO TO L1: END;
```

Form 2: |label:| DO variable-ref = exp^1 TO exp^2 [BY exp^3]
                        [WHILE(exp^4)] ;
                            |statement| END [label] ;

The remarks about the label following the END for Form 1 apply here also. If "BY exp^3" is missing, "BY 1" is implied. "TO exp^2 BY exp^3" may also be written as "BY exp^3 TO exp^2".

Execution: Let V1, V2, and V3 be variables with the type attributes of exp^1, exp^2, and exp^3 respectively, which are not used elsewhere in the program. Execution is exactly equivalent to executing the sequence:

```
    Determine variable-ref -- say it is to variable VAR;
    V1 = exp¹; V2 = exp²; V3 = exp³;
    VAR = V1;
    LOOP:       IF (V3>=0) & (VAR>V2) THEN GO TO NEXT;
                IF (V3<0)  & (VAR<V2) THEN GO TO NEXT;
      WHILETEST: IF ¬(exp⁴) THEN GO TO NEXT;
                |statement|
                VAR = VAR + V3;
                GO TO LOOP;
    NEXT:;
```

where if "WHILE(exp^4)" is missing, statement WHILETEST is deleted.

Form 3: |label :| DO variable-ref = spec |, spec| ;
                    |statement| END [label] ;

The remarks given for Form 1 about the label following the END apply here also. Each spec (specification) has the following form (see Form 2):

exp^1 TO exp^2 [BY exp^3] [WHILE exp^4]

Execution: This is exactly equivalent to executing the following sequence of loops, where variable-ref and |statement| are as above, and the superscript on the specs denote the order of the specifications above:

DO variable-ref = $spec^1$ |statement| END;
DO variable-ref = $spec^2$ |statement| END;
DO variable-ref = $spec^3$ |statement| END;
                    . . .

NOCHECK statement   Form: NOCHECK;

This is <u>not</u> a PL/I statement, and is included <u>only</u> in PL/C.

Execution: Execution causes suppression of any printing that would occur from raising the CHECK condition. See the CHECK statement.

NOFLOW statement   Form: NOFLOW;

This is <u>not</u> a PL/I statement, and is included <u>only</u> in PL/C.

Execution: Execution causes suppression of the printing that occurs from raising the FLOW condition. See the FLOW statement.

NOSOURCE pseudo-statement   Form: NOSOURCE;

This is <u>not</u> a PL/I feature and is included <u>only</u> in PL/C.

Execution: At runtime, it is equivalent to a null statement. It affects <u>only</u> the output listing, as follows: Printing of the source program listing is suppressed, beginning with the line containing NOSOURCE; until a SOURCE pseudo statement is encountered.

Null statement   Form: ;

Execution: Execution of the null statement does nothing.

ON statement

Form 1: ON condition [SNAP] SYSTEM ;
Form 2: ON condition [SNAP] ON-unit

The possible conditions are given in Appendix A.7. The ON-unit may be any unlabeled statement except a compound, iterative, IF, RETURN, or another ON statement. It may be an unlabeled BEGIN block.

Execution: Execution of an ON statement indicates how an interrupt for the specified condition is to be handled. If Form 1 is used, or if no ON statement has been executed for a certain condition, the standard system action is taken. This is usually to print an error message and stop execution. In PL/C, the standard action is usually to print a message, to attempt to fix the error, and to continue execution.

If Form 2 is used, the condition's occurrence causes the ON-unit to be executed. After it has finished executing, control usually returns to the point where the interrupt occurred. (This varies according to the condition; see IBMFM for complete details.)

In effect, the ON-unit is a procedure, which is called into action not by an explicit call, but by the raising of some condition.

The presence of SNAP causes a list of all procedures active at the time the interrupt occurs to be printed, just before executing the ON-unit or the standard system action.

Note that execution of an ON statement does not cause the ON-unit to be executed; it causes the ON-unit to be associated with the condition. After execution of the ON-statement, the ON-unit is said to be "pending". That is, the ON-unit is awaiting the occurrence of the condition. If SYSTEM was specified, then the "standard system action" for that condition is pending. (When the program begins execution, the standard system action is pending for each condition.)

We use the term "ON-action" to mean either a programmer-defined ON-unit or the standard system action. Only one ON-action can be pending for any condition at one time. However, each block or procedure in the program can have a different pending ON-action for each condition. When a block or procedure begins execution, the pending actions are what they were just before execution began. When that block or procedure is finished, the ON-actions revert to what they were before entry. If the exit is by way of a GO TO, the ON-actions are those of the block containing the statement jumped to.

Execution of an ON statement within a block or procedure changes the ON-action <u>only</u> for that block or procedure. Executing a second ON-statement within the block or procedure completely cancels the previously pending ON-action. It is possible to recover the ON-action of a surrounding or calling block using the REVERT statement.

See Appendix A.7 and IBMFM for more details on the ON-statement and conditions.

<u>OPEN statement</u>   Form: OPEN FILE(file-name) |options|
                           |, FILE(file-name) |options|| ;

In PL/C the possible options are: SEQUENTIAL STREAM RECORD INPUT OUTPUT TITLE(exp) PRINT LINESIZE(exp) and PAGESIZE(exp) . All exps must yield scalar values. These options need not be present; they augment the attributes specified in the file declaration.

Execution: Each file is opened by associating the file-name with the data set. The option INPUT or OUTPUT is used to indicate whether the file will be read or written.

Usually, the first eight characters of the file-name are used as the dd name of the data set. If the file-name is a parameter, the identifier of the <u>argument</u> and not the parameter, is used. If the option TITLE(exp) is used, the ddname for the data set is assumed to be the first eight characters of the string expression.

The LINESIZE option can be used only with a STREAM OUTPUT file. The value of the expression is used as the length of each line of the file. If no LINESIZE is given for a PRINT file, 120 is used.

PAGESIZE(exp) is used to indicate the number of lines on one page. The default is 60. PAGESIZE can only be used for PRINT files.

This is admittedly a sketchy description. See IBMFM for complete details.

PL/C Restrictions: The default attributes for all PL/C files are STREAM and EXTERNAL. The maximum number of files that may be open at any one time is a local installation option.

<u>PROCEDURE, PROC</u> This is not a statement. See "Procedure definition" in Appendix A.4.

PUT statement

    Form 1: PUT   [output] position ;

    Form 2: PUT LIST(exp |, exp|)   [output] [position] ;

    Form 3: PUT EDIT(exp |, exp|) format [output] [position] ;

    Form 4: PUT DATA (variable-ref |, variable-ref|)
                                         [output] [position] ;

    The order of the options "output" and "position" is
    immaterial; they may also be placed directly after PUT.

Execution: Execution of all these have to do with writing
    data on an output file or into a variable. In the normal
    case, "output" is missing and the standard output file
    SYSPRINT is used. If "output" has the form "FILE(file-
    name)" the data are written out on that file. If "output"
    has the form "STRING(variable-ref)" then the data are not
    written out on a file, but are assigned to the string
    variable referenced, beginning with its first character.
    In the latter case the position option may not be present.

    The forms for "position" are

        PAGE [LINE(exp)]   (only for PRINT files)
        SKIP [(exp)]
        LINE(exp)   (only for PRINT files)

    where the exps must yield integers. SKIP is equivalent to
    SKIP(1).

    Execution proceeds as follows:

    1. If PAGE is present, the current output page is ended
    and a new one is begun.

    2. If LINE(exp) is present, exp is evaluated and converted
    to an integer w. If $w \leq 0$, it is changed to 1. Blank
    lines are written out so that line w of the current page is
    the next one to be formed and written out.

    3. If SKIP(exp) is present exp is evaluated and converted
    to an integer w. w lines are then skipped. For non-PRINT
    files, w must be greater than 0. For PRINT files (like the
    standard one) $w \leq 0$ has the effect of writing at the
    beginning of the current line again.

    4. If Form 1 is used no transfer of data takes place.

    5. The data are written out, depending on the form used.
    The form to use depends on the format of the output
    desired, as explained below:

Form 2: PUT LIST(exp |, exp|)

For PRINT files (like the standard output file
SYSPRINT) the values of the expressions are written out,
24 columns each, in a standard format.   Each line has
five fields and each field contains one value. If an
exp is missing (but not the corresponding comma) a blank
field is written. If a string value covers exactly 24
characters, the next field will be left blank.   If a
string value contains more than 24 characters, it uses
as many fields as necessary.

Form 3: PUT EDIT(exp |, exp|) format

The values are written out according to the format.
See Appendix A.9 for details.

Form 4: PUT DATA(variable-ref |, variable-ref|)

Each reference may be to a scalar value, an array, or
a structure variable.   For PRINT files (like the
standard output file SYSPRINT), the values are written
out in the form

variable-name = constant

with a blank between each. The last one is followed by
a semicolon. Arrays are written in row-major order.

PL/C Additions: PL/C allows an additional form of the PUT
statement:

PUT option |option| ;

where the options are ON OFF FLOW SNAP ALL ARRAY and
DEPTH(exp) , and the PAGE SKIP and LINE options discussed
above. If ON or OFF is used, it must be the only option on
the statement.

FLOW, SNAP, ALL and ARRAY can appear in any combination
with each other, and with the standard SKIP, PAGE or LINE
options of PL/I. They are used as follows:

OFF -- suppresses printing of execution output on
SYSPRINT.

ON -- resumes printing of execution output on SYSPRINT.

FLOW -- displays the recent FLOW history of the program.

SNAP -- displays the recent calling history of the
program.

ALL -- displays the SNAP output as well as the current
values of all automatic, scalar variables in the blocks
active at the time of execution, and the current values
of all static or external scalar variables.

ARRAY -- same as ALL but includes array as well as
scalar variables.

DEPTH(exp) -- specifies the depth of block nesting for
which the display is to be produced. It is used only
with the SNAP, ALL and ARRAY options.

RETURN statement   Form: RETURN [(exp)] ;

   Execution: RETURN; is to be used only within a procedure
      invoked by a CALL statement. Execution causes immediate
      termination of the procedure and the procedure call.

      RETURN(exp); is to be used only within a procedure
      called as a function. Execution causes immediate
      termination of the function; the value of the expression is
      returned as the value of the function. (It is of course
      first converted to the attributes specified by the RETURNS
      option of the procedure definition. See Appendix A.4.)

REVERT statement   Form: REVERT condition;

   Execution: This statement is used in connection with the ON
      statement. Execution causes cancellation of the pending
      ON-action for the condition. The pending ON-action of the
      last block executed becomes pending again. See the ON
      statement.

SIGNAL statement   Form: SIGNAL condition;

   Execution: This statement simulates the interrupt specified
      by the condition. If the condition is enabled, the current
      ON-action for that condition is executed.

SOURCE pseudo statement   Form: SOURCE;

   Execution: This is not a PL/I feature and is included only in
      PL/C.   Provided the NOSOURCE option has not been given on
      the *PL/C card or the last preceding *PROCESS card, source
      program printing resumes with the line containing the
      SOURCE statement. While the program is executing, the
      SOURCE statement is treated as a null statement.

STOP statement   Form: STOP;

   Execution: Execution of the program is terminated.

Appendix A.4 <u>Definitions and Declarations</u>

Definitions and declarations are used to define attributes of

1) variables, arrays, structures, and files
2) procedures and entry points to procedures
3) parameters of procedures

Except for the entry point definition, declarations and definitions may be placed anywhere within a block or procedure; they are <u>not</u> executable statements but just descriptions of things. However, it is suggested that these definitions and declarations be placed as described under "BEGIN block" (Appendix A.3) and "Procedure definition" (Appendix A.4), so that they may be easily found by the reader.

<u>Declaration (simple)</u>
Form: DECLARE (name |, name|) |attribute| ;

1. If there is only one name, the parentheses are not needed. Thus the following two are equivalent:

   DECLARE (A) FIXED DECIMAL;   DECLARE A FIXED DECIMAL;

2. Each name has the form "identifier", in which case it is a simple variable name, a file-name, a label or an entry-name; or the form

   $identifier(exp^1:exp^2 |, exp^1:exp^2|)$

in which case it is an array named "identifier" of subscripted variables. It has as many dimensions as there are pairs "$exp^1:exp^2$". The exps are evaluated and converted to integers at the time the array is created. For each dimension, exp^1 must not be greater than exp^2. The subscript range is exp^1, exp^1+1, ..., exp^2.

   In a bound pair "$exp^1:exp^2$", "exp^1" can be omitted if exp^1 is the constant 1. Thus, A(50,20) is equivalent to A(1:50,1:20).

3. The typical attributes that will be used, together with their meanings in PL/C, are:

   FIXED DECIMAL   The variable can contain integers in decimal notation from -99999 to +99999.

FIXED BINARY   The variable can contain integers in
binary notation from (in decimal) -32767 to
+32767.

FLOAT DECIMAL   The variable can contain a floating
point number of the form

    ±.ddddddE±dd

where the d's are digits 0-9.   The exponent dd
has the range -78 to +75 (approximately).

FLOAT BINARY   The variable can contain a binary
floating point number ±.bbbbbbbbbbbbbbbbbbbbbE±dd
where each b is a bit 0 or 1, and the d's are
digits.   The exponent represents a power of 2.
Binary floating point numbers range from 2^{-260} to
2^{252} (approximately).

CHAR(x)   where x is an integer between 1 and 256.   The
variable can contain a string of x characters.

CHAR(x) VARYING   where x is an integer between 1 and
256.   The variable can contain a string of 0 to x
characters. Upon creation of the variable, it is
initialized to contain 0 characters (the null
string).   The number of characters in   the
variable at any point depends on the last
assignment to it.

BIT(x)   where x is an integer between 1 and 256.   The
value of the variable is a string of x bits.

BIT(x) VARYING   As in CHAR(x) VARYING, except that the
value is a string of bits instead of a string of
characters.

4. Two (or more) declarations may be written as one by
replacing the semicolon of the first and the DECLARE of the
second by a single comma. For example,

   DECLARE (A,B) CHAR(10), C FIXED BINARY;

is equivalent to

   DECLARE (A,B) CHAR(10); DECLARE C FIXED BINARY;

5. PL/I allows implicit declaration of variables, but it
is advisable to explicitly declare every name used in the
program. It is also advisable to specify all the data
attributes for each variable; the defaults are too ad hoc
to remember. See the beginning of Appendix A.5 for a list
of default attributes.

6. See "Procedure definition" and "BEGIN block" for a discussion of where declarations go and what effect they have.

7. Possible attributes are listed in Appendix A.5.

Declaration (of structures)   A structure is a hierarchical collection of names. The names at the bottom of the hierarchy are names of simple variables or arrays. The name at the top is called the structure name. Space does not permit a full, lucid explanation of structures, and we restrict ourselves to discussing an example. Consider the declaration

```
DECLARE 1 STUDENT,
          2 NAME CHAR(20),
          2 ADDRESS,
             3 STREET CHAR(20),
             3 CITY CHAR(20),
             3 ZIP_CODE FIXED DECIMAL,
          2 TRANSCRIPT,
             3 NO_OF_COURSES FIXED DECIMAL,
             3 COURSE_NAME(50) CHAR(10),
             3 GRADE(50) CHAR(1);
```

The name of the structure is STUDENT. It can be used to refer to the whole structure. STUDENT.NAME refers to the part of the structure containing his name -- a CHAR(20) variable. STUDENT.NAME is called a qualified name -- it consists of the sequence of names in the hierarchy, beginning with the structure name, which ends up at that variable name. The qualified name STUDENT.ADDRESS refers to a minor structure of the whole structure. To reference the various parts of the address, use STUDENT.ADDRESS.STREET, STUDENT.ADDRESS.CITY, and STUDENT.ADDRESS.ZIP_CODE.

Note that two parts of the TRANSCRIPT structure are arrays of character variables. The (qualified) name of one of these arrays is STUDENT.TRANSCRIPT.COURSE_NAME. To refer, say, to the Ith element, use STUDENT.TRANSCRIPT.COURSE_NAME(I).

To declare an array of 100 structures, each capable of holding the record of one student, change the first line of the declaration to

```
DECLARE 1 STUDENT(1:100),
```

We could then refer, say, to the Ith grade of the Jth student using

```
STUDENT(J).TRANSCRIPT.GRADE(I).
```

Structures are useful in collecting several items of information together under one name. For example, to pass the student record to a procedure we need only give the argument STUDENT; it is not necessary to pass each of the individual parts as arguments.

It is not always necessary to use the complete qualified name to reference part of a structure. Only enough of it must be present to make the reference unambiguous. For example, if there is no identifier GRADE being used, except in this structure, then one can used the name GRADE instead of the qualified name STUDENT.TRANSCRIPT.GRADE. Generally, one should include the name of the structure; for example, write STUDENT.GRADE, OR STUDENT.CITY.

The only difference in structure declarations and normal declarations is in the use of <u>level numbers</u> just preceding the name of a part of the structure. The structure name must have level 1; all its immediate subparts should have level 2, <u>their</u> immediate subparts should have level 3, and so on. The immediate subparts are generally referred to as immediate <u>items</u>.

PL/I gets its idea for structures from COBOL. More recent languages, for example PASCAL and ALGOL 68, have a much more useful, flexible way of declaring structures.

<u>Entry definition</u>

Form: entry-name : |entry-name :|
              ENTRY [(parameter |, parameter|)]
              [RETURNS(|attribute|)] ;
              |parameter declaration|

Use: This definition defines the entry-names to be "secondary entry points" of the procedure in which it appears. The procedure may be called using one of the entry-names, in which case execution begins at the statement following the entry definition. The placement of this definition is therefore important.

The parameters, RETURNS phrase and parameter declarations are as described under "Procedure definition".

Each parameter must be described in the parameter declarations, <u>unless</u> it has the same name as a parameter of the main procedure entry point or an earlier secondary entry point. In this case, the parameter has the attributes as specified in that earlier parameter declaration.

Care must be taken that execution of a procedure only references those parameters of the entry point for which it was called. Consider the procedure

```
A1: PROCEDURE (X, Y);
    DECLARE (X,Y) FIXED DECIMAL;
      ...
    A2: ENTRY (X,Z);
        DECLARE Z FIXED DECIMAL;
        IF Z=0 THEN X=X+1; ELSE X=Y;
    END A1;
```

If the procedure is called with CALL A2(B,0); execution proceeds without an error and the value 1 is stored in B. If it is called with CALL A2(B,1); an error results during execution, because the statement X=Y cannot be executed since no argument exists for parameter Y.

Procedure definition (simple)

Form: entry-name: PROCEDURE [(parameter |, parameter|)]
         |parameter declaration|
         |declaration|
         |statement|
         END entry-name ;

1. The entry-name is used to call the procedure. The entry name after END must be the same as the one preceding PROCEDURE. Be careful; the PL/I rules state that any ENDs omitted from within the procedure definition will automatically be inserted, without warning, just before the procedure END. Therefore, omit no ENDs.

2. This simple form of the procedure definition does not apply to the main program definition. See Appendix A.2 or the general procedure definition which follows.

3. Each parameter is an identifier.

4. The parameter declarations describe the attributes of the arguments corresponding to the parameters when the procedure is called. All parameters should be specified here. The parameters are not variables and never receive a value of their own.

   Parameter declarations look exactly like normal declarations, except that

   a) The length of a string or bounds for an array may be specified by using *. Thus CHAR(*) would be the attribute used for a character string, while A(*,*) would describe a two-dimensional array. In PL/C one must use * in these positions for parameters.

   b) Since a parameter is not a variable, it may not have storage attributes STATIC, AUTOMATIC, or BASED. PL/I allows a parameter to have the attribute CONTROLLED, but this attribute is not included in PL/C.

5. The declarations describe variables which are internal to this procedure, or EXTERNAL variables that the procedure may use. The non-STATIC variables (the usual ones) are created when the procedure is called, and are destroyed when its execution ends.

6. When the procedure is invoked, the statements are executed, in order, until either a RETURN; is executed or until the last statement has been executed. See also the GO TO statement. Upon termination, all variables created at the beginning of the procedure execution (see step 5) are destroyed.

Procedure definition (general)

Form: entry-name: |entry-name :|
      PROCEDURE [(parameter |, parameter|)]
         [OPTIONS(MAIN)] [RECURSIVE]
         [RETURNS (|attribute|)] ;
         |parameter declaration|
         |declaration|
         |statement, or entry point definition|
         |procedure definition|
         END [entry-name] ;

All the points discussed under "Procedure definition (simple)" apply here. In addition,

1. OPTIONS(MAIN) is used to designate the main procedure which the system should call to begin execution.

2. RECURSIVE must be specified if the procedure is to be invoked recursively -- if it may be called while it is still executing.

3. The RETURNS phrase is not used if the procedure is to be invoked using the CALL statement. It is used only if the procedure is a function. The attributes in the RETURNS phrase specify the attributes of the value that will be returned as the value of the function. Only type attributes for arithmetic and string quantities are allowed; a function cannot return an array, structure, file-name, label or entry point.

4. The entry point definitions are used to describe other points where execution of the procedure may begin. For example, consider the procedure

```
X1: PROCEDURE ...
       ...
    X2: ENTRY ...
        S¹  S²  S³
    X3: ENTRY ...
        S⁴  S⁵  S⁶          END X1;
```

If the procedure is called using the name X1, the whole procedure is executed. If it is called using the name X2, statements S^1, S^2, S^3, S^4, S^5 and S^6 will be executed. If X3 is used, only S^4, S^5, and S^6 will be executed. (See also the GO TO statement.) See the CALL statement for a complete description of the procedure call.

5. The procedure definitions define procedures which can only be called from within this procedure.

6. If the entry-name appears after the END, it must be the same as one of the entry-names preceding the PROCEDURE phrase. (In PL/C it must be the same as the <u>first</u> one preceding PROCEDURE.)

Appendix A.5 Attributes

We list here a brief summary of the more important attributes of variables. Each scalar variable has a set of attributes which help describe it. These are called type, scope and storage attributes. In addition, an _initial_ attribute can be given. These classes of attributes are described below:

1. _Type attributes_. These indicate what kind of value the variable can contain.

   a) For arithmetic variables, these attributes fall into the following classes:

   1. A _base attribute_, DECIMAL or BINARY. One should always be given.

   2. A _scale atribute_, FIXED or FLOAT. One should always be given.

   3. A _mode attribute_, REAL or COMPLEX. The default is REAL. Almost all variables are REAL so there is no need to give this attribute explicitly.

   4. A _precision attribute_. In general, this is not needed.

   b) For character variables, the attribute is CHARACTER, and perhaps VARYING.

   c) For bit strings, the attribute is BIT and perhaps VARYING.

   d) For labels, the attribute is LABEL.

2. _Scope attributes_. These are INTERNAL and EXTERNAL. They help indicate in what part of the program the variable can be referenced by its name.

3. _Storage class attributes_. These are AUTOMATIC and STATIC. They help indicate when and where the variable is to be created and destroyed.

4. _INITIAL attribute_. This specifies what the initial value of the variable is. This can be used only if the initial value is to be a constant.

PL/I provides defaults, in case a variable is not declared or in case only a partial list of attributes is given. For variables, the scope definition default is INTERNAL, while the storage class attribute default is AUTOMATIC. These are the usual cases and there is no need to give these attributes explicitly.

The default for the other attributes defining a variable are rather ad hoc (they are historically grounded in FORTRAN), and should not be used, except for REAL. Default attributes for base, mode and type depend upon the identifier name. For identifiers beginning with any letter I through N, the default attributes are REAL FIXED BINARY (15,0). For identifiers beginning with any other character, the default attributes are REAL FLOAT DECIMAL (6). If BINARY or DECIMAL and/or REAL or COMPLEX are specified, FLOAT is assumed unless FIXED has been specified. If FIXED or FLOAT and/or REAL or COMPLEX are specified, DECIMAL is assumed unless BINARY has been specified.

Got it? Now forget it and give the attributes explicitly.

Several attributes are not described here, either because they are not in PL/C, because they are beyond the scope of the book, or because they are not that useful for the space the explanation takes. They are:

1. "Parallel processing" or "multi-tasking" attributes. They are EVENT, EXCLUSIVE, and TASK.

2. File-name attributes. These are BACKWARDS, BUFFERED, DIRECT, KEYED, RECORD, SEQUENTIAL, STREAM, ENVIRONMENT and UNBUFFERED.

3. Attributes concerning programmer-control of storage and "pointer" variables. These are ALIGNED, BASED, CONTROLLED, DEFINED, OFFSET, PACKED, POINTER, POSITION, UNALIGNED, and UPDATE.

4. Attributes used to help the compiler "optimize" the program. These are IRREDUCIBLE and REDUCIBLE.

5. The LIKE attribute, which is used to help abbreviate structure definitions.

6. The PICTURE attribute, which is used to define special internal formats of data and to specify editing of data.

The following description of attributes is based on the version of PL/I defined by the IBM F-level compiler. See IBMFM. If no form is given for an attribute, then the form is just the symbol itself. For example, the AUTOMATIC attribute is written "AUTOMATIC". Abbreviations for attributes are given in parentheses.

AUTOMATIC (AUTO) and STATIC attribute   Two other storage class
attributes, CONTROLLED and BASED, are not included in PL/C.

1.   AUTOMATIC means that the variable is created when the block
in which it is declared is entered, and destroyed when execution
of the block is finished.   This is the conventional default
attribute, and it need not be given for any variable. An
EXTERNAL variable may not be AUTOMATIC.

2.   STATIC specifies that the variable is to be created when the
program begins execution, and is to be destroyed only when the
program terminates. The bounds of any STATIC array or string
variable must be given as integer constants, since the variables
are to be created before program execution begins.   A STATIC
variable can only be referenced within the block in which it is
declared, but remains a variable and retains its value after the
block execution is finished.

   Note that STATIC affects only the storage class of the
variable, and not the scope of its name (which is INTERNAL or
EXTERNAL). For example, there can be several STATIC variables
named X, each internal to a different block.

BINARY (BIN) and DECIMAL (DEC) attributes   Arithmetic values
   may be stored in the computer in decimal or binary
   representation. The number of bits (digits) of accuracy
   depends on the attributes of the variable as follows:

   FIXED BINARY   15 bits plus sign.
                     The range in decimal is -32767 to +32767.
   FLOAT BINARY   21 bits plus sign for the mantissa.
                     The range is approximately 2^{-260} to 2^{252}.
   FIXED DECIMAL   5 digits plus sign (-99999 to +99999).
   FLOAT DECIMAL   6 digits plus sign for the mantissa.
                     The range is approximately 10^{-78} to 10^{75}.

   See also the "Precision attribute".

BIT and CHARACTER (CHAR) attribute

   Form 1: BIT(length) [VARYING]
   Form 2: CHARACTER(length) [VARYING]

   "length" must be an expression which when evaluated can be
   converted to an integer.

   Use: The value of a variable with this attribute is a string
      of "length" bits for Form 1, or "length" characters for
      Form 2. In PL/C, "length" has a maximum of 256.   If
      VARYING is present, the string consists of 0 to "length"
      characters, depending on the last assignment to it.   Upon
      creation of the variable, its length is set to 0 -- the
      variable contains the null string.

For parameters, in PL/C use "*" instead of "length",
since the length depends on the corresponding argument.

BUILTIN attribute   Any reference to a name with this attribute
is a reference to the built-in function or pseudo-variable
with the same name. The name can have no other attributes.
A parameter may not have this attribute. This is used to
reference a built-in function in a block contained in another
block in which the name has a different meaning.

CHARACTER (CHAR) attribute   See "BIT attribute".

COMPLEX (CPLX) attribute   See "REAL attribute".

DECIMAL (DEC) attribute   See "BINARY attribute".

Dimensioning of Arrays   See "Declaration" in Appendix A.4.

ENTRY attribute   In PL/C, this attribute need be explicitly
given only for a parameter which is to be a procedure or
function. Otherwise, it is not needed.

Form: ENTRY [(|attribute| |, |attribute| |)] ;

   A name associated with the ENTRY attribute is an entry
   point of a procedure. The first set of attributes
   describes the first parameter of the entry point, the
   second set of attributes the second parameter, and so on.
   If a parameter is an array a special attribute (*) for a
   one-dimensional array, (*,*) for a two-dimensional array,
   etc. must be used as the first attribute in the list.

Use: There are three reasons for using this attribute:
   1.   In PL/I an external procedure can be compiled
   separately. In this case, when a program contains a call
   on that procedure, it cannot know what its parameters are.
   The ENTRY attribute serves to indicate the attributes of
   the parameters. For example,

      DECLARE P ENTRY(FIXED DECIMAL, (*,*) FLOAT DECIMAL) ;

   indicates that procedure P has two parameters, a fixed
   decimal variable, and a float decimal two-dimensional
   array. The procedure P does not have to appear in this
   program, but may be compiled at a later time.

   2. An argument may be the name of a procedure. In this
   case the declaration for the corresponding parameter must
   describe the procedure and its parameters using the ENTRY
   attribute.

   3. In PL/I (but not in PL/C), argument attributes must
   match parameter attributes exactly unless an explicit ENTRY
   attribute is given for the entry point. If we want to call
   a procedure P(X) where the parameter X is fixed binary,

with CALL P(2);, then we must write

```
PROGRAM: PROCEDURE OPTIONS(MAIN);
  DECLARE P ENTRY(FIXED BINARY);
      ...     CALL P(2);
      ...
  P: PROCEDURE(X);
    DECLARE X FIXED BINARY;
      ...
    END P; END PROGRAM;
```

PL/C Restrictions:

1.   Dimension and length attributes in the parameter   list that follows ENTRY must be given as *.

2.   The ENTRY and RETURNS attributes cannot be nested. That is, neither ENTRY nor RETURNS attributes can be specified in the list that follows the initial ENTRY.

3.   Structure parameters cannot be declared in the list after ENTRY.

4.   Note that 2 and 3 imply that an entry-name cannot be passed as an argument if any of its parameters is itself an entry or a structure.

5.   In the absence of explicit attributes PL/C supplies a scalar parameter with FLOAT, DECIMAL and REAL attributes, where under the same circumstances PL/I-F makes   no assumption as to attributes.

EXTERNAL (EXT) and INTERNAL (INT) attributes   These are called scope attributes.   They specify in which part of a program a name may be referred to. INTERNAL means that the name can only be referenced within the block in which it is declared (and of course within contained blocks). It is not necessary to give the INTERNAL attribute; it is the conventional, default scope attribute.

EXTERNAL specifies that the variable can be referred to within any block containing an external declaration for it. For example, if two external procedures and the main program all contain identical EXTERNAL declarations for the same variable I, then each can reference that same variable. There are not three variables I, but just <u>one</u> variable I which they can all reference. An EXTERNAL variable must be STATIC;   its name can contain no more than seven characters.

FILE attribute   This indicates that the identifier is a file-name.   The default attributes for all PL/C files are STREAM and EXTERNAL.

FIXED and FLOAT attributes   FIXED specifies that the value of the variable is to be kept in fixed point form. Typically, this means the value is an integer, but see the "Precision attribute" for more information.

FLOAT specifies that the value is to be kept in floating point.   The number of digits (bits) of accuracy remains the same no matter what the value, but the value need not be in any certain range.   See the "Precision attribute" and the "BINARY attribute".

FLOAT attribute   See "FIXED attribute".

GENERIC attribute   This attribute allows different procedures to have the same name; which one is called will depend on the attributes of the arguments.   It is not included in PL/C.

INITIAL (INIT) attribute Form: INITIAL (item |, item|)

Each item in the list can be a signed or unsigned constant (see Appendix A.2 for constants). The INITIAL attribute can be associated only with a variable or array. Only one constant can be specified for a simple variable; the multiple items are used for arrays.

Use: The constants are assigned as initial values to the corresponding variables at the time the variables are created. Thus, all three variables A, B and C in the following declaration are initialized to 3:

        DECLARE (A,B,C) FIXED DECIMAL INITIAL(3);

For arrays, the constant values are assigned to the subscripted variables of the array in row-major order. Consider for example the declaration

        DECLARE (A(1:2), D(1:2,1:2)) INITIAL(1,3,5,7);

Upon creation, the variables will be

    A(1)   1   A(2)   3
    D(1,1) 1   D(1,2) 3   D(2,1) 5   D(2,2) 7

If not enough constants are supplied, the left-over array elements are not initialized. If there are too many constants, then the left-over constants are ignored.

One can supply an asterisk * instead of a constant for an item. This means that the corresponding array element will not be initialized. For example,

    DECLARE E(1:3) FIXED DECIMAL INIT (3,*,2);

creates   E(1) 3   E(2) ///   E(3) 2

Iteration specification: To abbreviate a sequence of identical items an "iteration factor" may be used. For example, the item (4) 3 is equivalent to 3, 3, 3, 3.

The iteration factor is any expression that can be evaluated and converted to an integer. (For STATIC variables it must be an unsigned integer.) There are two forms for this:

1. (iteration-factor) item
    (this is equivalent to "iteration-factor" items.)

2. (iteration-factor) (item |, item|)
    (this is equivalent to the list of items repeated "iteration-factor" times.)

An iteration factor less than or equal to zero causes the item(s) to be skipped. For example, the following two are equivalent:

```
INIT( (2)*, (3)(*,3,6), 0(*), (3)8)
INIT(*,*, *,3,6,*,3,6,*,3,6, 8,8,8)
```

The item (2)'AB' is equivalent to 'ABAB', because (2) implies string repetition and is not an iteration-factor. With a string constant, to get an iteration-factor the string repetition must be there also. Thus (2)(1)'AB' specifies two elements and is equivalent to 'AB', 'AB'.

PL/C Restriction: Iteration factors, but not string repetition factors are allowed in the INITIAL list. This means that the phrase (x) (1) '---' in PL/I-F would have to be given as (x) ('---') in PL/C. The phrase (x) '---' is not allowed.

LABEL constants: A label constant assigned an initial value must be known within the block where the declaration occurs.

INPUT and OUTPUT attributes   These are attributes of a file-name (see "FILE attribute"). INPUT specifies that the file is to be read; OUTPUT that it is to be written.

INTERNAL (INT) attribute   See "EXTERNAL attribute".

LABEL attribute   A variable or array with this attribute can contain only a label constant. It may <u>not</u> contain an entry-name of a procedure.

Length of String Variables   See "BIT attribute".

OUTPUT attribute   See "INPUT attribute".

Precision attribute for arithmetic variables

Form: (number-of-digits [, scale-factor])

1. The number-of-digits is an unsigned decimal integer;
the scale-factor is an optionally-signed decimal integer.

2. The precision attribute must immediately follow a
FIXED, FLOAT, DECIMAL, BINARY, REAL or COMPLEX attribute.

Meaning: The number-of-digits specifies the minimum number of
decimal digits (or bits for binary) to be maintained for
the value of the variable. The maximum allowable number is
15 for DECIMAL FIXED, 31 for BINARY FIXED, 16 for DECIMAL
FLOAT, and 53 for BINARY FLOAT.

The scale factor may be specified only if the variable
is FIXED; it must be in the range -128 to +127. It
specifies the assumed position of the binary or decimal
point -- that is, the number of fractional bits or digits.
If omitted, 0 is assumed and the value is an integer.

Typically the precision attribute is omitted. The
default in this case is

(5,0) for FIXED DECIMAL   (15,0) for FIXED BINARY
(6)   for FLOAT DECIMAL   (21)   for FLOAT BINARY

Examples: We give below some sample attributes and indicate
to the right the corresponding format of a value with those
attributes. In the examples, d stands for a digit, and b
for a bit.

```
FIXED DECIMAL(5,0)        ddddd
FIXED DECIMAL(5,2)        ddd.dd
FIXED DECIMAL(5,7)        .00ddddd
FIXED DECIMAL(5,-2)       ddddd00.
FIXED BINARY(6,7)         .0bbbbbb
FLOAT DECIMAL(8)          .dddddddd*10**dd
FLOAT DECIMAL(6)          .dddddd*10**dd
FLOAT BINARY(10)          .bbbbbbbbbb*2**dd
```

PRINT attribute   The data file associated with a file-name
with the attribute PRINT will eventually be printed. Each
line (record) is written out with an extra character at its
beginning, which is used by the printer to determine when to
skip to a new page, to a new line, etc. See Appendix B.3 for
the USASI codes and their meaning in the extra character.

REAL and COMPLEX (CPLX) attributes   REAL specifies that the
value of the variable is a real number. REAL is the default
attribute and need not be explicitly stated if FIXED, FLOAT,
DECIMAL, or BINARY are used. COMPLEX specifies that the
value is a complex number, consisting of real and imaginary
parts.

RETURNS attribute   This is used in connection with the ENTRY
   attribute to help describe an entry-name. It indicates that
   the entry-name is called as a function, and describes the
   attributes of the value returned as the result of the
   function. The form of the RETURNS attribute is exactly the
   same as the form of the RETURNS phrase in a procedure
   definition (see Appendix A.4).

STATIC attribute   See "AUTOMATIC attribute".

VARYING (VAR) attribute   See "BIT attribute".

Appendix A.6 <u>Variables, Values and Expressions</u>

We consider how variables are referenced and changed. The kinds of values that can be assigned to variables have already been listed in Appendix A.4 under "Declaration (simple)", and in Appendix A.5 in the discussion of the Precision attribute. Constants for the different kinds of values have been described in Appendix A.2.

Appendix A.6.1 <u>Scope and Recognition of Names</u>

Assume for the moment that all identifiers are explicitly declared or defined. Note that the presence of a label preceding a statement, or an entry-name preceding PROCEDURE or ENTRY, constitutes its definition. "Block" means either a BEGIN block or a procedure definition.

The use of an identifier in a program always refers to a declared or defined identifier; it represents some entity -- a variable, array, entry point in a procedure, etc. That part of the program where an entity may be referred to by its identifier is called the <u>scope</u> of that entity. The scope has nothing to do with the question of when that entity is created or destroyed; it only indicates where it may be referred to by its name. The scope of an entity depends on where it is declared or defined relative to the blocks of the program.

The scope of an entity named with an identifier is the block in which its declaration or definition appears, including any contained blocks, <u>except</u> those blocks (and blocks contained in them) where another declaration or definition of that same identifier occurs.

For example, consider the program below, where the lines to the right show the scope of the corresponding identifiers. The identifiers X, W and B are each declared twice; we use superscripts to distinguish them.

PL/I allows the use of identifiers without having to declare them. For such undeclared identifiers, PL/I inserts a declaration with default attributes which are determined from the way in which the identifier is used. For an explanation of "contextual" and "implicit" declarations see IBMFM.

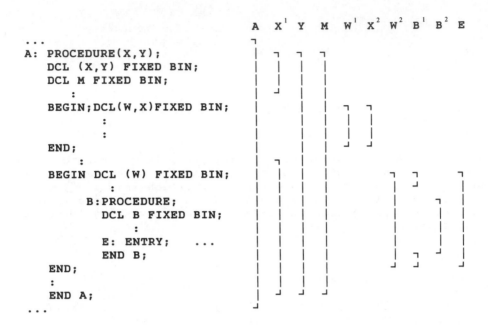

```
                                    A   X¹  Y   M   W¹  X²  W²  B¹  B²  E
    ...                             ⌐
    A: PROCEDURE(X,Y);              |   ⌐   ⌐   ⌐
       DCL (X,Y) FIXED BIN;         |   |   |   |
       DCL M FIXED BIN;             |   |   |   |
          :                         |   ⌐   |   |
       BEGIN;DCL(W,X)FIXED BIN;     |       |   |   ⌐   ⌐
              :                     |       |   |   |   |
              :                     |       |   |   |   |   |
       END;                         |       |   |   ⌐   ⌐
          :                         |   ⌐   |   |
       BEGIN DCL (W) FIXED BIN;     |   |   |   |           ⌐   ⌐       ⌐
            :                       |   |   |   |           |   ⌐       |
          B:PROCEDURE;              |   |   |   |           |       ⌐   |
            DCL B FIXED BIN;        |   |   |   |           |       |   |
               :                    |   |   |   |           |       |   |
            E: ENTRY;   ...         |   |   |   |           |       |   |
            END B;                  |   |   |   |           |   ⌐   ⌐   |
       END;                         |   |   |   |           ⌐   ⌐       ⌐
       :                            |   |   |   |
       END A;                       |   ⌐   ⌐   ⌐
    ...                             ⌐
```

Appendix A.6.2 <u>Referencing Variables, Arrays and Structures</u>

In Appendix A.1 we discussed variables, arrays and structure references   briefly.   We   elaborate   a   bit   more   here.   We illustrate assuming the declarations

```
    DECLARE (A, B(1:20,1:20)) FIXED DECIMAL,
         C CHAR(20),
         D CHAR(20) VARYING;
    DECLARE 1 PERSON,
         2 NAME CHAR(20),
         2 ADDRESS,
             3 STREET CHAR(20),
             3 CITY CHAR(20),
             3 ZIPCODE CHAR(5);
    DECLARE 1 UNIVERSITY,
         2 NAME CHAR(20),
         2 ADDRESS(5),
             3 CITY CHAR(20),
             3 ZIPCODE CHAR(5);
```

Within the scope of a declaration, one references variables, arrays and structures declared in that declaration as follows:

1.   To reference a simple variable use its name (e.g. A , C).

2.   To reference an array, use its name (e.g. B).

3.   To reference a subscripted variable, use the form

     array-name (exp ⌊, exp⌋)

The number of exps must equal the number of dimensions of the array. To find out which element of the array is referenced, evaluate the subscripts and convert to integers, from left to right. For example, if I has the value 1 and J the value 2, then A(I,J+1) refers to the subscripted variable A(1,3).

4. To reference a cross section of an array, use a form like that of a subscripted variable, but use an asterisk * for a subscript for which a whole "row" is wanted. For example, B(*,1) is the one-dimensional array consisting of B(1,1), B(2,1), ..., B(20,1). B(7,*) is the array consisting of B(7,1), B(7,2), ..., B(7,20). B(*,*) represents the whole array. A cross section is an array with as many dimensions as there are asterisks in the cross section reference.

The following program segment stores in array T(1:20,1:20) the transpose of the array B:

    DO I = 1 TO 20; T(I,*) = B(*,I); END;

5. To reference a structure, use its name (e.g. PERSON).

6. To reference a part of a structure use a qualified name. This is the sequence of identifiers, starting from the name of the structure and leading down to the name of the structure part desired, separated by periods. For example, to refer to the value of STREET of the substructure ADDRESS of the structure PERSON, use

    PERSON.ADDRESS.STREET

Note that the declaration for UNIVERSITY allows for 5 different addresses; UNIVERSITY.ADDRESS is a qualified name which refers to an array. UNIVERSITY.ADDRESS(1).CITY refers to the city for the first address.

It is not necessary to fully qualify such a reference; only enough names must be given to make the reference unambiguous. Thus STREET, PERSON.STREET, or ADDRESS.STREET would be equivalent to PERSON.ADDRESS.STREET. ADDRESS, however, is ambiguous since it could refer to either PERSON.ADDRESS OR UNIVERSITY.ADDRESS.

7. Pseudo-variables. A pseudo-variable is a phrase which allows one to reference a subpart of a variable, or two variables which are thought of as being one. For example, the SUBSTR pseudo-variable allows one to use part of a string as a variable, just as we use A(3) to reference part of an array.

Most of the pseudo-variables allow arrays as arguments, in which case the pseudo-variable refers to an array of values. Pseudo-variables may not be nested. Thus UNSPEC(REAL(A)) = '00'B is invalid.

The pseudo-variables COMPLETION, ONCHAR, ONSOURCE, PRIORITY, STATUS and STRING are beyond the scope of this book. The other pseudo-variables are:

1. COMPLEX(a,b) -- In an assignment statement like COMPLEX(A,B) = 1+2I; the real part "1" is assigned to the variable A, while the imaginary part "2" is assigned to variable B. If either A or B is an array, they both must be arrays with identical bounds.

2. IMAG(c) -- This refers to the imaginary part of the complex variable c. If c is an array, IMAG(c) refers to the array of imaginary parts of c.

3. REAL(c) -- This refers to the real part of the complex variable c. If c is an array, REAL(c) refers to the array of real parts of c.

4. SUBSTR(string, i [, j]) -- This refers to the subpart of the character string or bit string "string", beginning with character (bit) i and ending with character (bit) i+j-1. No other characters (bits) of the string are changed by an assignment to SUBSTR. The pseudo-variable is always non-VARYING. Thus, execution of SUBSTR(C,1,1) = ''; does not delete the first character from C, but just sets it to a blank. If j is missing it is assumed to be i+LENGTH(string)-1.

   If one argument is an array, they all must be, with identical bounds.

5. UNSPEC(s) -- s can be a string or arithmetic variable or array. The value being assigned to it is evaluated, converted to a bit string (if possible), and assigned to s without further conversion to the attributes of s.

8. To reference a function, use the same format as the call of a procedure, except that the keyword CALL and the semicolon are omitted.

Appendix A.6.3 Expressions

An expression is something which, when evaluated, yields a value. The expression "2" yields the value 2; if A is a variable with current value 3, then the expression "A" yields the value 3 while the expression "A+2" yields the value 5.

An expression can be a single constant, a reference to a variable, or a combination of "operators" and "operands", with perhaps parentheses to indicate the order in which the operators should be evaluated.

Operands of Expressions

These may be

1. Constants.

2. References to variables, as described in Appendix A.6.2.

3. References to built-in functions, as described in Appendix A.8.

4. References to user-defined functions (procedures with RETURNS attributes).

Operators

PL/C allows the following operators:

```
+ - * / ** < ¬< <= =
> ¬> >= ¬= | & and ||
```

Their descriptions appear below:

1. Arithmetic operators -- These operators have only arithmetic operands. Unless otherwise specified, if the operands of an operator have the same arithmetic attributes, so does the result. Thus addition of two fixed decimal numbers yields a fixed decimal number. The result of an operation in which the two operands do not have the same attributes is discussed in Appendix A.6.4. Remember that a constant like 3 or -2.45 is fixed decimal.

    a) + x   -- The result is the value of x.

    b) - x   -- The result is the negative of the value of x.

    c) x + y   -- This is conventional addition: 1+5 is 6.

    d) x - y   -- This is conventional subtraction: 2-5 is -3.

    e) x * y   -- This is conventional multiplication: 2*5 is 10.

    f) x / y   -- This is conventional division. Be very careful if both operands are fixed point. In this case the result is also fixed point but is not rounded to an integer. Because of the PL/I precision rules, 25+1/3 is 5.333333 and not 25.333333.

    g) x ** y   -- This is conventional exponentiation. That is, x is multiplied by itself y times. If y is not an unsigned integer constant, then x is converted to floating point and floating point exponentiation is performed. Some special cases are:

1. If x=0 and y>0 the result is 0.
2. If x=0 and y≤0 an error results.
3. If x≠0 and y=0 the result is 1.
4. If x<0 and y is not fixed (an integer) an error
    results.
5. If x=0 and y is complex with real part >0 and
    imaginary part =0, the result is 0.
6. If x=0 and y is complex but does not fit (5), an
    error results.

h) x < y,   x ¬< y,   x <= y,   x = y
    x > y,   x ¬> y,   x >= y,   x ¬= y

These are the arithmetic <u>comparison</u> operators. They
yield   the   value   "true"   ('1'B) or "false" ('0'B),
depending on whether the relation is true or not.   "¬="
stands for not equal, "<=" for less than or equal, etc.
For example,

```
1  < 2 yields true      1 ¬< 2 yields false
1 <= 2 yields true      1  = 2 yields false
1  > 2 yields false     1 ¬> 2 yields true
1 >= 2 yields false     1 ¬= 2 yields true
```

2. <u>Character string operators</u>

a) x || y   -- The result of this concatenation is a
    character string consisting of the characters of x
    followed by those of y. For example,

```
'ABC' || 'DXY' yields 'ABCDXY'
'ABC' || ''    yields 'ABC'
'AB ' || 'DXY' yields 'AB DXY'
```

b) x < y,   x ¬< y,   x <= y,   x = y
    x > y,   x ¬> y,   x >= y,   x ¬= y

These are the character string comparison operators.
They have the same form as the arithmetic comparison
operators. A comparison is evaluated as follows: first,
the shorter of the two operands is extended with blanks
until the two have the same length.   Then a left-to-
right character by character comparison is performed
until the result is determined. The result is '1'B if
the relation is true; '0'B otherwise. The collating
sequence given at the end of Section I.9.2.2 is used to
make the comparison. Examples are:

```
'A' <= 'A'       yields true
'A' <= 'AB'      yields true
'AB'<= 'A'       yields false
'A' = 'A '       yields true
```

3. <u>Bit string operators</u>   -- These always take bit strings
    as operands, and always yield a bit string result.

    a) ¬ x   -- The result is a bit string the same as x but
        with every bit reversed. ¬ '10011'B yields '01100'B.

    b) x | y   -- If one operand is shorter than the other,
        the shorter is extended on the right with zeros until
        they are the same length. Then a bit-by-bit operation
        is performed to yield a bit-string with the same length.
        For each bit, the result is 1 if either operand has a 1
        in that position, and is 0 otherwise. For example,

        '1010'B | '1100'B yields '1110'B
        '1'B | '1101'B yields '1101'B

    c) x & y   -- The shorter operand is extended with zeros
        until both operands have the same length. Then a bit-
        by-bit operation is performed to yield a value with that
        length.   For each bit, the result is 1 only if both
        operands have a 1 in that position. For example,

        '1010'B & '1100'B yields '1000'B
        '1'B   & '1101'B yields '1000'B

    d) x || y   -- The result is a string of bits consisting
        of those in x followed by those in y.

    e) x < y,   x ¬< y,   x <= y,   x = y
        x > y,   x ¬> y,   x >= y,   x ¬= y

        These bit comparison operators yield '1'B if   the
        relation is true, and '0'B otherwise.   The shorter
        operand is first extended with zeros until both operands
        have the same length. Then a left-to-right bit-by-bit
        comparison is made of the two operands until the result
        is determined.   See also the arithmetic and character
        string comparison operators.

Expressions and the Priority of Operators

Expressions follow conventional mathematical notation, where
parentheses may be used to indicate the order of evaluation of
the operators. For example,

    - A + B * C + D * (E + F)   is evaluated as follows:

    1.   Evaluate -A
    2.   Evaluate B*C
    3.   Evaluate -A + B*C (using the results of steps 1 and 2)
    4.   Evaluate E+F
    5.   Evaluate D*(E+F) (using the result of step 4)
    6.   Evaluate -A+B*C + D*(E+F) (using the results of
                                       steps 3 and 5)

Operations are performed using the following table of priorities
of operators:

```
prefix +  prefix -   ¬   **    (highest)
*  /                            |
infix +  infix -                |
||                              |
<  ¬<  <=  =  ¬=  >=  >  ¬>      |
&                               V
|                              (lowest)
```

   If two or more operators on the same level appear next to
each other, the operations are performed in left-to-right order.
The exception to this rule is the top line.   If two or more
operators from the top line of the table appear next to each
other, the operations are performed in right-to-left order. For
example,

```
A * -B is evaluated as A * (-B)
A + B + C is evaluated as (A + B) + C
A ** -B is evaluated as A ** (-B)
A ** B ** C is evaluated as A ** (B ** C)
```


Array and Structure Expressions

   PL/I allows array expressions which yield arrays of values,
and structure expressions which yields structures of values. An
array expression is evaluated element by element.   Thus if
A(1:3) is (3 8 2) and B(1:3) is (2 1 2), then A*B is the array
(6 8 4). This is _not_ conventional array multiplication.

   Any operator described for conventional expressions can also
be used for arrays, but be careful. An array operation implies
that same operation being applied to the individual elements of
the array (or array operands), to yield an array of the same
size. Read "Assignment to arrays" and "Assignment to
structures" in Appendix A.3 before using array expressions.

   In an array expression all array operands must have identical
bounds.   In a structure expression, each structure operand must
have the same structure.

Appendix A.6.4 <u>Data Conversion</u>

Quite often, values have to be converted from one form to another -- FIXED DECIMAL to FLOAT DECIMAL, bit string to character string, etc. These conversions occur when evaluating an expression, when assigning a value to a variable, and in similar situations. In PL/I, evaluation of operations and conversion of values is a difficult problem, mainly because of the way precision attributes are defined and used. The typical programmer will not use these precision attributes; instead he will rely on the default attributes given by PL/I and PL/C. Fortunately, PL/C retains as many significant digits as possible, which greatly simplifies the explanation of conversion of values.

We describe only data conversion as it is done in PL/C, and assume that the precision attributes are not explicitly used. Those people who want to understand why 25+1/3 = 5.33333 are encouraged to read IBMFM.

Remember that constants like 3.14 are actually fixed decimal values. To be sure of results, when using a constant as an operand of a division, write it with an exponent: 3.14E0.

Conversion During Arithmetic Operations

During evaluation of an operation like x*y, if the arithmetic attributes of the operands differ, some conversion must be performed before the operation can take place. The rules for the order of this conversion are:

1. If one operand is binary and the other decimal, the decimal operand is converted to binary.

2. If one operand is fixed and the other floating point, the fixed point operand is converted to floating point form. The one exception to this rule is with exponentiation. If in x**y, x is FLOAT and y FIXED, no conversion is necessary; the result is still FLOAT. If in x**y, both operands are FIXED, then x is converted to floating point form <u>unless</u> y is an unsigned integer constant.

3. If one operand is REAL and the other COMPLEX, the REAL operand is converted to COMPLEX. The one exception is exponentiation. If in x**y, y is a fixed point integer, no conversion is necessary.

Results of Conversion

<u>Bit string to character string</u>   -- Each bit 1 becomes the character 1; each bit 0 becomes the character 0. The length of the result is the length of the original value.

<u>Character string to bit string</u>   -- The character string
should contain only the characters 1 and 0; any other
causes an error message to be printed (the CONVERSION
condition is raised). Each character 1 becomes the bit 1;
each character 0 becomes the bit 0.

<u>Mode conversion</u>   -- Conversion from complex to real is done
by deleting the imaginary part of the complex number. When
converting from real to complex, a zero imaginary part is
added to the real value.

<u>Base conversion</u>   -- Converting from DECIMAL FLOAT to BINARY
FLOAT, or vice versa, causes no changes in the number,
since both are internally stored in the same
representation. Conversion from DECIMAL FIXED to BINARY
FIXED can cause the number to be truncated, so <u>significant</u>
digits may be lost. This is because DECIMAL FIXED has the
range -99999 to +99999, while BINARY FIXED has the range
-32767 to 32767. For example, the fixed decimal number
32769 will be converted to 1000000000000001B and then
truncated to 1B. An error message will be printed if a
significant digit is lost. (The SIZE condition will be
raised.) Conversion from BINARY FIXED to DECIMAL FIXED
causes no problems.

<u>Scale conversion</u>   -- Conversion from FIXED to FLOAT causes
no problem in PL/C, since the FLOAT representation allows
more digits (or bits) than the FIXED representation.
Conversion from FLOAT to FIXED may cause the least
signicant digits (bits) to be discarded. Truncation, not
rounding, is performed.

Appendix A.6.5 <u>Parameter-Argument Correspondence</u>

Suppose we have a call CALL P(A1); of a procedure defined as

```
P: PROCEDURE(P1);
   DECLARE P1 ...;
      :
   END P;
```

The parameter-argument correspondence is set up before the
actual execution of the procedure statements. Once this link
between parameter and argument is made, it is not changed for
the duration of the procedure execution.

The way the correspondence between P1 and A1 is set up
depends on the attributes of both P1 and A1. In general, it
must be remembered that P1 is <u>never</u> a variable and consequently
never possesses a value of its own. The declaration of P1 does
not indicate that P1 is a variable; it just indicates what the
attributes of the corresponding argument must be. In the above
example, an assignment to P1 changes A1 immediately.

We have generally indicated parameter-argument correspondence by an arrow from the parameter to the argument:

We might also have the case that A1 is also a parameter of a procedure, so that we have to follow a sequence of arrows to discover what a parameter represents:

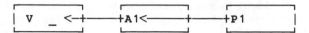

We now describe the way in which the parameter-argument linkage is done when a procedure is called, depending on the attributes of the parameter.

Scalar parameter   The parameter represents a variable that is neither an array nor a structure. The argument must be an expression (a constant, scalar variable, or more general expression). The linkage is drawn as follows: if the argument is a simple or subscripted variable whose data attributes match those of the parameter exactly, then the arrow is drawn from the parameter to the argument:

Note that the arrow is drawn before the procedure statements are executed. If the argument is a subscripted variable, the subscripts are evaluated just once, before execution of the procedure statements, in order to determine which variable is being passed to the procedure.

If the argument is anything else (a constant, an expression which is not a variable, a variable in parentheses, like (I), a variable with different attributes from the parameter), the following happens:

1. A new variable, say TEMP, is automatically created; its attributes are those of the parameter.

2. The argument is evaluated and assigned to TEMP. Normal conversion rules for an assignment statement apply.

3. An arrow is drawn from the parameter to TEMP:

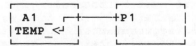

TEMP is called a "dummy argument".

If the parameter is a fixed length string and the argument a VARYING string, a dummy argument is created with a length equal to the maximum length of the argument.

If the parameter has the attribute LABEL, then the argument must be a label or a label variable.

<u>Array parameter</u>   If the parameter is an array, the argument must be an array expression or a scalar expression. (Note: In PL/C the argument must be an array expression; we cover only this case here.) The array operands of the array expression must have the same number of dimensions as the parameter.

If the argument is an array or a cross section of an array with the same attributes as the parameter, then an arrow is drawn from the parameter to the argument:

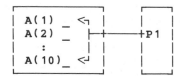

In <u>any other case</u>, an array TEMP (say) with attributes of the parameter and dimension of the argument is created, the argument is assigned to the array TEMP and an arrow is drawn from the parameter to TEMP. Any conversion is performed as in an assignment statement. TEMP is called a "dummy array argument".

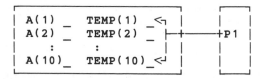

<u>Structure parameter</u>   If the parameter is a structure, then the argument must be a structure expression or a scalar expression. (In PL/C it may only be a structure expression.) The correspondence is similar to the correspondence for array parameters.

<u>Entry-name parameter</u>   If the parameter is an entry-name, the argument must be the name of a procedure (or function). It can be the name of a mathematical built-in function, like SIN. The number of parameters declared for the parameter and the argument must be the same.

<u>File-name parameter</u>   The argument must also be a file-name. The attributes of the parameter are ignored.

Appendix A.7 Conditions and Prefixes

During execution of a program an exceptional condition such as OVERFLOW (a floating point number becoming too large) or ZERODIVIDE (division by zero) can cause an <u>interrupt</u> to occur. Execution of the program is temporarily halted, a certain statement is executed, and then the program terminates or execution resumes, depending on the condition and what the programmer wants. Generally, a standard system action is performed when the interrupt occurs. However, the programmer himself can indicate what should take place, using the ON statement. We will call the statement to be performed when the condition occurs the "ON-action" for that condition.

The typical programmer will usually use only the CHECK, FLOW, and ENDFILE conditions.

Appendix A.7.1 Prefixes and Their Use

For each possible condition that can occur, the programmer can indicate whether or not the ON-action should be executed if the condition occurs. The programmer does this by placing a "condition prefix" before the statement in which the condition may occur. If the ON-action should be executed, it is said to be "enabled"; of not, it is "disabled". For example, suppose we do not want an ON-action to execute if division by zero takes place in a statement A=B/C;. Then we should write

    (NOZERODIVIDE) : A = B / C;

If division by zero does occur, the programmer won't know about it, and some undefined value will be stored in A.

The complete form of a statement is

    |prefix :| |label :| statement

A prefix has the form

    (cond |, cond|)

where each "cond" is a condition as specified in Appendix A.7.2. A "cond" may also be a condition with the letters NO immediately preceding it (no intervening blanks). A prefix attached to a statement signifies that each condition is to be enabled (if just the condition is used) or disabled (if NO precedes the

condition).   The statement can be any simple statement, BEGIN
block, IF statement, or loop. A procedure definition may also
be prefixed, which means the condition applies to the execution
of the whole procedure. There are some restrictions on which
conditions may be used as prefixes; these will be explained
under the particular conditions.

One may of course enable a condition for a block, and disable
it for part of that block. For example,

```
(ZERODIVIDE): BEGIN; ...
             (NOZERODIVIDE): A=B/C;
             ...
             END;
```

A prefix applies to the statement to which it is attached,
but not to any procedure called by that statement. The scope of
a prefix is statically defined, like the scope of an identfier
in a declaration.   Prefixes attached to IF, ON, compound, and
iterative statements are treated differently:

1. A prefix attached to an IF applies only to the evaluation
of the expression following the IF, and not to the statements
following THEN or ELSE.

2. A prefix attached to an ON statement does not apply to
the ON-unit.

3. A prefix attached to a compound statement has no effect.

4. A prefix attached to an iterative statement does not
apply to the substatements of the loop (except for FLOW).

A.7.2 Conditions

Unless otherwise noted, the following three points hold for
an interrupt:

1. The standard system action when an interrupt occurs is to
print a message and raise the ERROR condition. In PL/C, a
message is printed, some sort of error recovery is performed,
and execution continues. There is a limit to how many such
errors can occur before execution terminates.

2. In PL/I, the result of the operation causing the
interrupt is undefined. In PL/C, the result will be
described in the error message.

3. Upon normal termination of a ON-unit, control returns to
the point following the operation which caused the interupt.

The conditions are listed below.   Permissible abbreviations
are shown in parentheses. The PL/C default states are shown by
underlining, and the differences in default between PL/C and
PL/I are noted.   Unless otherwise noted, the form of the
condition used in a prefix or as a condition is the keyword
itself.   For example, the form of the FLOW condition is "FLOW".

The following conditions are not discussed here;   see   IBMFM
for details: AREA, KEY, PENDING, RECORD and TRANSMIT.

CHECK   Form: CHECK(name ¦, name¦)

   where each name is the name of a simple variable, array (but
   not a subscripted variable), a structure, an entry-name, or a
   label. A name cannot be a parameter in PL/I, but this is
   allowed in PL/C.

      This particular prefix may only be attached to a BEGIN
   block or a procedure definition. The names appearing in the
   CHECK prefix refer to names known within that block or
   procedure.

      The CHECK condition is raised in the following cases:

   1. If a name is a variable, array or structure, the
   condition is raised whenever it is assigned a value, or
   whenever part of it is assigned a value, or after a return
   from a user-defined procedure which had that name as an
   argument which was not a dummy argument.

   2. If a name is a label, the condition is raised just
   before execution of the statement with that label.

   3. If a name is an entry-name, the condition is raised
   when the entry-name is invoked.

Raising CHECK has no effect on the statement being executed;
it is used primarily to obtain output to help debug a
program. The standard system action is to print out the name
on SYSPRINT together with its value if it has one. If an ON-
unit is given, upon its termination, execution continues at
the point where the interrupt occurred.

   CHECK is not raised if

   1. An assignment occurs because of an INITIAL attribute.

   2. An assignment is made through a parameter. (But CHECK
   will be raised upon return from the corresponding procedure
   if the argument is not a dummy argument.)

In PL/C the system action is different than in PL/I. When an
element of a "checked" array is changed, only that particular
element is displayed, and not the whole array.   A similar

action occurs when an element of a structure is changed. The
timing of the PL/C display is also not exactly the same; PL/C
displays the results immediately after the check condition is
raised, and not after the whole statement has been executed.
In addition, PL/C has additional CHECK and NOCHECK
statements. See Appendix A.3.

<u>CONDITION</u>   Form: CONDITION (identifier)

    The identifier is given by the programmer. No declaration
or definition can be given for it; its appearance with a
CONDITION in an ON, SIGNAL, or REVERT statement constitutes
its declaration. It is given the attribute EXTERNAL.

    CONDITION is raised by execution of a SIGNAL statement
that specifies the appropriate identifier.   It cannot be
disabled.

<u>CONVERSION (CONV)</u> NOCONVERSION (NOCONV)   This occurs whenever
an illegal conversion is attempted on a character string
value. (For example, when a character other than 0 or 1
occurs in a string being converted to a bit string.) Upon
termination of an ON-unit, control returns to the beginning
of the statement and the conversion is retried.

<u>ENDFILE</u>   Form: ENDFILE(file-name)

    This occurs when an attempt is made to read when no more
data exists on the file. Another attempt to read from the
same file will cause another interrupt.   Upon normal
termination of an ON-unit, the statement that caused the
interrupt is immediately terminated. This condition cannot
be disabled.

<u>ENDPAGE</u>   Form: ENDPAGE(file-name)

where the file referred to is a PRINT file.

    This occurs when an attempt is made to start a new line
beyond the last line specified for the current page. The
last line is the limit given when the file was opened, or the
default of 60.   When ENDPAGE is raised, the current line
number is 1 greater than that specified. ENDPAGE is raised
only once per page, and it is possible to continue writing on
the same page by specifying a null ON-unit. An ON-unit can
start a new page by executing PUT PAGE for that file.

    The standard system action is to start a new page.   Upon
normal termination of the ON-unit, control returns to the
point of the interrupt and the operation is performed again.
If it is raised while data is being written, the data is
written on the current line <u>after</u> the ON-unit is executed.
If ENDPAGE results from LINE or SKIP this action is ignored.

ENDPAGE may not be disabled.

ERROR   This is raised in the following cases:

1. As a result of the standard system action for an
interrupt which is "print a message and raise the ERROR
condition.

2. As a result of an error during execution for which there
is no ON condition.

3. As a result of execution of SIGNAL ERROR;

    The standard system action is to raise the FINISH
condition. ERROR cannot be disabled. If there is an ON-unit
associated with ERROR, upon its normal termination the
standard system action is taken.

    The PL/C ERROR condition is not entirely compatible with
PL/I. In PL/C, the standard system action is to apply the
automatic error correction and then continue execution.

FINISH   This is raised by execution of STOP and EXIT, and by
    execution of a RETURN in the main procedure. The standard
    system action is to do nothing. If an ON-unit is associated
    with FINISH, it is executed before program termination
    occurs. The ON-unit can _avoid_ termination by jumping out of
    the ON-unit and continuing execution. FINISH cannot be
    disabled.

FIXEDOVERFLOW (FOFL) NOFIXEDOVERFLOW (NOFOFL)   This occurs
    when the length of a FIXED arithmetic operand exceeds 15
    digits (or 31 bits).

FLOW NOFLOW   This is not a PL/I condition; it is included
    only in PL/C. See the FLOW statement in Appendix A.3.

NAME   Form: NAME(file-name)

    This is raised during execution of GET DATA when a name in
the input cannot be referenced at the point GET DATA appears.
The standard system action is to ignore the input item, print
a message, and continue. Upon normal termination of an ON-
unit, execution of GET DATA continues with the next item in
the input. NAME cannot be disabled.

OVERFLOW (OFL) NOOVERFLOW (NOOFL)   This occurs when the
    magnitude of a floating point number exceeds approximately
    10^{75} or 2^{252}.

<u>SIZE</u> NOSIZE   This occurs when the high-order (leftmost) significant bits or digits are lost in an assignment to a variable or temporary, or in an input-output operation. SIZE is raised when the size of the value exceeds the size declared for that variable, while FIXEDOVERFLOW is raised when the maximum allowed value for the computer is exceeded.

In PL/I the default is NOSIZE; in PL/C, SIZE.

When SIZE is raised the arithmetic results in PL/C will differ from those produced by PL/I. PL/I-F may truncate results to the user's specification, while PL/C always retains the implementation-defined maximum precision. That is, in PL/C there may be loss of precision due to OVERFLOW or FIXEDOVERFLOW, but not because of SIZE.

<u>STRINGRANGE (STRG)</u> NOSTRINGRANGE (NOSTRG)   This is raised whenever the lengths of the arguments of SUBSTR don't follow the rules. The standard system action is to change the SUBSTR reference to fit the rules, by increasing or reducing the position and length arguments in a fairly obvious manner. See IBMFM. In PL/C the default is the opposite of PL/I's.

<u>SUBSCRIPTRANGE (SUBRG)</u> NOSUBSCRIPTRANGE (NOSUBRG)   This is raised when a subscript is evaluated and found to be outside its bounds. The PL/C default is the opposite of the PL/I default.

<u>UNDEFINEDFILE (UNDF)</u>   Form: UNDEFINEDFILE(file-name)

This occurs if a file cannot be OPENed by execution of an OPEN statement. This may be caused by a conflict of attributes, no blocksize specified, no DD statement in the JCL for the file, and other similar reasons.

Upon normal termination of the ON-unit, control is given to the statement following the statement that caused the interrupt. UNDEFINEDFILE cannot be disabled.

<u>UNDERFLOW (UFL)</u> NOUNDERFLOW (NOUFL)   This occurs when the magnitude of a floating point number is smaller than the minimum allowed -- approximately 10^{-78} or 2^{-260}. A 0 is used instead.

<u>ZERODIVIDE (ZDIV)</u> NOZERODIVIDE (NOZDIV)   This occurs when a division by zero is attempted.

Appendix A.8 <u>Built-in Functions</u>

We describe briefly the PL/I built-in functions. More
complete details can be found in IBMFM. Unless otherwise
specified, an argument may be an array as well as a scalar
value. The result is then an array with the same bounds. The
values in the array are the result of applying the function to
each of the individual values of the original array. If two or
more arguments are arrays, they must have identical bounds.

We describe the functions as they are evaluated in PL/C,
where the values are always maintained in the largest precision
possible.

String handling built-in functions

BIT(exp, [size])   -- The exp is converted to a bit string of
    length "size". "size" must be a decimal integer constant.
    If "size" is missing, the length of the result depends on
    the attributes of the exp. As with the CHAR function, the
    argument cannot be arithmetic in PL/C.

BOOL(x, y, z)   -- This is beyond the scope of this book.

CHAR(exp, [size])   -- The exp is converted to a character
    string representing the same value, of length "size". The
    same conventions apply for "size" as do with the function
    BIT. In PL/C, CHAR cannot be used to convert an arithmetic
    quantity to a string. Use the PUT statement with the
    STRING option for this.

HIGH(i)   -- The result is a character string of length i, each
    character of which is the highest character in the
    collating sequence. i must be a decimal integer constant.

INDEX(string, config)   -- string and config are bit or
    character strings. The result is a fixed binary integer
    which gives the leftmost position in string where the
    config begins. If config does not appear as a substring of
    string, the result is 0.

LENGTH(string)   -- The result is a FIXED BINARY integer giving
    the length of the string.

LOW(i)   -- The result is a character string of length i, each
    character of which is the lowest character in the collating
    sequence. This is hexadecimal 00.   i must be an integer
    constant.

REPEAT(string, i)   -- string is a character or bit string; i
    is a decimal constant. The result is "string" concatenated
    with itself i times. Thus REPEAT('ABC',3) is 'ABCABCABC'.

STRING(x)   -- x is a variable, array name, or structure,
    composed entirely of character strings or entirely of bit
    strings. The result is the string resulting   from
    concatenating all the elements of x together.

SUBSTR(string, i [, j])   -- The result is the substring of
    string beginning at character i and ending with character
    i+j-1. If j is missing, it is assumed to be
    LENGTH(string)-i+1.

TRANSLATE(s, r [, p])   -- All arguments are bit strings or
    character strings. If p is missing, the string consisting
    of all 256 possible EBCDIC characters in ascending order is
    used (from hexadecimal 00 to FF).

    If r is shorter than p, r is extended with blanks (or
    zeros). The result is a string identical to s, except that
    any character of s which is also in p is replaced by the
    corresponding character in r. Thus if character i of s is
    the same as character j of p, then character i of s is
    replaced by character j of r. For example, the result of

        TRANSLATE('XYZW', 'ABCD', 'VWXY')

    is the string 'CDZB'.

UNSPEC(x)   -- x is any expression. The result is a bit string
    containing the internal representation of x. The length
    depends on the attributes of x.

VERIFY(string, config)   -- string and config are both
    character strings or both bit strings. The result is a
    FIXED BINARY integer which indicates the position of the
    first character in string which is not in config. If all
    characters are in config, the result is 0. For example,

        VERIFY('ƁƁƁƁBC', 'Ɓ')   yields 5, while
        VERIFY('ƁƁƁƁBC', 'ABCƁ') yields 0.

Arithmetic Built-in Functions

The result of an arithmetic built-in function is always an arithmetic value. Unless otherwise noted, the attributes of the result are the same as the attributes of the argument. If conversion is necessary because arguments differ, the conversions are performed as outlined for arithmetic operations in Appendix A.6.4.

Unless otherwise noted, an argument may be an array as well as a scalar value, as explained in the introduction to Appendix A.8. The argument to the functions BINARY, DECIMAL, FIXED, and FLOAT may not be strings. Use the GET statement with the STRING option to convert strings to arithmetic quantities.

We omit descriptions of the functions ADD, DIVIDE, MULTIPLY and PRECISION.

ABS(x)   -- The result is the absolute value of x.

BINARY(x)   -- The value of x is converted to the binary base.

CEIL(x)   -- x must not be complex. The result is the smallest
     integer that is greater than or equal to x. CEIL(3.5) is
     4; CEIL(-3.5) is -3.

COMPLEX(x, y)   -- The result is a complex number with real
     part x and imaginary part y. X and y must be real.

CONJG(x)   -- The result is a complex number which is the
     conjugate of the complex number x.

DECIMAL(x)   -- The argument is converted to base DECIMAL.

FIXED(x)   -- The argument x is converted to fixed point.

FLOAT(x)   -- The argument x is converted to floating point.

FLOOR(x)   -- x must not be complex. The result is the largest
     integer not greater than x. FLOOR(3.5) is 3; FLOOR(-3.5)
     is -4.

IMAG(x)   -- The result is the imaginary part of x.

MAX(x1, x2, ..., xn)   -- The result is the maximum value of
     the arguments x1, x2, ..., xn. The resulting value is
     converted to conform to the highest characteristics of all
     the arguments. No argument can be complex. (FLOAT is
     higher than FIXED, BINARY is higher than DECIMAL, and
     COMPLEX is higher than REAL.)

MIN(x1, x2, ..., xn)   -- The result is the minimum value of
     the arguments. The resulting value is converted to the
     highest characteristics of all the arguments. No argument
     may be complex. (FLOAT is higher than FIXED, BINARY is

higher than DECIMAL, and COMPLEX is higher than REAL.)

MOD(x, y)   -- x and y may not be complex. The result is the
   remainder when dividing x by y. If x and y have different
   signs, the operation is performed on their absolute values,
   and the result is then ABS(y)-remainder. For example,
   MOD(29,6) is 5, while MOD(-29,6) is 1.

REAL(x) -- the result is the real part of the complex value x.

ROUND(x, n)   -- n is an optionally signed integer constant.
   If n is 0, x is rounded to the nearest integer. If n > 0,
   x is rounded at the nth digit to the right of the decimal
   (binary) point. If n < 0, x is rounded as the n+1th digit
   to the left of the decimal (binary) point.

      If x is floating point, n is ignored and the rightmost
   bit of the internal representation of x is set to 1.

SIGN(x)   -- x must not be complex. The result is a fixed
   binary value equal to 1 if x>0, 0 if x=0, and -1 if x<0.

TRUNC(x)   -- x must not be complex. If x < 0 the result is
   CEIL(x); if x > 0 the result is FLOOR(x).

Mathematical   Built-in   Functions All arguments   to   the
mathematical built-in functions are floating point. If not,
they will be converted to floating point.   Unless specifically
stated otherwise, an argument can be real or complex. The
result is always a floating point value, with mode, base and
precision attributes the same as those of the argument.

   An argument may be an array, as described in the introduction
to Appendix A.8.

ATAN(x)   -- The result is the arctangent of x.   x must not be
   ±1I.

ATAN(x,y)   -- Both x and y must be real; they must not both be
   0. The result is the arctangent of x/y.

ATAND(x,y)   -- Both x and y must be real; they must not both
   be 0. The result is the arctangent of x/y, expressed in
   degrees.

ATANH(x)   -- The result is the hyperbolic tangent of x.
   ABS(x) must be greater than or equal to 1.

COS(x)   -- The result is the cosine of x, where x is expressed
   in radians.

COSD(x)   -- The result is the cosine of x, where x is
   expressed in degrees.

COSH(x)   -- The result is the hyperbolic cosine of x.

ERF(x)   -- x must be real. The result is 2/SQRT(PI) multiplied by the definite integral from 0 to x of e**($-t^2$) dt.

ERFC(x)   -- x must be real. The result is 1-ERF(x).

EXP(x)   -- The result is e**x, where e is the base of the natural logarithm system.

LOG(x)   -- If x is real, it must be greater than 0. If x is complex, it must not equal 0+0I. The result is the natural logarithm of x.

LOG10(x)   -- x must be real and greater than 0. The result is the common logarithm of x (base 10).

LOG2(x)   -- x must be real and greater than 0. The result is the logarithm to the base 2 of x.

RAND(x)   -- RAND produces a sequence of pseudo-random numbers, one each time it is called. It uses the method of Coveyou and Macpherson in ACM Journal 14 (1967), 100-119. x should be FLOAT; if not it will be converted to FLOAT. It must be in the range 0 < x < 1. The initial value of x should have nine significant digits, and be odd; this maximizes the period of the sequence. RAND is usually used as an assignment: X=RAND(X). RAND is not included in PL/I.

SIN(x)   -- The result is the sine of x, where x is expressed in radians.

SIND(x)   -- The result is the sine of x, where x is expressed in degrees.

SINH(x)   -- The result is the hyperbolic sine of x.

SQRT(x)   -- If x is real, it must be greater than or equal to 0. The result is the square root of x.

TAN(x)   -- The result is the tangent of x, where x is expressed in radians.

TAND(x)   -- The result is the tangent of x, where x is expressed in degrees.

TANH(x)   -- The result is the hyperbolic tangent of x.

Array Generic Functions

All these functions require array arguments and return a single scalar value.

ALL(x)   -- x must be an array of bit strings. The result is a bit string obtained by "and-ing" (as in the operator "&") all the bit strings of the array together.

ANY(x)   -- x must be an array of bit strings. The result is the bit string obtained by "or-ing" (as in the operator "|") all the bit strings in the array together.

DIM(x,n)   -- The result is a binary fixed integer giving the "extent" of the nth dimension of the array x. The extent is the upper bound minus the lower bound, plus 1.

HBOUND(x,n)   -- The result is the upper bound of the nth dimension of array x.

LBOUND(x,n)   -- The result is the lower bound of the nth dimension of array x.

POLY(a,x)   -- This is not included in PL/C.

PROD(x)   -- The result is the product of all the elements of array x.

SUM(x) -- The result is the sum of all the elements of array x.

Condition Built-in Functions

These are: DATAFIELD, ONCHAR, ONCODE, ONCOUNT, ONFILE, ONKEY, ONLOC, and ONSOURCE. They are beyond the scope of this book. Three other functions, ONORIG, ONDEST, and STMTNO are included only in PL/C.

Based Storage Built-in Functions

These are ADDR, EMPTY, NULL, and NULLO. They are beyond the scope of this book.

Multitasking Built-in Functions

These are COMPLETION(event-name), PRIORITY(task-name), and STATUS(event-name). They are beyond the scope of this book.

Miscellaneous Built-in Functions

ALLOCATION(x)   -- This is beyond the scope of the book.

COUNT(file-name)   -- This is beyond the scope of the book.

DATE   -- The result is a character string of length 6, with
    the form yymmdd.   yy is the current year, mm the current
    month, and dd the current day (e.g. 731225).

LINENO(file-name)   -- The result is the number of the current
    line in the named file.

TIME   -- The result is a character string of length 9 giving
    the current time of day. Its form is hhmmssttt, where hh
    is the current hour of the day, mm is the number of
    minutes, ss the number of seconds, and ttt the number of
    milliseconds in machine-dependent increments.

Appendix A.9 <u>Formats</u>

GET EDIT and PUT EDIT read and write values using a user-defined <u>format</u> to control the editing and formatting of the values. The format is a list of "data items" which specify the format of each individual value in turn -- how many characters it uses, where the decimal point should go, and so on. Interspersed between the data items may be "control items", which specify things like skipping to the next line or page.

Input-output is done under the control of the list of variables or expressions being read into or printed, as follows. The format is searched for the first data item; any control items encountered are executed immediately. When the first data item in the list is found, the first value is read or written using that data item. Next, if there is a second value to read or print, the format is searched again, beginning at the item following the one just used. Any control items encountered are executed immediately. Upon finding a data item, the second value is read or printed. This process continues until the last value has been read or printed. Any excess data items or control items in the format are not used.

To make formats more flexible, one may specify "iteration factors". Thus "3 A(2)" is equivalent to a list of three items "A(2), A(2), A(2)", while "2 (A(2), X(1))" is equivalent to the four items "A(2), X(1), A(2), X(1)". Simple examples of formats and their use are given in Part I.6.

A format has the form

(specification |, specification|)

where each specification may be one of the following:

1. item -- Items are described below.

2. integer-constant item -- This is equivalent to "integer-constant" replications of the item. Thus "3 A(2)" is equivalent to "A(2), A(2), A(2)".

3. (exp) item -- At the point the specification is to be used, the exp is evaluated and converted to an integer. If 0 or negative, the item is skipped. If exp > 0, this is equivalent to "exp" replications of the item. Thus, if I has the value 4, "(I) A(3)" is equivalent to "A(3), A(3), A(3), A(3)". The expression is evaluated <u>each</u> time the specification is to be used to control editing.

4. integer-constant format -- This is equivalent to "integer-constant" replications of the format. Thus, "2 (A(2), X(1))" is equivalent to "A(2), X(1), A(2), X(1)". Note that this defines a format in terms of another format.

5. (exp) format -- The exp is evaluated as explained under specification 3 above. This is equivalent to "exp" replications of the format. If exp ≤ 0, the specification is skipped entirely.

The following items may be used. Any expressions in the item are evaluated each time the item is to be used. w, d, and s are used for expressions.

1. A -- Print a character string, in the next n columns.   n is the current length of the string being written out.

2. A(w) -- Read or print a character string. For input, the next w columns of the input stream are assigned to the variable. If w ≤ 0, the null string is assigned and no columns are used in the input stream.

   For output, the character string value is printed, left-adjusted, in the next w columns of the output stream. The string is truncated if too long. If w ≤ 0, no output results.

3. B -- Print a bit string in the next n columns of the output stream. n is the length of the value being printed.

4. B(w) -- Read or print a bit string. For input, the next w columns of the input stream are read in and assigned to the corresponding bit variable. Blanks may occur before or after the bit string value in the input, but they may not be imbedded within the value. Only 1's and 0's are allowed in the input value. If w ≤ 0, the null string is assigned and no columns are skipped.

   For output, the corresponding bit string value is printed, left-adjusted, in the next w columns. If too long, the value is truncated on the right. If w ≤ 0, no output results.

5. C(real-format-item [, real-format-item]) -- Read or print a complex number. Each real-format-item is either F or E, as described below. If the second one is missing, it is assumed to be the same as the first.

   For input, two numbers are read in and assigned to the real and imaginary part of the corresponding COMPLEX variable. No letter I may appear in the input. For output, the complex value is printed according to the format. No letter I is appended to it.

6. COLUMN(w) -- This control item causes columns to be skipped
    until column w of the current line is reached. On input,
    skipped columns are ignored; on output, they are filled
    with blanks.   If the current line is already positioned
    <u>after</u> column w, the current line is completed and a new one
    started, in column w. If w ≤ 0, it is assumed to be 1.   If
    w is greater than the size of a line, 1 is assumed.

7. E(w, d [, s]) -- Read or print a floating point number, in
    w columns. w must be large enough to include <u>all</u> parts of
    the number, including the preceding sign and the exponent.
    If the variable to be assigned or the value to be printed
    is not floating decimal, conversion will be performed on
    the number.

    For input, the value on the line should have the form

        [+ or -] mantissa [E [+ or -] yy]

    where yy is any 1 or 2 digit number.   The mantissa is a
    fixed point constant.   If the mantissa has no decimal
    point, the decimal point is assumed to be just before the
    rightmost d digits of the mantissa. If the exponent is
    missing, a zero exponent is assumed. Blanks may precede or
    follow the number in the field of w columns, but may not
    appear within the number.   "s" is not used for input.

    For output, the number is printed in a field of w
    characters in the form
        [-] <s-d digits> . <d digits> E <+ or -> exponent

    s represents the number of significant digits and d the
    number of fractional digits.   If s is missing, it is
    assumed to be d+1. Thus, one digit will be printed to the
    left of the decimal point. If d is 0 no decimal point is
    printed. s must be less than 17.

    If necessary, the number is rounded to fit the format.

8. F(w, d [, s])   -- Read or print a fixed-point decimal
    number, in w columns. If the variable being assigned or
    the value being printed is not fixed decimal, suitable
    conversion will be performed.

    For input, the number is an optionally-signed decimal
    fixed-point constant.   It may be preceded or followed by
    blanks, but can contain no embedded blanks. If the entire
    field is blank, the number is 0.

    If the number contains no decimal point, an implied
    decimal point is inserted d digits from the right of the
    number. If s appears, the number is multiplied by 10**s,
    <u>after</u> it is read in but before it is assigned to the
    variable.

For output, the value to be printed is first converted to fixed decimal form. It is then rounded to fit the format and printed out, right-adjusted, in a field of w columns. If d does not appear, the integer part of the number is written without a decimal point. If d appears, d digits will be printed to the right of the decimal point. If s appears, before writing out the value, it is multiplied by 10**s.

9. LINE(exp) -- This control item causes blank lines to be inserted so that the current line is the expth line on the page. If exp ≤ 0, 1 is assumed. If the current line number ≥ exp, the ENDPAGE condition is raised (which usually causes a new page to be started).

10. PAGE -- This control item causes a new page to be started. It may be used for output only.

11. SKIP [(exp)] -- This control item causes exp lines (records) to be skipped (the current line counting as 1 skip). If exp is missing it is assumed to be 1. SKIP may cause the ENDPAGE condition to be raised (which usually causes a new page to be started on output).

    On output, if exp ≤ 0, SKIP causes the same current line to be used, starting at the beginning. This does not erase the previous contents of the current line, but can be used to cause overprinting of characters.

12. X(w) -- This control item causes w columns to be skipped (on input) or w blank characters to be printed (on output). If w ≤ 0, it it is assumed to be 0.

Appendix A.10 A Comparison of PL/I and PL/C

PL/C is a compatible processor for a subset of the PL/I-F language. Some features of PL/I-F are not included in PL/C and certain features that are included are slightly restricted. However, with the minor exceptions noted below, processing under PL/C is equivalent to processing the same program under OS PL/I-F, Version 5. This means that PL/C is "upward-compatible" with PL/I-F-- that is, a source program that runs without incurring diagnostic messages under PL/C will run under PL/I-F and yield the same results. The converse is not true: a PL/I-F program may or may not run under PL/C since it may use features not included in the PL/C subset or may violate the additional restrictions placed on certain PL/C statements.

Summary of PL/I Features not included in PL/C (Release 7)

1. Direct-access auxiliary files are not included. Both STREAM and RECORD sequential files are implemented, but the RECORD I/O is limited since the list processing features of PL/I have not yet been implemented. This means that the DELETE, LOCATE, REWRITE and UNLOCK statements, and the BACKWARDS, BUFFERED, DIRECT, EXCLUSIVE, IRREDUCIBLE, KEYED, PACKED, REDUCIBLE, UNBUFFERED and UPDATE attributes are not included. The DIRECT, TRANSIENT, BUFFERED, UNBUFFERED, UPDATE, KEYED, EXCLUSIVE and BACKWARDS options on the OPEN statement are not included.   The KEY and PENDING conditions are not included.

2. Controlled and based storage, and list processing features are not included. This means that the ALLOCATE and FREE statements, the AREA, BASED, CONTROLLED, OFFSET and POINTER attributes, and the AREA condition are not included.

3. There is no multi-tasking in PL/C. This means that the DELAY and WAIT statements, and the EVENT and TASK attributes are not included. It also means that the TASK, EVENT and PRIORITY options on the CALL statement are not included.

4. The standard PL/I-F compile-time facilities are not included in PL/C. A source library and a macro facility, both incompatible with PL/I-F, are provided. See PL/C User's Guide.

5. The 48 character set input option is not included.

6. Message display to the computer operator is not possible under PL/C-- the DISPLAY statement is not included.

7. Sterling and picture data-types are not included in PL/C.

8. The DEFINED and LIKE attributes are not included.

9. Some of the PL/I-F built-in functions and pseudo-variables are not included in PL/C. See Appendix A.8.

Additional Restrictions Imposed by PL/C

1. Thirty-three statement keywords and six auxiliary keywords in PL/C are reserved, and cannot be used as identifiers. See Appendix A.2.

2. The names of built-in functions and pseudo-variables are not reserved and may be used as identifiers, but if they are to be used in this way they should be explicitly declared--contextual declaration of these particular identifiers may succeed (depending upon context) but will produce a warning message.

3. Parameters cannot be passed to the MAIN PROCEDURE of a PL/C program from the OS EXEC card.

4. Constants and comments must be contained in a single source card unless the PL/C NOBOUNDARY option is specified. See Appendix B.2.

5. There is no implied conversion between string and coded-arithmetic data types in expressions. String constants cannot have repetition factors.

6. There are restrictions on the END, ENTRY, FORMAT, PROCEDURE, READ and WRITE statements. See Appendices A.3 and A.4.

7. There are restrictions on dimension, ENTRY, INITIAL, LABEL, length and RETURNS attributes. See Appendix A.5.

8. Not all of the PL/I-F condition codes are used by PL/C and the default condition states under PL/C are not exactly the same as under PL/I-F. See Appendix A.7.

9. The files SYSIN and SYSPRINT are implicitly OPENed before execution begins and cannot be CLOSEd. This means, in particular, that the default attributes for SYSPRINT cannot be changed during a run. (The PAGESIZE and LINESIZE defaults for SYSPRINT are installation, but not user, options.)

PL/C Additions That Are Not Part Of PL/I

1. A built-in function to generate sequences of pseudo-random numbers has been added. See Appendix A.8.

2. SOURCE and NOSOURCE statements have been added to give more selective control over the printing of the source program. See Appendix A.3.

3. CHECK and NOCHECK statements have been added to give more flexible control over the output printed by the CHECK condition. See Appendix A.3.

4. A FLOW condition and FLOW and NOFLOW statements have been added to permit the automatic tracing of the execution of a program. See Appendices A.3 and A.7.

5. Several diagnostic options have been added to the PUT statement. See Appendix A.3.

In order to permit these non-standard features to be used in a PL/C program and still preserve upward-compatibility with PL/I, PL/C has a capability of selectively including the contents of certain comments as part of the source program. This is described in Section III.4.4 of the text.   Incompatible features can be enclosed in such "convertible comments" and in this way hidden from the PL/I compiler.

Dimensional Limits In The PL/C Compiler

The internal structure of the PL/C compiler is very different from that of the PL/I-F compiler and it was not feasible to limit certain critical dimensions of the source program in exactly the same way.   There are probably some unusually large and complex programs that would be accepted by PL/C but would exceed some dimensional limit in PL/I-F.   (The opposite is certainly true.)   The limits in PL/C are the following:
1. Maximum nesting of IF statements is 12.
2. Maximum static (syntactic) nesting of PROCEDURE,
    BEGIN and DO statements is 11.
3. Maximum nesting of factors in DECLARE is 6.
4. Maximum number of label prefixes on a statement is 87.
5. Maximum depth of parenthesis nesting in expressions is
    14.
6. Maximum number of identifiers in a factor or structure in
    DECLARE is 88.
7. Maximum number of identifiers, constants and literal
    strings in a program is 1024. Of this number approximately
    270 keywords and constants have been predefined so that the
    user can add about 750 more.
8. Maximum number of identifiers that can be declared in a
    single block is approximately 400.
9. No single expression can contain more than 256 symbols.

These limits are fixed by the structure of the compiler and cannot be relieved by increasing the core made available to the compiler. In most other respects the compiler's limits are related to the amount of core available--for example, length of program and size of arrays. In these cases when the compiler indicates that a limit has been exceeded the user can resubmit the program with a larger core specification.

Appendix B

OPERATING PROCEDURES FOR PL/C

Appendix B.1 Program Deck Structure

1. The control cards described below are those required or permitted by the PL/C compiler. Other control cards (i.e. OS job-control-language) must precede and follow these cards. Three PL/C control cards are used to identify the beginning of different sections of the program:

        *PL/C or *PLC
        *PROCESS
        *DATA

The first character "*" can be changed by the installation. Control card format is described in Appendix B.3.1.

2. A *PL/C card must precede the first card of the program. If the program includes external procedures (in addition to the main procedure) each external procedure is preceded by a *PROCESS card.

3. If data is required for execution, it follows the program, preceded by a *DATA card. If no data is required, the *DATA card is optional. If data is present it starts on the card following the *DATA card, and not on the *DATA card itself.

4. No special control cards are required to invoke PL/C batching. Each *PL/C card reinitializes the compiler to process a new program, so that a job consists of one or more programs back-to-back. Each program begins with a *PL/C card, may include *PROCESS cards, and may include data preceded by a *DATA card. A separator page precedes each program to facilitate separating the programs in a batch-job. If the ID option is given on the *PL/C card the text from this option will appear on the separator page. (An installation may elect to suppress the separator page.)

5. A fourth type of control card, *INCLUDE, permits source card images to be inserted in a PL/C program deck. See the PL/C User's Guide for a description of this facility.

6.   A fifth type of control card, *MACRO, invokes a compile-time
macro facility.   See the <u>PL/C User's Guide</u>. This PL/C macro
feature is not compatible with the PL/I compile-time facilities.

7.   PL/C will use whatever amount of memory (called "region") is
allocated to it by the operating system.   The method of
specifying the region size varies from one installation to
another.   The minimum necessary region size depends upon the
particular form of PL/C that has been installed.   With the
fully-overlayed form a region of 110K will accommodate a typical
program of more than 200 statements. For longer programs, or
programs with large arrays or very large numbers of different
identifiers more core must be provided.   Very short programs
(approximately 50 statements) can be run in a region as small as
96K.

Appendix B.1.1 <u>Examples of PL/C Card Decks</u>

   1.   Single program without data:
   *PL/C options
      source program cards

   2.   Single program with data:
   *PL/C options
      source program cards
   *DATA
      data cards

   3.   Program with 2 external procedures and data:
   *PL/C options
      source program cards for 1st external proc
   *PROCESS options
      source program cards for 2nd external proc
   *DATA
      data cards

   4.   Three independent programs run in batch-mode:
   *PL/C options
      source program cards for program 1
   *DATA
      data cards for program 1
   *PL/C options
      source program cards for program 2 (main proc)
   *PROCESS options
      source program cards for program 2 (ext. proc)
   *DATA
      data cards for program 2
   *PL/C options
      source program cards for program 3

Appendix B.2 <u>Program Options</u>

The programmer can specify various options on the *PL/C card
to control the manner in which his program is processed. The
standard, or default, action is indicated below by underlining.
If this is the desired action then no option need be specified.
Options are given only to <u>override</u> these defaults. (The default
actions can be altered by each PL/C installation, so it is
possible that yours will differ from what is shown below.) The
option phrases may be given in any combination, in any order,
separated by commas and/or blanks.

ID='programmer name' specifies up to 20 characters of
    identification used in the program heading line and on the
    PL/C batch separator page. (Single quotes around the name
    are required.)

XREF or <u>NOXREF</u> controls the printing of an alphabetical listing
    of identifiers, indicating where each is declared and used.
    See Section I.7.2.2.

ATR or <u>NOATR</u> controls the printing of an alphabetical list of
    identifiers giving attributes assigned to each identifier.
    See Section I.7.2.2.

<u>DUMP</u> or NODUMP controls the printing of the post-mortem dump.
    See Sections I.7.2.4 and III.3.3.

DUMPARRAY or <u>NODUMPARRAY</u> specifies whether or not arrays are to
    be included in the post-mortem dump.

TIME = (m,s) or TIME = m specifies an upper limit on total
    processing time (compilation plus execution). This limit
    is given as m minutes and s seconds. The default values
    (usually just a few seconds) are determined by each
    installation. Note that this is a PL/C time limit. There
    is usually another time limit superimposed by the operating
    system. If PL/C terminates a program for having exceeded
    the PL/C time limit it will end with the usual post-mortem
    dump. If the operating system cuts the program off, PL/C
    does not have a chance to provide the dump.

COMMENTS=(list) or COMMENTS or <u>NOCOMMENTS</u> controls whether the
    content of "pseudo-comments" is to be considered as program
    text or comments. See Section III.4.4.1. The list
    consists of any selection of the integers from 1 to 6,
    separated by commas. For example COMMENTS=(1,4,5)
    indicates that all comments whose first character is a 1 or
    4 or 5 or ":" should be regarded as program text. When

given without a list COMMENTS indicates that all comments whose first character is a ":" should be regarded as text.

SOURCE or NOSOURCE controls the printing of the source program listing. See Section III.4.3.

SORMGIN = (2,72,1) controls the margins of the cards for the source program (not including control cards or data cards). The default is to use columns 2 through 72 for program, and column 1 for printing control characters. See Appendix B.3.2.

BOUNDARY or NOBOUNDARY controls whether or not comments and literals in the source program can be continued across a card boundary (boundary as defined by SORMGIN). NOBOUNDARY permits continuation and is compatible with PL/I. BOUNDARY terminates comments and literals automatically at the card boundary. See Appendix B.3.2.

FLAGW or FLAGE controls whether or not warning messages will be printed. In the case of a warning, PL/C does not make any change in the source program. FLAGW will print warnings and errors; FLAGE will print only errors.

ERRORS = (c,e) specifies error limits. If c or more errors are encountered during compilation, the program will not be executed. (The compilation will be completed regardless of error count.) Execution will be terminated when e execution errors have been encountered. See Section III.3.1.2. Default values for both c and e are 50.

This limit provides a mechanism to permit a "compile only" run. ERRORS=(0,0) will suppress execution regardless of the outcome of compilation; ERRORS=(1,50) will permit execution only if no compilation errors were encountered.

UDEF or NOUDEF indicates whether or not PL/C should check for the use of a variable before it is assigned a value (an undefined variable). See Section III.3.1.2. NOUDEF suppresses this checking (and hence is compatible with PL/I).

LINECT = nn specifies the number of lines to be printed on each page of source listing. The default value for nn is 60; nn must be greater than 20.

PAGES = nn specifies a page limit on printed output (total of all types of printing -- source listing, execution, etc.). See Section I.7.2. The standard PL/C default is 30 pages, but this is usually altered at each installation.

LIST or NOLIST controls whether or not a listing of the object program produced during compilation is to be printed.

For example, the following card specifies production of a cross reference and attribute listing, with a 30 second time limit and 50 page output limit for a student named Ezra Cornell:

```
*PL/C ID='CORNELL, EZRA',XREF,ATR,TIME=(0,30),PAGES=50
```

The following abbreviations are accepted for option keywords:

```
        ID        I
        XREF      X          NOXREF        NX
        ATR       A          NOATR         NA
        DUMP      D          NODUMP        ND
        DUMPARRAY DA         NODUMPARRAY   NDA
        TIME      T
        COMMENTS  C          NOCOMMENTS    NC
        SOURCE    S          NOSOURCE      NS
        SORMGIN   SM
        BOUNDARY  B          NOBOUNDARY    NB
        FLAGW     FW         FLAGE         FE
        ERRORS    E
        UDEF      U          NOUDEF        NU
        LINECT    LN
        PAGES     P
        LIST      L          NOLIST        NL
```

These are not exactly abbreviations, but simply indicate which characters are significant to the PL/C scanner. Other characters may be present, which means that many spelling and keypunch errors will be overlooked. For example:

```
  ATR, A, ART, ATTRIBUTE, ATRIBUT, AX
```

all request an attribute listing, without producing an error message. Commas are optional and spaces may be added except in the parentheses after TIME, COMMENTS, ERRORS and SORMGIN which must be strictly as shown above. The following examples will both yield exactly the same results as the example shown above:

```
*PLC I='CORNELL, EZRA' X A T=(0,30) P=50
*PLC IX='CORNELL, EZRA',,XRFE , ATTRIBUTE TIM=(0,30),  PAGE=50
```

Any error detected in the processing of options terminates scanning of that control card.

All of the desired options must be given on a single card -- no continuation of the *PL/C card onto a second card is permitted.

*PROCESS Options

The following options (from those listed in Appendix B.2) can be specified on a *PROCESS card as well as a *PL/C card:

    COMMENTS=(list) or COMMENTS or NOCOMMENTS
    SOURCE or NOSOURCE
    SORMGIN
    BOUNDARY or NOBOUNDARY
    FLAGW or FLAGE
    LINECT

By specifying options on *PROCESS cards, different options can be applied to different sections of a program. If options are not given on a *PROCESS card, the <u>previous options are continued</u>; the default options are <u>not</u> reestablished for the new section.

Appendix B.3 <u>Card Formats</u>

For all types of cards the contents of columns 1 and 2 may be significant to the operating system under which PL/C operates and cause a card to be intercepted by the operating system and never reach PL/C. The characters // in columns 1 and 2 are significant to most IBM systems, and the characters /* are significant to some. Both of these combinations should be avoided in columns 1 and 2 of all cards (data cards as well as program). A <u>very common error</u> in PL/I is to <u>begin a comment in column 1</u> (with a /*).

If a card with // in columns 1 and 2 reach PL/C the following action is taken:

1. If columns 3-80 of the card are blank it is treated as an end-of-file and it terminates the PL/C program. The compiler expects to either begin a new program (with a *PL/C card) or have the job ended by the operating system. Any number of consecutive // cards with blanks in 3-80 have the same effect as one.

2. If columns 3-80 are not completely blank the card is ignored. PL/C just reads the next card as if the // card did not exist.

B.3.1 <u>Control Cards</u>

Control cards are recognized by a * in column 1. (The control card recognition character is an installation option and some installations may use another character instead of *.) The control keyword -- PL/C, PROCESS, DATA -- should begin in column 2. Control cards are not considered part of the source program and thus are not affected by the SORMGIN option.

The option phrases on control cards can, in general, appear in any order, in full or abbreviated form, separated by blanks and/or commas. However, options must fit on the single control card -- continuation onto a second card is not permitted. If necessary, use the abbreviated form of the option phrases (Appendix B.2).

Appendix B.3.2 <u>Program Cards</u>

1. The standard default card field for source statements is
columns 2 thru 72. PL/C will ignore the contents of 73-80 but
these contents will appear on the source listing.

1a. The portion of the card to the right of the right margin
(normally columns 73-80) is intended to be used for program and
card identification. A four-character abbreviation of the
program name can be punched in columns 73-76. (This can be
automatically duplicated from one card to the next. See
Appendix B.3.4.) The cards should be serially numbered in
columns 77-80. Initial numbers should be in intervals of ten or
more to leave room for later insertions. For example, a sorting
program might be identified and initially numbered as follows:

                SORT0010
                SORT0020
                SORT0030
                . . .

This will seem unnecessary until the first time you (or the
computer operator) drop one of your card decks.

2. The default position for the specification of carriage
control for the listing of the source program is column 1. Only
5 of the USASI codes are recognized for this purpose:

  blank   space 1 line before printing (normal mode)
  0   space 2 lines before printing
  -        space 3 lines before printing
  +   do not space before printing (overprint)
  1   skip to channel 1 (page eject)

Carriage control characters do not appear on the source listing.

2a. If any character other than these five appears in column 1
PL/C assumes that the writer neglected to skip column 1 and the
scan will begin in column 1. A warning message will be issued.

3. The default source card format can be altered by specifying
the SORMGIN option on the *PL/C or *PROCESS card. The form is:

        SORMGIN = (a,b,c)

   where: a is the leftmost column to be included
            b is the rightmost column to be included
            c is the column for carriage control

The maximum column specification is 100, and the carriage
control column must be outside of the a,b field. If the SORMGIN
option is used the description in paragraphs 1 and 2 above must
be altered accordingly. The correction in paragraph 2a will
only take place when a=2 and c=1.

4. When the default BOUNDARY option is in effect PL/C does   not
permit any element to be split over a card boundary. That is,
keywords, identifiers, constants and <u>comments</u> cannot start   on
one card and be continued on the next. This limits the length
of literals that may be included in a PL/C program.   It also
means that in program documentation with long comments each card
must be a separate comment-- with an opening /* and a closing
*/.   This is more restrictive than PL/I-F which will allow very
long comments.

    When the NOBOUNDARY option is specified literals and comments
may be continued over a card boundary. The maximum length of a
literal is then 256 characters. There is no limit on the length
of a comment. Note that the card boundary is as defined by the
SORMGIN option and not the physical card boundary. For example,
with the default SORMGIN of (2,72,1) column 2 of a card is
considered to directly follow column 72 of the previous card --
no blank is supplied.   Note also that the NOBOUNDARY option
applies only to literals and comments. In PL/C one still cannot
continue a keyword, an identifier or an arithmetic constant over
a card boundary.

Appendix B.3.3 <u>Data Cards</u>

    The card field for data cards is always 1 to 80. Data cards
are not affected by the SORMGIN or BOUNDARY options (see
Appendix B.2). Data cards are considered to be a continuous
stream of characters and the card boundary is of no significance
whatever. That is, column 1 of a card directly follows column
80 of the previous card, and any element may be continued over a
card boundary.

Appendix B.3.4 <u>Format Control on the Keypunch</u>

    We have recommended (in Section I.4.6.2) using program format
to display the structure of a program. The use of such format
conventions requires a convenient means of indenting   the
beginning of each program line to indicate its relationship to
the lines preceding and following.   The keypunch offers a
facility comparable to the "tab stops" on a typewriter for this
purpose.

    The "stops" are set by punching a control card which is
placed around a drum in the upper center of the IBM 029
keypunch. When the "star wheels" are lowered onto the face of
this drum (by depressing the left side of the toggle switch just
below the drum), pushing the SKIP key on the keyboard will cause
the card to advance to the next "stop" position. A stop
position is specified by punching a 1 in the corresponding
column of the drum control card.

The drum control card can also control automatic skipping, automatic duplication (copying from one card to the next), and the alpha/numeric shift of the keyboard. To describe the control characters for these different actions, consider the control card to be divided into sets of adjacent columns called "fields". One character is used to start a field (in the left-most column), and another to continue the field:

Type of Field:	To start:	To continue:
alpha	1	A
numeric	blank	+
automatic skip	-	+
automatic duplicate	/	/

The alpha/numeric indication in the control card is the default type for the column. This can be overridden by the ALPHA and NUMERIC keys on the keyboard. For the automatic skip and auomatic duplicate to be effective the AUTO SKIP DUP switch at the left top of the keyboard must be ON (in the up position).

A useful drum control card for PL/I would have the following fields:

```
1; automatic skip
2-5, 6-9, 10-13, 14-17, ...; alpha fields with
        stops every four columns
73-76; automatic duplicate (for program identification)
77-80; numeric (for card serial number)
```

The control card would be punched as follows:

```
                    1         2         3         4
columns     1234567890123456789012345678901234567890
cont.char   -1AAA1AAA1AAA1AAA1AAA1AAA1AAA1AAA1AAA1AA

            4         5         6         7         8
columns     1234567890123456789012345678901234567890
cont.char   AAAAAAAAAAAAAAAAAAAAAAAAAAAAAAAAA/// ++++
```

With this drum card, in order to punch a PL/C control card with a * in column 1 you would have to turn the AUTO SKIP DUP switch off momentarily to suppress the skip over column 1. If you do not want to use columns 73-80 for card identification, columns 73-80 of the control card would be punched as follows:

```
                                            7    8
columns                                     34567890
cont.character                              -+++++++
```

This will cause the keypunch to automatically release the card as soon as column 72 is punched, and to feed a new card.

Without an automatic skip or duplicate in column 73 it is
very easy to accidentally continue punching program text beyond
column 72. The result can be very mystifying. Characters
punched in 73-80 are not scanned by PL/C (unless directed to by
the SORMGIN option), but since they are printed on the source
program listing, it is not obvious that they have been ignored.
This usually produces a number of error messages for a statement
that looks correct on the listing.

PL/I and PL/C References

Conway, R. W. and T. R. Wilcox, "Design and Implementation of a Diagnostic Compiler for PL/I", Communications of the ACM, March 1973

IBM System 360 PL/I Reference Manual, Form C28-8201

IBM System 360 OS PL/I-F Programmer's Guide, Form C28-6594

IBM System 360 DOS/TOS PL/I Programmer's Guide, Form GC24-9005

IBM PL/I Language Specifications, Form C28-6571

IBM: A Guide to PL/I for Commercial Programmers, Form C20-1651

IBM: A Guide to PL/I for FORTRAN Users, Form C20-1637

PL/C User's Guide, Release 7, Department of Computer Science, Cornell University, 1973

PL/C Installation Instructions, Release 7, Department of Computer Science, Cornell University, 1973

Pollack, S. V. and T. D. Sterling, A Guide to PL/I, Holt Rinehart Winston, 1969

Weinberg, G. M., PL/I Programming: A Manual of Style, McGraw-Hill, 1970

Weinberg, G. M. et al, Structured Programming Using PL/C, Wiley, 1973

INDEX